HUMAN INTELLIGENCE

HUMAN INTELLIGENCE

BY

Jack Fincher

*What we are learning about human intelli-
gence may do more than double what we know.
It may compel us to redefine it altogether.*

G. P. Putnam's Sons
New York

Especially to Claire,
and to Erica, David, and Emily
—loving partners in all the
sacrifice that made it possible—
this book and its author
are dedicated

SBN: 399-11487-4
Library of Congress Catalog
Card Number: 75-37114

PRINTED IN THE UNITED STATES OF AMERICA

Contents

Acknowledgments

WHEN I told a teacher friend that I was going to write a book, her reaction could not have been more prophetic. "What about?" she asked. Human intelligence, I told her. There was a pause, then she added, "Who with?" Who with, indeed. The list is long. Over 200 scientists and academics in six countries either sent me their papers, answered my questions, or graciously granted me interviews—a phenomenal 95 percent of those I contacted. To them, including those whose names do not appear but whose views helped shape these pages, my warmest thanks. Thanks also to Carroll and Charlotte White and Marilyn Marcus for their association and insights; to Barbara Kaplan for her research and instincts; to Ingrid Rempel for her translation; to George Leonard for advice in setting the original tone and direction; to Fred Schmidt, Tom Place, and the late Don Kase for technical help; to Gene Turtle for access to ERIC at the jumping-off point; to Bob and Judy DeVito for their comments in the early going; to Steve Kaufman for a place to put my typewriter during a critical summer month; to my editor, Harvey Ginsberg, and my agent, John Hawkins, for their unrelenting patience. Thanks also to Linda Hickman, Suzanne Caster, Julie Schmidt, Mary Ann Shaffer, Barbara Hughes, Susan Banfield, and all the other stalwarts of the library.

Thanks also to Professor Mike Brailoff of Indian Valley colleges whose chance remark gave me the courage to keep at it: "Listen. They can talk all they want to about human intelligence, but no one really knows."

Finally, I would like to make more formal acknowledgment of my gratitude for permission to make use of quotations to the following:

7

8

9

Foreword

DIPPING its toes as it does into such deep and diverse pools of thought and knowledge as psychology, psychiatry, pharmacology, neuroanatomy, neurophysiology, physical psychology, psychobiology, endocrinology, anthropology, electroencephalography, microbial genetics, population statistics, and computer science, this book is neither the first nor the last word on anything—except, perhaps, how eclectic can be the browsings of a journalist whose gift was once described by Eric Berne as that of an "omnivorous reader." Alas, even that may be suspect when readers start coming out of the wings to cry, "How could he overlook . . . ?" and, "why would anyone write a book like this without once mentioning . . . ?"

In defense, the journalist can join the expert in pleading that there are literally hundreds of thousands of publications in each field every year and no one can possibly read them all. He can also cast himself in the role of excited messenger, leaving it to the experts to soothe the aroused with, "Well now, that's all right as far as it goes, but. . . ." Finally, he can note that even the experts are not immune to dispute and revelation. When the world's leading neuroscientists met to compare notes on the brain a few years ago, even they went home afterward and at the chairman's invitation, for publication rewrote the papers they had given.

'Tis the mind that makes the body rich.
—PETRUCHIO
The Taming Of The Shrew

Prologue

INTELLIGENCE AND ANXIETY

The monster is what people who are afraid of intelligence think intelligence would look like if it were a person.

—*Mel Brooks on his movie* YOUNG FRANKENSTEIN

SEVERAL YEARS AGO a team of psychologists and psychiatrists from San Francisco's Mount Zion Hospital moved into the city's Haight-Ashbury district and set up housekeeping. They were there, figuratively, to put under a microscope that vexing new life form, the Street People. For a dollar an hour, hippies, acid freaks, runaways, drifters, and dropouts allowed their psyches to be poked and prodded in a massive effort to find out what made them tick. For eighteen months they were interviewed, asked to write intimate personal sketches, subjected to intensive psychiatric workups, and bombarded with every test in the arsenal of psychology. When it was over, the Mount Zion team had not only amassed a Matterhorn of data but had made a totally unexpected discovery. True, the Street People would confess their most far-out ideas, fantasies, and sexual practices with an easy freedom that would have shamed their elders. But in one startling way they were hardly different. Tests of their intelligence disturbed them no end. Balked by a block design problem, one of them grew so frustrated he barely refrained from hurling the hard wooden blocks point-blank at the examiner. In a test of sorting, another blew up, seized two nails, and glaring across the table, jammed them murderously into corks. On days their IQ's were tested, most of the Street People were gripped by a gnawing anxiety more common to the classroom than the laboratory.

"Knowing their philosophy—you know, hang loose, nothing matters—you wouldn't have expected them to apply themselves very much," remembers one researcher. "But almost all of them were trying, damned hard. They were more concerned about their IQs than anything else. We expected them to be different. I guess we should have known better."[1]

15

Indeed they should have. We are all of us prisoners of our own experience, our children included, and Americans, perhaps more than any people on earth, have become a nation of inchworms measuring the marigolds. It is one of the most impressive and, some would say, least attractive things about us, this obsession with exactitude, this unslakable thirst for quantification. We are inveterate and addicted stop watchers, slide rulers, tabulators, counters, computers, and above all, testers. We test aptitude, we test ability, we test achievement. Foremost, we test intelligence. We not only test it, we can reduce our assessment of it to precise numbers: our Intelligence Quotient, or the IQ. So we like to think. So we have always thought.

Today the intelligence test is seventy years old, a senior citizen in the growing American family of psychometrics (psychological measurements). Until recently it had enjoyed a career both busy and distinguished. If you hoped to get through public school, go on to college, graduate into a profession—in brief, pursue the good life as advertised—you could scarcely escape its imperious eye. Even the student radical, that hairy harbinger of the coming change, was no exception. Alongside everybody else he docilely submitted the contents of his brain to periodic inspection like so many suitcases at a customs desk. The issue of IQ he left alone, this disenchanted child of the establishment, if he even recognized it as an issue. For as nearly as anything in American education, in American life, in fact, the IQ test was beyond secular question. The high priests in the temples of psychology had, for ostensibly the loftiest of motives, done their job well. Fearing what harm such a seemingly sharp instrument might do in the hands of the uninstructed, they had begun by reserving its use on the body public to those best equipped by training: themselves, naturally. They had ended, like surgeons before them, by deciding that the results of the operation should never be shared in understandable detail with the patient. Indeed, their concern for secrecy reached the rarefied point where the American Psychological Association drew up a code of ethics forbidding its members to tell people their scores—or anything else about the tests for that matter—except how to take them. Even though a client sometimes paid out of his own pocket for what he believed to be an accurate diagnosis

16

of his innate mental prowess, he usually had to be content with the bland assurance that he had done well, was weak on this or that, or—the most he could hope for as his twentieth-century soothsayer peered profoundly into the chicken entrails—that he was "well within the top five percent" of the population.

The inevitable result was what scientists call the "Black Box" mystique, a vague sense that such arcane matters were miles beyond the comprehension of mere mortals, whatever their IQ. The intelligence test had become a ritualistic exercise in darkest voodoo, one best left to the local witchdoctor and taken with a wafer of faith.

But that was yesterday. Today the top is off the box, the IQ tests under fierce and growing fire on all fronts. Charging the tests are loaded with crippling middle class bias, blacks are going into courts and legislatures across the land to block their use in education. Citing the language barrier, Chicanos are pressing hard-strapped school systems for costly new Spanish translations. Condemning testing as the tool of an unjust status quo, the disenchanted are picketing bookstores, breaking up classes, and shouting down speakers whenever and wherever they rise to suggest that social inequities are caused by race and class differences in native intellect as IQ scores define it. Even the suburban grade school is becoming a battleground. There, the special treatment at public expense of high-IQ children—a pitifully short-funded effort at best—has run into mounting opposition from earnest parents of the rank and file. They cry "unwarranted elitism," while families of the designated gifted question the program's wrenching effects on child and parent friendships alike, and wonder if the handout can possibly be worth the everlasting hassle.

Politics aside, the IQ test is increasingly criticized by the professionals themselves. Many now agree that a new test, a better test, a different kind of test—in the words of educator Robert Sears, "a test to tell us what to test"[2]—is badly needed if testing is to continue at all. Only such a test, they believe, can justify testing as an academic or scientific end in itself, much less as a tacit instrument of social policy all the more powerful for being unspoken. Other experts contend the whole set of assumptions underlying their use must be revamped first. Says Stanford theorist Lee J. Cronbach in a trenchant summary of how far behind the times the state of testing has fallen: "We do a nice 1940 job of using what we learned in the twenties."[3]

All in all, they seem to be saying, the standardized IQ test is more than showing its age. It has become a decrepit and despotic old wheeze, ripe for retirement.

For all the current ferment, our disenchantment has a short history. My generation, which went to school in the forties, was not the least anxious about the purpose or validity of the IQ test. On the contrary, we accepted its legitimacy at face value and pondered instead what dread or delightful secrets it might reveal. Why, it could quantify our brains in a twinkling. After such tests, always an exciting break in the daily routine, we guessed and gossiped and wondered. Once a girl I knew even found out her score—with results that have the gravest implications for the situation in which we now find ourselves.

Sally, I'll call her, was one of the most popular girls in my high school class, a bubbling extrovert whose boundless energy enabled her both to make straight A's and pursue a schedule of club meetings, dates, and dances that for sheer stamina would fell a draft horse. I never thought of her as smart or dumb. She asked stupid questions sometimes, but then, it seemed to me from the Olympian perspective of a sixteen-year-old male chauvinist, all girls did. She was blessed with personality, money, status. She was as warm and friendly as a pretty girl can be when she has an equally good opinion of herself and others. Above all she was, in the treacly teen talk of the time, "cute." What else could such a girl possibly want?

I found out after our IQ test my junior year. In a decision apparently prompted by the insistence of the more influential parents, we were told we could see our scores if we brought a letter from home requesting it. Most of us demurred. We were not about to profane the temple and anger the gods. The deadline came and went. That next afternoon I ran into Sally coming out of the principal's office. She tried to smile when she saw me but her eyes were so stricken I realized at once why she couldn't. "I knew I was no brain," she managed to say at last. "But I never knew I was"—her jagged little laugh was a half-stopped cry of pain— "*that* dumb."

18

When she gradually grew before my eyes into a stooped and mousy drudge, I knew, if I had ever doubted, the power of the IQ to affect our lives. I would see it again years later in a young matron who had thrown over the love of her life because, she said, she had looked up his IQ while working in the university registrar's office and found him in the lowest 10 percent of their class. (He went on to quite a career in state politics.) I saw, finally, its potential effects on my own emotions when, braving the injunction against it, I wrote my high school and asked at last for the score I had been too intimidated to request. Back came the results, not only for my junior year but for the seventh grade as well. The letter code and raw numbers meant no more to me than a doctor's prescription, but there was a percentile and that I understood. I had ranked in the top 5 percent of my seventh grade class, a heady whiff of deferred eminence that was instantly dispelled by the discovery that I had ranked in the top 22 percent the year before my high school graduation. My high school had four times as many students, but proportionately four times as many who were brighter? I doubted it. By an accident of geography I had gone to the junior high where the rich southside kids went, and everybody knew they were smarter than the northside kids, who were poor. We wouldn't have known a socioeconomic index from a Sears Roebuck catalogue but we knew that. Or so we thought.

I was also aware that I had been on the highest "track," the high school's informal system of ability echelons. All of us who were members of that secret elite knew it, just as children do today. No, statistics could not explain two IQ scores so at odds. Simple test error might, or an off-year due to stormy pubescence. But had I known then that in four years I had evidently slipped and tumbled 17 rungs down the intellectual ladder, I might have been as crushed as Sally. For some reason, a tumor on the brain, perhaps, that sapping mental disease male adolescents were told in those days menaced them, my intellect was marching backward toward certifiable imbecility.

It would never have occurred to me to question the test. The test was Holy Writ, the first and last word straight from the Oracle at Delphi. Nor would I have had any cause to suspect what I learned researching this book: That back at the temple there was a priestly difference of opinion. Some psychologists saw the group

19

test we had taken as overly involved, lacking in variety, arbitrary in its scoring, and structured to penalize excessively the low motivation its very tedium encouraged in the quick of mind. (Today many psychologists regard any group test as no more than a preliminary screening device to weed out the clearly defective before getting down to individual testing.) Most damning of all, one prominent professional journal of the day concluded that some of the questions, whatever they were, were not a reasonable test of intelligence.

So the validity of my score—and Sally's—indeed, everyone's in the class of '48 wherever in the land that test had been taken—was open to honest doubt. Unlike Sally, mercifully, most of us had never known our scores. But what about our teachers? A sizeable literature has since sprung up around the subtle, often unconscious effects of teacher expectancy. The finer points of that research remain controversial but its essential thrust is undisputed. Teachers tend, most humanly, to teach those they think will learn. What of those among us the test had, in effect, decreed with the full weight of scientific authority would not?

A good teacher, of course, is not about to rely on an IQ test if it contradicts her own instincts and experience. Nor should she. But at best such a contradiction muddies the academic waters. Sally had been a top student. Was the test all that wrong in her case or was she simply superbly motivated and self-disciplined to make the most of her modest abilities in the conventional classroom setting? Either way, her confidence was shattered. What of the converse, the poor student who scores high in IQ? Does it mean the test is wrong or does it mean the student lacks motivation, has troubles at home, or is turned off by the teacher's methods, personality, or subject?

If test and teacher concur that a good student is bright, how splendid. That student is assured the attention he or she needs. But if they agree a poor student is dumb, what if they are wrong? The same psychological factors that contaminate classroom performance can undermine the IQ test, too. And whatever the cost, in untapped human potential, in tragically undermined Sallys, it must ultimately be shared by all of us.

In the end our concerns about the IQ test are only symptoms of a deeper anxiety. It is the same anxiety so openly betrayed by the hung-up inhabitants of the Haight, a fundamental anxiety about intelligence itself. Tell a man he has no soul and you get a vacant stare or a philosophic argument. Tell him he has no brain and you're liable to get your head broken. About few things in life are we so emotional, so primitive, so unreasonable, so unintelligent. (A Republican Senator from the South held a press conference last year to *deny* a magazine poll that unanimously picked him the dumbest member of Congress.)

What is intelligence anyway? Why should it obsess us so? How does it relate to imagination, intuition, creativity? What has it to do with the arts, with athletic ability, with any of the other special talents to which we pay homage? We know intelligence exists, just as we think we can detect in any situation its appalling absence. We see it around us every day, just as we see people painting, composing, juggling, inventing the water bed, hitting home runs by the hundreds, and cheating brilliantly on their income tax. We even recognize that genius can exist without our comprehending it, much as we recognize the bumblebee can fly despite violating every law of aerodynamics. ("So you can make your child a genius, can you?" challenged Norbert Wiener, who was probably one. "Yes, as you can make a blank canvas into a painting by Leonardo or a ream of clean paper into a play by Shakespeare."[4] Yet when an executive recruiting firm dummied up a résumé on the nineteenth-century electromagnetic genius Faraday, no corporation approached wanted to interview him.)

But what, really, do we know about the natural laws of intelligence? At the risk of skirting the question, we know a larger answer: Whatever intelligence is, its importance in our lives cannot be exaggerated. Intelligence is human behavior at its highest, the epitome of millions upon millions of years of evolutionary response to the brutal pressures of an implacably changing environment. It will not be overthrown by any rebellion of feeling, however deep. Nor will it be undermined by any uprising of our senses, however strong. Drugs can color it, emotions cloud it, but neither can destroy its primacy in man's affairs without eventual death to the self and society. The need to use our heads, in sum, is as invincibly natural—and as savagely imperative—as the need to breathe, to eat and drink, to survive as human being and human-kind.

But to say that intelligence cannot safely be toppled by either our emotions or our perceptions is not to say that its role in our lives cannot be changed. Evolution *is* change. As our brains evolve so must our intellect, whether we wish it or not. Human destiny has never demanded it more than now. As psychobiologist Roger Sperry of the California Institute of Technology points out, the radical shift away from the checks and balances brought about by technology has elevated man's mind to "the dominant control force on our planet; what moves and directs the brain of man will, in turn, largely determine the future from here on."[5] For all our sakes, what moves and directs the brain of man had better be a higher order of intelligence, not simply the childlike indulgence of unrestrained emotion or the orgiastic celebration of our senses—or the destructive antiintellectualism dangerously inherent in both. In Sperry's visionary words, the future that starts tomorrow requires nothing less than our fullest use of "the relatively untested mental capacities and impulses of the human brain."[6]

Our knowledge of those capacities and impulses is, to put it mildly, more than incomplete. It is tantamount to ignorance. Indeed, as astonishing new lines of scientific (and not so scientific) evidence suggests, our traditional concept of intelligence is at once static, lopsided, and sterile. It has twisted our scale of values, warped our ways of educating, and perverted our system of rewards until we stand at the brink of catastrophe. It pits the old against the young, the black against the white, the haves against the have-nots, the "dull" against the "bright" in a bitter social war none can possibly win, all may possibly lose.

Yet paradoxically, today perhaps more than ever before, salvation can come from the very chaos that confronts us. It can come in an infinitely more feeling, vastly more perceptive, intelligence than we have ever known. It can come if we are sensitive enough to seize the opportunity that beckons, wise enough to use it in building a better world for all.

That kind of intelligence, and the abysmal lack of it that currently afflicts our everyday lives together, is what this book is about.

Part I
INTELLIGENCE AND THE BRAIN

The Universe is in God's Brain

—Poster caption by
David Fincher at age seven

Chapter 1

What's Wet and Dry and Stores Everything Everywhere?

THE AUDITORIUM is packed. The crowd has spilled into the adjoining hallways and classrooms to listen over loudspeakers, to watch on closed-circuit television. At the lectern stands Buckminster Fuller, genius of the geodesic dome, inventor of the Dimaxion car, one of planet earth's most persuasive apologists for technology. Beneath the glare of television lights, under a sparse frizz of snow-white hair, Fuller's head gleams as bulbous as an onion. As he talks, his voice as rough and raspy as his native New England limestone against a grinder, his ideas showering down in a Niagara of words, his eyes snapping shut now and again to permit his mind to concentrate on cornering some elusive concept, you can almost see Bucky Fuller's brain within its taut casing of translucent skin and shadowy underbone bursting with raw cerebration.

Fuller is, in his words, "thinking out loud"—about man's dead past, his dying present, his dawning future. He admits as much and more when he suddenly pauses and says, "I'm quite confident that one thing about you and I [sic] is unique. What's going on in this room between us is absolutely weightless, purely metaphysical.

"All the meaning of life, all our awareness, is completely abstract."[1]

Yet for all his words, the experience remains ineffable. He is there and we are here. We are, he and each of us, excited, stimulated, feverish with the heat of our shared awareness, an awareness of *something* somehow more tangible than matter let loose upon the teeming air, but what? It tells us little of what it is and less of where it comes from. Information is information, not matter or energy, cyberneticist Norbert Wiener once reminded us. But what our brain does with information, while involving both matter and energy, as yet defies our comprehension. It is the coin of the realm we call intelligence, and that is a mystery.

The soul, a Swedish doctor claims to have found through sensitive before-and-after deathbed measurements, weighs three quarters of an ounce. The gasp as it leaves the dying body, if we dare entertain the satiric fantasies of novelist Romain Gary, could, if harnessed, end forever the earth's growing energy crisis. But such a force if it exists would be as nothing compared to the power of a single, weightless human thought. Thought and thought alone, translated into purposeful action, has raised up a towering technology. Intelligence informed by our instincts, appetites, and emotions has created civilization as we know it—and produced in the process those very problems of survival that Gary would whimsically employ the endless transport of souls to solve.

Yet despite centuries of speculation and research, that fabulous factory of our intellect, the brain, remains almost as mysterious as our soul. In view of all we still don't know, it seems presumptuous to the point of arrogance that less than a century ago people of outstanding intellectual and creative accomplishment bequeathed their brains to medical schools for posterity's study. (In one memorable instance the results were macabre. A lab assistant dropped Walt Whitman's on the floor, swept up its shattered remains, and threw them away.) In those days biologists erroneously believed that the brain's size, as well as gross individual differences in its configuration, reflected both intelligence and talent in the arts. Highly corrugated temporal lobes signified a Toscanini, bulging frontal lobes another Einstein. Women, naturally, were the inferior sex in mental power because their brains, like their bodies, were smaller.

Today we know the size and structure of the human brain have no obvious relationship to individual intellect, though we have lately learned that its fissures and folds are more distinctive than fingerprints, as uniquely our own as the features of our face, and may yet yield up subtle variations meaningful to individual differences in mentality. But only the most jingoistic Anglophile would

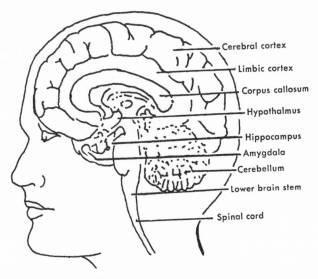

FIGURE 1.
Components of the brain

venture to say that Cromwell and Lord Byron, whose brains weighed almost five pounds, were twice as gifted as Anatole France, whose brain weighed only half as much. That conceit, like the brain collections themselves, has long since been stored away in a dusty bell-jar.

What, then, do we know about how the brain generates intelligence?

We know, in the crudest way, the brain's key components (Figure 1). We know that at the core lies the brain stem, with its blind instincts for self- and species preservation. Behind that sits the cerebellum, monitoring and correcting without our conscious control the simplest movements of the body. Above and in front of it cluster the amygdala, the hippocampus, and the hypothalmus. These are glands and suborgans which, together with the limbic cortex that forms a protective cowl over the brain stem, comprise our "emotional brain." We know that it contains our capacity for pleasure and pain, anger and joy, sex and hunger. All these parts of our brain, while in themselves indispensable, obviously influence our intelligence enormously but do not produce it.

27

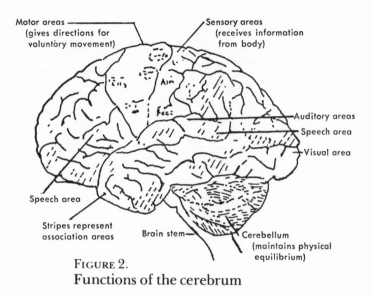

Motor areas
(gives directions for
voluntary movement)

Sensory areas
(receives information
from body)

Auditory areas

Speech area

Visual area

Speech area

Stripes represent
association areas

Brain stem

Cerebellum
(maintains physical
equilibrium)

FIGURE 2.
Functions of the cerebrum

Wrapped around the limbic cortex and divided into two hemispheres by a bridge of nerve fibers called the corpus callosum lies the actual seat of our intellect: a thick, crumpled gray sheet of richly pleated matter known as the cerebral cortex, or cerebrum. It is here we think, learn, remember, fantasize, dream and hallucinate.

We know something about the cerebrum (Figure 2) but what we do know, unfortunately, does not get us very far toward understanding the deepest roots of intelligent behavior. The fundamental nature of our memory, learning, thinking, and creating continues to elude us. Those who apply mathematician Kurt Gödel's celebrated proof to the brain may be right: No machine or system can ever divine its own inner workings, not even the most complex and miniaturized machine—or system—life on earth has ever known.

This has not, however, stopped us from trying to find out all we can in a multitude of ingenious ways. We have studied the brain-damaged and mapped the curious geography of their attenuated abilities. We have experimented with and dissected the brains of laboratory animals, and where feasible applied the results to the

28

human condition. We have traced the anatomy of brain tissue under electron microscopes that can magnify its minutest features a millionfold. We have attached electrodes to the scalp and crudely deciphered by computer the varied, ceaseless hum of the brain's electrical energy; pierced the living brain itself with electric needles to stimulate memory; implanted radio microprobes finer than a human hair to listen in on the neural singsong of a solitary cell while it works. As neuroscientist Robert Galambos puts it, "No little boy curious about what makes a clock tick ever showed greater ingenuity. . . ."[2]

The Neuron

From all this we have learned something and, like the little boy, guessed at much. We know, for instance, that every thought, every memory, derives from an electrochemically complex sequence of neural events. That sequence, whether it ends in Einstein conceiving that $E = MC^2$ or in your daughter remembering her appointment with the orthodontist, is essentially the same. It involves the systematic and instantaneous firing, or deliberate failure to fire, of *neurons,* the basic operational units of our brain and nervous system. Neurons, or nerve cells, are spidery filaments whose incredibly intricate networks shuttle within and between our brain and body, carrying those messages that enable us to think and survive an otherwise implacable environment.

Vastly oversimplified, they work like this. When, for instance, a stimulus strikes a receptor cell in one of our senses—touch, sight, hearing, taste, or smell—it triggers a tiny chemical secretion that launches a minute pulse of electricity up the fibrous pathway of our sensory nervous system. Somehow freighted with information—about heat, light, vibration, pressure or an invading chemical substance—the pulse of electricity shoots up the neuron's sensitive branches, called *dendrites.* Converging through its succoring cell body, it collects in the trunk end, or *axon.* The axon is attached to a branch or the cell body of another neuron. That connection, a fantastically swift, specialized, and efficient clearing house of information, is called a *synapse.* As it happens, there are two kinds of

29

synapses in our body, excitory and inhibitory, in about equal ratio. If the synapse is inhibitory, the stimulus pulse is delayed and sharpened, refined, filtered, or suppressed altogether to prevent the sensory overload that would otherwise turn all our conscious moments into a bewildering multimedia light show. If, however, the synapse is excitory and the stimulus pulse strong enough, certain transmitter chemicals or hormones are released in minuscule amounts and the original pulse of electricity, renewed, sent surging on with its cargo of information through the next neuron, in a relentless relay.

Parenthetically, some biochemists are beginning to believe that functional defects in these transmitters which block or distort nerve impulses may lie at the root of mental illness. Many of them—a tiny drugstore in our head that may contain thirty chemicals in all—are structurally similar to psychoactive drugs such as hallucinogens, amphetamines, and mood elevators. Too much or too little of one or the other have been shown in isolated instances to accompany schizophrenia, manic depression, and violently aggressive behavior.

Arriving at the brain, the relayed stimulus—in the case of our daughter's braces, a chance glimpse of her appointment card tacked to the family bulletin board—incites a relatively straightforward response in much the same fashion. Almost without conscious decision the response is translated into another electrochemical burst and sent coursing instantly back down the motor nervous system to start her legs moving, toward the bicycle that will take her to the dentist's office. At best, short of a reflex act like removing your hand from a hot stove, this basic neural process is never simple, except in the strictest relative sense. Even then, as many as a hundred thousand neurons may fire in several hundred thousandths of a second. In the instance of an Einstein smitten by sudden insight, the stimulus may not be sensory at all, but a fleeting thought lost to consciousness even as we apprehend it. Such a thought, perhaps sprung full-blown from a barely conscious association of diffuse ideas, can touch off a firestorm of prolonged neural excitation whose varied and sweeping patterns are believed to carry in uncracked (and perhaps uncrackable) code all our thoughts, memories, feelings. These patterns involve untold

30

millions of neurons at once. They are as yet complex beyond all understanding.

"Analogy!" cried the mathematician Polya. But how is analogy to capture the operative essence of that hive of neurons packed into our skulls—as many as a hundred million to the cubic *inch*—cells with which we mesh neural input to output and act upon our perceptions of the world through such mental behavior as language, reasoning, decision-making, problem solving, hunch, habit, and insight? Analogy, moreover, does not invite the remotest grasp by that same brain of the staggering numbers involved, almost ten billion neurons, or three times the world's population. Nor can it suggest to our vaguest comprehension the astronomical extent of synaptic connections possible in a single human brain: some three hundred to five hundred trillion, the distance in miles across the United States times the number of stars in the Milky Way, if not double that. The mind reels, if it can be cudgeled to think in such Brobdingnagian terms at all. For the problem is not merely (merely!) additive or exponential, though that would be problem enough. In theory, the function of one neuron we faintly fathom. In practice, the interrelated functioning of all the brain's neurons soars to a pinnacle of synergy, the principle that says the whole is infinitely more than the simple sum of its parts. And that we may never grasp.

This is not to say we have no idea how the brain produces intelligence. We have lots of ideas, each of which seems eminently reasonable to the very brain we are attempting to understand, though quite obviously not all these ideas, despite their reasonableness, can possibly be right. But of this we are sure: Memory is the indispensable matrix of the mind in which all else is embedded. Without it, there can be no learning, no thinking, no creating, no intelligent behavior as we know it.

Memory

Although we now know that simple one-cell bacteria have a rudimentary memory, the phenomenon of remembered experience in all its ramifications is uniquely man's. There are basically two

31

kinds of human memory, psychologists have found, short-term and long-term. Some prefer to split short-term memory into two parts.) The first they see as a sort of sensory anteroom, where arriving stimuli can be sized up and identified subliminally (beneath the threshold of conscious awareness) in the split second before being granted an audience with the second part, our brief but full attention. Visually, for example, they believe the first phase is what allows us to sustain perceptual continuity between such discrete but related stimuli as the disrupted train of images seen by our blinking eye. Other psychologists see these distinctive phases as simply differing ends of the same continuum. In either case, they agree that short-term memory manifests itself most consciously in those chunks of information we apprehend on the fly; that precise and finite amount of data we can, as Toronto's Fergus Craik disarmingly puts it, "keep in mind"[3] without rehearsal for up to thirty seconds if undistracted: A freshly looked-up telephone number, an address of momentary interest, the blurted name that accompanies a stranger's hurried handshake. Like a word written in your breath on a winter windowpane, it will be gone in less than a minute unless something happens, or you make something happen, to fix it further in your memory. Despite its evanescence, psychologists believe short-term memory is active in immensely important ways. It helps us perform calculations where the rapid manipulation of symbols is essential, but the resulting mechanical exercise is secondary to the outcome. If, for instance, in using pi to calculate the area of a circle, we could not put each step in multiplication firmly out of our mind after executing it, our head would soon be a jumble of useless digits. Short-term memory also retains the sequence of sounds or syllables in a spoken or written sentence until their meaning can be extracted, then banishes them from our consciousness. If it did not, our brain would ring with the day's accumulation of words even more than it does now. In the plethora of perceptions that constantly assails our senses, short-term memory detects features and recognizes patterns, stages a stimulus for our full attention when warranted, and keeps the stimulus around for the mind to ponder until its significance, or lack of it, is preliminarily decided. If it failed to do so, one thing would weigh equally on our mind like another. A clock tick would be as pregnant with possibilities as the ring of your phone or the unexpected sight of an old friend. Without the full-time filtering of sensory priorities that short-term memory gives us, consciousness would be chaos.

All in all, then, short-term memory has crucial importance to our intelligence. But it pales in the end beside the miracle of the brain's permanent storehouse, that prodigiously crammed, seemingly bric-a-brac-strewn Xanadu basement belonging to the Citizen Kane in all of us—long-term memory.

What do we keep there? A better question would be, what don't we? Judging from both accidental and experimental descents into its most subterranean chambers, all that we have ever consciously experienced is meticulously filed away there, and maybe more. Long-term memory holds, in effect, a lifetime of living. A sudden random stimulus—the smell of roasting chestnuts that flings you back onto a Paris streetcorner you knew twenty years ago—can unlock its deepest vaults as if by magic. People regressed to early childhood under hypnosis can often recall long-forgotten feelings and events in vivid detail. A tiny trickle of electricity from a microprobe surgically inserted in the brain can release memories of aching immediacy and fidelity to fact, as well as provoke an uncontrollable flood of authentic sensation, and behavior without benefit of thought or direct sensory stimuli.

All our memories, we know, are tantalizingly *there*. They pile up like miser's gold, teasingly accessible to ready withdrawal if only we knew how, until or unless something extraordinarily traumatic happens to foul the unknown mechanism of access. Such cases are rare—and fascinating. England's Elizabeth Warrington reports one bizarre anomaly in which the twenty-eight-year-old victim of a motorbike accident was rendered all but incapable of repeating verbal stimuli. He could manage two digits at most, often only one, and sometimes none. He also had comparable trouble with letters and words. But given a series of any one of them and asked afterward to point out the fourth, sixth, and so on, he readily complied—dramatically demonstrating that the train of information had entered his memory but could not get out.

In another classic instance, a young American airman suffered a wound at the base of the brain when a miniature fencing foil,

33

wielded by his companion in a mock duel, penetrated the back of his nostril. He promptly lost his ability to put anything into long-term memory. Attempts to test him clinically read like a bad joke. After being briefed on the procedure, he would nod his head eagerly and say, "Fine. Let's go." The researcher would then start his tape recorder and say, "Okay. Ready?"

"Ready for what?" the young airman would inevitably reply.[4]

The Wets and the Drys

How is what we know and feel unerringly stored away, and where? If only because of its proven perishability, most theorists tend to agree, short-term memory is primarily electrical, a kind of diminishing echo in the neurons that have been activated. But when it comes to the character of long-term memory, they part company. The Wets, or advocates of a biochemical basis, contend that such infallible and enduring storage can only be achieved through permanent but modifiable chemical changes in the brain. These changes, they believe, must occur at the level of the individual molecule, since the normal brain seldom reveals any gross constitutional changes with age, much less the sort of massive alteration that might be expected from the accumulating impact of lifelong learning were its effects multiply cellular. On the other hand, the Drys, those apostles of electrical primacy, argue that it is perfectly plausible for memories to be written indelibly if amendably into brain waves, although they cannot agree among themselves how. The debate is debonair but intense. The Wets archly compare the more avant garde electrical approaches to "placing electrodes on the surface of a computer to find out what problem it is working on."[5] The Drys in more private moments murmur about radical chemical experimentation being, in the acid words of one, "oozings from the stressed seams of cracked pots."[6]

Polemics aside, each faction has its points. They even share one fundamental area of agreement. There is no argument whatever that an incoming stimulus makes a distinct and lasting mark of some kind on the impressionable brain. If it did not, all stimuli

34

would be more or less the same, their differences a matter of degree rather than type. A taste might be less than a smell, the sight of a sunset simply greater in magnitude than the sight of an orange, like the graduated reading on a voltage meter. But no, each sense, and every stimulus that arouses it, is as uniquely different in character as they appear to us. The proof of this, if anything so obvious requires proof, lies more clearly with electricity than chemistry. It can be found in a wealth of exciting new work with the electroencephalograph (EEG), the machine that measures the brain's electrical activity.

Although the EEG has a long history in diagnostic medicine, the Drys aim their research at quite another sphere of interest, one called *cortical potentials.* Cortical potentials are curtains of high-frequency waves that flicker incessantly across the cortex in a hurricane of activity the Drys think holds the secret to how specific stimuli are registered in the brain.

In a typical study, the subject sits in a silent, darkened room. Electrodes are pasted to his scalp, and the EEG hooked up to an electronic averaging device that, in effect, establishes a background level for the brain's ongoing electrical activity. There is nothing to see, nothing to hear. Sensory stimuli have been reduced to an absolute minimum. The pressure of flesh against chair and floor, a faint metallic taste of apprehension are about all. Now, suddenly, a brilliant flash of patterned light or a loud noise is introduced. It triggers a burst of localized electricity in the brain that the EEG's drum-and-pens record in their Himalayan mappings as a tiny, jagged sawtooth. This the Drys call an *evoked* potential. In the absence of other strong stimuli, they claim, this small, spurting departure from the norm can be conclusively tied to the test stimulus.

The Wets dismiss this as nothing more than a reliable indicator that the staging-and-holding action of short-term memory is in progress, rather like the busy signal of your telephone. They insist it is of no use in deciphering the nature and content of the stimulus, in showing as a consequence that the core of the brain's unique information-processing capability is electrical instead of chemical. In short, they say, the medium is not the message.

Ah, but it is, retort the Drys. In such environmentally con-

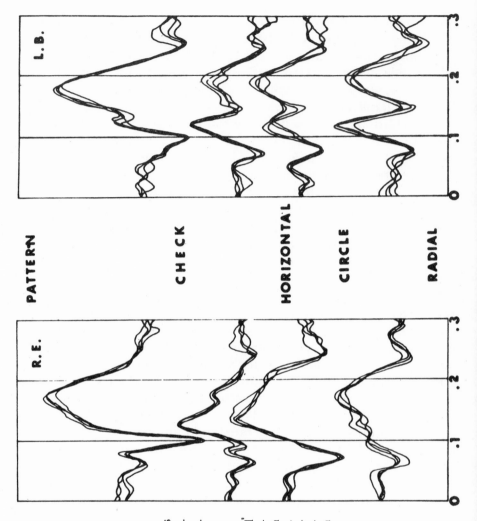

FIGURE 3

Visually evoked responses from two subjects presented with four types of patterned stimuli

(CREDIT: "The Visual Evoked Response and Patterned Stimuli," by Carroll T. White, in *Advances in Psychobiology*, G. Newton and Austin H. Riesen, eds. Reprinted by permission of the author and John Wiley & Sons, Inc. 1974.)

trolled experiments with induced visual stimuli, they report, the scribbly, dribbly aftermath of the sawtooth, as innocuous-looking as a tadpole's tail, when magnified and analyzed for contour proves consistently and systematically unique for each image. In other words, the different shapes seen—a checkerboard, a horizontal grating, a concentric circle, an outsized asterisk—yield distinctive electrical "signatures" (Figure 3). By signature, the Drys mean to convey that while no one visual stimulus registers exactly alike in different brains, it is registered the same by any one brain, no matter how many times it is repeated, and can be recognized as such.

The Drys are not yet ready to call this brain "language." That would suggest they were closer to cracking the brain code than anyone dares dream. But the hint is unmistakable. If a signature can be read, can the alphabet in which it is written, however abstruse, remain forever outside our comprehension?

The Wets declare themselves unimpressed on other grounds. These electrical signals, they charge, are limited to sensory stimuli, and reveal nothing of value about motor response or symbol manipulation in the brain itself. The Drys reply that the Wets just haven't done their homework. They point out that what they refer to as a *phase discontinuity* has been found in the EEG immediately prior to the subject flexing, on request, a given set of muscles. Put another way, the response is preceded by a short, sharp pulse that appears on careful study to be a mental precursor to the physical act. Hence, declare the Drys, even the decision to respond is at its base electrical.

(Neuroscientists on both sides of the question would do well at this point to investigate the Japanese martial art of aikido. Founded on the philosophy that all matter is energy—an idea entertained in the Orient millennia before nuclear physics—aikido teaches its disciples to anticipate an opponent's next move and turn it against him by sensing the flow of energy he generates in consciously formulating the act.)

As for symbol manipulation, chimpanzees taught to play tic-tac-toe for banana pellets show one novel configuration in their brain waves the instant before they make a winning move, another the instant before their opponent does. What could be more abstract, more information-laden—more weightless and metaphysical, in Bucky Fuller's terms—than the sudden realization of banana, yes, banana, no?

For that matter, add the Drys, nothing in chemistry, not even the psychedelics, can produce without bewildering distortion and disorientation the kind of legitimate if shorthand reliving of experience that local stimulation of neurons in the brain with an electric microprobe can.

Finally, E. Roy John of New York Medical College, the recognized father of evoked potentials research, goes even further. On the basis of repeated clinical studies of reversible lesions in laboratory animals, John now formally rejects the concept of a specific memory trance, or as a French scientist in 1904 enduringly christened it, the *engram*. Reversible lesions, as their name implies, refer to small, precise areas of the brain temporarily knocked out with chemicals or surgery. They are inflicted deliberately to see what effects occur, and inferentially to learn through the resulting deficits how the neurons there ordinarily function. Such research, John argues, proves that a purely localized neural response to stimuli can be everything the textbooks have always said brain cells in action are not. It can be variable, nonspecific, overlapping, arbitrary, ambiguous, erratic, and at the risk of hyperbolic redundancy, downright unreliable.

This, however, John believes, is entirely beside the point, a case of being unable to see the neural forest for the dendritic trees. He contends that a memory is not an isolated cellular happening at all but, in effect, a facsimile of the brain's total electrical state at the precise instant the new experience makes its impact, with all the brain's gross alignments of huge cell populations caught in the act of responding variously or not to the sensory-motor continuum. Seen that way, a memory becomes a frozen slice out of neural space and time, a single stop-action frame from a lifelong motion picture, one that must at the molecular level surpass all the thunderous battle scenes ever filmed rolled into one. If John is correct, the contents of our mind, though we have no conscious key as yet to the projector, can not only be reeled backward but can also be made to do filmic loop-the-loops.

To the Drys, such manifestations are exclusively electrical. No researcher, they point out, has ever unveiled a pair of neurons or neuron populations he could identify with impunity as having been chemically changed in different ways by exposure to specific stimuli. Unique character is the exclusive property of the brain's electricity, not of its chemistry.

But must it follow, then, that the permanence of such variable manifestations, such unique character, is electrical?

Not in the least, say the Wets. Frozen drunks pulled off skid row in the dead of winter without a detectable trace of electrical activity in their brains have no trouble remembering the good old days when thoroughly thawed. Extreme heat prostration and electroconvulsive shock therapy used to treat some types of mental illness can also erase or disrupt the brain's electricity. Although such traumas often obliterate all knowledge of the prior few days—the interval our brain seems to need for consolidating recent experience in long-term memory—it seldom touches the endless galleries of permanent recall. If long-term memory is in essence electrical as the Drys claim, where does it go when the current is shut off?

Moreover, John himself concedes that changes of "an undetermined nature" occur in the participating neuron populations to bring about a dependable "rerun" of unique experiential moments. And as the Wets never tire of telling, significant biochemical changes have been repeatedly and indisputably shown to accompany the consolidation of long-term memory, at least in laboratory animals. In a classic series of microscopic experiments, the distinguished Swedish neurobiologist Holger Hyden cut open by hand the individual neurons in the rat brain, scraped out their protoplasm, and analyzed it—a feat one of his admirers euphemistically described as "demanding rather more steady nerves than most of us coffee drinkers can manage."[7] For his pains Hyden was rewarded with a riveting discovery. He found that learning in rats both increased the amount and altered the critical makeup of RNA (ribonucleic acid) in the brains. It also reduced concomitantly the amount of RNA in the glia, those tens of billions of auxiliary cells in the brain believed to feed the neurons. Similar findings have since been reported in rabbits, monkeys, and goldfish.

39

Now, in human chemistry the RNA's principal role is to distribute the genetic code carried in molecules of DNA (deoxyribonucleic acid). This it does by manufacturing throughout our body, in an incredibly orderly and timely manner, a rich array of proteins loaded with coded information. This information contains the legacy of our heredity, the blueprint from which each of us is built, down to eye color and hair thickness. When the manufacture of such proteins in the brains of lab animals is inhibited by the injection of killer chemicals, its memory for a learned task such as maze-running can be disrupted.

Can it be, as Hyden believes, that such proteins may, in addition to their more basic genetic duties, act as "executive molecules" to supervise what he describes as the "necessary transition in millions of brain cells" needed to produce the "new state" that consolidates long-term memory? If RNA can unendingly and almost unfailingly (save for genetic anomalies such as birth defects and albinoism) replicate millions of years of that cell-to-cell memory we call species adaptation in man, what is to stop it from doing the same to achieve the infinitely more modest goal of mastering for a single lifetime the multiplication table?

On the profound significance of Hyden's work the Wets are largely agreed: Long-term memory is somehow linked to the changing chemical constituency of RNA and its protein-producing capacity. They concur too with Cal Tech's Roger Sperry that the brain's billions of neurons in their growth, assembly, and organization express chemical affinities far too elegant and selective to give the game away to electricity once it is played. The outgrowing fibers are guided by a chemically probing touch system that leads them along exact pathways in an enormously intricate program. Writes Sperry: "By selective molecular preferences (they) are guided correctly into their separate channels at each of the numerous forks or decision points which they encounter as they travel through what is essentially a three-dimensional, multiple Y-maze of possible channel choices."[8] And all for what, ask the Wets rhetorically, to retire to the sidelines when the real action begins?

United though they be behind Hyden and Sperry, the Wets are considerably less sanguine about the implications of another line of investigation started in the late 1950's by James V. McConnell, a research psychologist at the University of Michigan. In a decade-long sequence of experiments with, of all things, the planarian or common freshwater flatworm, McConnell churned up a controversy that haunts the world of biochemistry to this date— and gives the Drys not a few risible moments.

The flatworm has two intriguing attributes that McConnell yoked to extraordinary purpose. It is the simplest animal to have both a brain and true synapses, and it possesses startling powers of regeneration. Filet a planarian and you soon have up to a hundred new ones on your hands. Such characteristics made it the perfect living test tube in which to study learning at its purest and simplest—if the planarian could learn. McConnell set out to see if it could. To do so he took a well-thumbed page from Pavlov, the Russian physiologist and father of conditioning, who proved years ago that you could train a dog to salivate at the sound of a bell, provided you "paired" the sound with the sight and smell of meat enough times beforehand for the two stimuli to become entwined in the dog's mind. McConnell paired a flashing light with electric shock, and trained the planarian to respond to the flashing light alone with contractions of its body. Ergo, the lowly flatworm could learn.

If he chopped the flatworm in two and allowed both pieces to regenerate, wondered McConnell, would the brain retain a vestige of conditioning? McConnell did, and showed that the regenerated piece could learn the same response to flashing light in half the time. To his own surprise, the tail learned as well as the head. Ergo, he decided, memory was spread chemically throughout the flatworm's body.

But how was he to prove such a sticky point? The answer, or so he thought, was simple. The planarian is a voracious cannibal. McConnell merely dropped his trained subjects into a blender and fed the resulting pablum to ravenous, untrained planarians. When tested on light conditioning, the well-fed cannibals significantly outperformed their untrained peers. Ergo, concluded McConnell in published papers, rudimentary intelligence had been transferred by chemical means.

The furor was immediate and lasting. McConnell's most charitable critics decided the unbroken molecules of the eaten planarian had been incorporated directly into the cannibal's digestive walls, where it had excited some primitive response that created chemical conditions to facilitate learning, without actually transmitting it. *Sic transit* memory molecule. The initial failure of other investigators to replicate McConnell's experiments only strengthened the prevailing skepticism. But in subsequent work here and abroad, researchers have minced, mashed, diced, and pureed the brains of trained rats and mice, extracted from them RNA, and injecting it, gotten what they believed to be a transfer of behavior in an encouraging number of cases. By mid-1972 a grand total of 133 published reports of success had appeared in the professional literature.

Another academic furor occurred when two scientists, one of them the eclectic E. Roy John, demonstrated that the chemical crossover could be erased in the flatworm's regenerating tail, if not its head, by submerging it continuously in a weak soup of ribonuclease. Ribonuclease is the body enzyme, or chemical catalyst, that ordinarily is secreted in judicious amounts to stop production of a specific protein when enough has been made. It acts as an automatic chemical brake on the RNA engine. Why had the flatworm's tail succumbed to chemical overkill when the head had not? Evidently either the stuff of learning was not uniformly distributed or, as McConnell was moved to speculate, the embedded brain was safely cushioned by surrounding tissue against the soup's lethal effects. In either event, the importance of RNA and its protein production to the worm's trained behavior was plain.

A gradually abating storm swirled around the question of whether the flatworm really had any intelligence, whether McConnell's conditioning should even be called learning. But even more controversial was the ensuing revelation by pharmacology professor Georges Ungar at the respected Baylor College of Medicine in Houston, Texas. Ungar claimed to have isolated and purified a coding substance he called *scotophobin* from one such transfer. It involved a most unlikely behavior he had trained into rodents: avoidance of the dark. After conditioning them with electric shock, Ungar made an extract of the brains and injected it into untrained mice. When the mice demonstrated a higher-than-chance learning curve on dark avoidance, another highly purified extract was made of their brains. From it, Ungar isolated, analyzed, and finally synthesized scotophobin (from the Greek *skotos,* dark, and *phobos,* fear), a "coded molecule" of protein he maintains induces the highly unrodentlike phenomenon of dark avoidance. It does this, Ungar said, by modifying synaptic connections directly, without benefit of actual experience—or it might be more fitting to say, with borrowed experience, a kind of short-circuit learning.

Many biochemists questioned Ungar's grasp of molecular chemistry. They found it impossible to believe that a fragment of protein could be freighted with that much information (although Hyden hypothesizes that a single molecule of RNA could encode at least 10,000,000,000,000,000 bits of information). The American referee of his article in the British journal *Nature* blistered its technical weaknesses as so grave that it rendered his conclusions "more likely false than true."[9] Unperturbed, Ungar continues to work on synthesizing more coded molecules.

McConnell, meanwhile, might have escaped with a minimum of adverse attention had he limited himself to his observation that the planarian discovery, together with corresponding indications from studies of the simple-celled paramecium, suggested chemicals mediating memory in some invertebrates were widely diffused through the body. There was little threatening about that. But no, he dared speculate publicly that man might someday make in the laboratory artificial molecules containing the sum total of the world's knowledge, and enthused: "What a change it will make in our educational system if much of what a man must learn during his too-short lifetime can be injected into him chemically!"[10] The eyes of the scientific community glazed over. There was a chorus of muffled coughs, a discreet rattling of papers in the back row. McConnell packed up his flatworms and his blender and went back to Ann Arbor. There, a self-depicted prophet before his time, he has laid aside the tumultuous work of a decade and taken up a subject only slightly less incendiary: behavior modification.

Today, the war between—and within—the ranks of the Wets and the Drys over the ultimate mechanisms of human intelligence, and how to leash them more tightly to our needs in the future, continues to rage fitfully. On occasion the pitch of battle obscures equally important issues. For example, precisely where in man's brain is his memory stored? Why is it we can surgically whittle away at random parts without specific memories, however they are stored, ending up on the cutting room floor? If we knew that, we could take a giant step toward comprehending the brain's code.

Holographic Theory

Back in the 1920's, the eminent American psychologist Karl Lashley, having cut up countless rat brains and failed utterly to eradicate their maze-running memory, came to two conclusions that have been stiffly disputed ever since: Long-term memory is distributed equally throughout the brain, and the intensity of recall depends on how much brain remains to process it. Cut out a chunk and you blur long-term memory—but expunge it? Never.

Nonsense, cried Lashley's critics. There was no physical precedent for such equipotentiality. Besides, sensory and motor abilities could fall to the knife or accidental injury in the brain; why should memory be any different? The explanation surely lay elsewhere. Then, in 1971, at Indiana University, researcher Paul Pietsch performed a series of operations on the brain of a salamander named Punky that made Lashley look post facto like a prophet.

The salamander is a marvel of organic plasticity. You can transplant its brain to its tail for months, then move it back without loss of either life or function. Pietsch wanted to test whether he could wipe out Punky's reflexive, life-giving hunger for the tubifex worm by cutting it out of his brain. His eloquent conclusion: "In more than 700 operations I rotated, reversed, added, subtracted, and scrambled brain parts, I shuffled. I reshuffled. I sliced, lengthened, deviated, shortened, apposed, transposed, juxtaposed, and flipped. I spliced front to back with lengths of spinal cord, of medulla, with other pieces of brain turned inside out. But nothing short of dispatching the brain to the slop bucket—nothing expunged feeding!"[11]

Pietsch embraced Lashley's point of view. Memory was everywhere. Anomalies such as the young American airman he regarded as proof that entry into long-term memory could be blocked, not memory itself abrogated or deranged. The fault lay in the bucket, not in the well. But suppose, just suppose, the salamander's impulse to feed resided elsewhere in Punky's jellified body?

Pietsch next shuffled in a few brain parts from the tadpole, a vegetarian. The tadpole tissue survived, but so did the salamander's eating instinct. The substitution of various-sized bits of alien brain did not in the least depress, much less destroy, its host's appetite. It was like "adding a zero to a string of integers,"[12] Pietsch wrote. Maybe the feeding instinct *was* located elsewhere. Pietsch took a deep breath and transplanted the entire brain of a frog.

As he had foreseen from the earlier experiments, the frog brain survived the salamander's crude rejection mechanism, but Punky's taste for the tubifex vanished. In 1,800 trials, Pietsch reported, the salamander never made "so much as a single angry pass"[13] at its natural prey. Its instinctive behavior had disappeared with the last speck, and only with the last speck, of its original brain.

Again, how was this equipotentiality possible? In the vernacular of science, the 1920's had offered Karl Lashley no "model" anywhere for his vision of the brain as a bottomless container, unless you accepted uncritically the trick glass from which the magician Blackstone could pour an unending stream of water. Today, however, we have it, the technological prototype of Blackstone's bottomless glass. It is a fascinating instrument called the optical holograph (from the Greek *holographos,* meaning "written in full"). Using a beam of laser light instead of a lens, the holograph can capture on film and project the three-dimensional image of any object with flawless fidelity. In its eerily exact manifestation, it is not unlike tonight's bright image of a distant star that died a million years ago. The star, as such, is dead, but another installment of the light that has always defined it is only now, as we gaze unknowing at its burned-out source, arriving to deceive anew our eye. So it is with the holograph. The object it photographs and projects appears to be there, a few feet away. We know we can

45

INTELLIGENCE AND THE BRAIN

reach out and touch it. But as we do, our hand closes on empty air and we find that it is gone. All we are looking at is the object's image as the laser light defined, trapped, and staged it for our perception. The object has been frozen forever as it appeared; matter made light of.

An explanation of the holograph's technicalities would take more pages than their pertinence is worth. What is pertinent can be stated briefly, if not much more simply: The laser light captures on film not a photographic positive or negative but a sketchy hieroglyphic that contains, in effect, a set of translatable rules to use in reconstructing how the light behaved when it struck the object. The result is less a picture of a cake, to use another metaphor, than an instantly realizable recipe for its perfect visual recreation from one specific vantage point in space. By varying slightly the angle at which the laser light strikes, hundreds of different objects can be recorded on a single piece of film. The entire *Encyclopaedia Britannica,* in fact, might be stored on one about as big as a sheet of typing paper—just as a lifetime of knowledge and experience can be cryptically written into a sheet of cerebral cortex no larger than a good-sized woolen muffler.

Most significant of all, only the optical holograph in the physical world outside our heads is known to demonstrate the property of *distributedness* that lies behind Karl Lashley's long-disputed conclusions about memory. Science writer Isaac Asimov might be talking about the brain as he describes the peculiar staying power of the hologram. (The holograph produces holograms just as the telegraph produces telegrams):

> If you cut a hologram in half, you are *not* left with two halves of a complete picture. Each half of the hologram can be used to produce the complete holographic image. If you tore the hologram into ten ragged pieces, each piece could be used to produce the complete holographic image. If you scratched the hologram, the part actually scratched would be spoiled, but all the rest would still produce the complete holographic image with no signs of a scratch upon it. If you punched a hole in the hologram, you would still get an image with no sign of a hole.[14]

But, adds Asimov, as the hologram is torn into smaller and

46

smaller pieces, or marred by more and more scratches, "the dimmer and fuzzier the image becomes."[15] In other words you can blur it, but you cannot expunge it, not this side of total destruction.

The concept of distributedness, then, like memory itself, defies quick and easy understanding. It says nothing less than this: that each rule contains the entire set of rules, every ingredient the complete recipe, all coded parts the whole.

Those rules—that recipe—that *code*—is what fascinates brain researchers. As cyberneticist Philip Westlake of the University of California at Los Angeles points out, when both processes are reduced to mathematical equations and compared, the oscillation and fluctuating amplitude of laser light in the optical holograph as it codes resemble the wave forms in the brain as *it* codes. So in spite of their physical differences—the one composed of discrete electrical pulses, the other of continuously flowing electromagnetic radiation—the two methods of coding may be momentously similar.

The evidence, however, remains distressingly meager and indirect. We know, for instance, that our ability to see and distinguish patterns can survive even when the optic nerve is riddled with lesions or the visual cortex removed altogether. Without intact point-to-point neural pathways between the retina of the eye and the region of the brain that processes visual information, Westlake asks how is such a thing possible except holistically through alternate reconstructing sources? His view is strengthened by the existence of a form of brain damage called *polyopia,* which manifests itself in multiple visual images that suggest at least a holographic stage in the perception of sight.

There, for the moment, the matter dead-ends, pending another empirical step that will take us closer to finding out if the two codes share a common base and are, perhaps, decipherable in the same way. All things considered, it is an awesome burden for the empirical to carry. As Holger Hyden is fond of quoting mathematician Michael Polanyi about empiricism, "It relies on clues which are largely unspecifiable, integrates them by principles which are undefinable and speaks of a reality which is inexhaustible."[16]

47

So: Human memory, the matrix of all our intelligence, may be at bottom chemical, electrical, or both. It demonstrates holographic properties of ubiquity, economy, and survival, but relies in the end upon that common denominator of all our mental processes, the nerve cell or neuron. The neuron, a microscopic bit of living tissue, is present in our brain and nervous system in numerically fantastic constellations and complexity. Neurons grow and die and can be destroyed in radical amounts without erasing what the brain knows. That knowledge is stored for a lifetime, yet readily accessible to instant retrieval and amendment, in a code still beyond our remotest comprehension.

Man's brain, in sum, is no optical holograph, just as man himself is no salamander, flatworm, mouse, or rat. But the parallels give us cause to pause and ponder. Sensory and motor abilities fall to the knife, but the memory lingers on. As what, an electrical echo with a chemical voice box? Can we even be sure that everything in it, words and images, abstract symbols and concrete impressions, are couched in the selfsame code? If by some technical sleight of hand we could extract a fragment of that code, or those codes, as it is—raw, intact, finite, undeciphered by our conscious awareness—and bring it quivering with life into the bright arena of our full scrutiny, would we have something for the microscope, the oscilloscope, or both?

For that question, as for others of comparable magnitude in brain research, there is as yet no clear answer. Are there, then, as we seem to be saying, no new or recent answers in the neurosciences as monumental to our knowledge of intelligence as the questions that remain?

On the contrary, in at least one area of neurophysiology there are exciting indications that research borders on a tremendous breakthrough. There, what we are learning about human intelligence may do more than double what we know. It may compel us to redefine it altogether.

48

Chapter 2

A Brain Divided

In 1844 an obscure British physician named A. L. Wigan published a curious report. He told of three cases in which men who had led apparently normal lives until their death had been found on autopsy to have lost one entire side of their cerebrum to wasting disease. In two cases the hemisphere was "gone, annihilated— and in its place . . . a yawning chasm," wrote Wigan. In the other case it was "reduced . . . to a thin membrane . . . the whole solid contents . . . absolutely gone."[1] Yet personhood, personality, consciousness had remained. How was such a thing possible?

Wigan came to a startling conclusion. "If [one hemisphere] be a perfect instrument of thought," he wrote, "if it be capable of all the emotions, sentiments, and faculties which we call in the aggregate, mind—then it necessarily follows that Man must have two minds with two brains."[2] Before the century was out several better-known scientists were moved to embrace Wigan's novel concept, among them the English surgeon and pathologist, Sir Victor Horsley. With a very un-British lack of reticence, Horsley proclaimed, "we are not single animals: We are really two individuals joined together in the middle line."[3]

Despite their revolutionary implications—or perhaps because of them—the views of Wigan, Horsley, and their supporters made no more than a ripple on the rising tide of neurology. For in the meantime two European neurologists had hit upon related discoveries that were to give rise to quite a different doctrine, even as they laid to rest for a lifetime Wigan's troublesome findings. In 1865 France's Paul Broca reported that injury to certain areas of the cerebrum's left half led almost invariably to speech disorders, while damage to the same area of the right half did not. Nine years later Germany's Carl Wernicke traced another type of speech impairment to a region of the cerebrum outside Broca's area. But again, in case after case, it proved to be lodged only in the left hemisphere. Neither area, Broca and Wernicke found, had anything remotely to do with the motor system controlling the muscles that shaped speech. Rather, each area was intimately related to a basic mental process underlying the manufacture of spoken language. In Broca's area it was word formation, in Wernicke's, sentence coherence. Did this mean, then, that the power to generate speech was located exclusively in the left hemisphere? Subsequent research into the speechless condition, known as *aphasia*, showed it to be so in 97 out of 100 cases. Clearly, neurologists decided, in expressive language the left hemisphere was dominant. Was it dominant in anything else of comparable importance?

At this point their attention turned to another human phenomenon, right-handedness. By and large nature in her myriad workings shows no overriding preference for either the left or the right. Stars spin in either direction; so too, in their way, do the whorls of seashells. Man alone among animals is overwhelmingly right-handed; the ratio today is a resounding nine to one. Nowhere at any time in modern history has there been a left-handed culture. Right-handed tools predominated as far back as the Bronze Age, thousands of years before Christ. In all things the right hand was plainly ascendant. What if anything could be the connection with language?

Anatomically, we know, both our sensory and motor nervous systems are lateralized. That is, one side of our body feeds its neural signals predominantly to, and is in turn mainly controlled by, the opposite side of the brain. Therefore, neurologists concluded, since man appeared fundamentally right-handed the neurons engaged in learning various manual abilities lay in the opposite, or left, hemisphere too. (Remember, this was decades before Karl Lashley raised the issue of ubiquitous memory.) And if language and handedness *both* issued out of the left hemisphere, went the accepted reasoning, the left must have functional preeminence in the great mass of men. We are right-handed, Broca concluded, because we are left-brained. Thus developed the classic theory of *hemispheric dominance,* which held that one half of the cerebrum, the left, contained all our higher faculties, including what brain theorist Michael Arbib calls the spotlight of consciousness.

The right hemisphere, in contrast, was believed to be not only ingloriously mute, but dominated, trancelike, automatic, and all but unconscious. Since this was patently untrue of those millions of left-handers in the world who made up the one-in-ten exception, the advocates of one-hemisphere dominance hastened to add that their dominance for some obscure reason must lie on the right side of the cerebrum, their passive hemisphere on the left.

What of Wigan's patients? Wigan, providentially, hadn't said which hemispheres were missing. He had said the men led apparently normal mental lives, which meant that their speech, manual and mental abilities were apparently intact. So in all cases it was assumed that either the remaining hemisphere was the naturally dominant left or the man was left-handed, thus right hemisphere-dominated. Any other conclusion had been safely interred.

Much, however, has happened during the last fifty years to suggest that the theory of one-hemisphere dominance to the exclusion of the other should be drastically modified if not discarded altogether. For one thing, as psychiatrist Abram Blau pointed out in his book *The Master Hand,* no one has yet proved that right-handedness is the natural condition of man. Many primitive peoples still engage in work with a marked left-hand preference, and sources as diverse as early paintings and the Bible depict large numbers of left-handed in action. As for the marked shift to right-handed preference that undeniably occurred in the Bronze Age, Blau attributes it to a growing cultural need to prevent needless duplication—both of rare materials used and teaching effort expended across the generations—by incorporating uniformity of hand into the social code and transmitting it tribally down through time. All the moral and ethical injunctions that have followed since, Blau believes, emerge as a means of influencing peoples, of directing their behavior, of indoctrinating a preference.

To Blau, and to other more clinical researchers as well, the issue is now and forever confused by a further question: right-handed in what? Estimates of left-handedness in the scientific literature range from 30 percent down to 1 depending on the criteria used.

Of 250 students tested by one investigator, only nineteen were right-dominant in all tasks. The question, Blau decided, was further confounded by socialization and training. Of 500 high school boys he tested, the ratio of left to right use approached fifty-fifty in simple skills, but was skewed dramatically to the right on those requiring long and careful instruction, such as handwriting.

Handedness, moreover, has proved to be by no means as neurologically clear-cut as it first appeared. No one has yet been able to show that the hand links up with a collection of cells having for hand preference anything like the language center's unique capability for generating speech. For that matter, if handedness were an expression of natural dominance on the part of either hemisphere, would that dominance be expressed manually in terms of skill or preference? In an overwhelmingly right-handed society, no left-hander needs Blau to tell him the two are not always the same. (A cloudy notion of dominance still persists in the canons of education today. It says that if language is fixed, and not the stakes in a floating neural crap game, we needn't worry about it.)

Then too, an investigation of over a hundred left-handers who had lost their speech to injury revealed the unexpected fact that more of them had suffered lesions on the left side of the brain than on the right. The concept of one-hemisphere dominance as it stood could hardly be stretched to fit such a discrepancy as all three—handedness, language, and dominance—existing simultaneously on the same side.

Finally, as research expanded and testing techniques improved, it was discovered that people, all unknowing, usually favor one *eye* almost as preponderantly as they do one hand. In almost half the population examined, that eye was the left, which of course is directed in its movements primarily by the right hemisphere. To confuse matters further, when these two most important extensions of man's brain for learning—the hand and the eye—were tested together, a high incidence of crossed-lateral expression was found, a marked preference for the opposite hand and eye. What did this mixed state of affairs say for unwavering one-hemisphere dominance?

At best the concept was clouded, most neurologists agreed, especially since other evidence continued to mount that the right hemisphere was far from asleep—just as, in life-or-death situations, the left hemisphere was anything but indispensable. By painstakingly paying attention to what abilities were lost or impeded when either side of the cerebrum was damaged, researchers gradually pieced together, by clinical inference, a crude map of a brain hemispherically divided in its labor. From studies of deficits in hundreds of half-brains, they learned that the right hemisphere was better than the left at recognizing faces, pictures, and other objects. It was also better at perceiving and understanding spatial relationships. From the tragic creative losses of such composers as Ravel, they learned that while language issued from the left hemisphere, the wellsprings of music were in the right. (Ravel was struck down by a left-hemisphere stroke at the peak of his career. Although his "analytic recognition"[4] of musical notations was so grossly disabled he could no longer write music, his sense of rhythm, melody, style, and musical memory were largely unimpaired.) The right hemisphere was even better at constructional tasks under visual control, such as arranging and building. On top of everything else, the maligned right hemisphere retained at least a passive comprehension of language, if not the means to use it actively in formulating abstract ideas, the exclusive—and almost all-encompassing—province of the left.

By clinical inference, then, it could be shown that either hemisphere was vibrantly alive to the world of self and the world outside. Each was dominant in its own way but neither was dominant in all things, certainly never to the total and lasting exclusion of the other when both halves were healthy. The name of the neural game, evidently, was not an overweening dominance by either hemisphere but a specialization on the part of each—though whether it was more pronounced in the normal brain, or less, remained moot. The ghostly musings of another Wigan contemporary, the leading American neurologist Hughlings Jackson of Harvard, rang down the corridors of scientific inquiry: "If . . . it should be proved by wider evidence that the faculty of expression resides in one hemisphere, there is no absurdity in raising the question as to whether perception—its corresponding opposite—may not be seated in the other."[5]

Though reluctant to divide function as neatly as Jackson had speculated, most neurologists were now ready to admit that a vital schism, a fascinating split, or at least a localization of function, apparently existed. The more enthusiastic hailed it as a true bilateralization of function.

Had Wigan been alive in the 1950's, moreover, he would have seen himself vindicated. By then, removal of either hemisphere had become an accepted if last-ditch surgical practice for treating otherwise fatal tumors and certain types of disabling, intractable epilepsy. At most, hemispherectomy was found to produce a more rapid rate of mental fatigue and a lessened adaptability in meeting new problems. Although some sort of neural compensation or subtle substitution of function undoubtedly must occur, expressive language excepted, the loss of half a cerebrum apparently did not grievously detract from either the patient's basic intelligence or his acquired capacity for correct social behavior. If one hemisphere were lost, the other could carry on in its place. As Wigan noted, there remained "a person" no matter which hemisphere was removed.[6]

Deficit studies of anomalies, of course, are negative ways of determining anything. They work indirectly, by inference, by subtracting losses, by emphasizing what is not rather than what is, by keeping a sedulous eye not on the doughnut but on the hole. In studying hemispheric differences, researchers always found themselves comparing one functioning half-brain to another, each of which was trapped in a different head with a half-brain that wasn't working. Scientifically speaking, such a methodology was considerably less than elegant. What they needed to further fathom the functional secrets of a brain whose parts were so superbly organized was a means of isolating in the same brain a functioning right hemisphere from a functioning left. In that way, the two could be compared most naturally. Such a tool was found almost by accident. With it came the most provocative brain discovery of our lifetime. It reduces our psychology texts of ten years ago, as one writer wrote, to "medieval simplicity."[7]

The Surgically Split Brain

The corpus callosum is the biggest and most centrally located of the cerebral commissures, those thick fibrous bridges that connect the hemispheres. The callosum has been called "the largest and most mysterious information transmission system in the world." Narrow and nonfunctional at birth, it appears to grow along with the cortex, in blind obeisance to a timetable of natural development. It activates the sparse sensory and motor connections between the two hemispheres first, the rich linkages of higher intelligence last, just as we learn to transfer a rattle from one hand to another before we learn to turn written music into the sound of melody. From microelectrodes implanted in its neural pathways, we know the callosum is hyperalive electrically. But until recently we could only speculate that it somehow mediated and dovetailed a constant flow of information from one hemisphere to the other, or simply served as the master conduit for Lashley's holographic code.

For years, surgeons had known that the callosum, whatever its principal role in our mental processes, also helped spread certain kinds of epileptic attacks. They knew this because some seizures originally confined to one hemisphere would ultimately envelop both, unless blocked by disease in the callosum. That meant the callosum had to be the route of choice. In severely disabling epilepsy, when all else had failed and only hemisphere removal appeared to remain as a means of stopping its spread, what would happen if the commissures were cut?

The first such operation, performed in 1940, was a success. Subsequent seizures were limited to one side, and were not disabling. A growing number of cases over the next fifteen years confirmed that commissurotomy could indeed abolish generalized convulsions. All well and good, but what was the price? Although patients could easily go through a routine medical checkup without revealing anything wrong, there were two curious, readily detectable, but often dismissed or overlooked clues that a price had been paid. The "split-brain" patient, as he came to be called, initially favored his right side when he moved. He also continued to deny the presence of unseen objects placed in his left hand. Otherwise he seemed to lead a life every bit as normal as those of Wigan's half-brains, which is to say, as normal as anyone's. Personality, temperament, and intelligence appeared untouched.

Yet something vital must normally flow across those thick neural bridges. The callosum alone contains two hundred million neurons, twice as many as the body's entire sensory and motor systems combined. When those bridges were down, some highly important kind of traffic between the hemispheres had to stop.

Using an ingenious series of tests concocted for the purpose, Roger Sperry and his chief assistant at Cal Tech, Ronald Meyers, in the early 1950's set out to examine the surgically split brain more closely. In so doing they put into motion a burst of studies by others, notably members of the original research team, J. E. Bogen, and Michael Gazzaniga, then a graduate student, at New York University. The momentum of that work grows to this day. Taken together, the experimental results are beginning to alter forever our basic knowledge of human intelligence.

These investigations, in keeping with the complexity of their subject, have been far from simple. In his book *The Bisected Brain* and other writings, Gazzaniga marvels at the ability of man, this "endlessly clever primate," to maintain a "façade of perceptual unity" by "jumping the split" with a variety of involuntary behavioral strategies—strategies that amount to nothing less than an attempt to fool us into thinking that the cerebrum's higher capacities were still intact.[8] As Gazzaniga cautions in gargantuan understatement, "We must remember we are examining half of the human brain, which can easily learn from a single trial—and learn how to cheat, if necessary, to preserve its options." There were other problems, too. As Sperry notes, since the speechless right hemisphere is unable to communicate in words what it is experiencing, the nature and quality of its inner life remained, under the best of circumstances, less accessible to examination. Furthermore, Sperry points out, the task was complicated by other unifying factors, notably the "great overlap of common, almost identical experience resulting from the fact that these two separate mental spheres have only one body, so they always get dragged to the same places, meet the same people, and see and do the same things all the time. . . ."[9] Nevertheless, the results were astonishing.

Initially, on testing, the right hemisphere appeared stunned by the radical separation, almost as passive and unconscious as tradition would have it. That explained why patients would bump into things with their left side, and preferred to lead from their right, controlled as it was by the more expressive left hemisphere. But soon the right hemisphere revived and came around, to join in revealing a brain that commissurotomy had literally and dramatically divided against itself. Each half, according to Sperry, had become a separate entity, with "its own private sensations, perceptions, thoughts, feelings . . . memories . . . its own inner visual world."[10]

Touch

Sperry and his associates quickly discovered why split-brained subjects steadfastly denied the presence of objects placed in their unseen left hand. That hand was controlled by the speechless right half of their brain, and lacking the crucial integration of the commissures, the linguistic left half had no idea it was there. Objects identified by touch with either hand could later be retrieved by the same hand from a grab bag, but even that little bit of learning, the simplest sort of tactile discrimination, could not be transferred to the other hand. Each hand might as well have belonged to a different person. If the task was one that the hand and its controlling hemisphere were not equipped by neural specialization to perform, moreover, the result was fumbling failure if not outright neural anarchy. In one instance when a subject was asked to do with his right hand a jigsaw puzzle that was beyond the left hemisphere's limited spatial abilities, the right hemisphere, like the more facile of two children vying for its parents' approval, was unable to restrain itself and moved the left hand to do it.

Each hand further betrayed the specialized functions of its controlling hemisphere when given a pencil. (The subjects were right-handed, incidentally.) The right hand, having access to language but not to art, could still write but could hardly draw (Figure 4). The left hand, having access to art but not to language, could draw with practice, but could write nothing, however hard it tried, except the subject's signature, an automatic act more like duplicating a remembered design than manipulating language.

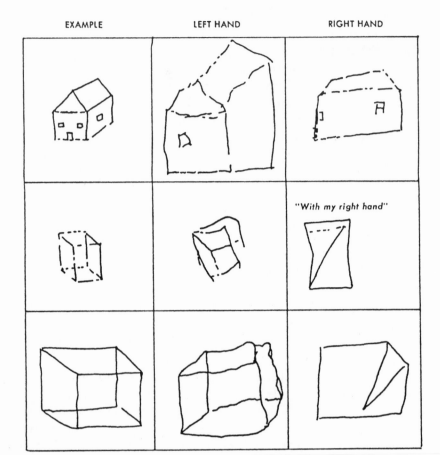

| EXAMPLE | LEFT HAND | RIGHT HAND |

"With my right hand"

FIGURE 4

Redrawn from original illustration as it appeared in "The Split Brain in Man," by Michael Gazzaniga, *Scientific American* (August, 1967). Reprinted by permission of the author and of *Scientific American*.

Despite practice, the hand controlled by the left hemisphere, in contrast, balked at even the most childlike figures. Given a square to copy with his right hand, Bogen found, the subject gave up after a few ineffectual squiggles, or more dramatically, drew four corners stacked together, as if the left hemisphere knew the geometric principles of a square but was at a loss to relate them spatially!

Time and again, tests in the purely tactile realm revealed a

58

striking superiority in the hand controlled by the right hemisphere when it came to discriminating complex patterns. Recognizing strange shapes bent out of wire, replacing segments of circles, sorting mixed objects for weight, size and shape—the hand controlled by the right hemisphere consistently excelled when it came to comparing and contrasting the unknown purely by touch. By the same token, the hand controlled by the left hemisphere performed best in those touch tests involving familiar objects with distinctive features that could be easily talked about.

Such distinctions, researchers decided, were anything but academic. Man is replete with talents that can be neither learned nor expressed wholly in language. Many important, useful physical forms in life can hardly be captured in words at all. As one psychologist says, "try to describe a spiral staircase without using your hands."[11]

Sight

Even more provocative, vision was literally torn in two; all it told of the world outside rendered schizoid in a stroke. How this occurs is not as simple as it might seem. Contrary to what we might expect, the eye does not feed all its neural signals to the opposite hemisphere. Although we are unaware of it, each eye is vertically split into two visual half-fields. Everything seen to the left of the vertical midline in both eyes is sent to the right hemisphere, and vice versa. Normally, the two fused fields of sight thus formed— the combined left-half fields and the combined right-half fields— are knit by the commissures into a seamless, unified whole. But in the split-brain, Sperry's team found, they functioned independently, as two separate and distinct perceiving systems, each totally outside the awareness of the other.

For instance, when images were flashed to a half-field in one eye for a fraction of a second—too fast for the eye to fudge by shifting its glance minutely—only the controlling hemisphere knew what had been seen. Since only the left hemisphere could trigger a spoken response, the subject verbally confirmed what he saw in the right visual field and denied the presence of what he saw in the left. Curiously, however, some subjects were able to describe the position of lights flashed into the left visual field. Without expressive language in the right hemisphere, how was this possible?

Gazzaniga decided the left hemisphere was plotting the directional cast of the left visual field in the test eye from the parallel cast of the left visual field in the other eye, whose movement it could peripherally see.

In another test, this one to see whether the right hemisphere could distinguish between red and green lights, the split-brain was again caught cribbing. To the surprise of the researchers, the subject began to speak up and answer correctly for the visual field not controlled by the language hemisphere, usually on the second try. Since that hemisphere should not have had access to the color information, something fishy was going on, and researchers soon found out what. The left hemisphere was guessing. If it guessed correctly, the right hemisphere let the answer stand. But if it guessed wrongly, the right hemisphere would incite a frown or a shake of the head, adroitly tipping off the left hemisphere to change its oral response. As a cheating tactic, it was as effective as a knowing friend in the classroom flashing an agreed-upon signal from the back row.

When researchers simultaneously flashed a green light to one hemisphere and a red light to the other, however, neither hemisphere was able to indicate with a shake or nod of the head whether the colors were the same or different. And if a dollar sign was shown to the left visual field and a question mark to the right, both at the same time, the subject would draw the dollar sign but reply "question mark" if asked to say sight unseen what he had drawn. The one hemisphere, the talking hemisphere, simply did not know what the other hemisphere had seen, or vice versa, any more than two people would if they had gone to different movies.

Not only were the hemispheres of two distinct minds, each capable of constructing a perceptual whole without the other, both would stop at nothing—including sheer fantasy—to do it. When the image of a square was flashed across the vertical midline of either eye, half on either side, each hemisphere "saw" not a half-square but the square completed. Sperry called this phenomenon, which has yet to be explained, "hallucinated completion."[12] To nail down its eerie existence, he and his associates confronted their subjects with "chimeric" images, fanciful apparitions composed of two boldly different half-faces (an old man's and a young woman's, etc.) joined in a line from forehead to chin, so that when the image was flashed, each half-face fell into a different visual half-field. In their perceptions of such a patent unreality, the disconnected hemispheres routinely resorted to a physical impossibility. Each "saw" the half-face in its visual half-field of the tested eye complete and alone and occupying the whole facial space. Verbally or by pointing, subjects reported first one completed face, then the other, depending on which half-field of the eye was covered, without in the least noticing anything odd about their visual perception (Figure 5).

Sperry's visual studies also indicated that the two hemispheres perceived objects in ways quite different. They not only saw different things when split, they saw things differently. "In dealing with faces," Sperry reported, "the right hemisphere seems to respond to the whole face directly as a perceptual unit, [while] the left hemisphere seems to focus on salient features like the moustache, the hair—to which verbal labels are easily attached."[13] The right hemisphere saw the forest, the left hemisphere the trees. The redundant right-left doubling, then, of which the normal brain is blissfully ignorant, assumed a significance in Sperry's view far beyond simple duplication: "If, as we now suspect, each hemisphere processes its sensory input in distinctly different ways, then such a doubling begins to make sense. In the normal intact brain the right and left contributions to any given perceptual experience become fused, making it difficult or impossible to determine which hemisphere is contributing what."[14]

Even if perceptions involved a transfer from one sense to another, such hemispheric specialization persisted. Subjects given wooden blocks to feel sight unseen and asked to point them out from a visually displayed array of opened up, two-dimensional drawings did three times better with the left hand, controlled as it was by the nonlanguage hemisphere. When their left hand was feeling a block, the subject's execution tended to be rapid, direct, and of course silent. When their right hand was at work, they took

NORMAL
FACES

CHIMERIC
STIMULI

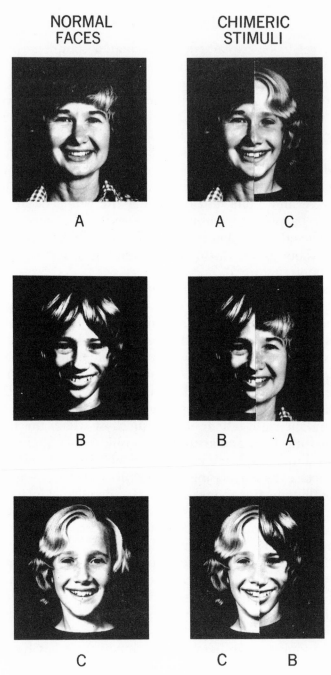

A

A   C

B

B   A

C

C   B

FIGURE 5
Chimeric stimuli. Test for recognition of faces

STIMULUS
IMAGE

C   A

VOCAL
NAMING

VISUAL
RECOGNITION

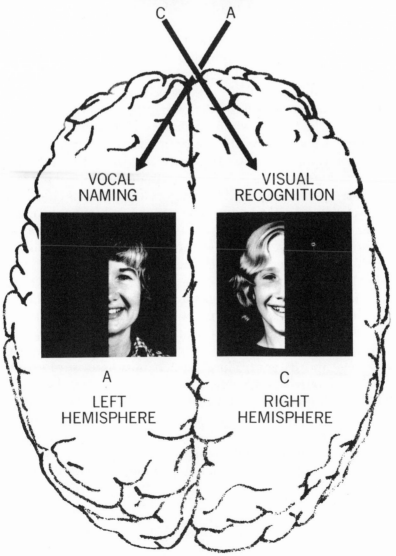

A

LEFT
HEMISPHERE

C

RIGHT
HEMISPHERE

as long as forty-five seconds to make a decision, responded hesitantly, and despite instructions not to, kept up a running verbal play-by-play of their reasoning as if it were a necessary part of the selection process.

All in all, the researchers concluded, "it appeared that the two hemispheres were processing the same information in entirely different ways, the left . . . in verbal, symbolic, analytic terms while the right utilized simple visualization."[15]

Capture and Control

When the word "heart" was flashed across the center of the combined visual field, impinging on that of either hemisphere, the right of course saw "he" and the left "art." Asked what he had seen, the subject replied "art," which was to be expected. But asked to point to the flashed word among several on a card, he pointed to "he." Why, when no choice of hands was involved, did he prefer what was seen by the right? As Sperry interprets it, the right hemisphere is naturally dominant when the task requires only direct visual matching and no language or meaning is needed. Indeed, it was found, if the subject was given his choice of how to respond, the right hemisphere proved fully capable of capturing and controlling both the split-brain's sensory perception and its motor response, provided the task depended on abilities in which it was superior. On chimeric tests, for example, subjects overwhelmingly demonstrated a preference for the face seen in the left visual field, which registered in the right hemisphere only. They did this by habitually pointing to the face on the left as the one seen, even when they were required to use the right hand. This was convincing evidence, the researchers felt, that the left visual field and its controlling right hemisphere were calling the shots perceptually. Only when asked to name what they had seen rather than point it out did they respond to the face in the right visual field. As long as language was not involved, Sperry concluded, the brain's primary tendency was for all visual stimuli to be perceived in the nonlanguage hemisphere.

The speculation by Hughlings Jackson, it appeared, had been

right. The nonlanguage hemisphere was superior in sight and touch if not in the other senses, which fused in the whole brain and fell apart without significant discrimination in the half. The nonlanguage hemisphere, in brief, dominated in perception.

Intellectual Skills

In addition to its lack of expressive language, the right hemisphere demonstrated its most dramatic deficits in another field of symbol-manipulation, mathematics. It was even something of a dullard in simple arithmetic. Given wooden blocks with pegs to manipulate, it could add numbers totaling less than twenty, but no more. It was utterly at a loss to subtract or multiply. Since it could neither speak, write, spell, nor calculate beyond the most primary level, was it a complete ignoramus? Not at all, the Cal Tech team decided. It could draw, build, arrange, and make the subtlest of spatial distinctions. Despite its exalted ability to manipulate symbols, the left hemisphere could not even produce a square. The two hemispheres, then, simply differed in their ways of behaving intelligently (Figure 6).

Duplication

Investigators found evidence, in addition, that each hemisphere was equipped with a scaled-down and simplified version of the other's specialized skills. The left hemisphere could not copy a design but could direct the right hand to select it from a collection. It could then confirm that correctness verbally. So it was clearly capable of recognizing a given spatial configuration. The right hemisphere, on the other hand, repeatedly demonstrated a rudimentary understanding and usage of the simplest language. It could direct the left hand to pick from a pile of unseen objects one described, alluded to vocally, or named on the screen. Given ample time, like a backward child it could slowly read aloud words like "cup," "clap," and "six." It could also select from a flashed series of nouns one to fit a descriptive phrase spoken by the examin-

65

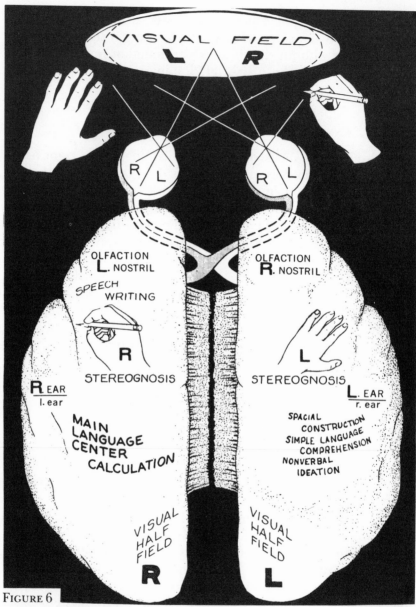

Figure 6

Lateralization of function in the two hemispheres as tested in the surgically split brain.

(Credit: "Perception in the Absence of the Neocortical Commissures," by R. W. Sperry, in *Perception and its Disorders*. Reprinted by permission of the author and The Association for Research in Nervous & Mental Disease, publishers, 1970) er, such as: "Used to tell time: Clock." (The kibbitzing left hemisphere, working solely from the verbal clue, spoke up: "Watch.") Slowly and with effort it could spell words like "pie" and "hat" and "love" using block letters, but it could not remember even one of them moments later. When pressed, at such times, it could even swear as pyrotechnically as a drunken sailor.

In sum, each hemisphere appeared to retain a sort of short-hand expression of the other hemisphere's abilities, both passively adequate at a superficial level, neither capable of a complex voluntary act that would require it under normal conditions to seriously challenge, much less usurp, the specialties of the other.

Parenthetically, such a duplication hints at the massive neural compensation that may take place in dire emergencies to enable either hemisphere to do the work of both, much as a single kidney can assume the lifesaving function of two. Indeed, we know that in children a pervasive compensation is the rule, a happy fact since brain tissue does not regenerate. Children, in fact, have expressive language on *both* sides. From a wealth of case histories we have seen that when gravely injured in the left hemisphere they often regain full speech and grow to maturity as if nothing had happened. Adults, in contrast, almost never completely recover linguistically. The limited language usually remaining to the adult right hemisphere, moreover, may very well be but a vestigial remnant of the basic childhood grammar, which prompts an intriguing question. Once laid down, why should this ground plan for a language begin to atrophy in one hemisphere around age four? Why should something once established be shut down if not dismantled on one side while developing freely on the other? Seldom if ever is nature so spendthrift with her resources. Nowhere else in the brain—that we know of—is the principle of parsimony so flagrantly violated. For that matter why should the two hemispheres be so rigorously specialized? Would it not make more sense in the long run, from the standpoint both of compensation and efficiency, to have each replicate the other?

Research to date has yielded no hard and fast answers to any of these questions. Again from studies of anomalies—"alexics" or word-blind persons, whose language is not crisply lateralized to one hemisphere or the other—Sperry concludes that a mutual and natural interference of function exists between the two hemispheres. They get along, in brief, like dogs and cats, and must be separated, he thinks, if the brain is to operate with optimum intelligence. As he puts it: "A distinct operational advantage can now be seen to having these two rather different and somewhat antagonistic mechanisms for the cerebral processing of information set apart . . ."[16]

Sperry's hypothesis is supported by the fact that distinct anatomical differences between the two hemispheres have recently been detected, both in stillborn babies and postmortem in adults. Wernicke's area, the area responsible for sentence coherence, has been shown to be larger in the left hemisphere than in the right. It is bigger by a third—almost half an inch—in the mature brain, which suggests at least a predisposition to language in the left hemisphere, if not outright genetic determination.

Otherwise, when it comes to why the hemispheres should grow to be so specialized, and precisely how, a thicket of clues leads to a swamp of conflicting theory.

"A Vast Unknown"

The core meaning of the split-brain experiments, to their researchers anyway, seems monumentally clear. A single pass of the surgeon's knife, as Michael Gazzaniga poetically puts it, leaves us according to Roger Sperry, with two separate minds, that is, two separate realms of conscious awareness, two separate sensing, perceiving, thinking and remembering systems.

One of these, located in the left hemisphere, is as familiar to us as our own sense of self-awareness. The other, located in the right hemisphere, is a shadow presence more discernible to us in its absence, when the left hemisphere is tested in isolation.

Neither invariably dominates, or is superior to, the other. The right hemisphere, J. E. Bogen believes, is working just as hard and intricately, doing "just as important work."[17] The difficulty in evaluating it arises largely from our ignorance. Says Bogen: "We have barely scratched the surface of a vast unknown."[18]

A Brain Divided

Bilateralization in the Normal Brain

Couldn't the very act of severing the commissures bring into play some latent mechanism for rechanneling the brain's neural workload, some backup system for granting each hemisphere autonomous control when, and only when, the integrative bridges are down?

To be sure, the concept of hemispheric specialization, or more properly, bilateralization of function, still has its foes. They prefer the term *localization* of function, because it has the virtue of implying specialization without raising the troublesome issues inherent in the concept of one hemisphere operating entirely independently of the other, much less pitted against it for mastery of the brain's response. The advocates of localization insist, moreover, that while capture and control of the sensory and motor nervous systems by either hemisphere has been satisfactorily demonstrated in the split-brain, this by no means proves it to be our normal condition. The right hemisphere's initially stunned condition upon separation, the phenomenon of hallucinated completion, both can be equally seen as artifacts of surgery that are otherwise meaningless. The very act of disconnecting the hemispheres, they argue, introduces yet another variable into the equation, just as deficit studies did.

The advocates of bilateralization would agree, but are quick to point out additional indications that in the intact brain most if not all cerebral activities are lateralized to one hemisphere or the other, and with them control of the entire brain-body response for each function. Working with the normal brain, for example, Gazzaniga has found that when the symbols *A* and *a* are flashed only to the visual field controlled by the right hemisphere, it takes the subject thirty milliseconds longer to say whether both represent the same letter than it does when the same stimuli are flashed to the visual field controlled by the left hemisphere. To Gazzaniga, the consistently timed delay when the right hemisphere is involved means the information has to be relayed across the commissures to the left hemisphere for processing because more than simple pattern recognition is needed. A knowledge of language is. A corollary discovery has been reported by Robert Ornstein and

69

David Galin of Langley Porter Neuropsychiatric Institute in San Francisco. When an EEG is taken from the skull over both hemispheres while a normal subject is busy at a task tailored to one—speaking, say, or drawing—Galin and Ornstein have determined that the other hemisphere will show a very slow, increased brain wave denoting inner relaxation. In effect, it will idle. Depending on the task at hand, they concluded, the two hemispheres, either alternate work shifts depending on the task at hand, or the brain's higher faculties are *time-shared,* computer parlance for the condition in which a computer works with such blinding speed in generating outputs that several human inputs when programmed can be handled all but simultaneously.

Furthermore, in a dramatic proof that speech and music are lateralized to different sides when the commissures are functioning, researchers have injected the anesthetic sodium amytal in the carotid artery on either side of the neck and put half the brain briefly to sleep while the subject was singing. Depending on which hemisphere was anesthetized, the subject, in midtune, would suddenly lose all sense of the melody or of the lyrics, but not both.

Finally, Montreal's Doreen Kimura has adapted to the intact brain many of the testing measures the split-brain researchers used on their commissurotomy patients. In subtle laboratory discriminations of sight, sound, and touch pitting one eye, ear, and hand against the other, she found that the two hemispheres consistently outperformed each other perfectly in keeping with the theoretical superiority of each. In dichotic tasks (one sense tested on both sides simultaneously, each with a different, competing stimulus) the left-side senses excelled on spatial and music perception, the right-side senses on spoken and written language perception only. The commissures, though uncut, changed nothing.

Indeed, more recent research indicates that the normal right hemisphere responds to melody holistically, as a gestalt, while the left, if that of someone musically sophisticated, dissects its passages in a manner analogous to the feature-detecting capacity of the left-hemisphere visual fields. In other words, the right hemisphere, in effect, thinks "Ah, yes, *Silent Night,*" two Columbia University psychologists report, but the educated left hemisphere thinks, "two sequences, the first a literal repetition, the second a repetition at different pitch levels—ah yes, *Silent Night* by Franz Gruber, typical pastorale folk style."[19]

In sum, Sperry writes, ". . . differential balance and loading between these right and left hemisphere faculties . . . could make for quite a spectrum of human intellect—from the mechanical or artistic geniuses on the one hand who can hardly express themselves in writing or speech, to the highly articulate individuals at the other extreme who think almost entirely in verbal terms."[20]

Who's in Charge Here?

If either hemisphere directs the brain in the performance of its specialties, depending on which is the more gifted, a perplexing question arises. Where is the boss mechanism for the brain's so-called normative system? Which hemisphere, if either, occupies the priority-setting, value-determining, judgment-rendering "executive" office? Which part of our brain makes the endless stream of decisions in matters great and small without which, as one experimental psychologist puts it, "the world would seem flat and any activity would be like any other?"[21]

In most of its behavior, this side of insanity anyway, the brain does not metaphorically leap upon two horses at once and gallop off in opposite directions, although a sane philosophy requires an enduring awareness that different directions do exist. In the corporate vernacular, who or what, exactly, is in charge here?

The question is obviously crucial, because on this point the advocates of bilateralization and their critics further part company. The advocates believe that each hemisphere has its own normative control. Their critics, on the other hand, continue to see a unity of purpose, of control, of effort. Above all—and here the two factions are as wrenched apart in their thinking as the most dramatically realized commissurotomy—they see in the living, waking brain, divided or not, the indomitable unity of individual consciousness. In J. E. Bogen's words, they see "The inner conviction of Oneness . . . [the] most cherished opinion of Western Man."[22]

71

It is on this rock that the concept of bilateralization at its most extreme comes closest to foundering. How can we conceive of ourselves as Sperry's "two separate realms of conscious awareness" coexisting beyond the bounds of our own knowing? How can we have two "thinking and remembering systems" that share control time for the total, higher brain, as Ornstein and Galin would have it, or alternate, each without suspecting the existence of the other? When the commissures are cut, how can there abide within us two distinct and separate "sensing, perceiving" entities that persist in alternating smoothly and effortlessly between two different perceptions of chimeric stimuli, as speech and gesture dictate, without once catching each other in the act? And when our "two separate minds," as Sperry conceives them, are informed of it after the fact, how can we reply without the tiniest tremor of apparent hemispheric conflict, "I must have done it unconsciously"?

The problem is partly semantic. Not only does "conscious" mean having an awareness of one's own existence, it also means being capable of complex response to the environment. Exponents of extreme bilateralization, needless to say, tacitly opt for the second definition. Gazzaniga claims that while the experiential world of the right hemisphere is conscious, it is private. Ornstein sees in the two "modes of consciousness" a possible parallel to Freud's concept of the conscious and the unconscious, as expressed in the psychoanalytic symptoms of repression and denial, when what the patient says obviously is not congruent with what he feels. Sperry refers to the "introspective consciousness" of a right hemisphere not above provoking a scowl or a wince or executing an exasperated shake of the head when words generated by the left hemisphere are in error; a right hemisphere that the left hemisphere often obliquely talks to by "thinking out loud," but whose separate existence it stubbornly fails to recognize except spectrally. For example, on one occasion when a split-brain subject's right hemisphere unexpectedly directed the left hand to perform a task intended for the right, the subject blinked and blurted in a convincing show of amazement: "Now I know it wasn't *me* that did that!"[23]

What difference does it make? Why should we care if the hemispheres function locally or laterally, with or without a shared consciousness, independently or under a central control?

It matters and matters mightily, say the split-brain researchers, because the evidence indicates that each hemisphere not only cooperates with and complements the other when the commissures are intact, it also responds to reinforcement or the lack of it. It is on this ground that Sperry and his growing army of disciples hand down a devastating indictment of civilized life today: Our society, they charge, especially in the fields of science and education, is inherently prejudiced against the intellect of the right, or nonlanguage, hemisphere. It is the linguistic, the abstract side of ourselves we test and educate and reward—and by such powerful social strategems catapult to an overarching prominence in the human scheme of things.

"What it comes down to," declares Roger Sperry, "is that modern society discriminates against the right hemisphere."[24] We are, in short, neglecting fully half our thinking brain, not just quantitatively but qualitatively.

Since Western culture with its Judeo-Christian tradition is primarily verbal and abstract, Robert Ornstein reminds us in his book *The Psychology of Consciousness,* it is only human that we regard the loss of language or the ability to manipulate mathematical symbols as the ultimate crippling. It is only human, but is it intelligent? Ornstein has the courage to say the obvious: To a writer, scientist or mathematician, injury in the left hemisphere may indeed be disastrous. But it is no more disastrous than injury in the right hemisphere to a musician, artist, or craftsman. Dominance, he declares, must be defused as the semantic boobytrap it is. Each hemisphere must be free in our mind to do its thing.

But what *is* its thing?

In the language hemisphere the answer could not be more obvious. In the nonlanguage hemisphere, however, the answer, while as familiar to us as sunshine, has been as little thought about by most of us in the context of intelligence as the dark side of the moon. A study of aphasia for the Commonwealth Fund said it as far back as 1935:

[There is] ample evidence that language plays a tremendous part in thinking and intelligent behavior [but] at the same time it is evident that purposeful and effective thinking may be carried on when language is extremely inadequate or confused, and must therefore depend on nonlinguistic symbols such as visual or kinesthetic images.[25]

The authors meant visual and kinesthetic images in the brain. They meant, in fact, mental images.

Chapter 3

Evolution, Imaging, and Language

In the beginning was the Word, says the Bible. But the Bible is a book and may be forgiven its bias. If modern brain research is right about the first man, in the beginning was not the word but the mental image: an internal impression of the external event. Indeed, the brain's ability to manufacture mental images was originally more important than its ability to produce language. As we will see in the remaining chapters of this section, it still is—a fact largely lost sight of in the surfeit of symbols from our overbearing left hemisphere.

Drawn large, declares social philosopher Kenneth Boulding, the mental image is "the sum of what we think we know and what makes us behave as we do." By that he means that each of us has in his mind a picture of the way the world is, a neural mosaic made up of thousands of millions of smaller mental images that are constantly being changed by new events and modified by our perceptions of, and reactions to, them. It is this internal picture we live by, Boulding believes, not by the words of any high-flown tenet or dog-eared maxim. Indeed, tenets and maxims are but pale efforts to capture in symbols the full and rich panopoly of this image, these images.

Contrary to what the words immediately suggest, mental imagery is not the exclusive property of the sight and sighted. It is the brain's highest gift to any and all our senses. In her autobiography, for example, the deaf and blind Helen Keller speaks joyously of how a word traced on her hand in Braille could "revive an image that some earlier experience had engraved on my brain,"[1] without resonating with meaning in and of itself. Everything that could hum, buzz, sing, or bloom, she wrote,

75

had a part in my education—noisy-throated frogs, katydids and crickets held in my hand until, forgetting their embarrassment, they trilled their reedy note, little downy chickens and wildflowers, the dogwood blossoms, meadow violets and budding fruit trees. I felt the bursting cotton-bolls and fingered their soft fiber and fuzzy seeds; I felt the low soughing of the wind through the cornstalks, the silky rustling of the long leaves, and the indignant snort of my pony as we caught him in the pasture and put the bit in his mouth—ah me! how well I remember the spicy, clovery smell of his breath![2]

From scent, touch, texture, and vibration, Helen Keller constructed a mental picture of a physical world so richly alive that we almost forget she could neither see nor hear. Language was necessary to unify those impressions in the absence of her other senses, to communicate the wealth of that experience to others. But as she herself admits, it was not needed to store up the treasure of impressions her remaining senses had harvested. They existed in mental images.

In his book *Evolution of the Brain and Intelligence,* Dr. Harry Jerison of UCLA's Institute of Evolutionary and Environmental Biology declares that what we call human intelligence may be nothing more—or less—than the unique ability of our nervous system to piece together continuously Boulding's internal picture of the physical world out of the myriad splinters of information provided by our senses. As he sees it, consciousness is this picture, a simplifying device, really, a "model of a possible reality"[3] held in our heads and subject to ceaseless revision. Every waking moment, he believes, the brain generates the miracle of this intelligence—instantly, endlessly, and usually without obvious effort (although it requires a fifth of our blood and oxygen to do so).

In tracing its evolutionary history, Jerison recognizes mental imaging as the crucial linkage that enables us to make sense of our senses. He assigns to it much of the credit for the growth of our brain. His analysis is noteworthy because it is the first attempt to build a case for intelligence as biology, not out of life as we know it, but from the fossil record, casts made inside the cranial cavities formed by the reassembled skulls of vertebrates dating back 400 million years. Such a passage of time, he confesses, renders his work "a chain of speculation."[4] Its technical details would interest only a paleontologist. But Jerison's conclusions merit our attention because, while his theory is frankly a new and unorthodox hybrid born of biology, psychology and neurophysiology, it issues out of data that comes as close to the actual evidence as we are ever likely to get.

Evolution

In Jerison's view, three kinds of sensory information combine to create our possible perceptual world. The first is the internal information from the subtle systems that regulate our organic states, such as visceral contractions, muscle and joint positions. Although not perceptual in the strictest sense, such information is part of that experience of physical reality we call *kinesthetic* (having the sensation of bodily movement) and *somesthetic* (having the sensation of surface and internal feeling). It is obviously the least important to understanding external events. The second kind of sensory information is proximal, that arising out of touch and taste. While important, in most life situations it is less vital than the third kind, which Jerison believes essential to the survival of higher forms of life: sensory information about events at a distance. Distance information can be acquired through hearing or smell but Jerison feels it was, and remains, primarily visual. Without it, man would have been doomed to blunder shortsightedly into early destruction.

As Jerison sees it, the story of man's intelligence begins with the early land-dwelling reptiles. From the marvelously intricate structure of the present-day reptilian eye, Jerison concludes that these early reptiles lived in a predominantly visual world, if hardly in the human sense of the word. Their responses to visual stimuli were rigidly stereotyped. Indeed, they comprised little more than a locked-in system of reflexes, answering all but automatically to a set range of vital needs such as detecting food, avoiding danger, and finding shelter. These responses were not only programmed by nature into their small brains but, significantly, judging from reptiles now, the neural machinery required to process the incom-

77

ing visual information was fixed at birth and housed almost wholly in the retina of the eye, outside the brain itself. In short, not only did the creature know just one game with a limited number of plays to choose from, it was playing with a genetically stacked deck.

The same is still true of reptiles today. Roger Sperry once showed that if you cut and scrambled the optic fibers in a frog, then surgically rotated its eyeballs 180 degrees in their sockets, the fibers would grow back oblivious to the altered visual environment, exactly as they were. The poor frog, left with permanent upside-down and backward vision, would continue vainly to strike out with its tongue at the vacant spot where the errant eye told it the fly was—until it starved.

In contrast, if you put distorting lenses on a man's eyes, his brain will straighten out what they perceive. This is only possible, Jerison thinks, because the distortion is checked, rechecked and finally corrected against input from our several senses that has been incessantly cross-referenced by mental imagery—perhaps even in our dreams, one theory has it—and firmly indexed in that "possible reality" we call consciousness. Even then correction does not occur quickly. After all, the brain constantly monitors our perceptions to update its mental picture of the physical world. In this instance it must be sure that it is not the model that needs changing, but the visual perception. Only then will it act in ways we cannot explain to override the engineered distortion of its eye—perhaps by a breathtaking refinement of Sperry's "hallucinated completion." In man this happens, in frogs, never. Nothing remotely like our consciousness intervenes to mediate for the frog between stimulus and response, to amend its surgically altered perception of visual reality.

Restricted though it was, the early reptilian vision was at least adequate to the requirements of daylight living on the land. The first stage in man's intellectual development, Jerison believes, occurred when the first mammals came on the scene 175 million years ago. These were little more than small reptiles that hunted at night, in deference to their more powerful relatives. As such, they needed a fine distance sense that would work in the dark, where their vision would not. From changes in the size and shape

78

of their cranial casts, Jerison theorizes that in response to the problem they evolved good distance hearing. For that hearing to perform at night the same function its vision had in the day, the nocturnal mammal had to be able to create from a sequence of sounds an auditory image. For example, the snapping of twigs growing ever louder had to come to mean "prey or predator approaching," depending on the sound's nature and magnitude. This was not simple. Some idea of the neural complexity involved can be seen in the way accomplished musicians today can "hear" the music when they scan a written score. Even the crudest beginnings of such a sensory transformation were clearly beyond the bounds of the early mammal hearing mechanism. New and more elaborate neural machinery for it had to be packaged in the head, which dictated a corresponding increase in the brain's size. All unnoticed by the pinheaded dinosaur thundering placidly through the swamp, the first mental image was born.

The second significant stage in man's mental development happened about the same time, Jerison believes, when the limited reptilian eyesight of the first mammals began to change under the pressures of its new environment. Gradually it evolved into the typical mammal night vision we have today, one that can roughly determine position and keenly detect movement in either moonlight or twilight, if not in total darkness. No major neural elaboration in the brain would have been needed for such a straightforward sensory adaptation, Jerison thinks. But now that both hearing and seeing were good for distance, the nervous system's natural hunger for parsimony and efficiency demanded the two senses be integrated to ensure that the simuli each perceived either had or hadn't a common source. Sights became fused to both related sounds and their mental images in a recognizable blend that was reliably the same wherever they chanced to occur. The sound of twigs snapping louder and louder gave rise to an auditory image which, when coupled with the sight of a large and growing gray mass having a certain contour, meant "predator coming" whether it happened at the water hole or a more unlikely place such as the animal's own burrow. As the mental image gained at least another partial dimension—visual confirmation—the beast's intellect took on added flexibility. And the brain got bigger to make room for the complicated neural apparatus required by such a sensory integration.

The mental image, however, was still auditory and incomplete. The mammal's night eye faithfully mapped what it saw for immediate processing and use. If that coincided with the deeper imagistic meaning of sound, well and good. But the eye's neural equipment, Jerison's fossil studies suggested, was still mostly lodged outside the brain, so it stored nothing. The information it collected perished instantly. Not until some 60 million years ago, after the great dinosaurs died and the mammals crept out of their holes into the prehistoric morning, did the third stage of their mental development dawn. Now they began to evolve a new distance daylight vision to complement their sophisticated hearing. Indeed, Jerison's theory assumes, it was modeled on it and required the same sort of expanding neural elaboration in the brain. Just as their hearing could unify a string of sounds into an auditory image, so could their sight now put together patterns of light into meaningful pictures having mental counterparts. But mammalian daylight vision gradually went one step farther, as the growing size and changing shapes of mammal brains over the next 59 million years suggests. Its mental images came not only to bloom in unthinking response to the pressures of the moment, they could also be summoned up on demand—unlike the auditory ones, which still had to await the physical presence of the stimulus. Reality was no longer a thing or things apart, randomly run up against and spontaneously dealt with. It became a growing set of references in the brain, images that from visual stimuli, at least, made up a filing cabinet of catalogued information in the head to live by.

The last evolutionary stage of perception, Jerison's findings suggest, occurred in man himself during the last million years, with the corresponding refinement of the auditory system to produce the same enduring, accessible mental imagery as the visual system; mental imagery equally immune to the onslaughts of passing time and changing place. One distant day to come, writers of radio drama would stretch and compress time all out of shape, erect totally synthetic space, to create whole worlds in our heads by the skillful exploitation of just such auditory images, as anyone old enough to remember *The Shadow* knows. But for now the blizzard of sensory information that showered early man's central nervous system from both distance senses could be shaped by mental imagery into constant, larger neural assemblages—Jerison throws up his hands and calls them clumps—more quickly, easily, and economically coped with than the raw perceptions themselves. Eventually such clumps would be organized into the big picture, the model of a possible reality itself. Endlessly checked and rechecked and modified where needed, that unique perceptual world in each of us, Jerison reasons, would at length become so intuitively real, so persuasive, so fixed, that man would learn to interpret the restless kaleidoscope of his sensory experience as the product of his *own* movement and fluctuating sensibility rather than the ceaselessly changing face of a fickle world whirling around him.

At this point enter intelligence as we know it—not as a trait apart, Harry Jerison insists, but as one more aspect of our response to the perceptual world, one having two dimensions: an unsurpassed talent for integrating our perceptions through mental imagery and, unlike the lowly frog, the flexibility to adjust to the inevitable inconsistencies in the flow of life-giving sensory information.

These mental images, man soon found, could be magically extended over time in either direction, not only into time past but into time future. He could harvest the bitter fruits of yesterday's experience: When without your club, keep away from the saber-toothed tiger! He could also project events to come, particularly those he could cause to happen. A stone deftly chipped or broken became an imaged tool. (Some of them dating as far back as 600,000 years are not as primitive as we might expect. In the Berkeley laboratory of archaeologist Desmond Clarke at the University of California, no student has yet been able to make one in a semester.) The future, early man must have seen further, would surely exist after he died, just as the past surely had existed before he was brought screaming into consciousness. Now he knew fear, not the hackle-raising fright of present physical danger but the deep and abiding dream of the inescapable end to come that he could clearly foresee, saber-toothed tiger or not. And looking into himself, perhaps he saw a glimmer of hope that somehow, some way, beyond all primitive understanding, he might survive. Could not such a thing be imagined (mentally imaged)?

So moved, perhaps, and warmed by rough fur or fire or the comforting nearness of his mate, he opened his hairy mouth and uttered expressive sounds; gestured in rude semaphore against the darkling air; sought to draw on the cave wall with a charred stick a crude picture of what was on his mind.

Exactly when these gestures and utterances became speech, these drawings writing as well as art, is unanswered by either the cranial casts or Jerison's hypothesis. In evolutionary terms, Jerison is fond of pointing out, language for all its wonder is nothing more than a species adaptation, as natural to man as the fantastic eighty-wingbeats-per-second flight mechanism is to the hummingbird. Man's reality could now be represented—modeled—with the external symbols of language, with the external images of art, as it had been with the internal images of sight, sound, touch, taste, and smell. In a monumental understatement, Jerison calls this "a reasonable extension of a conscious perceptual world."[5]

More importantly, although Jerison does not pursue it in so many words, man's internal impressions of external events, his mental images—having been integrated through inputs from all his senses and their meaning exhausted within his crude brain—were now ready to be made external for group processing. For the first time, through language and art, there could be a reaching out to others for a common validation of the senses. The result was a larger vector on perceptual reality; a grander calibration of our senses; a confirmation of that "possible" world—attempted with ever-increasing sophistication but never to be perfectly realized—by one vast human consensus.

Now something new and momentous became progressively more possible: communication meaningful beyond the mere cries of flight or fight shared by other animals. Did all human brains share essentially the same mental picture of their world? The question and its answer could be exchanged through a common tongue and art, the mental images compared by producing not only their external versions in art but also the symphony of onomatopoeic sound ("splash," "roar," "sigh") necessary to evoke them in each other. As its meaning escaped the shackles of nature-emulating sound, then soared free of sound altogether, language would enable man to transmit from generation to generation the accumulated wisdom of his past and what it took to survive: a priceless legacy of information about tools, clothing, hunting, shelter, taboos, customs, and communal safety. (As the Great Oog writes, *When without club, keep away from the saber-toothed tiger!*)

In short, man could pass on his growing culture. Nothing worthy of that name could have been preserved, much less built upon, if each generation had had to go back and invent anew the full range of human knowledge for itself. So it was, concludes Jerison, that man strode onto the world stage equipped with his unique capacity for mental imagery, for language, for culture, in that order. Although language has since been refined to the point where, in Jerison's view, it has become more like the direct perceptual experience itself, "all the words in the world," says Marshall McLuhan, "cannot describe an object like a bucket."[6] Imagery, not language, had primacy. Language was fundamentally what Jerison calls "an image-construction mechanism."[7]

Imaging

Nevertheless, in today's undying din of words, the crucial importance of the mental image—the means by which our species lifted itself up out of the primordial dark and took its place in the sun—has been all but lost to popular attention. It endures, of course, in psychiatry, where Freud strove to achieve a healing release of repressed psychic pain and injury by prompting his patients to relive in images the buried memory of the causative event with all its attendant emotion. It flourishes too in a host of new psychotherapies, encounter techniques, and sensitivity groups, which owe their debt to Jung and the rich regard for imagination he found in the more fertile ground of Europe. In America, by contrast, expressions of vivid imagery such as daydreaming have until recently been looked down upon as, in psychologist Jerome Singer's words, "symptoms of neurotic dispositions."[8] That was probably Freud's fault. As we shall see later, he was "suspicious of fantasy processes," as Singer puts it, and "less willing [than Jung] to afford as free a scope to man's image-making capacities."[9] ("He is . . . 'a strange son of chaos,'" Freud once wrote Jung about a colleague he felt too embroiled in fantasies, "but what he says about the unconscious, with which he is on much better terms than we are, is usually right."[10]) Freud and the United States, one gathers, deserved each other. And the legitimacy of the mental image as a model of healthy reality was downgraded here as a consequence. Lost was any sense of the degree of importance Singer freely ascribes to it:

> The verbal system is . . . tremendously useful since it reduces complexity to simple abstract formulations and accounts for some of man's greatest achievements in science and mathematics. [But] the . . . imagery system has advantages for the recall of complex detail, for the reinstatement of emotion, and for communicating to another some of the same experience felt by the subject. . . .[11]

We experience mental images almost incessantly, of course, and nowhere more than in our dreams, which in the light of Jerison's theory of mental modeling, take on a far deeper significance. One researcher now suggests that dreaming is neither a meaningless discharge of pent-up neural energy nor an escape valve for the "unconscious" as once thought. Rather, he regards it as the means by which our brain "files away" its impressions of the day's events. Such nightly storage he compares to a computer's being "off line," that is, busy revising and updating its master program (Boulding's and Jerison's "big picture") and not available for further input and output. The notion is doubly fascinating because, if dreaming is indeed an index to the pace of the learning process, the younger we are, the more we need to learn and the more we ought to dream—which is exactly what happens. EEG studies of the rapid eye movements characteristic of dreaming proves that babies dream most of all, adults least.

But this, currently, is only the academic concern of scientists. Otherwise, the market value of the mental image survives only in the public's aimless if persistent fascination with visions and hal-

84

lucinations, in a vague appreciation for those awesome (and suspect) few who boast a "photographic" memory, and in an occasional random browsing back among the magazine truss ads when our eye is caught by a come-on for one of those aging memory improvement courses—courses merchandized with scant awareness, one suspects, of the profound role in human intelligence played by the mental imagery behind the bag of tricks they hawk.

Such mnemonic (memory-aiding) devices have been with us since Cicero. The granddaddy of them all was employed by the Greek poet Simonides. After a banquet in the poet's honor, Cicero tells us, the roof fell in, literally, killing all the guests and mutilating their bodies so badly that none could be identified. Simonides, having providentially been summoned outside by a messenger of the gods, returned to name each and every corpse where it lay. The occasion had made such an indelible impression on him that he recalled the face of everyone and where he sat. Thus, legend has it, originated "the Method of Loci" (the Latin word for places), a technique in which things to be remembered, usually names or other words, are mentally linked to images of geographic locations in some orderly fashion.

Are images really more effective than words as hooks in the mind? Undoubtedly the two do work best together, but the answer is more complicated than that. William James thought memory could be strengthened with exercise, like a muscle. When he tried to prove it by memorizing poetry, however, he found it wasn't so. After five weeks of rote practice for twenty minutes a day his performance not only failed to improve, it fell off. Listen, on the other hand, to the publisher Bernstein in the movie *Citizen Kane* reminiscing about a girl in a white dress, carrying a white parasol, that he saw on a passing ferryboat forty years before: "*I* only saw her for one second and she didn't see me at all—but I'll bet a month hasn't gone by since that I haven't thought of that girl."[12] The experience had been nothing more than a fleeting image, yet it was etched in his mind.

For the more practical, psychologist Gordon Bower of Stanford reports that college students using the loci method have remembered seven times more than college students relying on free recall, or on any pet learning strategies they might have devised in

85

their studies. Free recall—simply remembering without any conscious associations of any kind—Bower likens to trying to find a few specific volumes after all the books in the Library of Congress are dumped from their shelves and thrown in one enormous pile. Seen that way, it's amazing free recall works as well as it does. In one controlled loci experiment, on the other hand, students were shown a list of forty unrelated nouns and given an average of thirteen seconds to link each in their thoughts to the mental image of a different campus location. Not only were they able to recall an average of thirty-eight out of forty nouns right after the list was presented, and in order, they averaged thirty-four out of forty in order the next day despite being given a new list to study immediately beforehand. Compared to rote learning, Bower concluded, their performance was "quite exceptional, if not staggering."[13]

Generally, however, most of us stubbornly persist in defining memory, and, too often, intelligence, purely in terms of symbolic behavior. Perhaps we do this because language is *there*, something, figuratively speaking, that we can get out on the table, look at, and analyze. We tend to ignore even the most obvious evidence for a powerful independent memory based on mental images; images so real, yet so elusive, that words alone cannot begin to capture their richness and depth. It escapes us until a skilled writer evokes with deceptive plainness Bernstein's undying image of the white dress with the white parasol, or a psychologist like Gordon Bower demonstrates that concrete words for physical objects, like horse and dog, are remembered more easily than abstract words for intangible concepts, like horse sense and dogma; that pictures described or labeled are remembered even more easily; that the horse and dog themselves, in all their snorting, shaggy substantiality are remembered most easily of all, especially when vibrantly in action. Until such a revelation of imagery's power we are oblivious. After it, we wonder. Do we, in Theodore Roszak's beguiling words, know more than we can say?

Despite the importance Jerison attributes to it in the intellectual development of early man, mental imaging continues to be downplayed even by psychologists, Singer not withstanding. For one thing, it is hard to study. Obviously, we cannot confirm what is going on in each other's mind, not with the exactness that Western life sciences traditionally demand in their emphasis on behavior that can be observed, validated, and duplicated by others. Then too, mental imaging as a reliable learning tool, a reflection of Jerison's "possible world" grown increasingly complex and abstract, is hard to trust. Its more exotic offshoots keep getting in the way. Imagination, that intricate tapestry blended from bits and pieces of unrelated memories interwoven with the thread of our fancy, can by the very power of its plausibility confound honest recall with events that never happened. The same can be said for the delusions of a Don Quixote, the hallucinations of a Hamlet. In sum, familiar though mental imaging may be in all its manifestations, we scarcely know enough to examine it intelligently. As a result, says Bower, "an awful lot of nonsense"[14] gets bruited about by people discussing its vividness and usefulness in their own lives. Jerison's thesis notwithstanding, seeing by the mind's eye is often a sham seeing, Bower contends, one more artifact of our highly suggestible imagination. As such, many mental images are far from dependable interior simulations, or representations after the fact, of the possible reality our senses perceive. Often they are at best, in Bower's phrase, "hinted-at ghosts"[15] strutting a phantom stage.

But ghostly or not, Bower believes, mental imaging is not only scientifically valid, but one of the most lively and compelling fields of psychological investigation today. Indeed, the prospects for understanding it better are not at all as bleak as the foregoing may suggest. For it now appears that the "mental event," as some researchers prefer to call it, can, if patiently and cleverly handled, be made to jump through the same hoop of observable behavior that typifies the rest of the life sciences—at least inferentially. Design it a fitting external task, saddle that task with the proper parameters, mount a few shrewd assumptions to be tested, and the mental event itself can be effectively if indirectly timed, measured, and judged. In so doing, psychology, after a Dark Age of behaviorist-induced skepticism, is coming full circle back to one of its earliest philosophic underpinnings, a belief pithily expressed by two of Bower's colleagues, Roger Shepard and Lynn Cooper. In their massively documented paper on mental images, they observed that, ". . . The richness and structure of human behavior can never be fully and parsimoniously understood without reference to those inner states and processes that we all recognize within ourselves but can never directly observe in others."[16]

Ah, but recognition is one thing, critics would cry, description is another. We know that a mental image cannot normally be heard, tasted, smelled, touched, or really seen. When pressed, researchers say they are vaguely visual or kinesthetic. So describe what one looks or feels like, say their detractors. You can't? Then draw us a picture. You can't do that either, eh? Then how in the name of science do you presume to study such an amorphous phenomenon, if anything so "senseless" deserves to be called a phenomenon at all?

Undaunted, Shepard and his associates are doing just that. They have devised a variety of ingenious techniques, the most easily understandable to the layman being an exercise in what they call mental rotation. The basic test is simple. You are given perspective drawings of two complicated block figures differently aligned on the page, and asked if they are identical to or mirror one another (Figure 6). If the actual block figures were lying on the table in front of you, both face up or face down, as it were, the most natural approach would be to grasp one of them and turn it on the table top until one of its ends matched the corresponding end of the other block figure. Then you would look to see whether the other two ends matched or did not. Virtually the same thing happens when you are asked to do the problem from drawings and entirely in your head, Shepard found. You perceive the drawn figures as three-dimensional objects in space and, visualizing them, compare one to the other by mentally rotating it as required, either within or outside of the picture plane.

In either case, Shepard believes, you are literally "turning something over in your mind."[17]

This can be verified easily, if inferentially, by putting a stopwatch on the whole process. The greater the angle between the different orientations of the two objects visualized in space, the more time it takes to bring them into the proper alignment for mental comparison. In other words, mentally closing an 80-degree angle takes twice as long as a 40-degree angle, a 40-degree angle twice as long as a 20-degree angle, and so on. These are not just sloppy dollops of time but exquisite correspondences. No comparison ever takes anyone more than scant seconds.

How can we be sure the brain hasn't hit upon some unspeakably abstract calculating process of its own? For one thing, Shepard's subjects *said* they mentally rotated the visualized objects. And for another, we know that the brain by its nature would be likely to find a shortcut if one existed, yet not once in Shepard's four years of experiments has anyone broken the 60-degrees-per-second "barrier" derived by averaging the earliest responses. All in all, the performances seem too tightly locked into Shepard's simple angular relationships and mathematical correspondences to allow for any other explanation.

Shepard next devised a task in which you visualize and mentally assemble the sides of a flattened paper cube to decide whether two arrows marked on its edges belong to sides that meet (Figure 7). Such a mental operation, he points out, is more complex than rotating, and requires a sequence of distinct spatial manipulations. The more mental folding needed to complete the imaged cube, the more time it took, in perfect analogue—even when "extra baggage" was added in the form of irrelevant sides. Only when the arrows appeared at opposite ends of a straight string of four squares, one of them the base (shaded) square, did Shepard's subjects abandon mental folding and visualize instead the act of "rolling" the arrowed sides together in a single fluid maneuver. Although mental rolling failed to obey the same set of per-second correspondences as mental folding and rotation, Shepard believes it was equally spatial because, again, his subjects said it was.

In either case, the resulting array of timed responses established the existence of stored mental "templates"—Jerison's representational patterns of a possible reality; images we can call forth, manipulate, and compare to both reality and other mental templates with equal force and dexterity. But, the cynic persists, Shepard still has not described these mental images, these stored templates, not one of them. Don't tell us he intends to get off the hook by claiming they are, in some indefinable way, *like* what they stand for? Not in the least, Shepard would doubtless reply. They lack the vividness, the detail, the clarity of their perceptual counterparts. But while unquestionably abstract and schematic—dia-

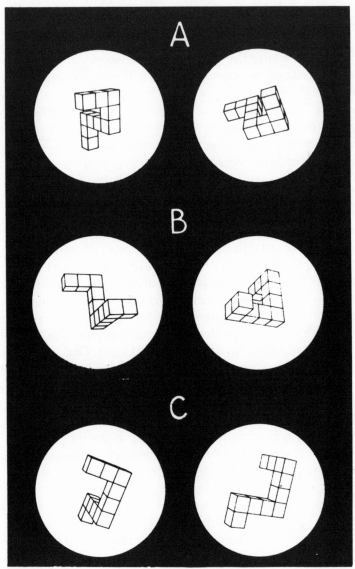

FIGURE 7
Block rotation in tests of the mental event

(CREDIT: "Mental Rotation of Three-Dimensional Objects," by R. N. Shepard and Jacqueline Metzler. Reprinted by permission of the authors and *Science*. Copyright 1971 by the American Association for the Advancement of Science.

gramlike—in contrast to the real thing, Shepard suspects they embody it "with enough fidelity to permit a quick and definitive comparison."[18] He calls these mental images *second-order isomorphisms (iso:* similar, *morph:* form). He concedes that the image of a square, for example, need not be a square, or first-order isomorphism. But he thinks whatever its configuration is should be more related to the image of a rectangle than to that of, say, as he puts it, "a green flash or the taste of persimmon."[19]

In that he may be unduly cautious. In at least one experiment, EEG researchers have found that the minute burst of electricity released in the brain when a geometric form is imagined—its evoked potential—closely resembles in wave shape that evoked by the geometric form itself when visually perceived. So the relationship of mental images to the perceptions they represent may be more isomorphic than Shepard suspects.

He is less cautious about the implications of mental imaging for intelligence. He thinks it may be indispensable in various mental processes that defy manipulation by language—everything from doing jigsaw puzzles and arranging furniture tastefully to assembling complicated mechanical devices and working out solutions to problems in geometry, electrical engineering, and theoretical physics. Rotating, folding, flipping, and rolling are just a few of the valuable spatial transformations Shepard has tested in our heads. If he's right, we can also stretch, shrink, bend, and do complex combinations of these and others involved in such spatially demanding activities as choreography, gymnastics, and sculpture.

What all this may mean, Shepard suggests, is that mental image is, in effect, one of the two operative languages of the brain. Proponents of linguistic supremacy to the contrary, this is not far removed in its deepest intellectual implications from Jerison's heretical position that language was first and foremost "an image-construction mechanism." Bower may be more accurate today when he says that mental imagery and verbal symbolism are the twin components of human thinking, the one "relatively more attuned to the task of representing and operating on concrete information," the other "better suited for processing abstract information".[20]

Shepard's research, preliminary though he stresses it is, sup-

91

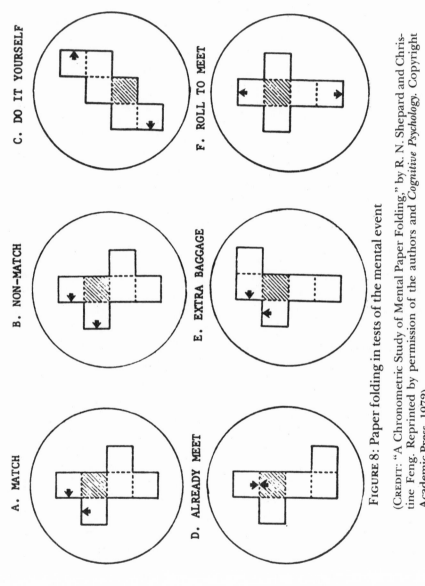

FIGURE 8: Paper folding in tests of the mental event

(CREDIT: "A Chronometric Study of Mental Paper Folding," by R. N. Shepard and Christine Feng. Reprinted by permission of the authors and *Cognitive Psychology*. Copyright Academic Press, 1972)

ports Bower's analysis. "At the very least," Shepard writes, "it raises a question about the advisability of formulating theories of human behavior solely in terms of . . . verbal mediation or symbol manipulation—as has been characteristic of experimental psychology. . . ."[21]

Such research, Bower thinks, points to "some kind of solid geometry program in the head,"[22] one highly developed in childhood but gradually pushed aside by our growing competence for language. This may be naturally so, he speculates, because language frees the acquisition of knowledge from the immediate sensory impressions in which all information initially is anchored. It enables us, in other words, to deal more abstractly with the concreteness of experience. Without language and math we would be chain-bound to our perceptions like Prometheus to his rock.

Just such a man was S, the Russian journalist turned stage performer celebrated by the eminent Soviet psychologist A. R. Luria in his book *The Mind of the Mnemonist*. S could remember and repeat verbatim years later everything he was told, or shown in writing. He could master trains of inconsequentia beyond Luria's expert capacity to measure: numbers, letters, and words without end, sense and nonsense; the metaphorical laundry list of the world.

Everything that entered S's mind, Luria found, lodged in mental images that were consumately vivid, enduring, and plastic beyond anything known. In his mind's eye he could make them larger or smaller, move their salient features around against their mental background, and if he wanted to focus on one, hang a visualized canvas around it to mask out distraction. Then too, his senses were suffused with synesthesia, a rare phenomenon in which one sense when stimulated evokes the sensations of another. As Luria poetically put it, for S there was, ". . . no dividing line between color and sound, between . . . taste and touch. Rather . . . smooth, cold sounds and rough colors; salty shapes and bright, clear or biting smells, all so intertwined and fused that it was hard to distinguish one sensation from another."[23] While not as central to his recall as the visualized mental image, synesthesia provided an invaluable extra dimension. As S himself once noted, "I recognize a word not only by the image it evokes but by a

93

whole complex of feelings that image arouses. . . . It's not a matter of vision or hearing but some over-all sense. . . . What I sense is something oily slipping through my hand . . . or a slick tickling . . . caused by a mass of tiny, light-weight points. When that happens I simply remember, without having to make the attempt. . . ."[24]

Early in his stage career S stumbled on the method of loci and made it eerily his own. When taxed to repeat a formidable sequence of words designed to trip him up, he simply took a stroll in his mind down a familiar Moscow street and distributed the images they suggested among the houses, gates, and store windows he remembered. On recall, he walked back down the visualized street and gathered them up as he went, much as Bower's college students would later do. He never got the words wrong but he sometimes omitted them because, as he told Luria with frustration,

> I put the image of the pencil near a fence . . . But what happened was that the image fused with that of the fence and I walked right on past without noticing it. The same thing happened with the word egg. I had put it up against a white wall and it blended with the background. How could I possibly spot a white egg up against a white wall? . . . Sometimes I put a word in a dark place and have trouble seeing it as I go by.[25]

After he took pains to place the mental image against a contrasting backdrop, under a convenient light, said S with the air of a man who suddenly sees how stupid he was not to have grasped the obvious sooner, his troubles ended.

Despite his strange gift, S was hardly a superman. He often seemed a dim-witted fellow, and in some ways he was. Faced with a "junk heap of impressions,"[26] as Jerome Bruner aptly analyzes it, S was helpless to get behind the surface of words and numbers and deal with their deeper meanings. As if to prove Bower's point, he was also woefully sterile in the normal exercises of higher intellect all of us take for granted and display, to a greater or lesser degree, in coping with life around us every day. Abstraction, logic, generalization, the gift of summary, the ability to contrive or understand complex or even simple reasoned relationships—all eluded him. For example S could and did methodically

94

memorize in his own astonishing fashion a table of numbers running from one to a hundred. He failed utterly to realize the principle of consecutive numbers that would have made the feat ridiculously beside the point even for a kindergartner. Figurative language, the touchstone of poetry, defied his comprehension. Expressions like "wind-driven clouds" and "weighing words" triggered him to paroxysms of imaging in an effort to pinpoint meanings that literally, to his mind, made no sense. Simple, concrete words could be as bad. To him, the lowly pig had little of the grace he saw in the sound of the Russian word *svinya*. Abstract terms were most baffling of all. What thinking S did, in Luria's estimation, "amounted merely to operations he would . . . perform on his images."[27] How then could the exalted philosophic concept contained in the word "nothing" be at all feasible when he could see, in all its scintillating multimedia imagery, that it was so clearly and magnificently something?

S, to be sure, was the rarest of anomalies. But he stands nevertheless in lasting testimony to the enthralling potential—and peril—of mental imagery once unleashed and somehow left unchecked by nature. Similarly, in a remarkable novel called *Spear in the Sand,* Raoul Faure turned the tables on Robinson Crusoe to show what would happen to man's left hemisphere if he were stranded on a desert island so idyllic no effort was needed to survive. In passages that ring with psychological rightness, Faure traces the disintegration of those symbolic processes that stamp the mind of civilized man. Out of his loneliness and his rampant images, Faure's protagonist concocts even the strange and primitive rituals that betray the kind of "illogical logic" that must lie behind the aborigine's superstition:

> Science is all right when there are other people who have learned the same science, but here? Why provoke unseen powers who were here a long time before you for the stupid sake of doubtful principles you learned in crowded and safe buildings. . . . What will you do? Throw your books at them? Don't take chances. . . . Go back and cross those twigs and for your doubts cross an extra set. . . .[28]

In desperation for the passing years, he decides to write a book, but

> . . . His hand had kept the memory of the letters [but] not his brain. . . . They were just scrawlings as if a fly had dipped its legs in an ink puddle and dragged itself across a white sheet. . . .[29]

Still, too much abstraction can have its cost too, as Faure's protagonist found when he attempted to transfer the fruits of his heightened sensitivity to paper. He realized

> . . . the poverty of words. There were four or five expressions for blue, and there were a hundred blues. . . . He was powerless in front of their innumerable shades. . . . Sensations were richer, far richer than expressions. . . .[30]

As Gordon Bower laments, in today's society the course of our intellectual development, its overweening cultural emphasis on the recognized symbolic gifts of the left hemisphere "leads to the gradual withering away of imaginal processes, which die from neglect and disuse. Visual impressions are no longer remembered in their full, vivid richness, but rather become conventionalized in . . . conceptual stereotypes."[31] The right hemisphere is co-opted, preempted, its gifts made symbols of. This in turn may be what leads to the stultifying, stereotyped thinking in the face of ample sensory evidence to the contrary that Robert Coles, for one, so eloquently deplores in our growing political polarity and social stratification. "To Coles," says sociologist David Riesman, "policemen are not pigs . . . southerners are not rednecks, and blacks are not all suffering in exotic misery. What he is saying is, 'People are more complicated, more varied, more interesting, have more resiliency and more survivability than you might think. I listen to them! You listen to them!' " Adds Coles himself, "I think that's the trouble with trying to generalize too much about the way people think—about trying to label them. Sometimes maybe they're that way, but sometimes they're different."[32] If Coles is correct, we are in danger of becoming in our own overly abstract way as set in our responses to life as the dinosaur in his—and as doomed.

Indeed, the deterioration in our ability to use mental imaging has gone so far we may have to develop techniques for teaching it, Bower believes, just as we do the three R's. Some commercial systems of "brainstorming" have taken the first tentative steps in that direction. Until their efforts are more widely realized and amplified in our modern society, however, Bower offers us a five-word prescription for breaking out of the prison of single-minded thinking and liberating the imagery of our right hemisphere. We must, he says, "become as a child again."[33]

Language

How the miracle of language began is still a mystery. We don't know if its origins were rooted in the consensus-seeking expressive behaviors of gesture, speech, and cave art, in the mental modeling of perception in symbols, or in both. There is, for instance, a curious resemblance between language and vision—and music. In all the world's 2,796 languages, notes the eminent language scholar Eric Lenneberg, words label not specific objects but a set of principles governing the relations between them. "Knowing a word is never a simple association between an object and an acoustic pattern," says Lenneberg. Rather it is "the successful operation of those principles that lead to the using of the word 'table' or 'house' for objects never before encountered."[34] Likewise, in a sense, as artist Tom McArthur writes in a glorious spoof of Gertrude Stein,

A rose is a rose is a rose,
So they tell us.
But a rose *and* a rose *and* a rose
Is a trellis.[35]

In much the same manner, says psychologist Irvin Rock, our visual perception of a form is based primarily on how parts of a figure are related to one another geometrically, rather than on absolute features. To take just one example, a square becomes a diamond to our perception when rotated 45 degrees from upright; unmoved, it remains to us a square whether its sides are one inch in length or one mile. Conversely, writes Rock, "A melody can be transposed to a new key, and although all the notes then are different, there is no change in the melody."[36]

97

Language and vision, moreover, appear to share a key characteristic called *categorical perception*. As the name implies, categorical perception is the instantaneous classification, or putting into a category, of a stimulus even as we perceive it. Ordinarily, we perceive a stimulus, then interpret it. But in speech, perception of sound and its interpretation as possible language are so meshed as to be inseparable. Subjects asked to listen to a sequence of synthetically generated electronic sounds reported they heard a continuous stream of unintelligible noise until a fragment of sound identifiably speechlike occurred, quite by chance. At that point, with a split-second speed that transcended their response to any other lifelike sound, their hearing automatically interrupted the rhythmic flow and plucked out that fragment for attention. It did so even though the sound had been produced at random and proved to be not speech at all.

Psycholinguists—scholars in the deeper intellectual meaning of language—have argued that such a phenomenon, like the capacity for language itself, is inborn and unique. But given a series of free-form line figures to scan, one researcher has found, visual perception does much the same. Our eye passes measuredly over meaningless two-dimensional shapes until, suddenly, instantly and without our willing, it seizes on and pulls out for inspection those seen as silhouettes of three-dimensional objects. In either case, then, speech or vision, an unthinking quest for information content occurs. It takes the form of an instantaneous staging operation in which the perception is simultaneously compared to what is already stored in the brain, whether that storage be in linguistic symbols or mental images, processed by one cerebral hemisphere in its unique fashion or the other.

If this be so, it could explain how a child grasps the practical rudiments and subtle intricacies of his own language long before he starts school and is formally exposed to it. He may perceive it, as linguistic psychologist David McNeill has speculated, through a process not fundamentally different from the perception of a line drawing—though it takes him 300 million times longer, two or three years instead of two- or three-tenths of a second. It would then be not something intellectually grafted on, like the knowledge of how to tie a shoelace, but an integral and growing part of the brain's organic organization and maturation of the perceptual

98

apparatus itself. No wonder, then, that a foreign language is readily learned but rarely mastered. It is peculiarly a product of the brain and a part of the culture in which it arose, reflecting, perhaps, almost cellular differences in perception and—at the risk of being redundant—philosophy. As a Spanish king once complained, no matter how long and hard he labored, he would never in his life be able to speak French half as well as a five-year-old Paris street urchin naturally does.

Thus there are differences between languages that shape the brain for a lifetime. But there are also universals in its native acquisition that stamp it as every bit as biological as the act of walking. Like walking, language is common to all cultures in its dynamics. Normally it begins around a certain age, when the body has reached a given stage of motor development and the brain has matured to 65 percent of the gross weight, neural density, and relative proportions it will have in adulthood. However varied its outward forms, furthermore, all language is based upon the same mental operating characteristics, that seven-eighths of the psycholinguistic iceberg we technically term its "deep structure." The step-by-step strategies by which we attain a working proficiency as a child, and relative mastery later on, are virtually the same everywhere, even in primitive societies. Linguistically speaking, we crawl before we walk and walk before we run. Language spontaneously occurs in children who hear little or none of it because their parents are congenitally deaf. But, cautions Lenneberg, this is not to dismiss the importance of environment. It also occurs in the seriously retarded, who will with equal spontaneity pick up an amazing amount just watching television.

Do we learn language consciously or do we perceive it unconsciously in the course of our normal development? Fundamentally, is it something we grow into or something we acquire? We do both, surely. But the arguments pro and con are intense, far-reaching in their implications for learning, and consequently better reserved for the next chapter.

As for the importance of language, just look what time has done. What started out in Jerison's evolutionary view as just another species adaptation, perhaps no more than one of man's many means of modeling a possible reality from his perceptions, has today become the linguistic tail that wags the dog of intelligence. By their absence as well as presence, words not only signify the presence of certain perceptions or their absence, they also reflect and even influence man's abilities to think and learn. Eskimos, for instance, have almost a hundred words to describe the differing textures of snow. This prolixity counts not for poetic purposes but for survival. With polar landmarks at a premium, the Eskimo's ability to discern the horizon through an Arctic blizzard in all its gradients of shifting white can mean the difference between a warm igloo and frozen death. Not surprisingly, Eskimos excel in background perception. No Eskimo ever coldly expired for want of a word, of course—but another to whom he wished to communicate the latest weather report very well could have. In a corollary vein, the primitive Trobrianders of the South Pacific do not have one word for each kind of fruit, but totally different words for the same fruit in various stages of growth—a telling mark of their deeply existential bias against anything becoming something else in time.

Words, moreover, have an undeniable power to harness complicated thought—or hopelessly obfuscate the lack or truth of it—as images cannot. They can do so against life's hard realities as well as on their behalf. In its heyday, to take one example, the Nixon administration embarked on a campaign to strike the word "poverty" from all government reports to avoid the "emotional complications" of a "value-laden, highly-politicized word." The move to make the word (and with it, the need for action?) go away by fiat failed, of course. (Advertising is more successful, as is slang. The slang term "trash food," for example—coined to describe the low-cost, quick-serve, mass-produced franchise product that keeps children and teen-agers alive and vice versa—is a contradiction that attests to the power of language.) Then again, as one researcher observes, the words "altruism" and "empathy" were not coined before the nineteenth century, when a surge of humanitarianism overwhelmed civilized man's barbaric indifference to men. This is not to say that neither condition existed before it was named. Most certainly it did, but probably not for very long, and not as anything more coherently formed and socially forceful than a nebulous string of loosely related images born of Biblical parables and Judeo-Christian commandments which, taken together, could hardly encompass such a grand concept.

100

Thanks to Gutenberg's invention of movable type, from there it was only a step, albeit a giant step, to the widespread belief typified today by one educator's statement that, "It is no accident that a stupid person is said to be 'dumb.' If he cannot think, the readiest way to convey the fact is to say that he has no language . . . language not only conveys thought but also controls thought and, finally, *is* thought."[37]

Today, if Marshall McLuhan and others of his ilk are right, we are in imminent danger of the corollary assumption: that thought *is* language, and cannot exist or function without it. In his prophetic book *Understanding Media,* McLuhan levels an accusing finger not at Gutenberg but at the phonetic alphabet itself. All the alphabets of the Western World are derived from Greco-Roman letters, he emphasizes, in which semantically meaningless symbols are wedded to semantically meaningless sounds to achieve a meaningful synthesis of virtually unlimited abstraction. Psycholinguist Noam Chomsky calls this open-ended quality *generative.* That is, with twenty-six finite letters an infinity of expression is possible. As laudable as this is, McLuhan thinks, these alphabets must share the guilt of starkly dividing man's senses, of diminishing his intuitive awareness, of undercutting his collective consciousness, even as they extend and amplify in space and time his grasp of the perceptual world.

As French philosopher Henri Bergson wrote, says McLuhan, speech

> . . . enables the intellect to detach itself from the vastly wider reality. Without language, Bergson suggests, human intelligence would have remained totally involved in the objects of its attention. Language does for intelligence what the wheel does for the feet and the body. It enables them to move from thing to thing with greater ease and speed but ever less involvement.[38]

All of which sounds, one is tempted to think, ominously like the modern life effects of the automobile. McLuhan goes on:

> . . . it can be argued, then, that the phonetic alphabet, alone, is the technology that has been the means of creating "civilized man." . . . As an intensification and extension of the visual function, the phonetic alphabet diminishes the role of the other senses of sound and touch and taste . . . the fact that this does

101

not happen in cultures such as the Chinese, which use nonphonetic scripts, enables them to retain a rich store of inclusive perception in depth of experience that tends to become eroded in civilized cultures of the phonetic alphabet. For the [Chinese] ideogram is an inclusive gestalt [a unified physical, psychological or symbolic configuration having properties that cannot be derived from its parts], not an analytic dissociation of senses and functions like phonetic writing.

. . . The same separation of sight and sound and meaning that is peculiar to the phonetic alphabet also extends to its social and psychological effects. Literate man undergoes much separation of his imaginative, emotional, and sense life, as Rousseau (and later the romantic poets and philosophers) proclaimed long ago. . . .[39]

Rational, of course, has for the west long meant "uniform and continuous and sequential." [But] each mother tongue teaches its users a way of seeing and feeling the world, and of acting in the world, that is quite unique.[40]

Eden, then, was not Adam's downfall. The Tower of Babel was.

Chapter 4

Learning, Thinking, and Creating

So the evidence is in for two vastly different, specialized, independently functioning cerebral hemispheres. And from its outlines emerges a revolutionary new way of looking at intelligence. One side of our brain is verbal and mathematical. It formulates the theory of relativity and drafts the Magna Carta. The other side is spatial, musical, and integrative. It paints the Sistine Chapel, composes "The Flight of the Bumblebee" (with help on the notation from its opposite number), and learns to ride a bicycle. One half is analytical, sequential, logical, and linear; it produces Descartes ("I think, therefore I am") and the true-false question. The other half is tactile, relational, holistic, and simultaneous; it prompts Picasso, on impulse in a Riviera restaurant, to mold the beard of Moses in his mashed potatoes. One hemisphere is as precise and discrete as the formula for a headache remedy, the other as unfocused, as diffuse, as a psychedelic light show. One is abstract and gives us the deft drama of ideas that is Shaw's *Pygmalion*. The other is kinesthetic and gives us the silent, spinning majesty that is Nijinsky's pirouette. One defines what a friend is (in symbols), the other recognizes him unerringly in a crowd a block away.

That its labor is hemispherically divided, however, is hardly the last word. As we have seen, intelligence begins when a neural stimulus triggers a neural response. Stimulus and response in turn are modeled in images or symbols, and thereby embedded in our brain electrically, chemically, or both. But at what point does perception become, or fail to become, learning? When the thing perceived either does or does not become consciously modeled in memory? And what about thinking? Does it commence as we be-

103

gin consciously to reinforce, replace, modify, or manipulate those mental models which make up our perceptual world? And when we start to use these models in constructing new left-hemisphere concepts or in making explicit our imagistic right-hemisphere perceptions—or in fusing the two in novel forms—is this what we mean by creating?

What Kenneth Boulding once remarked about learning appears to apply equally to thinking and creating: All we really know can be written on three pages. That observation, fortunately, hasn't kept Arthur Koestler from writing seven hundred wise and witty pages on the act of creation alone. In that spirit, if no other, all three invite further scrutiny and speculation, especially in the illuminating new light of the hemispheres.

Learning

Everything from talking to dying, said Flaubert, must be learned. Indeed, from the beginning of life something very like learning appears to go on in the basic growth and support systems of our body. Preeminent is the protoplasmic stuff of life itself, DNA (deoxyribonucleic acid), which contains in genetic code all the information required to reproduce our kind. DNA can be said to display cellular "memory" of a most crucial sort, and learning through selective evolution as well. A kind of biologic learning and memory occur too in the body's immune system, which yields up as needed specific antibodies to fight infection, repelling selectively and for a lifetime the invasion of any alien matter—including, unfortunately, unless medically suppressed, lifesaving transplants. An invading organism, it now appears, is like an organic "key" that selects from tens of billions of biochemical "locks" in our bodies the one that will unerringly bind up and destroy it—not just once but every time thereafter.

For that matter, even perception must be learned, in the sense that it is inexorably shaped by the selective pressures of the environment. We know, for instance, that animals experimentally raised from birth in vertically striped boxes develop an abnormal preponderance of vertical line detector cells in the nerve tissue of their retinas. Indeed, in response to these visually constricted surroundings, the retina actually transforms—the vertical line detector cells actually recruit into their number—edge- and horizontal line-detecting cells. In human terms, we know further that Pygmies raised in dense rain forests, when transported to grassy plains of contrastingly unrestrained lateral distances, lack the perspective to make accurate size discriminations between, say, a small antelope fifty yards away and a huge bull elephant a hundred yards away. To the Pygmy, both are virtually the same size. Similarly, another African tribe which lives in conical huts on gently hilly terrain cannot distinguish straight lines in certain rigorous perception tests. Marshall McLuhan writes about an anthropological film in which a Melanesian carver cut out a decorated drum with such skill, coordination, and ease that the audience broke into applause—yet when asked to build simple crates to ship the carvings in, he and the other native craftsmen struggled futilely for three days to make two planks intersect at a right angle.

In the book *Space and Sight* by Marius Von Senden, writes Annie Dillard, cataract patients blind since birth, when operated upon had no visual sense of space as something to be intelligently understood whatsoever. Form, distance, and size were meaningless. A patient could identify a cube or a sphere by touch before the operation but afterward he had no clue whatever as to what he was seeing. A house a mile away was considered nearby but requiring a lot of steps. Elevators gave no more sense of vertical distance than the train did of horizontal. A room was known to be part of a house but the patient could literally not conceive of the whole house being bigger! "Vision," wrote Dillard, "was a pure sensation unencumbered by meaning." "At best," Von Senden reported, "space was conceived as ending with visual space."[1]

Patients had no notion that a larger object, say a chair, could mask a smaller one such as a dog, or that the dog, for that matter, could still be present though not seen. Only gradually, according to Von Senden, did patients come to realize that they had "a space" behind them too.

As Annie Dillard muses in her book *Pilgrim at Tinker Creek,* a lyric celebration of the senses, "a nightmare network of ganglia, charged and firing without my knowledge, cuts and splices what I do see, editing it for my brain"[2]—and that brain alone. Which may explain both the human yearning for consensus and the corollary phenomenon that every lawyer worth his shingle knows: that no two witnesses to a crime ever see the same thing or tell the same story. Dillard adds philosophically,

> Donald E. Carr points out that the sense impressions of one-celled animals are *not* edited for the brain. . . . "This is . . . interesting in a rather mournful way [he says] since it means that only the simplest animals perceive the universe as it is."[3]

Yogis, moreover, have long demonstrated a bizarre form of learning by clotting their blood at will, reversing peristalsis to nourish themselves on fluids sucked up through their anus, and slowing their rate of metabolism to survive for hours in airtight boxes on a fraction of the oxygen believed necessary to sustain life—in short, by exotic variations in biofeedback. Although there is much we don't yet know about it, biofeedback depends upon learning to duplicate by an act of will the precise electrical states of the brain needed to induce and regulate spontaneously a host of involuntary behaviors. Patients of no metaphysical persuasion whatever, notably victims of chronic hypertension, have learned to control their own blood pressure.

Does this mean the autonomic nervous system can be made to "remember"? It must. For without memory, how can there be recall on demand of ideas, feelings, or states? Where teaching and learning go, some kind of "memory" must follow.

What kind of memory can it be that persistently, perversely eludes our waking awareness? As Andrew Weil notes in his absorbing book *The Natural Mind,* the sensory nerves that transmit information from the internal body to the brain—the somesthetic and kinesthetic sensation Jerison makes little of in tracing the evolution of our intelligence—remain an enigma. We don't know much about the nature of that information or how it is meshed with that coming from our outside senses. This may be why our "gut feeling" about something remains indefinable, if far from fuzzy in its impact. Putting aside for now altered states of aware-

106

ness such as those of drugs, dreams, and mystic highs, we are still left with two ordinary kinds of consciousness, left-hemisphere and right-hemisphere.

Science has always supposed that most inner sensory information has no direct connections to consciousness, says Weil, "but if we ask, what kind of consciousness? the [limitation] of this conception becomes clear." For the autonomic nervous system, he goes on, seems to be cut off *only* from "the ordinary [consciousness] of the ego"[4]—that exclusive domain of the linguistic "I," the left hemisphere. The right hemisphere, with its proven ability to juggle and integrate simultaneous and diffuse spatial inputs, then, would seem an ideal locus for the somesthetic and kinesthetic "memories" necessary to biofeedback.

Weil thinks they may be stored in the "emotional brain" of the limbic system instead. But in a dramatic series of electric probe experiments, Canadian neurosurgeon Wilder Penfield has shown that direct stimulation of the cerebrum results in an eerily exact "replay" of events lodged in our memory, not only as initially experienced by our senses but with every shade of our original mood and nuance of emotion intact. In other words, emotions may be generated by the limbic system but they are forever one in our cerebral memory with the conscious experience that gave rise to them. So too, one suspects, since it is "conscious" to our right hemisphere, would be the inner sensory information of the autonomic nervous system.

Seen in that context, hunches, "gut reactions," feelings "in our bones," may be as close to using our full experiential intelligence as we are ever likely to get in a state of ordinary waking consciousness. It may even be a method of decision-making far more effective than the piling up of empirical facts or the rational deduction of the left hemisphere can ever be.

But none of this is what we normally mean by learning. We mean the mental modeling of perception in images and/or symbols, the apprehension of Jerison's possible reality that includes ourselves and the rest of the world. Where, when, and how does it start?

Noam Chomsky speaks for psychology at large when he characterizes the two major views of learning as *rationalist* and *empiricist*.

107

The rationalist regards learning as a process occurring essentially from the inside out. The empiricist regards it as a process occurring essentially from the outside in. The rationalist sees the newborn as a seed bursting with enfolded promise. The empiricist sees it as John Locke's *tabula rasa,* a clean slate upon which nature writes her always unique but ever unchanging story.

Jean Piaget's general theory of mental development is at once the most organic and coherent of the rationalist approach. Piaget believes intelligence develops sequentially, starting with the sensorimotor stage of the first two years when the child learns to act directly upon reality in the absence of language. In this stage, the child's mind "operates" on reality to establish in a world of dynamically changing position and context a set of reliable constants—a ball is a ball is a ball, despite its frequently differing size, texture, color, bounce, and angle of visual exposure. Its firm, round, rolling reality comes to resist perceptual transformation. Gradually the child learns to separate himself from the external world as well as from his own actions. He does this by learning to split the actor away from the action, the behavior away from the object or event it represents. During the early phase of this initial learning stage, says Piaget, the action and its actor are fused. The opening of the nursery door is one in the child's mind with the appearance of its mother and the imminent satisfactions of its wants and needs.

The second stage, Piaget continues, begins around one and a half when, having successfully made the separation between actor and action (the sound of the nursery door does not in itself mean its mother; it may even mean his father has come to spank him for crying) the child now learns to internalize the external world and its growing web of relationships. Mental imagery comes into play as a means of representing an object or event, often through deferred imitation. The child can make one object stand for another that shares common perceptual features: For purposes of play he can turn a shoebox into a doll bed. The relationship between actor and action has become abstract as well as physical.

Piaget's third stage of learning development occurs between seven and twelve, and is marked by further consolidation of the symbolic, or representational. Deferred imitation is joined by outright fantasy, drawing, and symbolic play language, all of which free the child to construct a substitute reality when, as Donald Morehead fetchingly puts it, "reality isn't around."[5] Now the child can learn things, primarily from language, that he could not know if he were forced to depend entirely upon his own direct contact with the outside world. From eleven on, the child enters the formal stage of learning that characterizes adulthood. No longer is he tied to the concrete. Abstract symbols get "wired in" and he can reason by pure hypothesis.

Although Piaget agrees that the idea of childhood learning locked into static stages is "disastrous," the suggestion that his methods could be used to accelerate development, not just demonstrate it, he dismisses as "idiotic." To encourage intellectual progress, he says, teachers should give children "rich, open" educational materials to interract with, to ask endless questions about. But they must never forget that "behind what we observe there are ten times more things than we suspect. . . ."[6]

At the opposite pole stands behaviorist B. F. Skinner, who rejects the rationalist concept of an inner autonomous man having an engine of feeling and thought that propels him to behave as he does. Skinner sees behavior as an empirical force shaped and maintained by its own consequences, good and bad, positively or negatively reinforced. As he sees it, learning is not at all the pre-programmed outgrowth of the brain's maturation. Rather, it is the traceable result of successive environmental contingencies, a complex train of cause and effect extended steadily until its locomotive cannot be seen for the caboose. As he quotes George Eliot, "Our deeds determine us as much as we determine our deeds."[7] To change man, change and control his environment, not only before but after, he responds:

> We change the way a person looks at something, as well as what he sees when he looks, by changing the contingencies; we do not change something called perception. We change the relative strengths of responses by differential reinforcement of alternative courses of action; we do not change something called a preference. We change the probability of an act by changing a condition of deprivation or aversive stimulation; we do not change a need. We reinforce behavior in particular ways; we do

not give a person a purpose or an intention. We change behavior toward something, not an attitude toward it. We sample and change verbal behavior, not opinions.[8]

Continuous, or operant, conditioning is by Skinner's definition a vital part of life in any civilized society. As he sees it, we already live in a world of illusory freedom, one hedged in by a host of positive and negative reinforcers ranging from praise, money, and status, to traffic lights, jail, and community disgrace. He would merely have us use these more intelligently by elevating them to a managerial technology in preplanning environments. Piaget's internal world of unseen drive mechanisms to a strict behaviorist like Skinner is utterly beside the point, if it exists at all.

Nowhere is the battle between these two schools of thought more fiercely fought than in the arena of language. Skinner claims verbal behavior can be accounted for purely in terms of the speaker's personal history, without reference to its ideas and meanings. He points to such evidence as the work of the scholar who dissected Coleridge's *Kubla Khan*—long touted as a classic of inspiration—and exhaustively traced every line to something that had happened to the poet in his lifetime. Psycholinguists vigorously disagree. Chomsky sees language as "a kind of latent structure in the human mind, developed and fixed by exposure to specific linguistic experience."[9] Neither data analysis nor principles of formal thinking, he contends, can totally fathom the system of rules that must underlie its normal usage. When the number of word combinations a child uses can explode from fourteen to 2,500 in seven months, adds David McNeill, the feat of imitation and memory implied by behaviorist theory becomes untenable.

In the midst of this, Canadian research psychologist Donald Hebb and two colleagues have sought to establish "A DMZ in the Language War,"* and with it a middle ground in the rancorous dispute over the true nature of human learning. Chomsky and those like him, the Hebb faction asserts, are guilty of "indefensible nativism,"[10] as much for leaving the field of learning to the behaviorists as for their "naïve" reaction against what the behaviorists

*Psychology Today, April, 1973.

have made of it. The notion that children, like rats or pigeons, learn only from conditioning and reinforcement of overt response strikes Hebb and his colleagues as "primitive."[11] Man learns in different ways, he believes, not the least of them a subtly latent learning in which the thing perceived is remembered and only later expressed in response to a related stimulus. A forecast of rain at breakfast, for example, can spark a decision hours later not to have the car washed. Here, the time gap between stimulus and response is so great, so filled with other stimuli, other responses, that it invalidates the stimulus-response arc as an explanation.

In its place, Hebb and his associates offer a *cell assembly* theory, which postulates a hierarchy of neural assemblies graduated from first-order perceptions (directly related to a specific stimulus) on up to a pinnacle of the holistic sounding suspiciously like Jerison's "neural clumps" become mental models. They get considerable support from the new field of information processing, which has as its model the computer. Earl Hunt of the University of Washington has compared the learning brain to a computer whose memory bank is surrounded by an ingenious hierarchy of sensing and classifying buffers. In an orgy of incessant checking and filing, these buffers (neurons, neuronal clumps, cell assemblies) rapidly graduate an incoming stimulus from level to level. At every level they successively contact the memory bank and progressively match, for likeness and contrast, an ever higher order of the stimulus features to information already stored. Appropriately and scrupulously they recode it in this new light without further interpretation (same or different), then quickly pass it on up the chain of command. If the match is successful, recognition is swiftly confirmed by the memory bank with an identifying code, the butterfly of known meaning caught in a neuronal net of finespun discrimination. If the match is not successful and a recheck shows no transmission mistake has been made, a description of the mismatch is sent winging through channels to consciousness where learning, defined as error-correction, immediately begins.

If Hunt is right, it is all a most instantaneous process, lovely with harmony and synchrony. Thus, by such continuous feed-

111

back, do lines become letters, letters become letter groupings, letter groupings become recognizable as words, and words become the miracle of learning we know as *War and Peace.* Thus too do lines become contours, contours become configurations, configurations become recognizable as representations of objects, and objects in their pattern of depiction become the "Mona Lisa." Thus, in brief, does the miracle of perception become the miracle of learning.

Such learning is never static or merely additive. As Peter Lindsay and Donald Norman argue in their book *Human Information Processing:*

> Classical learning theories typically rely on repeated exposure to specific stimuli as the basis of acquiring information. They have difficulties dealing with the fact that the understanding of a concept continues to be elaborated and embellished, even though the concept may never directly be encountered again. . . . As more information about the world is accumulated, the memory system's understanding continues to grow and become elaborated. As an automatic by-product of this changing structure, our knowledge continually changes. . . .
>
> This continual evolution of the stored knowledge within the memory system has very profound effects on the way that new information is acquired. It suggests that there must be a tremendous difference between the way a message is encoded into a child's memory and the way that same information is encoded by an adult. For children, each concept encountered has to be built up from scratch. A great deal of rote learning must take place during the initial construction of the data base: Understanding is only slowly elaborated as properties [of various stimuli] are accumulated, as examples are learned, and as [relationships] evolve. At first, most of the concepts in memory will only be partially defined and will not be well integrated with the other stored information.
>
> Later in life, when a great deal of information has been accumulated and organized into a richly interconnected data base, learning should take on a different character. New things can be learned, primarily by analogy to what is already known. The main problem becomes one of fitting a new concept into the preexisting memory structure: Once the right relationship has been established, the whole of past experience is automatically brought to bear on the interpretation and understanding of the new events.[12]

112

Individual differences and idiosyncrasies are the rule, of course, rather than the exception.

> . . . Understanding evolves through a combination of the external evidence and the internal operations that manipulate and reorganize the incoming information. Two different memories would follow exactly the same path of development only if they received identical inputs in the identical order and used identical procedures for organizing them. Thus it is extremely unlikely that any two people will evolve exactly the same conceptual structure to represent the world they experience.
>   . . . What a person believes depends on what he has experienced and what sequence of inferences and deductions has been applied to the stored information. Even very subtle differences in the environment can produce different memory products, despite the fact that the underlying machinery for interpreting and remembering information may be common to all. . . .[13]

Such a system, they conclude, has its dangers.

> . . . It is seldom that an adult encounters an entirely novel event—one that is totally unrelated to his existing conceptual structure. Almost everything he experiences can be related to what he has encountered in the past. Even when he experiences clearly discrepant information, his conceptual structure is made up of such a complex and interdependent set of relationships that it resists revision. Thus, an adult is more likely to reject a discrepant input or change its meaning than to modify or change his beliefs. With children, the conceptual structure is not nearly so elaborate or so highly interconnected as that of adults. New experiences can be taken in stride, since contradictions seldom arise.[14]

Parenthetically, the phenomenal success of a melodramatic potboiler like the movie *The Poseidon Adventure* may be due in large part to its having literally, visually, turned our mental models of a possible reality upside down, like the capsized ship itself. As the characters hazardously made their way "up" to the "bottom" of the stricken ocean liner and to the safety of the surface of the sea, the audience shared with them to an almost unbearable degree the eerie sense of almost total disorientation.

What, finally, are the implications of hemispheric specialization

113

for conscious learning? Can the right hemisphere learn when we remain unaware of it? Of course it can, because it is conscious, if by conscious we mean capable of complex response to the environment. The split-brain experiments have proved that. Can the two hemispheres learn wholly independently of each other? Again, split-brain experiments confirm that they can, simultaneously and even in opposition. Must they? The question is moot. Much to the surprise of the Cal Tech team, efforts to help one disconnected hemisphere help the other, when limited to pure information input, were counterproductive. Sperry and his associates had long suspected that even though the commissures were cut, there might be some valuable "neural leakage" across the lower brain structures. Could it be used to pass an answer? It could, they found, but the message interfered to such a degree that learning was all but impossible. For example, flashing the word "correct" to the left hemisphere when the right was performing on one of its specialties sent the right hemisphere's scores into a tailspin. Only when the subject was chided for poor performance and aggressively informed that anyone with half a brain could do it better, did he buckle down and get the answer. Emotional involvement appeared to stimulate a more general systemic reaction and bring about a joint effort. That kind of cooperative strategy under pressure—or its absence—may say something about the importance of personality factors such as motivation, anxiety, and tension when tackling intellectual tasks.

In the split-brain, we know that learning specialized to one hemisphere is usually "laid down" on that side only. But what about the adult whose brain growth and health are normal, whose commissures are intact and ticking away? Can and do his two hemispheres learn separately, not just now and then, but all the time?

The question is crucial. If the answer is yes, then the impact of early environment, of society's permeating systems of reward and punishment, may be even more important than the most rabid behaviorist suspects. It could mean that each hemisphere learns in the presence of stimuli tailored to its abilities and withers in their absence, so that one hemisphere becomes dominant in an even more decisive—and insidious—sense of the word. It could even mean that when both kinds of stimuli are competing for attention and the two hemispheres are in conflict, the mature brain takes from even the most balanced environment what our dominant hemisphere—the product of early social conditioning—deems to be perceptually important, at the expense of what it decrees is not. This initial reinforcement of one side of the brain, cyclically repeated, could provide an intellectual "set" for a lifetime of learning. Such a cycle would be not only self-sustaining but also stubbornly resistant, if not impervious, to the best and worst of a later environment's ideal offerings to the other hemisphere.

It could be equally argued, of course, that both sides of the brain pursue a simultaneous cooperative strategy in most normal learning situations, each extracting those facets it processes best, each producing and filing for future reference its piece of the mosaic. Sperry admits as much when he concedes that the two hemispheres function better together than apart. But the components contributed by each needn't be equal. In most learning opportunities, in fact, parity would be improbable. The intellectual content of a lecture is almost exclusively verbal, that of an art exhibit almost exclusively not. Humans, London's Eunice Belbin has shown, learn some things better by observation than by either verbal instruction or actual experience. (So do cats.) Depending on a complex of family factors—cultural bent, economic circumstance, parents by inclination verbal or imagistic—a definite predilection for learning in one hemisphere or the other could be shaped at the outset for a lifetime.

It could also be argued, and probably will be, that whichever hemisphere is naturally more endowed in innate gifts will dominate through just such a selective interaction with its surroundings. But the paramount point of such speculation, and it is only that, still stands. If our hemispheres do learn separately, whichever does the lion's share may determine the direction our brain takes us. Given our disparate talents and opportunities, it may determine the eventual distance as well. How can it be otherwise in a society which engineers itself to reward or punish according to its perceived needs?

Thus we become what we learn. And what we learn inexorably shapes, and is shaped by, how we think.

115

Thinking

"The brain thinks too much," someone once said. "That's what it's supposed to do." Indeed, when it comes to thinking—modifying and manipulating his mental models—man is in a class by himself. His superiority to other mammals, and their superiority to lesser creatures, can be traced out in a hierarchy that depends upon the proportionate amount of cerebral cortex available to each. As the cortex develops, so does his ability to think.

Again, it is Piaget who has perfected a simple set of parameters to demonstrate that this growth occurs in definite stages. Faced with a problem to solve beyond his brain's organic competence, Piaget has proved, the young child resorts to precausal thinking. Why does the nail sink to the bottom of the bucket? "Because it's tired." Why then, does the toy boat not sink when the nail, which is lighter, does? "To keep people from drowning."[15] Precausal thinking, clearly, has less in common with rational thinking than it does with one of the Little Moron jokes that swept this country in the forties. "Why did you shoot?" one little moron asks the other as they watch a duck the second one has bagged plummet into the lake. "The fall would have killed him."

But gradually that same child abandons the precausal and begins to cope more intelligently with those perceptual clues to reality his senses bring him. Piaget illustrates this in his experiment with two identical glasses, his half full of orange soda, the child's half full of lemonade. As the child watches, Piaget transfers the lemonade to a tall, thin glass. Now, he asks, who has the most to drink? If the child is five years old he will probably reply without hesitation, "I have." Height appears to be his only perceptual clue to quantity. If he is six, however, confusion may set in. His glass is taller, all right, but Piaget's is somehow, well, bigger. Now he perceives two clues to quantity, but one remains rather vague. But ask him again when he is seven and suddenly the answer is crystal clear: The size of both drinks remains the same, regardless of how either is repoured. The new glass is taller, yes, but the old glass is wider. The spatial clues are no longer in conflict, but perfectly integrated. He now understands—whether through further cerebral maturation, another year's experience, or both, the issue is unsettled—what Piaget calls *conservation of amount.*

116

In more than thirty years of painstaking give-and-take with children of all ages about such deceptively simple problems, Piaget has charted the fascinating country of the young and growing mind, and mapped from their onset many such principles of conservation inherent in human mastery of changing dimension: number, substance, length, area, weight, and volume. All are vital to anchoring our mental models of the possible world in a stable and permanent, though flexible, reality. Without them, as Harry Jerison showed, our lives would be lost in an endless and bewildering blizzard of perceptual transformation.

Later on, of course, man learns to think symbolically, to learn such powerful stratagems as deduction (reasoning from the general to the particular), induction (reasoning from the particular to the general) and analogy (seeing—an important distinction—how one thing is like another). His ability is a matter not only of power but also of diversity. What psychologists call his *cognitive style*, the forms in which he habitually expresses his thought, varies from situation to situation and person to person. Some situations demand problem solving, others the raising of new questions. Some involve multiple tasks quickly and variously done, others a single consuming endeavor demanding total absorption over prolonged periods. Some, therefore, attract one kind of thinker, others another, and some—like professional writing—all kinds.

Many writers, for instance, are "bleeders" who can't get past a paragraph without seeing and too often trying a dozen different ways to do it better. That cognitive style, if it deserves such a euphemism, is epitomized by Camus' would-be author, Monsieur Grand, in *The Plague,* who spent seven years on the opening sentence of his first novel, seeking to catch in just the right words the clip-clop of hoofbeats on the cobbled streets of Paris. Other writers, like thirties novelist Thomas Wolfe, are afflicted with galloping logorrhea and must be wrenched from their pages, or vice versa. "But it's not finished!" Wolfe once bellowed at Maxwell Perkins when the editor picked up a huge cardboard box brimming with a million words of overdue manuscript and headed for the door. "Oh, yes, it is," replied the unflappable Perkins, not breaking stride as he made off with what became two books. An enviable few, on the other hand, can think and write their way straight through entire manuscripts from beginning to end without ever

117

looking back. Robert Heinlein, the dean of science fiction, confessed he kept the seed of a new book germinating in his mind until, like the irritating speck of sand that prompts the oyster to produce its pearl, he could stand it no longer. Then he locked himself in his bedroom, wrote it all nonstop, and collapsed in exhaustion. Georges Simenon, creator of over eighty Inspector Maigret detective novels and 200 other books, is an even more extraordinary case. When Simenon got an idea for a book, the barest idea, he rolled a sheet of paper into his typewriter, pecked out "Chapter one, Page one," and began. When he finished a chapter, he laid it aside unread and began another, letting his mind and the story take him where they would. He kept this up on a precise daily schedule until it was finished. Then he typed, "The End," mailed it off to his publisher, and forgot about it. "My last book was *Maigret et Monsieur Charles,*" he informed an interviewer when he retired at seventy, "which I wrote last February. . . ."[16]

Brains, in short, differ. As psychologist Howard Gardner of Harvard puts it, some people are tone-deaf, others are all thumbs. My wife, for example, cannot understand how I could patiently exchange the contents of salt and pepper shakers which had been misfilled, when merely reversing the lids with their different-sized holes would do. Absurd as it may seem, I have a blind spot in my thinking for things like that. I, in turn, cannot understand how she can plan a fifteen-mile car trip in rush-hour traffic with supreme assurance that it will only take her five minutes. She has a blind spot in her thinking for things like that. People, as a matter of fact, are constantly floored by how other people think—or in their opinion, fail to. One recent letter to the editor of our local newspaper compared another letter writer's thinking to "ten miles of tangled shoelaces." The only description better was possibly that of a sergeant I knew at a U. S. Air Force base in France. "The French," he would mutter when grappling with the Gallic minds of his civilian construction crew, "are wired backwards."

Is the character of our thinking, as well as its content, lateralized by hemisphere?

Split-brain researchers think so. J. E. Bogen likes to say that left-hemisphere thinking is predominantly *propositional,* or sym-

118

bolic and logical, while right-hemisphere thinking is *appositional,* or comparative and relational. Arthur Deikman, a colleague of Galin and Ornstein, believes the two hemispheres are dominated respectively by the *action* mode and the *receptive* mode. Such a basic division in theoretical thought about thinking is not new, for that matter. As long ago as 1956 Jurgen Ruesch and Weldon Kees in their book *Nonverbal Communication* described man's thinking as "computerlike," both digital (discursive, verbal) and analogic (nondiscursive, imagistic.) Thomas Hobbes, William James, even those archantagonists Freud and Pavlov, all agreed on the existence of two distinct types of thought. "Mental discourse" was either "unordered" or "directed" to Hobbes. Intellectual discrimination, added James, could be both "differential" and "existential." Pavlov decided thought hinged on two "signaling systems," one basically immediate and perceptual, the other abstract and linguistic. These two signaling systems, he concluded, divided humanity into three kinds of people: the thinker, the artist, and a salutary combination of the two.

Freud, for his part, divided man's "mental production" into *secondary process thinking,* that which begins with language, and *primary process thinking,* that which a disciple described as "carried out more in pictorial, concrete images." As we know, the father of psychoanalysis, and for a time after, his followers, had little good to say about the latter. Its images, the disciple wrote, were

> less fitted for objective judgment . . . relatively unorganized, primitive, magical, undifferentiated, based on common motor reactions, ruled by emotions, full of wishful or fearful misconceptions, archaic, vague, regressive, primal.[17]

Bogen finds this bill of particulars excessively harsh. Perhaps, he speculates with tongue firmly in cheek, it reflects not a sound objective judgment but the junior analyst's own "unconscious denial"[18] of their intrinsic worth.

"We are embarrassed by intuition," conceded physiologist Barbara Brown. "Security lies in conscious rational thought because only that is socially acceptable in our culture."[19] Freud himself, while obviously biased against some right-hemisphere processes,

119

paradoxically could not deny their power in his own life. With some embarrassment, he once admitted in a letter to Jung that he was "not cut out for inductive investigation . . . my whole make-up is intuitive."[20]

To which Jung might have replied but didn't, as he later would write,

> Imagination and intuition are vital to our understanding. And though the usual popular opinion is that they are chiefly valuable to poets and artists (that in "sensible" matters one should mistrust them), they are in fact equally vital in all the higher grades of science. Here they play an increasingly important role, which supplements that of the "rational" intellect and its application to a specific problem. Even physics, the strictest of all applied sciences, depends to an astonishing degree upon intuition, which works by way of the unconscious (although it is possible to demonstrate afterward the logical procedures that could have led one to the same result as intuition).[21]

Or as Bogen delights in quoting the author of—of all things—a highly successful cookbook, "Only a strongly intuitive person on speaking terms with his [sic] imagination has a chance of success."[22]

Andrew Weil makes a similar distinction today when he speaks of "stoned" and "straight" thinking. "Stoned" and "straight" are drug culture slang words Weil uses to label the strikingly different thought processes he believes typical of drug users and nonusers respectively. In his view, straight thinking deals in conceptual understanding, focuses on external reality, is alert to differences rather than similarities, and, true to its name, attempts to explain the world through a narrow-gauge cause-and-effect linearity. Stoned thinking experiences life directly and wordlessly, discerns the inner content beneath the outward form, relies on intuition rather than self-conscious cognition, and accepts as inevitable the essential mystery and ambivalence of the natural world. Despite its connotation, Weil is quick to emphasize, the use of drugs does not guarantee stoned thinking any more than abstinence guards against it. It simply connotes a strong tendency. "I know a great many persons who use a great many drugs and yet think in straight ways most of the time," he writes. "On the other hand, I know a number of people who are very stoned in their thinking and yet have never used drugs."[23]

Thus, though the words "cerebral lateralization" may never have entered their heads, thinkers from Freud on down to the present have detected and delineated, if often crudely and prejudicially, the two kinds of thinking that appear to go on in the hemispheres, one of them in symbols, the other in images. In so doing, they have left behind a teasing intimation that split-brain experiments have only strengthened: The right hemisphere *is* the Freudian unconscious, or at least the major expressive part of it, leaving to the limbic system the job of generating emotion as an inescapable component of memory. If so, as such maverick disciplines as scientology and est training would suggest, aberrant behavior may be "bad thinking" in the linguistically inaccessible right hemisphere (inaccessible in the sense of bringing about any changes there purely through verbal manipulation). Suspect to organized medicine though they may be, both scientology and est training mistrust and shun words to work with direct experience. They are more interested in what their disciples do than what they say. Scientology preaches that the essence of human experience is stored by our brains in mental pictures. Est founder Werner Erhard decrees that, "What you experience for yourself is the truth—something only believed is a lie."[24]

Although conventional psychiatry and psychology would scarcely go that far, they too recognize the persisting psychic dangers of language. "Words serve as screens to cover sensory or 'gut' memories," admits psychiatrist Lawrence Kubie, "with the inevitable consequence that every verbal symbol serves to screen a deeper meaning. . . . Without knowing it, this is what we have always meant when we have spoken of a patient's 'intellectualization' as defeating insight. . . . If this is true, then the ultimate answer to one of the riddles about the relation of insight to psychotherapy depends on our ability to penetrate the smokescreen of words."[25]

As a matter of fact, more and more psychotherapists are beginning to lay siege to these hidden bastions of speechless thought with techniques aimed at "desensitizing" feared or taboo situations with imagistic rehearsals and make-believe of the very things that disturb. For example, impotent men and frigid women have

121

successfully unlocked long-shut-away feelings that lie at the root of their problems by intensely visualizing, step by step, the rudiments of sex, from seduction through foreplay to coitus. Albert Ellis, to name one practitioner, traces the roots of emotional illness not to actuating events but to the patient's irrational belief system. It is not the situation itself but what the patient believes about it that warps his interpretation of what has happened to him, Ellis thinks, that triggers unfounded feelings of anxiety, worthlessness, and depression. An irrational belief system Ellis defines as one stemming from the all-too-human tendency of people to believe unrealistic ideas about themselves in relation to their needs and wants from the world. Change those ideas, he contends, and the power of universal events to unduly influence our lives will vanish (and with it, another researcher adds, the kind of stress that sickens and kills).

In that same vein, transactional analyst Fanita English writes in *Psychology Today* of "divergent pulls" within our minds from early on that must be resolved, pulls manifestly between the two hemispheres:

> . . . The young child's mental system is very different from the adult's. . . . It can maintain, side by side, contradictory combinations of feelings, goals and beliefs. The child thinks syncretically, pulling together incidental analogies, coincidental juxtapositions and approximations of imagery. This process serves him well, because it leads to . . . creative combinations and quick flashes of intuition unhampered by ponderous deductive logic. But it also maintains his magical beliefs and his archaic cause-and-effect conclusions that may some day steer [him] to disaster.[26]

In other words, while we may need to be as a child again to free our mental imagery from its prison of language, it is dangerous to dwell there indefinitely. Albert Ellis counters this failing with fantasizing techniques intended both to restore emotional balance to the patient's responses and alter his irrational beliefs. He gives the patient, as it were, mental practice on the very thing that's gone wrong. (Mental practice, for that matter, can also help your tennis strokes and your golf swing.) If imagery can get us into trouble, Ellis seems to be saying, it can jolly well get us out.

122

Fanita English goes on.

> At about the age of five or six the child actively seeks verbal
> content and imagery for the inchoate images, ideas, goals, mes-
> sages and conclusions he has collected. . . . Reality and fantasy
> are interwoven. . . . One day, a particular fairy tale or animal
> story turns him on. With a few changes here and there, perhaps
> some omissions, this story accommodates all the scraps he was
> trying to fit together. . . . Later, as an adolescent or an adult,
> he might suddenly vibrate to a more complex story—a myth or a
> novel or a biography or a movie. . . . The person may never re-
> alize that there, couched in new, more verbal symbols, is the
> theme he selected [for his life] long, long ago in another magic
> realm.[27]

That other magic realm is almost surely the right hemisphere.
But it need not be invoked only in therapy to correct what it has
caused to go wrong. It has far more positive powers. Which brings
us to the last and most fascinating arena where the functions of
our two hemispheres meet, interplay, and if properly fused, blend
into the highest mental expression of which man's intelligence is
capable: the act of creating.

Creating

University of California psychologist Donald MacKinnon tells
the story about a man who set out to find the greatest general who
ever lived. His search led him to the gates of Heaven, where Saint
Peter pointed out the soul he sought. "But that isn't the greatest
general," the man protested. "I knew him when he lived on Earth.
He was only a cobbler."

"I know," Saint Peter replied. "But if he had been a general he
would have been the greatest of them all."[28]

The moral of the story is all too clear. It isn't enough to recognize talent when it surfaces. For the good of society and the self
we have to go out and find it, or at least create optimum conditions for it to emerge this side of Saint Peter.

But what exactly are we to look for, prepare for, test for? Tests
of creativity, unfortunately, like tests of intelligence, are notori-

ously limited when used to predict future performance in the real world. Too often, says psychologist Frank Barron in his book *Creative Person and Creative Process*, they violate the very essence of the process, "which goes at its own pace, will not be hurried, is behaviorally silent for long periods of time and is easily aborted if someone is always blowing a whistle. . . ."[29] A better approach, says Duke University's Michael Wallach, is *persistence forecasting*, a term borrowed from meteorology to suggest that what the child does today outside the school curriculum—art, music, writing on the school paper—is the best bet for what he will do tomorrow. Wallach suggests that excellence in real-world pursuits has a different structure to it, one with a far more diversified range of products and performances than the classroom. Such circumstances, according to Wallach, depend heavily upon initiation by the person; he may generate and maintain activities that bring about particular outcomes, responding more to internal pressures than to the demands of his environment.

But such a method is far from infallible. For a complex of reasons, and despite those pressures from within, the potential artist may never pick up a brush, the potential general never join the Army. How then, shall we know him, or her?

Research has proven the obvious: We are not necessarily looking for high IQ or impeccable scholarship. In a study of architects whose work was judged most creative by a national panel of their peers, MacKinnon found "essentially a zero relationship"[30] to academic performance and intelligence as traditionally measured. Generally, his creative architects had attended college with "profound skepticism"[31] and earned no better than a B average. Similar studies of physicists, biologists, and psychology graduate students found that creativity in their professional achievement—as reflected by patents, prizes, projects, and the opinions of their professors and colleagues—was in no way predictable from their grades, aptitude tests, or achievement scores. In almost half the cases, in fact, research attainments were negatively related.

Indeed, studies of creative people have shown that while their academic skills and IQ scores are usually higher than average, the most "intelligent" and scholastically accomplished among them are no more creative than the least. Both criteria appear to be "threshold" phenomena: Once you step beyond a certain cutoff point, further progress is meaningless. Creativity then becomes, in Frank Barron's view, a unitary and pervasive dimension in its own right. Thus a reasonably high IQ is "necessary but not sufficient" for the act of creating, but once the threshold is crossed, other more critical factors take over. But what are they?

The *creativity syndrome*, as MacKinnon calls it, is characterized by two kinds of factors that are often overlapping and frequently fused: the cognitive and the personality. Time and again, researchers examining creative people have marveled at their "pristine innocence of perception,"[32] their fruitful insight, the breadth and depth and wealth and ease of their powers of mental association—an amalgam of attributes that leaves many of them, as a friend once described Franz Kafka, "constantly amazed."[33] One early researcher expressed a typical if perhaps extreme view when he reported that a famous woman poet who took a word association test gave "a higher proportion of unique responses than those of anyone outside a mental institution."[34]

Foremost, creative people are highly esthetic, particularly in the ancient Greek sense of being alive to their perceptions. They thrive on the complex, the intricate, the asymmetrical, the complicated. This trait permeates the nature of creative mathematicians and scientists as well as artists, and is totally unrelated to IQ scores and academic skills. Apparently the creative have an uncommon capacity to integrate this wealth of chaotic sensory experience into a higher order of mental synthesis. In plain words it makes them the kind of people who can turn junk into jewelry; who would rather put together a stained glass window than take apart a watch.

They tend too to notice what goes on around them more acutely, retain and retrieve sense impressions more readily, and—ah, the illogic of it all!—are slow to label and screen out the irrelevant. They perceive life rather than judge it, a stance that results in a heightened awareness not only of the outer world but of the inner self. People who judge, says MacKinnon, tend to lead a life that is orderly, controlled, and carefully planned. The perceptive approach, in contrast, engenders a life that is open, flexible, spontaneous, stimulating, and receptive. The majority of creative writers, mathematicians, and architects tested on esthetic sensitivity measures were perceptive types. Only among research scientists was a preponderance of judging found, which may have something to do with the distinction MacKinnon makes between artistic creativity, with its outward expression of inner states, and scientific creativity, with its need to mediate externally defined objectives and goals. Even so, the more perceptive among them were the more creative.

Then too, creative people proved more intuitive, both about what is and what, in the visionary sense, can be. MacKinnon found intuition strong in the mental makeup of over 90 percent of the mathematicians, research scientists, creative writers, and architects he tested. They put more stock in gut-level hunches and prophetic dreams. In addition, they were far more willing to inject formless fantasies into their thinking than the noncreative, who are by comparison mentally rigid, self-limited, and controlled. Not only were the men of arts and sciences more unrestrained in their fantasy than firemen, salesmen, and businessmen—a small test group of Air Force officers was too. Barron decided they felt freer to indulge in fantasy because their egos were strong enough to check its expression when needed, a safeguard other researchers generally found critical to fantasy's effective use in stimulating new avenues of thought. Their primary process, shades of Freud, was well integrated with their secondary process. The same must be said for, of all people, Einstein. "When I examine myself and my methods of thought," he acknowledged to his biographer, "I come to the conclusion that the gift of fantasy has meant more to me than my talent for absorbing positive knowledge."[35] Indeed, he traced his more creative impulses to "certain signs and more or less clear images . . . [in] combinatory play."[36]

What's more, in inventing fantasies the creative consistently produces more stimulus-free themes, incongruities, and unexpected endings. Even their dreams are more original. In one of Barron's experiments, subjects were hypnotized, fed a fictitious account of supposed events that day, and instructed to dream about them that night. The more creative not only dreamed more imaginatively, Barron reported, their dreams were clearly intended as solutions to the problems implied by their fictitional day.

Finally, in the cognitive area, Wallach found that creative people generate ideas more prodigally—perhaps, he speculates, because they are better at imagining hypothetical possibilities or letting their minds wander in an unfocused but ultimately fruitful fashion; a pronounced penchant for divergent thinking that sends their minds veering off into worlds of the novel and unknown. Again, this talent, like the others, appears to exist independently of academic skills, as Wallach and Nathan Kogan found in a study of fifth-graders. That richness, that prodigality, may explain their taste for greater mental risk-taking, especially in careers, where they lean more to the adventurous and flamboyant and less to the doctor-lawyer-professor triad that attracts the more conventional, straitlaced IQ performer.

Equally critical to the creativity syndrome, researchers agree, is a constellation of personality factors. As Barron writes, creative people have "an edge to them."[37] They are more aggressive, more rebellious, more nonconforming, more emotionally troubled, and more given to impetuosity and violence when their vitality—also more—is thwarted. They are also, simply, more emotional. In writers Barron found a much more intense sensibility than usual, more openness to feelings of awe and oneness with the universe, as well as ". . . feelings of horror, forsakenness, and desolation."[38] They dreamed more in color, had more nightmares. Overall, though, they were as sturdy in the ego as they were emotionally extreme. Compared to people in general, Barron decided, the creative "appear to be both sicker and healthier psychologically,"[39] imbued as they are with larger-than-life sensibility.

That "eccentricity," if such a loaded word is a fair description, may be as much the result of social climate as individual temperament, the result of pressures created by stereotyped, conformist notions of normality that have no biological basis in the brain. All that we have been talking about, of course—the esthetic, the spontaneous, the intuitive, the fantastic, the synesthetic, the divergent—are properties of the right hemisphere. And it doesn't take a PhD to see that, rightly or wrongly and for whatever reason, those mental characteristics and functions specialized to either hemisphere have strong connotations in our society of being divisible by sex, of being basically masculine or feminine.

127

Says MacKinnon, "The evidence is clear: The more creative a person is the more he reveals an openness to his own feelings and emotions, a sensitive intellect and understanding self-awareness, and wide-ranging interests including many which in the American culture are thought of as feminine. . . . Our creative . . . appear to give more expression to the feminine side of their nature than do [the] less creative. . . ."[40]

Man, in the socially potent stereotype, is rational, logical, and abstract; a thinker. Woman is not. She is intuitive, comparative, holistic; a feeler. Man, by definition, is a left-hemisphere creature, woman a right. And while all exceptions are not of course creative, researchers find that the highly creative are exceptional in exactly that way. The women are more "masculine" in their mode of thought than most women, the men more "feminine" than most men.

Neither sex, it must be added immediately, need strike a Faustian bargain with the devil or take a plane to Copenhagen and become like the other to be creative. The most creative men studied were neither effeminate nor homosexual. (According to one study by Albert Ellis, any degree of homosexuality is directly related to a loss of creative potential.) Nor were the women—mathematicians—open or closet Lesbians. The more creative retained their femininity, the less creative, as one study put it, ". . . seemed to have donned masculine armor as protection."[41] Nevertheless, as Marie Dellas and Eugene Gaier of the State University of New York at Buffalo noted in their paper on the identification of creativity, "It is the blending of the feminine and masculine, the integration of the necessary sensitivity and intuition with purposive action and determination, that is conducive to creativeness."[42] In short, it is a marriage of the two hemispheres too often lacking in our society, which tolerates, almost on a quota system like undesirable immigrants, comparatively few artists of either sex and exacts from them in return a terrible price in maladjustment, eccentricity, and neurosis.

As taboo as it is in technological America for a man to be like a woman, or a woman to be like a man, it is even more suspect for either of them to be like a child. Creative people are nonetheless more playful, whimsical, and childlike than most—and as Barron

128

observes wistfully, "The Muses seem to prefer children."[43] So do the hardheaded practicals, like Polaroid camera inventor Edwin Land. "Why can't you just develop the film in the camera?" a child once asked him. Ever since, Land has tried to keep a child around his laboratory. For it is axiomatic that children have a spontaneity, freedom, and imagination that most adults lamentably lack. As John Holt writes in *Escape From Childhood*, moreover, they "are the farthest thing in the world from spiritual. They are not abstract, but concrete. They are animals and sensualists; to them, what feels good is good."[44]

Is there a connection between this and the creative act? Barron is convinced there is. As he sees it, most of us as adults habitually employ the mechanism of classification to select what we need in life for our survival. We use it to see and avoid the destructive; to accentuate the positive and eliminate the negative. As a result we become conceptualizers rather than perceivers. We tend to seek out in every situation the familiar, the comfortable. We shun the hazards of honest observation and fresh inference with their threatening—and challenging—possibilities for contradiction and amendment (of our existing mental models). We pursue relentlessly the principle that like produces like. Otherwise, how are we to know who or where we are?

As growing children, however, we have drawn from our environment by "primitive . . . preverbal" means—visual, auditory, oral, tactile, kinesthetic—a fund of sensory information that comes to "occupy permanently the interstices of [our later] conceptual framework . . . effective though unnoticed and largely unverbalizable."[45] As we approach adulthood, Barron believes, we must choose between two paths. One remains open and vulnerable to this kind of perceptual experience. The other involves a blindered adjustment to the inevitable encroachments of maturity that is, alas, considered all too normal and expected. For when we put away childish things, says Holt, we put away the best things in childhood, things that needn't be the exclusive property of children.

They are *human* qualities. We are wise to value them in people of all ages. When we think of these qualities as childish, belonging only to children, we invalidate them; we make them into things we should "outgrow" as we grow older. Thus we excuse ourselves for carelessly losing what we should have done our best to keep. Worse yet, we teach the children this lesson: only "little kids" go around all the time looking enthusiastic and asking silly questions; to be grown-up is to be cool, impassive, untouched, invulnerable.[46]

On the other hand, in Barron's view, the person who remains open to both inner and outer perception does not separate himself from life but rather "gives himself over to the life processes within him," and, if lucky, "retains his innocence in the face of fate."[47] His unfettered intellect not only continues to accept the world's unending stream of novelty, but also is ever ready to reject the straits of rigid classification, with its perils of ossification and decay, to welcome an existence ever full of what W. H. Auden called "large, noisy feeling states." If he achieves that "love marriage of innocence and experience" while "moving ahead to the command and control that experience brings," Barron concludes, he can restore to our attention through his creativity what most of us have long since lost sight of at the crossroads: A world triumphantly "pregnant with unheard of possibilities. . . ."[48]

"Before the problem of the creative artist," Freud confessed, "analysis must, alas, lay down its arms."[49] But where is the problem if we recognize these hitherto mysterious aspects of creative arts as the normal functioning of the entire right half of the upper human brain? That half, when consciously conjoined with its opposite, routinely confronts us with what Barron calls the paradox of discipline and freedom, habit, and flexibility, order and disorder, integration and diffusion. For optimum creativity, he asserts, "the task we face is to avoid sacrificing one possibility to the other."[50]

Art speaks for itself, as philosopher Jacques Maritain said, and not in the voice of reason. Barron agrees with Maritain: Reason is a prison. Yet, he would add, the artist can learn useful things there, chiefly training and discipline: "The maturation of the talent, discipline in its exercise, must precede its full expression. The complex creative act can be expected to occur only rarely in childhood."[51] The same might be said of adults who haven't the patience to serve the requisite apprenticeship. Despite the Beatles' philosophy—*art is con, just do it*—the result of "letting it all hang out" is more often than not indifferent music, bad poetry, and worse pottery—pop culture in which, as Raymond Cattell laments, ". . . the thoughtful, subtle work of (serious creativity) is lost in monotonous drumbeats which assert that the individual has only to lose his inhibitions to become a da Vinci, a Beethoven, or an Einstein."[52] Delacroix's advice to young painters, Barron and Cattell would agree, still holds universally: "First learn to be a craftsman; it won't stop you from being a genius."[53]

The secret of creativity, then, would appear to lie in our ability to synchronize the complementary functions of our cerebral hemispheres, to pool the experience and talents of each half in producing an integrated whole. "The creative process allows for novel integrations, or gestalts, and creative ideas often emerge in drowsy or twilight states of consciousness," writes one observer. "But the expression of these ideas often requires activity, excitement and a good deal of rational and sequential thought."[54] To employ the metaphor of hi-fi, the creative person is one who plays the music of his life on both channels to the most soaring, full-bodied effect of which his stereophonic brain is capable. Most of us usually limit ourself mainly to one preferred channel. Increasingly, as we grow older, the other lies more and more idle, gathering more and more dust. As a consequence our life's music grows tinny, unbalanced, devoid of its natural richness, resonance and depth.

It more than lacks a critical dimension. It is worse than half-hearted. It is half-headed.

Is it accurate, or even fair, to define creativity as the intellectual product of both hemispheres when it fuses, as it must, what we have always thought of as intelligence and art? Perhaps a clearer perspective on the problem is possible if we compare the classic definitions. Intelligence, as defined by one typical writer, has as its chief purpose the conservation of knowledge, the discovery of principles, a fascination with ideas, the drive to know, to seek out, to solve—all for the satisfaction of synthesizing orderly, elegant, and inclusive conceptual systems. Art, says that same writer, is an ordering of our perceptual experience, one skillfully and sensitively expressed in patterns of behavior that esthetically satisfy both the artist and the beholder, extending and enriching mutually their experience of the world. A better working description of either hemisphere's function can scarcely be conceived (or imagined). Seeing how each is held in such high esteem, it seems a shame that intelligence and art must both stand semantically exposed as half-brained endeavors. Is there any intelligent (or artistic) way out of this dilemma?

One solution, likely to please neither artists nor intellectuals, might be to redefine the two modes. Intelligence could mean the full spectrum of mental modeling, both imagistic and symbolic, and art the fidelity of our expression to those inner models of the outer world, whether it be the art of music, literature, painting, and sculpture, or the art of diplomacy, decision-making, cooking, and conversation.

Such a philosophy is at least half implicit in the beguiling Balinese proverb quoted by Marshall McLuhan: "We have no art. We do everything as well as we can."[55]

Chapter 5

Athletics and Art

Among those many things most of us do as well as we can—without once considering them acts of intelligence—are athletics and art. The nonathlete has long derided sports as the doltish domain of mental laggards and meatheads, but there is at least inferential evidence that such surpassing motor skills are in the truest sense intelligent. The finest sort of spatial and kinesthetic intelligence may not be limited to dance and sculpture but may also be tautly at work on a circus tightrope, in the pert muscularity of an Olga Korbut, in the crack of Hank Aaron's bat against baseball, in the fifty-yard "bomb" a football quarterback lays in the outstretched arms of a racing flanker.

Just how bodily "configuration manipulations"—originating in the sensory images of the right hemisphere, as Stanford's Roger Shepard and others have found—could be translated into the split-second, superbly integrated movements of the athlete remain a matter of conjecture. There is also some cause for reservation. Contrary to what we once believed, microelectrode studies of single brain cells firing have shown that the motor cortex lying midway of each cerebral hemisphere does not initiate complex muscular action at the brain's highest level. It responds to massive impulses from the deeper brain, from the cerebellum and basal ganglia below the cerebrum. Still, research at the National Institute of Mental Health's Laboratory of Neurophysiology indicates that the coordinated involvement of all three neural areas is manifestly necessary. Since the basal ganglia appear to be preferentially active in slow movements and the cerebellum in quick movements—facts amply demonstrated by the selective effects of such brain disorders as Parkinson's disease—NIMH researchers have

133

postulated that the motor cortex may have the subtle function of "refined control,"[1] of balancing the mix, as it were. In any event, its role is critical. Damage to the lower brain's movement-related nerve cells causes only abnormality. Damage to the motor cortex causes paralysis.

Although the NIMH researchers won't say so, such a fine-tuning in the motor cortex might, if opportunity, training, and motivation were stripped away, conceivably be all that separates Hank Aaron from your neighborhood sandlotter. That's assuming, of course, that the right hemisphere of the intact brain were capable of something the commissurotomy experiments showed it could do in the split-brain: wrest motor control of the body's right side away from the left hemisphere in functions from which it is uniquely specialized.

Hints abound that it can. Athletes speak of a special feeling in their inner body, sharpened perceptions, a heightened sense of engagement with the here and now, a falling away of physical surroundings in the perfect merger of performer and performance—all suggestive of right-hemisphere function. When a juggler's skill is analyzed it proves heavily reliant on first the kinesthetic, then the visual. Interesting too is the psychological phenomenon called interference. That is, when the brain is sorting images, it finds it easier to signal the outcome of its search through speech; when sorting words, a spatial signal such as pointing is easier. Mixing metaphors, if "the line is busy" an alternate channel of communication is automatically switched on to avoid what an esoteric new computer-based field called human information processing refers to as "competition for limited processing capacity."[2] As Gordon Bower points out, two activities in different modes tend to be mutually less competitive, interruptive, and interfering. If the juggler is really "thinking" about what he is doing, as he claims, how can he exchange quips with his audience without disruption of his skill? And why is it if anyone touches him or grossly interferes with the gestalt of the whirling balls or machetes against the performing background, it causes him to falter? Finally, it seems he can pick out his girlfriend in the crowd as he performs, but only a visual detail at a time—adding up to a realization that it is her, and not as a holistic presence—

apparently utilizing what Sperry discovered to be the feature detection capability of the left hemisphere. In short, the right hemisphere is clearly busy. Under the circumstances it comes as an anticlimax that his personality is nonverbal, nonmathematical, artistic, and intuitive.

At best, however, such evidence is inferential, the hole in the doughnut again. The idea of athletics as a major aspect of right-hemisphere intellectual function has mixed professional appeal, even among the split-brain researchers. Sperry thinks it is "not really"[3] so. Bogen, on the other hand, believes that such a hypothesis makes sense, that athletic talents "are a good deal more than motor skills."[4] Gazzaniga is probably most typical of the scientific community at its more avant garde when he declares that such speculation is "well taken, and may even be true. It is still too early to say with any scientific confidence. . . . In some sense I react against it in that it all sounds far too simple."[5]

Perhaps it does. But some nonscientists are today pursuing athletics as if the anathema of the left hemisphere with its incessant abstraction were a foregone conclusion. Though the right hemisphere is never mentioned as such, they teach and play in the spirit of what the renowned Zen master D. T. Suzuki wrote in his foreword to the book *Zen in the Art of Archery*: "As soon as we reflect, deliberate, and conceptualize, the original unconsciousness is lost and a thought interferes. . . ."[6]

In his sprightly manual *The Inner Game of Tennis*, self-styled "yoga tennis" pro Timothy Gallwey echoes Suzuki. He counsels, "The important thing is to experience it. Don't intellectualize it."[7] Instead of teaching his students with longwinded oral instruction, Gallwey without a word lets them learn by first watching him make a stroke, then visualizing an image of it in their own mind, and finally letting their sense of feel take over in wordlessly, thoughtlessly duplicating the stroke themselves. The first time he tried his technique, the student watched wordlessly but then broke Gallwey's injunction of silence to remark that he realized now his feet were wrong. He thereupon hit ten balls perfectly except for one thing—his feet stayed wrong.

When the "ego-mind" and the verbal judgments of its running play-by-play are split away from the act of learning and playing,

Gallwey has decided, the "computerlike unconscious" can concentrate on silently absorbing such things as how high the ball bounces when hit at varying speed and spins, or how fast it falls and comes up off the court. The result of such "thoughtless" concentration, he claims, is the delightfully uncommon but memorable experience that ordinarily comes but rarely to the weekend tennis player: that of "playing over your head," of "not knowing what you're doing," of being "unconscious" in the staggering proficiency and repertoire of your shot-making. Like Suzuki's Zen archer, in fact, his pupils can hammer their serves to knock over buckets spotted on the backline—just by visualizing precisely where they want the ball to go and correcting now and then for a little psychic windage.

The common denominator in all this Gallwey calls *mindlessness*, ". . . An intuitive sense that the mind is transcended—or at least in part rendered inoperative."[8] Such an experience is equally implicit in the vicissitudes of the baseball player who, in a batting slump and having tried everything to break it including watching his swing on films, changing his lucky socks, and trying a dozen different stances, decides finally to stop thinking about it, steps up to the plate and, flailing away, knocks two balls out of the park. If the phenomenon still strikes as unearthly strange to those unversed in hemispheric function, Gallwey brings it home with an example familiar to all: Learning to dance.

> The steps were not complicated, but it was weeks before I was dancing without the need to play back the tape in my head: "Put your left foot here, right foot there, turn, one two, three; one, two, three." I would think out each step, command myself to do it, and then execute it. I was barely aware there was a girl in my arms, and it was weeks before I was able to handle a conversation while dancing . . . Contrast [this] with the way the modern twelve-year-old learns to dance. He goes to a party one night, sees his friends doing the Monkey, the Jerk, and the Swim, and comes home having mastered them all. . . . How does he do this? First, by simply *watching*. He doesn't think about what he is seeing. . . . He simply absorbs *visually* the image in front of him. This image completely bypasses the ego-mind, and seems to be fed directly to the body, for in a few minutes the kid is on the floor doing movements very similar to those he was watch-

ing. Now he is *feeling* how it is to imitate those images. . . . If the next day he is asked by his sister how to do the Monkey he'll say, "I don't know . . . like this . . . see?" Ironically, he thinks he doesn't know how to do the dance because he can't explain it in words.[9]

If the Monkey, the Jerk, and the Swim are expressions of spatial and kinesthetic intelligence, then surely football, tennis, and track, to name three different types of sport, are too. But do they, like the artistic attributes of the right hemisphere, as language does, extend our conscious perceptual world through human consensus?

Gallwey recognizes as much when he speaks of competition being "identical with true cooperation"[10] because each player benefits psychologically by his efforts to overcome the obstacles offered by the other. At its peak, he thinks, this results in a "superconscious state"[11] on either side of the net, in which each player resolves "the lack of harmony which usually exists between the two (inner) selves." Ideally, Gallwey believes, the player then shifts from being a "player of the outer game" to being a "player of the inner game." He plays tennis to improve his concentration instead of vice versa. Thus, competition—the crisp back-and-forth that is to tennis as language is to debate—becomes, like forensics at their most profound, an opportunity to "reach new levels of self-awareness."[12] The same would seem equally true of team sports like football, as well as those like track-and-field, with, of course, the added element of theater that makes any spectator sport or participant game, in McLuhan's words, a "dramatic model of our psychological lives."[13]

Whatever their deepest attraction, athletics and those who perform them are clearly better than ever. Scarcely a record that stood in any sport twenty years ago still stands today before the growing hordes of trained and motivated people that press themselves irresistibly against it. Those among us who would cite superior coaching, more participants and improved facilities as the reasons for such a record-breaking onslaught raise at least as many questions as they answer. For what are such factors but a natural response to an inner need that wells within us and will not be denied, one that might at bottom be the resurgent right hemi-

137

sphere reaching out anew with its spatial and kinesthetic intelligence for ever-greater perceptual consensus.

But nowhere is the right hemisphere more in evidence, ever and always, than in the world of the artist and his art. The creative act, as we have seen, demands the best energies of both hemispheres, especially the language arts with their requisite melding of symbols and imagery. The balance between these brain "languages" varies, of course. Some writing—Somerset Maugham's—is as lean and spare and devoid of images as the most sterile dinner-table conversation. Other writing—Lawrence Durrell's—is so shot through with images that following his characters through their exotic adventures, as someone once said, is "like trying to watch a street scene through a stained-glass window." The more creative the writing, the more right-hemisphere the mental investment. A poem in its formative stage, said Stephen Spender, is "like a face which one seems to be able to visualize clearly in the eye of memory, but when one examines it mentally or tries to think it out, feature by feature, it seems to fade."[14] That same amorphous, immediate, spontaneous pieces-falling-together quality is reflected further in the enthusiastic remark of one young author on the publication of his first novel: "It was like—do you remember when you first learned how to ride a bicycle? Remember that funny feeling when you finally got going and you realized, 'By god, I can ride that damn thing!' "[15]

All in all, as Jerome Singer writes, much of the world's great literature is characterized by a high degree of concrete imagery.

> The poetry of Keats, for example, draws heavily on almost every sensory modality. [A] painstaking count of the images used by Shakespeare in comparison with those employed by a number of his contemporaries showed that Shakespeare not only used much more concrete imagery but that he was especially prolific in his use of . . . references to taste, smell and touch. . . .[16]

As the same time many writers, notably Goethe and Huxley, betray a dissatisfaction with their craft not the least typical of the more right-hemisphere artist. Writes Goethe,

138

We talk far too much. We should talk less and draw more. I personally should like to renounce speech altogether and, like organic Nature, communicate everything I have to say in sketches. . . . The more I think of it, there is something futile, mediocre, even (I am tempted to say) foppish about speech. . . .[17]

Adds Huxley,

We can never dispense with language and the other symbol systems; for it is by means of them, and only by their means, that we have raised ourselves above the brutes. . . . But we can easily become the victims as well as the beneficiaries of these systems. We must learn how to handle words effectively; but at the same time we must preserve and, if necessary, intensify our ability to look at the world directly and not through the half-opaque medium of concepts, which distorts every given fact into the all too familiar likeness of some generic label or explanatory abstraction. . . .

. . . All our education is predominantly verbal and therefore fails to accomplish what it is supposed to do. . . . It turns out students of the natural sciences who are completely unaware of Nature as the primary fact of experience. It inflicts upon the world students of the humanities who know nothing of humanity, their own or anyone else's.

"I have always found," Blake wrote rather bitterly, "that Angels have the vanity to speak of themselves as the only wise. This they do with a confident insolence sprouting from systematic reasoning." Systematic reasoning is something we could not, as a species or individuals, possibly do without. But neither if we are to remain sane, can we possibly do without direct perception, the more unsystematic the better, of the inner and outer worlds into which we have been born.[18]

While the definition of art perhaps could and should be expanded to embrace the most humble expressive abilities of both hemispheres—Norbert Wiener called man himself a message—it is in the classic sense of the arts that right-hemisphere intelligence finds its most exalted expression. Music, painting, sculpture, dance, and the mimetic aspects of theater are all ineffable gropings toward self- and species awareness fully on par with the linguistic arts and philosophy in their efforts to extend human con-

139

INTELLIGENCE AND THE BRAIN

sciousness. Each in its own way communicates the uniqueness and commonality of our experience, pushes our perceptions into the always tentative realm of human consensus, and probes to the edge of mysticism and beyond for the deepest meanings of life itself. As ballet master George Balanchine says, "Our brains are a cemetery of words. There is no way except with inner vision to explain how you feel. . . . Be careful or you will think with words. That's why I can do ballet. I can't write. I can't even spell. I am made in silence. As soon as I start speaking, I stop seeing."[19]

Although most artists, like Balanchine, profess to be firmly convinced that what they do cannot effectively be talked about—"the only true comment on a piece of music is another piece of music,"[20] said Igor Stravinsky—that conviction, fortunately, has kept few of them from trying, Stravinsky included. From a sample of their amassed articulation, furthermore, emerges a kind of esthetic consensus in its own right, one that makes point by point a persuasive case for the arts being, if anything, the more enlightened measure of our mind.

First, there is virtually no argument, among artists and their critics at least, that art is communication at its zenith. Music is purposeful singing and a reincarnation of ideas, the most amorphous of arts, and a thing of sonorous images continually in danger of falling apart, says Aaron Copland. It is an emotional science that blends ideas and feelings (Gershwin). It is organized sound (Leonard Bernstein), a cry of the soul (Frederick Delius), a transcendental language (Charles Ives) that develops by new infusions of emotion into its vocabulary (Stravinsky). By the same token, sculpture gives tangible form to emotion (Auguste Rodin); painting is a tug-of-war between idea and image (Ben Shahn) which ends in the painting speaking (Vincent van Gogh); the art of acting is a psychophysical action that automatically involves the emotions, the images, and the inner monologue of man (Konstantin Stanislavsky); dance a language that tells of life and death and love and hate (Isadora Duncan), an organized beauty in which dancers grope with their own private grammar to say something not quite articulate (critic Arnold Haskell) and if successful, like Rudolf Nureyev, speak an art which Rodin and Leonardo would have understood (critic Alexander Bland).

* * *

"I turn my ideas into tones which resound, roar and range until at last they stand before me in the form of notes,"[21] said Beethoven of the elusive process of communicating through the right hemisphere. "My music must be an artistic reproduction of human speech in all its finest shades,"[22] wrote Modest Moussorgsky, to which Gustav Mahler counters, "so long as I can sum up my experiences in words, I can certainly not create music about it."[23] And Felix Mendelssohn adds,

> . . . people often complain that music is too ambiguous . . . whereas everyone understands words. With me it is exactly the reverse . . . these too, seem so ambiguous, so vague, so easily misunderstood in comparison to genuine music. . . . The thoughts which are expressed to me by music . . . are not too indefinite to be put into words, but . . . too definite.[24]

Stravinsky plainly regards composition as more a sensual pleasure than a means of communication: "Performances are but pale memories of creative arts. In music, as in love, pleasure is the waste product of creation."[25] He sometimes feels, nevertheless,

> like those old men Gulliver encounters [who] have renounced language and who try to converse by means of objects. . . . One never composes exactly the piece one sets out to compose, just as I am not now saying exactly what I had in mind . . . but what the extenuating word that comes to mind as I go along leads me to say. . . .[26]

The language of the right hemisphere, its artists agree, is fully as rich, varied, and individualistic as that of the left. The subtlety of dance is such, according to Arnold Haskell, that "six ballerinas will perform the same [movement] in an almost identical manner, and yet create an entirely different impression."[27] Similarly, when Rimsky-Korsakov would revise Moussorgsky's work because of the "awkward way he manipulated his abundant ideas and harmonies," critics conceded that though it was "easy enough to correct [his] defects . . . when this is done, it is impossible not to feel that the result is no longer Moussorgsky."[28]

The common denominator of artistic language—the unique quality that enables it to achieve both the open-endedness of a generative alphabet and the iconic wealth and idiosyncrasy of a

141

personal ideograph—has been captured in words by right-hemisphere talents as varied as composer Paul Hindemith, painter Ben Shahn and Stanislavsky drama teacher Sonia Moore.

Writes Hindemith,

> There is no doubt that listeners, performers and composers alike can be profoundly moved by perceiving, performing or imagining music, and that, consequently, music must touch on something in their emotional life that brings them to this state of excitation. But if these mental reactions were feelings, they could not change as rapidly as they do; they would not begin and end precisely with the musical stimulus that aroused them. If we experience a real feeling of grief—that is, grief not caused or released by music—it is not possible to replace it, at a moment's notice and without plausible cause, with a feeling of wild gaiety. . . . Real feelings need a certain interval of time to develop, reach their climax, and fade again; reactions to music, however, may change as fast as musical phrases do; they may spring up in full intensity at any given moment and disappear entirely when the musical pattern that provided them ends or changes. . . . The reactions music evokes are not feelings; they are the images, the memories of feelings. We can compare these memories of feelings to the memories we have of a country in which we have travelled. The original journey may have taken several weeks or months, but in conjuring up in our memory the events of it, we may go through the entire adventure in a few seconds and still have the sensation of a very complete mental reconstruction of its course. It is the same trick dreams play on us. They, too, compress the reproductions of events that in reality would need long intervals of time for their development into fractions of a second, and yet they seem to the dreamer as real as adventures he has when he is wide awake.
>
> Dreams, memories, musical reactions—all three are made of the same stuff. We cannot have musical reactions of any considerable intensity if we do not have dreams of some intensity, for musical reactions build up, like dreams, a phantasmagoric structure of feeling that hits us with the impact of real feeling. Furthermore, we cannot have any musical reactions of emotional significance, unless we have once had real feelings, the memory of which is revived by the musical impression. . . . If music did not instigate us to supply memories out of our mental storage rooms, it would remain meaningless. . . .[29]

Sonia Moore agrees. The actor, she writes, must create

142

. . . images in [his] own mind corresponding to those of the character. You must learn to see images . . . and to describe them so well to your fellow actors that they see them too . . . so that you also stir the images . . . of the audience. . . . You cannot say a word until you see the image and know your attitude toward it, . . . We see a continuous film of images . . . Life does not stop when we are silent. Thoughts flash through our mind all the time . . . If you do not use images and inner monologue, you will only be another prop . . . Words without images are dead . . . Have in your memory a reserve of images which you will be able to use as an artist uses sketches.[30]

Seeking to capture "some inner figure of primitive terror" for a painting, Shahn says, "the image that I sought to create [was] the emotional tone that surrounds disaster . . . the inner disaster. . . ."[31]

I do not doubt that those artists who work only for pure form (or look upon their art as therapy) . . . believe with equal fervor in what they are doing. . . . But . . . such art can contain nothing of experience either inward or outward It is only a painted curtain resting midway between the subjective and the objective, closing either off from the other. . . . How can one actually achieve a universality in painting . . . ? The universal is that unique thing which affirms the unique qualities of all things. . . . The emotional image is not necessarily of that event in the outside world which prompts our feeling; the emotional image is rather made up of the inner vestiges of many events. . . . It is of that company of phantoms which we all own . . . images that have the nostalgia of childhood with possibly none of the facts. . . . It is the underground stream of ideas. . . . With the practiced painter his inner images are paint images, as those of the poet are no doubt . . . word images and those of the musician tonal images. . . .[32]

In its potential for synesthesia, it would almost seem that the right hemisphere excels the most metaphoric flights of language. Rodin obliquely endorsed this point of view when he called Dante "a literary sculptor: he speaks in gestures as well as words."[33] Beethoven, in like vein, spoke of creating his music "in its breadth, its narrowness, its height, its depth. . . . I hear and see the image in

143

front of me from every angle, as if it had been cast. . . ."[34] Musical notes, moreover, "can be manipulated as if they were objects . . . made to do exercises, like a dancer,"[35] claims Copland, who marvels at the ability of some people to "see all around the structural framework of an extended piece of music" despite his feeling that "each separate moment presents a picture, not unlike that of the painter's canvas."[36] Goethe in turn described architecture as "frozen music,"[37] which prompted Stravinsky with his irrepressible wit to confess that he would be "frightened to enter some of the compositions I have heard. . . ."[38]

The more kinesthetically involving the art, the observations of ballet lovers suggest, the more synesthetic its nature. "A dancer 'reads' a ballet as if it were a poem," says Nureyev, and pure dancing is to "play on his body as though it were a musical instrument."[39] Adds Charles Louis Didelot, the French father of Russian ballet, "A true dancer must also be a good actor and a poet at heart."[40] So thoroughly steeped was he in his own self-image as the dancer that Nijinsky could boast, "I always see myself dancing. I can visualize myself so thoroughly that I know exactly what I look like, just as if I sat in the midst of the audience."[41] He never watched a mirror to correct his thoughts, yet Rodin could say of him, "[He] was a living Michelangelo, Donatello, Giovanna da Bologna."[42] Haskell eulogized the great prima ballerina as "a living and progressive museum of plastic art . . . an entire academy of music . . . if she has the necessary gifts . . . she will carry the work of musicians and painters around the world."[43]

Wrote music critic Ernest Newman on watching Leonide Massine dance to Brahms,

> There can, of course, be no question of a translation of the "meaning" of this music as a whole into terms of another art. . . . There is no real equivalent. . . . But . . . surely there can be parallelisms. . . . Certain elements in the musical design, certain gestures of the music, certain softenings and hardenings of the colors can be suggested quite well. . . . How any musical listener in the audience who knows . . . Brahms . . . and has any imagination at all could fail to perceive these extraordinary parallelisms I confess myself unable to understand. . . . The opening entry of these two figures . . . with their curious gliding, undulating motion seemed to me as per-

144

fect a translation into visible motion of the well known dip and rise of the first phase in the violins as could possibly be conceived. I could cite similar felicities of parallelisms by the hundred.[44]

Or as Romola Nijinsky wrote of her husband's "Dance of War" while interned in Switzerland during the First World War, as Nijinsky pirouetted on the brink of madness,

"Now I will dance you the war, with its suffering, with its destruction, with its death" [he said]. "The war which you did not prevent and so you are all responsible for." . . . He seemed to fill the room with horror-stricken suffering humanity. It was tragic; his gestures were all monumental, and he entranced us so that we almost saw him floating over corpses. The public sat breathlessly horrified and so strangely fascinated. They seemed petrified. But we felt that Vaslav was like one of those overpowering creatures full of dominating strength, a tiger let out from the jungle who at any moment could destroy us. And he was dancing, dancing on. Whirling through space, taking his audience away with him to war, to destruction, facing suffering and horror, struggling with all his steel-like muscles, his agility, his lightning quickness, his ethereal being, to escape the inevitable end. It was the dance for life against death.[45]

Just as the eighteenth-century German poet Daniel Schubart claimed to have found in some keys the characteristic expression of definite feelings—"He calls E minor a girl dressed in white with a rose-colored bow at her bosom!"[46] exclaimed Schumann—the Russian composer Alexander Scriabin was so suffused with synesthesia he experienced musical tones as actual colors.

Rimsky-Korsakov agreed in principle; Rachmaninoff did not, although he pointed out with relish that the other two composers could not agree on the points of contract between the sound-and-color scale. Rimsky-Korsakov saw E flat major as blue, Scriabin as red-purple. They agreed that D major was golden brown. They surprised Rachmaninoff, however, by challenging him on a passage of the *Miserly Knight* where the old baron opens his boxes and chests and gold and silver flash and glitter in the light of a torch. He had to admit that, surely, the passage was written in D major. "You see," said Scriabin, "your intuition has unconsciously followed the laws whose very existence you have

145

tried in vain to deny." Rachmaninoff felt, on the contrary, that the connection was due to his having unconsciously borne in mind the scene in a Rimsky-Korsakov opera where people draw a great catch of gold fish out of Lake Ilmen and break into a jubilant shout of "Gold! Gold!" This is written in D major. But he could not convince them.[47]

Concluded Schumann:

> In sculpture, the actor's art becomes fixed; the actor in turn transforms the sculptor's works into living forms; the painter turns a poem into a painting, the musician sets a picture to music. . . . If Liszt played behind the screen, a great deal of poetry would be lost.[48]

The target of art's communication, however, the intended recipient of its extended perception, remains a matter for enduring debate. Does the artist in man create for himself, for other people, for the other side of his brain—strange as that may seem—or for all three?

Like Stravinsky, some artists apparently create primarily for the benefit of their own perceptions: "As I see it," he says, "the metaphorical alignments, symbolizations, reflected thoughts and feelings are purely the listeners' without any 'real' basis in the music. . . . I doubt . . . the subjective regions of most metaphorically inclined listeners are as rich and varied as they suppose."[49] Van Gogh sought foremost intensity of thought. "The imagination is made sharper and more correct by continually studying nature and wrestling with it. . . . Is a calm, well-regulated touch always possible? . . . As little, it seems to me, as during an assault in a fencing match."[50] Each work brings with it "an element of self-discovery," says Copland. It is a "unique formulation of experience," one produced not by an act of will, but entirely spontaneous or "cajoled, induced and gradually perceived," the "antithesis of self-consciousness. . . ."[51] Despite its originality, when a piece is put in the hands of the wrong performer, Copland confesses, it frequently makes him think, "This is all very fine but I don't recognize myself."[52]

Ben Shahn shares that single-mindedness. In its "clamoring of images"[53] he feels that painting is able to contain whatever one thinks and all that he is. . . . It is . . . the wholeness of thinking and feeling within an individual; it is partly his time and place; it is partly his childhood or even his adult fears and pleasures, and it is very greatly his thinking what he wants to think. . . . It is the function of [art] to extend our consciousness, not to narrow it. . . . One does not judge an Einstein equation by its communicability but by its actual content and meaning. . . . Value [in art] "consists in some vague striving for truth." . . . Whatever one thinks as well as whatever one paints must be constantly re-examined, torn apart, if that seems to be indicated, and reassembled in the light of new attitudes, or new discovery. . . . Only the individual can imagine, invent, or create. . . . In the work of art he finds his uniqueness affirmed. . . .

Painting is both creation and response. It is an intimately communicative affair between the painter and his painting . . . a conversation back and forth. . . .[54]

Other artists, however, believe their work communicates to, and extends the perceptions of, their audience—one way or another, whether exactly as intended or not. Copland, for one, thinks it is interpreted according to some "unwritten Esperanto of the emotions,"[55] which enables the discerning to recognize,

not merely the joyous quality of a piece but the specific shade of joyousness—whether it be troubled joy, delicate joy, carefree joy, hysterical joy. . . . We [also] experience basic reactions such as tension and release, density and transparency, a smooth or angry surface, the music's swellings and subsidings, its pushing forward or hanging back, its length, its speed, its thunders and whisperings—and a thousand other psychologically based reflections of our physical life of movement and gesture, and our inner, subconscious mental life.[56]

Schumann agreed with Copland on emotion when he assessed the keyboard artistry of Liszt:

. . . Just as letters and concepts rise before us when turning the pages of a dictionary, so here there arises tones and emotions. Within a few seconds tenderness, boldness, exquisiteness, wildness succeed one another; the instrument glows and flashes under the master's hands.[57]

147

It was Schumann, moreover, who rejected the use of dummy keyboards to teach piano technique with a terse, "dumb people cannot teach us to speak."[58] Even Stravinsky, in pointing out that psychiatric patients who ignore verbal entreaties frequently respond to music, observed that such results prove "it *is* understood in correlative terms."[59] Sculptor-painter Albert Giacometti would have it both ways. In trying to "convey tangibly the intangible sensation of a visual perception of reality," James Lord wrote of him, Giacometti would complain, "if only someone else could paint what *I* see, it would be marvelous, because then I could stop painting for good."[60] Still, Giacometti made it clear, he was not implying that his efforts were for him alone: ". . . What I'm trying to do [is] to show you how things appear to me. . . ."[61] The transcendent, two-way nature possible in such wordless communication was exemplified in a story Romola Nijinsky told of a celebrated exchange between her husband, who spoke only Russian, and Rodin, who spoke only French. The young dancer had consented to pose for the aging sculptor. When problems in posing arose, Rodin made his wishes known by sketches; Nijinsky replied in body movements. "They understood each other perfectly," Romola Nijinsky reported.[62]

Finally, in recognizing the creative value of their "inner critic," there exist those artists who, however unwittingly, seem to suggest not only that the inner critic *is* the left hemisphere, but also that the left hemisphere is the final authority on the nature of reality, perhaps for all of us (a point of view surely shared by professional critics at large). Copland acknowledges the essential schizophrenia of the artist in everyone when he describes creativity as "an hallucinatory state of mind: One half of the personality emotes and dictates while the other half listens and notates."[63] Arnold Haskell said as much of the dance when he praised an admired ballerina for "the gift that makes her experiment so recklessly, and then step aside and coldly judge the result."[64] Said Russian actor Tommaso Salvini, "an actor cries and laughs, and at the same time watches his crying and laughing."[65] No one, however, has written more incisively on the subject than Ben Shahn:

> An artist at work . . . must be two people, not one. On the one hand, the artist is the imaginer and the producer. But he is

also the critic, [a critic] of such inexorable standards as to have made [the working professional] seem liberal. . . . When a painting is merely in the visionary stage, the inner critic has already begun stamping on it. . . . The artist is enthusiastic about some idea he has. "You cannot," says the inner critic, "superimpose upon visual material that which is not essentially visual. Your idea is underdeveloped. You must find an image in which the feeling itself is embedded. . . . Now, find that image!"

So the inward critic has stopped the painting before it has even been begun. Then, when the artist strips his idea down to emotional images alone and begins slowly, falteringly, moving toward some realization, then the critic is constantly objecting, constantly chiding, holding the hand back to the image alone, so that the painting remains only that, so that it does not split into two things, one the image, and another the meaning. . . . He continually rejects the contradictory elements within a painting. . . . He rejects insufficient drawing . . . forms and colors incompatible with the intention or mood of the piece. He rejects intention itself and mood itself often as banal or derivative. He mightily applauds the good piece of work; he cheers the successful passage; but then if the painting does not come up to his standards he casts aside everything and obliterates the whole.[66]

During his early career, Shahn goes on, when he painted post-impressionistic landscapes,

. . . The inner critic . . . began to play hara-kiri with my insides, with such ironic words as "it has a nice professional look about it." My inward demon was prone to ridicule or tear down my work in just those terms in which I was wont to admire it. [Such] work . . . did not contain the central person which, for good or ill, was myself.[67]

The artist's heroic attempt to heal the psychic split within him—and by extension advance toward spiritual wholeness all those that attempt touches—leads at the very least to extremes of empathy. That empathy can often breed an intense identification with the feelings of others unknown to those less sensitive. Mahler verged on it in a pejorative vein when he dismissed Brahms on the strength of his music as "really a little man with a narrow chest . . . when one has at the same time been buffeted by the blast from Richard Wagner's lungs!"[68] In practice for his ballet

Mephisto Valse, Nijinsky once assumed so perfectly all forty-five parts, everything from a fat old landlord to a lecherous rich merchant to the girls to the devil himself, that those watching quite forgot who—and how many—he was. "He had an inimitable way of throwing inviting glances," wrote Romola Nijinsky of her husband's fantastic ability to become a feminine role, "and undulating in such a lascivious manner as to stir up the senses of the spectator almost to frenzy."[69]

Giacometti, reports James Lord, experienced much the same sort of empathy to an even profounder degree in an eerie incident involving a Japanese who was posing for him. "Yanaihara was posing for me and suddenly [Jean] Genet came into the studio," Giacometti told Lord. "I thought he looked very strange, with such a round, very rosey face and puffed lips. But I didn't say anything about it. And then [my brother] Diego came into the studio. And I had the same feeling. His face looked very rosey, too, and round, and his lips looked very puffy. . . . Then suddenly I realized that I was seeing Diego and Genet as they must have looked to Yanaihara. I had concentrated so long and so hard on Yanaihara's face that . . . I could see white people the way they must look to people who aren't white."

Lord himself experienced the same uncanny sense of vicarious identity when Giacometti was painting his portrait. The artist's foot accidentally struck the catch that held the easel shelf and the canvas fell abruptly a foot or two.

"Oh, excuse me," Giacometti said.

Lord laughed and observed that Giacometti had excused himself as though he had caused Lord to fall instead of the painting.

"That's exactly what I did feel," Giacometti replied.

Another time the left side of Lord's face began to itch violently. When he scratched it, Giacometti asked why. "Because of all the little strokes of your brush on my cheek," Lord answered. Giacometti said he understood perfectly the sense of transmutation Lord's remark implied.[70]

At its most extreme, such intensity of extended perception tempts the artist to play at God himself, at creating man and matter alike. The actor, writes Sonia Moore, creates his work of art with technique "so thoroughly concrete that we will be able to see

150

objects that don't exist,"[71] much as the great ballerina Anna Pavlova, in one critic's words, generated "contact with the audience that was a definite, concrete thing."[72] The Stanislavsky-trained actor, in addition, bodily becomes "his own instrument" to "build a new person who has different thoughts, different images, different emotions—a completely different inner world. . . ."[73] Such a Godlike apprehension of life is likewise mirrored in Rodin, who exclaimed that

> lines and colors are only . . . the symbols of hidden realities.
> . . . Our eyes plunge beneath the surface to the meaning of
> things, and when afterward we reproduce the form, we endow it
> with the spiritual meaning which it covers. . . . The resem-
> blance which [the artist] ought to obtain is that of the
> soul. . . . The line of a forehead, the least lifting of a brow, the
> flash of an eye . . . [all serve to] read the soul within. . . .[74]

As Rodin describes his most famous statue, "The Thinker," you can easily imagine the sculptor inwardly regarding himself, much as Nijinsky did his own mental image: ". . . His feet drawn under him, his fist against his teeth, he dreams. The fertile thought slowly elaborates itself within his brain. He is no longer dreamer, he is creator."[75]

Equally to the point, Bernstein observes that Beethoven's *Eroica* funeral march "seems to have been previously written in Heaven, and then merely dictated to him,"[76] an echo both of the Biblical prophets and of the Greek concept of divine amanuensis, whereby the word of God or of the creative muse respectively was delivered to the mortal ear intact and entirely. "A masterwork awakens in us reactions of a spiritual order,"[77] writes Copland. "Just as the individual creator discovers himself through his creation, so the world at large knows itself through . . . the creation of its artists."[78]

Puccini declares with Italianate effusiveness,

> Almighty God touched me with His little finger and said,
> "Write for the theater." . . . Without fever there is no creation,
> because emotional art is a kind of malady, an exceptional state of
> mind, overexcitation of every fiber and every atom of one's be-

ing. . . . It is a question of giving life that will endure to a thing which must be alive before it can be born, and so on till we make a masterpiece.[79]

Something of the same fever must have seized van Gogh, the failed minister, to make him enter this uncharacteristically jovial—and curiously fraternal and condescending—remark about God the creator in his diary:

> We must not judge God from this world, it's just a study that didn't come off. If you are fond of the artist . . . you hold your tongue. . . . This world was evidently slapped together in a hurry on one of his bad days, when the artist didn't know what he was doing or didn't have his wits about him.[80]

(Rodin would not make the same mistake as God, even though he might labor more than seven days. When asked once why he failed to finish so many statues, Rodin snapped, "Are the cathedrals finished?"[81])

In attempting the divine, however, the artist stands in steady peril of veering off into unfathomable reaches of metaphysics, mysticism, and madness. Indeed, many would agree, the risk is necessary. "It seems to me important that we keep open what William James calls the 'irrational doorways . . . through which . . . the wildness and the pang of life' may be glimpsed," says Copland.[82] "My need to expose myself in music symphonically begins precisely where dark feelings hold sway," adds Mahler, "at the gate which leads into the 'other world,' the world in which things are no longer divided by time and space."[83]

More sublimely, writes Bernstein, when endeavoring to plumb the ineluctable deeps of music "we are stopped cold at the border. . . . We try to be scientific about it. . . . To employ principles, acoustics, mathematics and formal logic. We employ philosophical devices . . . to explain the 'shape' of a theme from a Beethoven quartet. . . . Words, words, words. Why is the theme beautiful? That's the rub. . . ."[84] A Harvard professor, he notes in his book *The Joy of Music,* tried to evolve a mathematical system of esthetic measure that could rate an object of art for beauty.

* * *

It comes to a dead end. . . . The five human senses are capable of measuring objects up to a certain point. (The eye can decide that X is twice as long as Y; the ear can guess that one trombone is playing twice as loud as the other); but can the senses' own aesthetic responses be measured? Form is only an empty word, a shell, without [the] gift of inevitability; a composer can write a string of perfectly molded . . . movements, with every rule obeyed, and still suffer from bad form. Beethoven broke all the rules, and turned out pieces of breath-taking rightness.[85]

The results of such efforts can—for the artist if not his art—be nightmarish rather than sublime. According to Axel Munthe's memoir, *The Story of San Michele,* French short-story master Guy de Maupassant raised the psychic split itself to a pinnacle of frightening manifestation. A man obsessed with death and insanity who produced one masterpiece after another while "slashing his excited brain with champagne, ether and drugs of all sorts," de Maupassant was hard at work one day when, looking up from his writing table, he saw a stranger enter his study despite the customary vigilance of his valet. To the author's amazement, the stranger sat down and began to dictate. De Maupassant was about to ring for the valet when he realized to his horror, wrote Munthe, that the stranger was himself.

But no one is more the bizarre embodiment of creative right-hemisphere excess than the fiery Russian composer, Scriabin. In the words of his biographer, Faubion Bowers, Scriabin traveled perilously "between the frontiers of reality and imagination"[86] while seeking the ideal of a universal transformation of the world through art. A frail, effeminate man barely five feet tall, Scriabin produced during his short career at the turn of the century a body of avant-garde music variously described at the time as "daring, original," "insane," and "depraved"—reflecting, in conductor Robert Craft's words today, "a species of psychedelic exultation."[87] Scriabin was a superb pianist, a goatish womanizer, the father of two children who died tragically at early ages, and a monumental drinker whose facial expression of perennial ecstasy led one contemporary to quip in later years that though his thirst had lessened, Scriabin remained "a drunk for the rest of his life."[88]

153

INTELLIGENCE AND THE BRAIN

Gifted at "thinking intuitively and expressing himself by analogy,"[89] Scriabin, in his voluminous notebooks, professed to believe that "all is my creation. The world is an activity of my consciousness. Consciousness determines being. All that exists, exists only in my awareness."[90] Unity within multiplicity, diversity out of sameness, were thoughts that obsessed him: he was afflicted with apocalyptic nightmares and a morbid interest in death. He was fascinated by the stories of a fellow artist who had reputedly drunk the blood of the wounded and eaten the flesh of the dead during World War I. An incorrigible mystic, he embraced yoga with such proprietary fervor that he publicly criticized one Indian expert for being "too rationalist."[91] A savant of sorts, he predicted sweeping socialist changes across the globe when the First World War broke out, changes that would eventually raise up China, India, and Africa.

Early on, Scriabin capitalized on his clinical synesthesia (words and emotions had colors for him too) by inventing an organ that played both in music and color. Before dying horribly at the age of forty-four of a strep infection stemming from a massive boil on his lip, he began but never finished a mighty synesthetic work called *The Mysterium,* "synthesizing sound, sight, color, lights, scent and touch,"[92] says Bowers, which he firmly believed when performed would signal the destruction of the civilized world and the birth of a new race of men.

Scriabin felt the electricity in the air, and reacted to its perturbations; he decided nature was matched by a "process of energy inside himself."[93] He thought he could fly, and actually tried. Once he attempted to walk Christ-like on the waters of Lake Geneva. He failed. Unperturbed, he settled for preaching to the fishermen from a boat.

But above all, he wrote lasting music. As his half-brother Apollon remembered,

He said he could express any idea, experience or appearance of nature in music. The "language of music" is limitless as it is with life and nature. He was absorbed in musical ideas, nuances, from everything around us . . . he jotted everything down in his little notebook. . . . We came to a bridge over a brook and

154

he looked at it for a long time. An automobile passed by and stirred up a lot of dust and a flight of birds. . . . Suddenly he took out the little book again and began writing with his pencil. . . . Then he began to sing and make gestures and nod his head to some rhythm.

. . . He explained . . . that he had notated in music all our feelings of that afternoon—our conversation, the moments standing on the bridge, the car, the sound of the flight of birds [94]

Even when the act is not creative in the artistic sense, there is reason to believe that the right hemisphere, with its ability to juggle and integrate all our perceptions in novel ways, is dominant. Perhaps history's greatest example of this is Leonardo da Vinci. Leonardo was, curiously enough, a "mirror" or backwards-and-upside-down writer, who would feel keenly for a lifetime his early lack of language, the poetic Greek and scholarly Latin of his day. But no one was more steeped in the experiential learning of the right hemisphere than Leonardo, who worked in an artist's workshop in Florentine Italy, where the tactile delights of wax, stone, wood, bronze, plaster, and gold stood at his fingertips.

As scholar Richard McLanathan traces his life, Leonardo thought that vision was the key to knowledge because it was the primary means of perception. He had the genius to show ideas, principles, and their application that could not be expressed in words. He saw similarities beneath the surface, understood things in terms of function, recognized by analogy the same mechanical principles operating in the structure and workings of living bone and muscle as in machines. Ever and always he encouraged others to see the big picture: "The more minute your description, the more you will confuse the mind. . . ."[95]

Leonardo was so wide-ranging in his imagination that he foresaw the airplane, the tank, the life preserver, the jack, the car, the helicopter, the parachute, and the machine gun. He was an observer, experimenter, illustrator. He made thousands of drawings of designs for an air-conditioning system as well as machines to mint coins, polish needles, and make files. Alongside those he sketched curious fables and futuristic drawings of deluges and earthquakes that suggested the destruction of the world in an atomic blast.

155

But beneath it all, writes McLanathan, lay a unity of purpose founded on the belief that through accurate observation man could understand the principles of everything in nature.

"All our knowledge," Leonardo wrote in his tight little mirror script, "has its origins in our perceptions."[96]

To which McLanathan adds, "He was the first to bring an artist's training, imagination and insight to the pursuit of knowledge. . . . For him art and science were the same. . . ."[97] Says scholar Carlo Pedretti, a man who has devoted his life to the study of da Vinci's genius: "You may well assume he had a right hemisphere dominance."[98]

Why did he appear in the Renaissance? McLanathan replies: "The Renaissance was . . . a period of synthesis, of putting things together and relating them, rather than of analysis, like our own age of specialization."[99]

Part II
INTELLIGENCE AND TESTING

Intelligence is what intelligence tests test.
—E. G. Boring

Chapter 6

In Search of a Science

In his early years Sir Francis Galton was an aristocratic dabbler, an indifferent schoolboy despite a prodigious IQ posthumously put at 200. He studied medicine, biology, astronomy, meteorology, and anthropology. He was a journalist, essayist, mathematician, geographer, explorer, boatsman, balloonist, and fastidious world traveler who wrote pedantic tips on how to fold shirts when packing a suitcase. An inveterate inventor, he produced some of the first weather maps, discovered anticyclones, developed a teletype machine, hit upon remote control, and perfected the first supersonic dog whistle. Jules Verne might have had him in mind when he created Phileas Fogg, the protean protagonist of *Around the World in Eighty Days.*

Undoubtedly here was career enough for several ordinary mortals, and if not for the fortunes of birth Galton might have been satisfied. But he was the younger half-cousin of Charles Darwin, whose theory of the origin of species burst upon industrial England like a thunderclap in 1859, when Galton was thirty-seven. So captivated was Sir Francis by his kinsman's achievement that he turned his gadfly brilliance at once and for the rest of his life to the corollary mystery of individual differences. In its pursuit he examined personal variations in hearing and smell, researched innate family disposition to talents such as art, invented composite photography to investigate facial types, and pioneered in fingerprinting. From it all he emerged fifty years later the founding father of intelligence testing in the English-speaking world, a fact which was to leave a mark on modern civilization every bit as indelible and distinctive as the whorls and ridges of the human thumb.

159

For although the sinews of today's testing movement grew out of the seminal studies of French psychologist Alfred Binet, who introduced the first effective mental scales in 1905, it was Galton who provided the conceptual spine. To many of testing's critics that was unfortunate because Sir Francis, for all his prodigious intellect, was a product of the monied upper class that graced a British Empire upon which the sun never set; a partaker of the same pukka sahib mentality that led the illustrious London physician John Langdon Haydon Down to coin the term "Mongolian" or "Mongoloid" for idiot because, he said, "there can be no doubt that these ethnic features are the result of degeneration."[1]

Faced with abysmal performance on his tests, Binet would later quietly counsel against "brutal pessimism" and prescribe "mental orthopedics."[2] He found it a "deplorable verdict" that any individual's intelligence could be looked upon as a "fixed quality."[3] Galton, in contrast, would lament: "The number amongst Negroes of those who we should call half-witted is very large. Every book alluding to Negro servants in America is full of instances. I myself was much impressed by this fact during my travels in Africa. The mistakes the Negroes made in their own matters were so childish, stupid and simpleton-like as frequently to make me ashamed of my own species."[4]

In his landmark book *Hereditary Genius* (1869), which Darwin greeted with a cousinly "I do not think I ever in all my life read anything more interesting or original",[5] Galton concluded that the mainspring of intelligence was inborn. Contrary to the popular doctrine of Horatio Alger, which even Darwin espoused, the self-made man in Galton's view was a myth. To prove it, he meticulously traced out over several generations the genealogies of some one thousand eminent British statesmen, professionals, and leaders in such things as rowing and wrestling to show an incidence of familial relatedness over a hundred times, he said, that of mere chance. Blood, he said, tells: "I have no patience with the hypothesis occasionally expressed, and often implied, especially in tales written to teach children to be good, that babies are born pretty much alike, and that the sole agencies in creating differences between boy and boy, and man and man, are steady application and moral effort."

In case anyone was still disposed to miss his point, he added:

> It is in the most unqualified manner that I object to preten-
> sions of natural equality. The experience of the nursery, the
> school, the university and of professional careers, are a chain of
> proof to the contrary. I acknowledge freely the great power of
> education and social influences in developing the active powers
> of the mind, just as I acknowledge the effect of use in developing
> the muscles of a blacksmith's arm, and no further. Let the black-
> smith labour as he will, he will find there are certain feats beyond
> his power. . . ."[6]

Eminence, of course, is by no means synonymous with genius,
nor was it in the fusty Victorian atmosphere of the private club
and old school tie. Four years later a Swiss botanist named Al-
phonse de Candolle issued the first in a line of rebuttals that extends down to this day and shows no sign of ending. De Candolle
compiled a list of environmental influences he felt proved that
nurture, not nature, was the chief instrument in producing scientific genius: wealth, leisure, scientific tradition, education, available libraries and laboratories, freedom to express opinion and
follow a chosen vocation, and geographic location in the temper-
ate zone—any and all of which would appear to wholly support
both the presence of a genius like Galton and the absence of an
Eskimo Einstein. De Candolle's countercontention, which would
make an Einstein of anyone with the wherewithal to finish a good
graduate school, was as patently questionable as Galton's first
flush of unbridled hereditarianism. But it underlined what Galton's earliest disciple, mathematician Karl Pearson, would later
concede to be the "crude extemporizations of the first settler."[7]
Galton was indeed breaking new ground with a very primitive
plow. Others better implemented would inevitably follow.

Galton's controversial work, however, did much more than just
shake the tinsel from England's finest family trees. It brought to
the infant and uncertain study of intelligence an arsenal of statistical methods that spanned a gamut of complexity almost as broad
as the range of human mentality itself. At his simplest, Sir Francis
borrowed from Belgian astronomer Adolphe Quételet the central
notions of "average" and "normal distribution." Both concepts

161

had been used traditionally to account for errors in celestial reckoning accruing from the subtle but steady accumulation of small numerical "accidents," exceptions best expressed as unavoidable but significant variations from a proven norm. Galton's use of these concepts, in retrospect, was a public relations stroke worthy of Madison Avenue. Man would be measured like the stars!

Technically put, Quételet had demonstrated that if you plotted on a graph any bodily measurement from a large population—height, for example—the array of resulting figures would tend to cluster about a midpoint and tail off at the extremes. In other words there would be a "normal distribution" of heights around an "average." In drastically diminishing numbers at either end would be found the anomalous giants and dwarfs, "accidental" variations from the norm. Galton found that such a bell-shaped curve, steeper or flatter depending on the range of diversity in whatever quality and population measured, was characteristic of almost every measurable physical property of living organisms. Hence, statistically speaking, it was more reliable than the mutable, messy laws of a febrile biology.

Since psychological traits presumably rested on physiological foundations, argued Galton, the phenomena of average and normal distribution must also be true of intelligence. Thus the same objective tool, the bell-shaped curve, could be applied. Sir Francis set out to prove it. Using eminence as his working index to brainpower, he made an assiduous study of a Britannic *Who's Who*, evaluated and ranked those it included and their accomplishments, and threw in a statistical leavening of types less successful from the rest of the British population—proportionately, one gathers—down to charladies and chimney sweeps. Sure enough, the result when plotted against the curve yielded up the expected profile (Figure 9). With slight adjustments, it is still with us.

So people did tend to perch around the middle rung of a theoretic ladder having its bottom in abject idiocy, its top in sublime genius (if, of course, you accepted Galton's highly subjective criteria). The intellect of any one man, then, could best be judged by comparing him with others—or to be more mathematical about it, by comparing him with the "average man." Statistics had created a mythic figure that plagues our perceptions of humanity to this day.

162

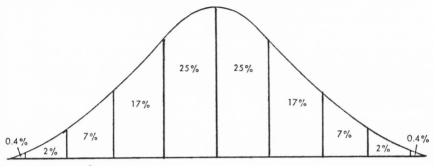

FIGURE 9
Galton's Bell-Shaped Curve

If intelligence was overwhelmingly inherited, as Galton insisted, something found only in the best families, why did parents often have children of noticeably differing mentalities? And if that fact were extended to the English population as a whole, how did the normal distribution remain stable, a mathematical constant, across the generations as Galton claimed?

Here Sir Francis, at his more abstruse, weighed in with his own statistical formulations of "correlation" and "regression to the mean." Parents, he said, did not impart their intelligence to children with complete correspondence, on a perfect fifty-fifty basis. There was only partial causation, what he called "positive correlation"; a strong tendency to likeness, a shared territory. As for the basic inviolability of distribution, the children of any family taken together tended to be more or less intelligent than their parents in the direction of the average. Bright parents generally had slightly duller children on the average, dull parents slightly brighter. In technical terms the generations regressed toward the mean. Excepting that rare fluke—the imbecile born to genius, a prodigy born to retardates—nature thus provided its own self-correcting genetic mechanism, an up-and-down escalator effect that slowly, continuously, balanced out over time.

Although Galton would have been the last to suggest, as his critics imply, that the average is everything, that the exceptional is defined by the typical, his formulation survives to the enduring detriment of an intelligent understanding of intelligence. For as any humanist would insist, there is more to intelligence, more to its role in life, more to its force in the minds of people, than a

163

bloodless abstraction. If there is not, then the typical too easily becomes the type and the type the stereotype.

Galton was unperturbed. The range of human intellect is vast, he said. Genius is to average as average is to idiotic; thus, to Galton, the least intelligent man is less endowed than the smartest dog. "The word generic presupposes a . . . collection of individuals who have much in common, and among whom medium characteristics are very much more frequent than extreme ones," he wrote. "No statistician dreams of combining objects into the same generic group that do not cluster towards a common centre . . . for if the attempt be made to do so the result is monstrous and meaningless."[8] So Galton understood the danger. Or did he? His attempt at reassurance takes on an iniquitous luster in the eyes of his critics in light of the missive he sent De Candolle when working on a pictorial composite of the "Jewish type" by facial features:

"It strikes me that the Jews are specialized for a parisitical existence upon other nations, and that there is need of evidence that they are capable of fulfilling the varied duties of a civilized nation by themselves."[9] Oh, Israel!

By a thunderous coincidence, *Hereditary Genius* came out the same year as *Das Kapital,* which Karl Marx dedicated to Darwin in the belief that evolution and socialism were commonly grounded on the inevitability of human change. As British botanist-hereditarian C. D. Darlington points out, the books of Marx and Galton were both concerned with improving mankind, but the methods they advocated were as organically opposed and as historically persisting as socialism and capitalism, communism and fascism. Marx, the environmentalist, preached change by political action against the evils of the prevailing social system. Galton, the hereditarian, urged change through intelligent control of man's evolution. Marx sought a solution without; Galton a solution within. Marx called for revolution. Galton, who was to die childless, favored "eugenics," or improving the breed by encouraging intermarriage of the more highly endowed.

With eugenics all the rage, an aggressive lady from Zurich wrote playwright George Bernard Shaw suggesting a sexual liaison to produce a child having her beauty and his brains. Shaw declined by return mail: "What if the child inherits my body and your brains?"[10]

Marx, in theory at any rate, championed the common man. Galton reduced him to a statistical starting point. And, the observer a century later is compelled to ask, for what? Nowhere did Galton analyze or even define what he thought intelligence was. Later he and his followers would set up "penny arcades" in museums, fairs, and railroad stations, where people with time on their hands could for a few cents test their reaction time, manual strength, digital dexterity, eyesight, and hearing against the implacable average. Because mental defectives were often deficient in sensory and motor skills, Galton thought these might be linked to higher mental skills. In his judgment this failed to prove out—though a related approach is one of the more provocative avenues in IQ testing today—and Sir Francis was left to fall back upon his own observations and theories, which were always metaphorically beguiling if sometimes unscientific by today's standards.

For instance, he hypothesized that color blindness was almost twice as prevalent among Quakers because members of that sect had for several generations segregated themselves and dressed in drabs to dramatize their belief that the fine arts were worldly snares. Thus, Sir Francis felt, genes influenced social behavior which in turn affected mating, which further reinforced the iron dictates of the genes. (Genes had not yet been named, but Galton, to give him credit, was thinking along precisely those lines.) Flowing from such an inference, Darlington would later claim, was nothing less than "the genetic analysis of civilization. . . . We can now see that . . . what is true of one gene in the Quakers is true of all genes in all communities of all plants and animals. . . ."[11]

And never mind, one supposes, that such a degree of social isolation as the Quakers contrived is more and more a thing of the past. Galton, at any rate, would have agreed with Darlington on the power of genetic selection. It was, he felt, especially true in the area of human intelligence. "The very foundation and outcome of the human mind," he wrote in *Human Faculty* (1883), "is dependent on race."[12]

How were family and race characteristics transmitted from generation to generation? Galton said it was by what he called "particulate inheritance."[13] Just as old Italian buildings often contained intact columns and lintels salvaged from an earlier day, he said, so in heredity were the "traits of feature and character,"[14] the protoplasmic shards of human architecture, passed down from our ancestors. Barring trauma in the womb, we are almost wholly derived from our genes at birth, so how could such an explanation accommodate both family likeness and individual variation? Galton thought long and hard about that. He decided finally that they were different effects of the same underlying cause—much as the forms of vegetation on barren sea-locked islands capriciously sown by wind, current, and birds from two common sources of variegated seed. The pattern of flowering would vary from island to island but the vegetation, having sprung from the same stock, would share a family resemblance.

In a more scholarly vein, Galton was the first to realize the hereditary significance of twins, an accomplishment that would secure for all time his place in psychology if nothing else did. The anecdotes he painstakingly collected from some eighty pairs revealed strong similarities between identical twins reared apart as well as strong differences between fraternal twins reared together. His explanation was as ingenious then as it is academically old hat today: Identical twins issue from the same egg, hence the same genes. Fraternal twins do not; they simply share the same placental sack. Hence the genetic bond can be stronger at a distance than the common experience of two closely related organisms growing up together. His inquiry, incidentally, elicited from one mother a remark that has since, in obeisance to humor's own laws of heredity, born fruit in a fearsome family of jokes. Her twins were so identical, she enthused, that each was often "more like his brother than himself!"[15]

In *Natural Inheritance* (1889), Sir Francis further refined his theories. It wasn't possible, he decided, for the offspring to get more than half his traits from either parent. More likely, half at most were determined by his parents together, a quarter by his grandparents, an eighth by his great-grandparents, and so on, diminishing mathematically with the remoteness of ancestry, compounded of all. His ideas went largely unchallenged at the dawn of what psychologists call bio-social science. Indeed, in the clamorous and concordant apotheosis of Darwin, Britannia embraced them as dogma. As Cambridge zoologist Raphael Weldon noted with invincible circularity: "The questions raised by [his] hypothesis are purely statistical, and the statistical method is the only one at present obvious by which that hypothesis can be experimentally checked." The modern scientist looks in vain for any intellectual cross-fertilization there. And a little later: "The unit with which such an enquiry must deal is not an individual but a race, or a statistically representative sample of a race. . . ."[16] Alexander Pope had been wrong. The proper study of mankind was not man, but men.

For a time psychometry and biometry—the measurement of mental and biological variables respectively by statistical means—dazzled the Darwinian world. According to one contemporary, they had demonstrated they could penetrate the mysteries of man through the application of complex multidimensional mathematical methods to the psychologists' "hard" data—just as physicists had conceived of atoms after Newton.

Mendel

Then, in 1885, came the Austrian monk Gregor Mendel's prosaic study of inheritance in pea plants, which Garrett Hardin thinks is the greatest purely intellectual work in nineteenth-century biology. Mendel, who was born the same day as Galton, was as poor as Galton was rich, as isolated as Galton was urbanely social, as unknown as Galton was celebrated. A peasant's son who had flunked the test for his teaching credential (he scored lowest in biology), Mendel was also as stubbornly single-minded as Galton had been eclectic. Their thinking, in fact, was all but antithetical. Sir Francis had said that inheritance was a straightforward matter of blending, of simple fractions. Mendel showed it to be a matter of calculating permutations and probabilities, of algebra. Genes could jump generations, dominate or recede, combine and recombine to produce variations of dazzling diversity and complexity. Intelligence, argued the Mendelians, was polygenetic (a combination of many genes), and not susceptible to the simplicities of Galtonian statistics.

The Royal Society Committee on Evolution became, to borrow

167

Darlington's quaintly descriptive term, "a bear garden." To prove their point the Galtonians bred moths, mice, and poppies, the Mendelians poultry, rabbits, and sweet peas. The controversy grew bitter. It finally culminated, Darlington reports, when Raphael Weldon spent the winter of 1905 in Rome going through the General Stud Book, a descriptive registry of thoroughbred breeding, trying to prove that chestnut horses could have bay or brown foals and that coat color in racehorses was not, therefore, Mendelian. Darlington's last dispatch from the front was Weldon's epitaph: "The effort killed him. He died . . . a martyr to the new belief that biology was a department of statistics; a martyr also to the old belief that heredity could be deduced from evolution."[17]

At that strategic instant someone should have handstitched and hung on the walls of the Royal Society a sampler bearing the sentiment of one battle-scarred participant: "We must take our genetics *with* mathematics, not *as* mathematics."[18] But no one did and the moment passed. With it went whatever chance might have existed for a proper peace between the two feuding camps. Mendel's biology and Galton's statistics remain essentially as incompatible as cats and dogs to this day, and our knowledge of intelligence and ways to test it suffer in consequence.

Binet

But getting back to bedrock, exactly what *was* intelligence, anyway? Binet in Paris had no more idea at the outset than Galton in London. But he supposed whatever it was had infinitely less to do with sensory and motor functions than it did with the actual psychological processes of thinking. Practically speaking, thought Binet, people displayed more or less of it not in how keenly they saw and heard, how quickly or adroitly their muscles reacted, but in how well among other things they comprehended, reasoned, rendered judgment, persisted in a train of thought, adapted to their immediate surroundings, and demonstrated a productive capacity to criticize themselves and their doings. In short, it depended upon how well they exercised those higher faculties that made

168

them uniquely human. To attempt to divine, as Galton did, these mental ingredients from the more easily accessible physical measurements was, as one observer humorously notes, to employ the tactic of the wily drunk who looks for his lost wallet under the streetlamp because the light is better there. No, the secret of intelligence had to be directly attacked. It had to be qualified and quantified. It had to be tested. But how was this to be done?

As director of the Sorbonne psychology lab, Binet drew for his subjects Paris schoolchildren. It was providential because, as since proved by Jean Piaget (then one of his assistants), the pyramiding stages of mental development go hand in glove with the normal processes of maturation. In the growing years, age was the one obvious tool that could be used to sort out intellectual differences between people, even if those differences at first glance appeared related to how old they were and not how smart. Adulthood resisted such a technique. There were, went the colloquialism, old fools, young fools and damn fools. But of course a twelve-year-old would usually outperform an eight-year-old. What was surprising about that? However, not always; that was what surprised. Did this mean the eight-year-old was far brighter than most children his age or the twelve-year-old far duller? Clearly this could only be determined by comparing each to his own age group, or more accurately, by comparing each to what was normal for his own age group, based on comprehensive testing that would establish the norm and what fell outside its boundaries. Binet had the first pale glimmer of an idea that was to transform the Western World.

For the next ten years, while Galtonians across the channel such as Weldon wrestled with statistical studies of heredity, Binet and his staff worked at perfecting their pragmatic mental norms. They stockpiled measures of them by testing the intelligence of young Parisians every way they could think of that seemed likely to yield such a sorting by age, a method still very much a part of IQ determination today.

In 1904, fifteen years after compulsory primary education was introduced in France, the government came to Binet for help. Too many children were incapable of following instruction. To save time and money some means had to be found to sift them out and into special programs before they failed. Binet and his collaborator, psychiatrist Théodore Simon, were ready with a battery of tests already standardized on the norm for each age from three to eleven. The tests ranged in difficulty from such basic developmental skills as the eye-head coordination needed to watch a lighted match move across the fields of vision up through such practical puzzles as arranging objects by weight, to the rational pinnacle of distinguishing between closely related abstract words.

The results, Binet declared when it was all over, could be expressed as the child's "mental age" regardless of how old he was in years. Our hypothetical eight-year-old might have passed all the tests up to and including those of the normal ten-year-old. If so, he would have a mental age of ten. So too would our twelve-year-old of manifestly the same intelligence. He could do the ten-year-old tasks but none beyond. Thus Binet further analyzed the intelligence of each. Neither was normal for his age; both were mentally ten. One was advanced, the other mildly retarded, but neither was as advanced or retarded as he would have appeared in the absence of an average ten-year-old. Intelligence was relative.

As a screening device, the Binet-Simon scales were more than sufficient for the French school system. Indeed, suitably revised as items were dropped and added to improve their effectiveness, they soon spread throughout Western Europe, the United Kingdom, and America. It remained, however, for a German psychologist, William Stern, to suggest that an "Intelligence Quotient" could be calculated by dividing the mental age by the chronological age and multiplying by a hundred to round off the result for Teutonic satisfaction. Our eight-year-old now had an IQ of 125 and our twelve-year-old one of, alas, only 83. Numerology was on the scene. Things were looking up.

Or were they?

An imbecile could pass at most the first fifteen test items, one more than the average five-year-old. Did this mean the average five-year-old was dumber than the brightest imbecile? Obviously not, said Binet. His intelligence clearly differed in character. How? Binet could not say. He simply declared it so by fiat. Moreover, foreshadowing the controversy to come, as the tests progressed up the scale in complexity, they became more loaded with demands for information, more dependent on the perks of culture, more tied to academic achievement. How better to assess the caliber of intellect than by examining its exercise in the absorption of knowledge, the assimilation of its surroundings, the acquisition of learning skills? But to ask, as Binet and Simon did in a test of adult mentality, three differences between a president and a king, was to suggest that intelligence resides in a history book for those who, whatever the reason—love of learning, motivation to excel—are diligent enough to dig it out and dogged enough to remember it. Conversely, that would suggest equally that those who have no history book or cannot read because they have never been taught are innately stupid.

The tests did predict later performance in school—for those already there. Binet made no claim to anything else. He did not pretend they were a touchstone of life success. Yet Binet's work, like the parallel research then going on in England, was to have profound effect on the future measurement of human intelligence. This was all the more ironic because Binet, like Galton before him, had finessed the crucial question. He had measured what he thought to be intelligence. He had not said what it was.

Burt and Spearman

Meanwhile, back at Oxford, Galton the indefatigable had persuaded the Association for the Advancement of Science to finance a survey of mental capacity among schoolchildren throughout the British Isles. A team of psychologists named to construct the tests in the early 1900's included two men destined to leave their mark on modern techniques of testing: Charles Spearman, a former army officer in the Boer War and India, and Cyril Burt, perhaps the first expert ever in juvenile delinquency and a man recognized today even by his critics as the most brilliant social engineer of the early twentieth century. Burt and Spearman, in the course of their mission, set out to solve the thorny problem their predecessors had ducked: the structure of intelligence. They agreed, Burt would later write, on the existence of a "kind of superfaculty"[19] pervading all intelligent behavior, one largely innate and varying with the individual. They differed at the outset in that Spearman rejected the concept of any additional special abilities that might in themselves have intellectual value, while Burt held out for a hierarchy of mental functions which the superfaculty potently but not totally informed. In his tests, Burt, like Binet, went straight at the highest forms of thinking. Spearman, curiously, clung for a time to Galton's conceit that the key might be found in the broadest range of general sensory and motor discrimination.

Both were strongly influenced in their approach by the statistical techniques of Galton and his protégé, Karl Pearson. Notably, they seized on something called the "co-efficient of correlation," a sort of exalted mathematical guilt by association whose more primitive beginnings had been handed down by Galton. Psychologists use coefficients of correlation a bit differently today. But what the term meant to Burt and Spearman was this: If a child scored roughly the same on tests of several diverse kinds of mental ability—vocabulary, math, problem solving, design drawing— despite the obvious lack of surface similarity in these abilities an underlying unity could be assumed. The closer the scores, the higher the unseen correlation; the higher the correlation, the greater the degree of underlying unity. Spearman christened that unity G, for general intelligence.

Analyzing these factors for large numbers of children, Spearman discovered that the tests most heavily loaded with G were not those of simple sensory discrimination but those involving reason and judgment. Ultimately he abandoned his sensory discrimination thesis and embraced the concept of two main factors: G and S, for special factors, a constellation of various abilities any of whose magnitude together with G determined both the depth and direction of intellectual bent. In other words, performance in mathematics depended both on a person's general intellectual ability, G, and his specific aptitude and training for it, S.

Significantly, for believers in bilateralization of brain function, the relation of G to any one S varied enormously. *General intelligence was by Spearman's reckoning four and a half times more important to mathematical ability than it was to music, and thirty-six times more important than it was to drawing.* In fact, G as he defined it had so

172

little relationship to some forms of S that it was almost schizophrenic. The right hemisphere of his brain was metaphorically nudging him in the ribs but his left hemisphere, predictably, was unaware of it.

Burt differed from Spearman in that he ultimately accepted not a two-factor theory but a hierarchical system composed of a general factor, group factors, and specific factors. The specific factors were for simple sensory and motor processes such as acuity of hearing, sight and touch, and manual skill. The group factors pertained to various perceptual processes such as pattern perception, and to mechanical kinds of intellect such as rote memory and habit formation. The G factor involved the higher apprehension and application of concepts, reasoning, and judgment. These were best deduced, Burt felt, not by such external criteria as the demonstration of memory-learning, but by internal critera implicit in "problems of the greatest complexity of which the [subject] was capable,"[20] those demanding the abstract manipulations of the left hemisphere. The die was cast, the seed planted. Intelligence was best examined by testing reasoning, judgment, and those informational skills most heavily freighted with that miracle ingredient, G. Those special aptitudes least loaded with information and G—music, art—those farthest removed from the strictures of reasoning and judgment—imagination, intuition—were the most remote from any true exercise of the intellect. The right hemisphere, by historical extension of this basic viewpoint, would be seen to hold nothing of any real significance to the issue of intelligence. Though, as we shall see, at the end of his long and illustrious life Cyril Burt would be honest and intelligent enough to admit that educational psychology had been asleep at the switch.

The Americans

At this point the relatively brief and placid history of intelligence testing on both sides of the Atlantic splits into two main streams. One grew into a broad, unswerving, irresistible rush to consolidate its modern role in society and education. The other, one of the darkest chapters in Anglo-American political annals, became an ugly roiling backwater of racism and nationalism that contaminated everything it touched. Modern psychology would like to forget those sad, bleak years in which its infancy played too full a part. But some idea of its wretched excess is necessary to understand the depth and vehemence of minority reaction against the IQ test today.

As the tide of European immigration swelled against the shores of the United States and Great Britain in the early twentieth century, eugenics, Social Darwinism and the issue of native intelligence became in turn the trenches from which a war against the unwanted—the foreign, the ill-born, the demanding poor—was fought with no quarter given. Eugenics decreed we were getting the dregs, the castoffs, the worst of an already bad lot. Social Darwinism preached survival of the fittest—and hadn't these, by definition, proven themselves unfit to survive in their own country, much less ours? And finally, as Leon J. Kamin, chairman of the Princeton University psychology department, has chronicled in scholarly detail, the experts on intelligence had their ill-starred day in court. England's Karl Pearson, Galton's right-hand man, had for twenty years collected and analyzed statistics on the racial stock flooding the British Isles. In particular he had paid attention to the Jews who had fled Poland and Russia to escape the pogroms. His beliefs were explicit: "We are not dealing with a mutable characteristic capable of being moulded by the doctor, the teacher, the parent or the home environment. . . . Taken on the average, and regarding both sexes, this alien Jewish population is somewhat inferior physically and mentally to the native. . . ."[21]

In the United States the testimony of psychology was little better. In Kamin's words the newly imported tests were warped into "an instrument of oppression against the underprivileged."[22] Even Stanford's distinguished Lewis Terman, the recognized father of IQ testing in America, was not immune to the virus of race-baiting. Faced with the poor performance of a pair of Mexican-Indian children, he wrote:

"Their dullness seems to be racial, or at least inherent in the family stocks from which they come. The fact that one meets this type with such extraordinary frequency among Indians and Negroes suggests quite forcibly that the whole question of racial differences in mental traits will have to be taken up anew . . . there

will be discovered enormously significant racial differences
. . . which cannot be wiped out by any scheme of mental culture." His prescription? "Children of this group should be segregated in special classes. . . . They cannot master abstractions,
but they can often be made efficient workers. . . . There is no
possibility at present of convincing society that they should not be
allowed to reproduce . . . they constitute a grave problem because of their unusually prolific breeding."[23]

Henry Goddard, another pioneer in the American testing
movement and research director of the Vineland, New Jersey,
School for the Feeble-Minded, felt the new science of "mental levels" justified the social and economic inequities between the working man and his boss: "That workman may have a ten-year intelligence while you have a twenty. To demand for him such a home
as you enjoy is as absurd as it would be to insist that every laborer
should receive a graduate fellowship. How can there be such a
thing as social equality with this wide range of mental capacity?"[24]
That question, purged of its bias, is as explosively pertinent today.

Goddard guaranteed himself a place in psychology when he
traced the two branches of what he called the Kallikak family (a
pseudonym derived from the Greek for good-bad), which together with the Jukes make up the two most infamous families in
American psychological literature. With the aid of the Kallikaks,
Goddard set out to show the awful preponderance of idiots, imbeciles, morons, epileptics, criminals, and the sexually immoral descended from one "Martin Kallikak" and a feebleminded girl. A
preachy sort, Goddard turned a stiff neck on the possible impact
of environment on the fortunes of the illegitimate. And in his
puritanical zeal to indict poor Martin in his dalliance, he never really nailed down the paternity beyond the dubious word of the ad-
dled tavern tart wooed and won in a night while Martin was a Revolutionary War militiaman. Goddard was always inclined to give
the legitimate lineage of Martin's later marriage all the best of it.
A few of its heirs, notably two doctors, had "an appetite for alcoholic stimulants," while offspring of the bastard branch were
rife with "public nuisances."[25] Speaking statistically, of course,
nuisance has a pronounced tendency to go public when the means
don't exist to sustain it privately.

But the blackest hour in American testing occurred when it was widely and openly used to promote what Kamin calls the overtly racist immigration law of 1924. The twilight began twelve years earlier, when the U.S. Public Health Service invited Henry Goddard to Ellis Island to apply the new mental tests to arriving European immigrants in the very shadow of the Statue of Liberty. Based on his examinations, Goddard subsequently informed his employers that 83 percent of the Jews, 80 percent of the Hungarians, 79 percent of the Italians, and 87 percent of the Russians were not just backward, they were feebleminded. Those fulsome figures evidently did not fall on deaf bureaucratic ears. By 1917 the number of aliens deported had vastly increased and Goddard claimed the credit.

As the nightfall of American conscience descended, more and more states (by 1932 the number would reach two-thirds of the Union) were moved to pass stiff eugenics laws. Many linked feeblemindedness to drugs, perversion, drunkenness, and insanity. Some made sterilization mandatory. The best were imbued with the enlightened social outlook of that day as expressed by Harvard's prestigious Robert M. Yerkes: ". . . Never should such a diagnosis be made on the IQ alone. . . . We must inquire further into the subject's economic history. What is his occupation; his pay. . . . What is the economic status or occupation of the parents?"[26]

At this point the other mainstream of American testing reached one of its periodic crests with the massive use of IQ criteria on some two million servicemen during the First World War. The herculean effort was directed by the selfsame Yerkes and marshaled most of the nation's leading experimental psychologists. Included was Lewis Terman, who in 1914 developed the Army Alpha test, a milestone in psychometry and by two years the forerunner of the Stanford-Binet, which today is one of the two most popular individual intelligence tests in the English-speaking world.

Even the Army Alpha, an awesome job of logistics and statistics if nothing else, did not escape pollution from the other stream. When the results were published in 1921 under Yerkes' editorship by the National Academy of Science the data showed blacks had scored lower than whites. This was predictable enough, considering the prolonged and stifling climate of social and economic inequality that had prevailed without a breath of civil rights amelioration. But in addition the test performance of immigrant draftees, rated by country of origin, found the Latin and Slavic countries at the bottom, exactly where their immigration foes had always said they would be. Poles, in fact, did not score appreciably higher than blacks. British draftees, of course, were at the head of the list, a weathervane fact which was apparently lost on Princeton psychologist Carl Brigham. Under a government research grant, Brigham took a long look at the mountain of statistics and noticed a curious contour: the scores of each geographic group seemed powerfully related to the number of years since its influx had been highest. Could it be that Italians, Poles, Russians, and Jews did worse because they hadn't been here and speaking the language as long as the Germans and Scandinavians?

Not at all, Brigham decided. It was simply a matter of Nordic blood being superior to Alpine and Mediterranean. He concluded with a gratuitous warning that has been with us ever since: ". . . We are incorporating the Negro into our racial stock, while all of Europe is comparatively free from this taint."[27]

Having earned his academic spurs, Brigham moved on to become secretary of the College Entrance Examination board, where he later devised and developed the Scholastic Aptitude Test. Less than a decade later, to his belated credit, he confessed that his findings had been "pretentious" and "without foundation"[28] because they ignored the crucial variable of adopted language. But by then the damage had been done. Aided by science, a red-baiting Congress had passed the 1924 law restricting the number of immigrants and assigning national origin quotas based on the 1890 census—before the human deluge from southeastern Europe. (One witness testifying before a Senate committee offered this marvelous non sequitur: "Some of their labor unions are among the most radical in the whole country."[29]) The vote came in the wake of testimony that for sheer racial and ethnic abuse has seldom since been equaled on the steps of any back-country courthouse, testimony that reached if not exceeded in scabby virulence the remarks of one Nathaniel Hirsch of Harvard, who had tested the native-born children of immigrants for the National Research Council. Wrote Hirsch:

"I have seen gatherings of the foreign-born in which narrow

and sloping foreheads were the rule. . . . In every face there was something wrong—lips thick, mouth coarse . . . chin poorly formed . . . sugar-loaf heads . . . goose-bill noses . . . a set of skew-molds discarded by the Creator."[30]

Times change. So do people, professions, and the state of our knowledge. It would be hard to imagine a psychologist worth his training today who wouldn't agree with Leon Kamin: ". . . We know now that the psychologists who offered 'expert' and 'scientific' testimony relevant to explosive social issues in the 1920s did so on the basis of pitifully inadequate data."[31]

For all its blatant abuse during the infamy of immigration, the concept of the IQ may have worked with ultimately more insidious effect on exactly those bastions of middle-class America it was invoked to protect. By adopting, as one critic put it, "a model derived from classical physics and chemistry"[32] rather than the life sciences, Galtonian psychometry ignored intelligence as an organic process of growth whose only constant was change. Instead it made of intelligence an all but fixed entity which, if the nut of it could be cracked, would reveal like the atom a complex world of constituent particles. Intelligence thus became not a splendidly various and changeable body of behavior to be understood only in relation to the human whole, but a thing apart, a constellation of near absolutes operating in accord with a mysterious set of inner dynamics resembling Kepler's laws of planetary motion in their unswerving reliability.

The trick of research, then, was not to accept, observe, learn, and leave ample room for amendment. The trick was to nail the thing down, break the code, find its key. The siren song of an intelligence that was stable, distinct, and independent caught the public ear as few seductive sounds from science have before or since. When the first nationally widespread test returns burst upon American education in the 1930's, the middle class had been given as scientific fact a distorted basis for its assumptive superiority that plagues its perceptions of society to this day.

Three men did most to carry forward this concept of intelligence as an end product and not a living process. In 1938 came Louis Thurstone, an electrical engineer who, like Charles Spearman before him, used the statistical technique of factor analysis to

178

fragment the concepts of *G* (for general intelligence) and *S* (for special factors such as music and art) into a handful of Primary Mental Abilities (PMA's). When clusters of correlations found among different answers were simultaneously compared across many tests, Thurstone argued, what emerged was no global, underlying quality of general intelligence with its satellites of special ability. Gaze deeper, insisted Thurstone, and the same territory showed a more varied topography of related mental faculties: memory, number, reasoning, word fluency, verbal comprehension, perception, and spatial visualization. The idea that you could be strong in one or more and weak in others, with all its inherent possibilities for a truly useful diagnostic test, seems largely to have escaped the notice of the embryonic profession that was psychology.

Enter at this point R. B. Cattell—physicist, chemist, mathematician, and protégé of Burt and Spearman. Cattell is a man who believes science will someday with the aid of computers "write in elegant equations"[33] the solutions to all of life's mysteries. Although he did not share Thurstone's enthusiasm for taking a scholarly wrecking ball to the shaky edifice of a single monolithic intelligence, he confessed himself both disturbed and intrigued to see flaws in the monolith. Principally what Cattell saw, in 1940, were two general factors propping up Thurstone's PMA's: intelligence that was *fluid* and intelligence that was *crystallized.*

Fluid intelligence Cattell defined as a capacity to perceive relationships and integrate them mentally, independent of our senses. It involved many of the same faculties contained in Guilford's ambitious structure, as well as some of Thurstone's more academically uncontaminated PMA's. According to Cattell's colleague, John Horn, both were combined into patterns "much the same way chemical elements are organized [by] the periodic law."

Crystallized intelligence Horn called "the precipitate out of experience"[34] that results when fluid intelligence is mixed with formal education and other raw materials of the culture. High in crystallized intelligence, said Cattell, was the man who would "recognize an engineering problem as requiring solution by differential calculus" and "diagnose a defective sentence by pointing to a dangling participle." These skills he could not have acquired,

179

however, without the fluid ability to master them. High in fluid ability, but low in crystallized, were those who would "astonish you in a game of chess, or by solving a wire puzzle with which you have struggled in vain, or in swift insights into men and motives."[35] This despite the fact that their vocabularies might be colloquial, their acquaintance with history negligible, their knowledge of geometry and algebra nonexistent. Both kinds of intelligence, Cattell found, followed different growth curves and were hopelessly confounded in most IQ tests.

Despite the obvious importance of such a schism, Cattell in recent years has shied away from further IQ research and turned his computer instead to a field no less fraught with human variables if less contentious: personality.

Last on the theoretical scene, in 1967, was J. P. Guilford, a psychologist and statistician who also set out to prove that Thurstone was wrong. PMA's, Guilford contended, were a fruitlessly mixed bag. Factors such as the verbal and spatial were related directly to the content of a question, but other factors, such as reasoning, were not. They reflected more what your brain did with content. They were really operations. And when your brain operated on the content of a question the result was something else entirely. It was a product. So every exercise of intelligence, Guilford decided, involved a content, an operation, and a product. Depending on the nature of the problem, any one of them might be more obvious than the others, but all were necessary. Moreover, Guilford went on, these were not three different elements but three different kinds of elements. He theorized that there were four kinds of content, five kinds of operations, and six kinds of product. Intelligence could most easily be thought of as the cube of these dimensions (Figure 10.).

Content, said Guilford, could be semantic (the critical meaning of verbal material), figural (perceptual images such as sound and sight), symbolic (letters and numbers) and behavioral (interpretation of human acts.) Operations included cognition (knowing, as of facts), memory (retaining information), convergent production (producing the one correct answer), divergent production (producing many answers or ideas), and evaluation (judgment). Product was expressed in a unit (for example, a word), a class of units

180

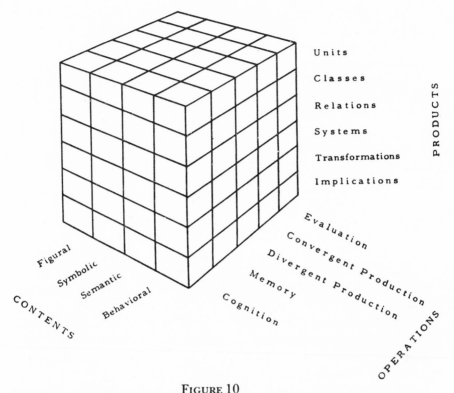

Units

Classes

Relations

Systems

Transformations

Implications

PRODUCTS

Evaluation
Convergent Production
Divergent Production
Memory
Cognition

OPERATIONS

Figural
Symbolic
Semantic
Behavioral

CONTENTS

FIGURE 10
Theoretical model for the complete "Structure of Intellect"

(CREDIT: "Intelligence Has Three Facets," by J. P. Guilford. Reprinted by permission of the author and *Science.* Copyright 1968 by the American Association for the Advancement of Science.)

(for example, a noun), a relationship between units (similar, different), a system of information (a plan), a transformation (a change), or an implication (a prediction). Intelligence, then, was composed of four contents times five operations times six products, or no less than 120 separate and distinct elements! Guilford had not further fragmented intelligence, he had pulverized it. Unfortunately, for the more organic theorists, his theoretical structure of human intelligence was almost too much like the subatomic world of whirling mesons and pi mesons for lasting comfort. A third of the particles his model predicts have never been found.

181

Although the analogy, like all those involving the brain, is by no means perfect, it may help to think of Guilford's model in terms of a symphony orchestra. Its harmonious effect is achieved by multiplying woodwinds, brass, strings, and percussion (content) times the four kinds of musician and the conductor needed to interpret the score (operations) times the resulting musical contribution of each in achieving the overall orchestral sound (products).

Apart from Guilford's grand scheme, the last quarter-century of research into intelligence has, in Cattell's words, been marked with little more than "trivial consolidation" and a "hardening of attitudes" as investigators shunned the tricky theoretical realm in favor of devising tests "to fill the holes in a subjective framework."[36] Perhaps some of them have grown sensitive to criticisms of factor analysis as a tool for psychological research. (Mathematician Lancelot Hogben accuses its adherents of too often confusing classification with cause and effect in arriving at arbitrary results that cannot otherwise be verified.) Perhaps too, in the dark of night, others among them despair of ever capturing on computer tape the elusive quality of creative intellect Galton marveled about in his twilight years as "an unusual and spontaneous flow of images and ideas" issuing from a brain "always pullulating [breeding rapidly and abundantly] with new notions."[37] Or perhaps, in their secret hearts, most instinctively agree that what E. B. White said about humor may in the end apply equally to intelligence:

"[It] can be dissected, as a frog can, but the thing dies in the process and the innards are discouraging to any but the pure scientific mind."[38]

Testing goes on, of course, but essential questions about it remain. As Sir Cyril Burt wondered in 1964, a half century too late, perhaps:

How can we best detect the individuals who are endowed by nature with creative ability . . . ? And what are the existing social and scholastic barriers which hide or hinder the emergence of creative talent?

Educational psychologists have of late woken up to the fact that the kind of examinations and intelligence tests which they still habitually employ tend to select the efficient learner and the verbal reasoner rather than intuitive observers or constructive and critical thinkers. With most of the mechanically scored tests handed out year by year, the child who gives an original answer, or hits on an alternative solution which the psychologists had missed (by no means a rare occurrence) is automatically marked wrong. Even when by some happy chance our methods of selection have picked out a potential inventor or a budding genius, we still have no notion how he should be encouraged and instructed so as to develop to the utmost his unusual latent powers.

The problem has at last been recognized; but the remedy is still to seek.[39]

Perhaps, one is emboldened to add, it has really been there all the time, mutely yelling across the commissures. In 1880 Francis Galton announced the astonishing results of a questionnaire on—his words—"mental imagery." His survey, the first large-scale questionnaire in psychology, began as follows: "Before addressing yourself to any of the questions, think of some definite object—suppose it is your breakfast table as you sat down to it this morning—and consider carefully the picture that rises before your mind's eye."[40]

Then came the questions. Was the image dim or fairly clear? Was its brightness comparable to that of the actual scene? Were all the objects pretty well defined, the colors of the china, the toast, mustard, meat, parsley, or whatever quite distinct and natural? The results, Galton found, were quite surprising. Many of his subjects, scientific men chosen as most likely to give accurate answers, were appallingly deficient. They had no more notion of the true nature of imagery than a color-blind man has of the nature of color. Some of his subjects, however, saw the breakfast table as clearly as if it were present. Who were they? Why, it was amazing, but—they were women and children!

"Our bookish and wordy education," Galton reported into the bottomless maw of enduring scientific obscurity, "tends to repress this valuable gift of nature."[41]

183

Chapter 7

Should Old IQ Be Forgot? *

"Do you realize," mused one thirty-year-old, "I've known you longer than anyone in my life except my parents and that you probably know me better than anyone and you still look pleased to see me when I come in?"[1]

That question, with all its incredulity and wonder, was directed at a staff member of the Oakland Growth Study, one of three epic and ongoing investigations into the physical and psychological maturation of 350 people begun by the University of California at Berkeley over forty years ago. Two of the studies, the Guidance Study and the Berkeley Growth Study, started with large samples of babies born in Berkeley in the late 1920's. One study focused on family influences from an early age, the other on individual physical, motor, and mental development from birth. The third, the Oakland Growth Study, drew children from the fifth and sixth grades at intervals beginning in 1932, and dealt primarily with physiological and social growth. All three studies continue in their quest for knowledge to this day, a periodic process involving testing, measuring, data-collecting and, as one now-grown subject described his end of the in-depth interviewing, "talking out loud and finding what I really thought—and having someone willing to listen."[2]

Such longitudinal field studies, as they are called, were one of the earliest crazes in experimental psychology. By their nature, if nothing else, they are also one of the most enduring. Thousands of people trailing untold volumes of statistics have since been tracked into adulthood with all the cheery persistence of Sherlock

*Parts of this chapter appeared in *Human Behavior* magazine.

Holmes and Doctor Watson pursuing the infamous Moriarty. Weary of attempting to reconstruct Galton's ephemeral average man from the random sample of humankind that passed through their doors, researchers hoped to do more than tap into the complex dynamic of what it means to grow up and live in a modern society. By following the human animal through life and watching what it gradually became, they hoped to seize and examine the teeming stuff of life itself. Psychologically speaking, they wanted to bottle lightning.

Nowhere did this kind of careful, prolonged observation appear more needed than in the ticklish area of intelligence. Binet's eight-year-old had an IQ of 125, his twelve-year-old one of 83. But what did these numbers, their ratio, signify with the passage of time? Did that mean that both IQ's had been the same three years earlier and would still be the same when the children were grown? Or did they mean that the IQ of each, if it changed, would bear the same fixed relationship to the other as before? Were their IQ's, shades of Galton and Mendel, locked into something immutably mathematical or were they merely a demonstration on demand of a trait that for all its importance was biologically—and perhaps undependably—in flux?

The distinction was vital. Either the IQ was relatively stable and could take its place alongside other reliable personal measurements such as height or weight, or it was not and could not. There was, in brief, no in-between. Or so, at least, it seemed.

The need for such long-term study, the dangers of easy generalization without it, could already be seen in the so-called cross-sectional studies of human intelligence over a lifetime. These studies showed beyond a shadow of a statistical doubt that the upward curve of man's intellectual development leveled out in his fourth decade and tailed inexorably away thereafter. When a man passed forty he had nothing to look forward to mentally, it seemed, but ossification, dissolution, and decay. Statistics did not lie—except that they did. In the absence of longitudinal data for any one population, the test scores of populations in all the different age groups had been patched together to produce a composite curve. The result was less a picture of the average man's IQ at different ages than it was a graphic comparison of the dramatic

185

difference in IQ found for succeeding generations. The average man did not fall 15 points in IQ between the ages of forty and sixty as a cursory look at the chart suggested. The average man of forty on the chart was simply 15 points higher in IQ than the average man of sixty on the chart. He always had been—a fact driven home by World War II soldiers when their average score on the Army Alpha test surpassed those made by more than eight out of ten of their World War I counterparts.

Galton's balancing up-and-down escalator theory to the contrary, why should the average man in 1941 have a decidedly higher IQ than the average man in 1914? That was another story, psychologists decided. His improved score reflected better health, increased education, and superior communications—in themselves an oblique commentary on just what it was intelligence tests were, in smaller or larger part, testing. But the development of intelligence from birth through maturity to old age—its trajectory, if it had one—remained an open question, one to be explored only as it unfolded in the fullness of time. This the coordinated growth studies set out to do.

One overriding problem resisted solution from the outset, the problem of testing itself. "Ideally," wrote Nancy Bayley, one of the team psychologists, ". . . we should be able to measure the same children from birth to maturity on a single test which is applicable over the entire age range. Such a test, furthermore, should be calibrated in absolute units, so that velocities of growth in individuals and over different segments of the span may be compared directly. However, in spite of repeated efforts to produce them there are no existing intelligence tests which meet either of these criteria."

She added a remark that stands as a caveat as pertinent today as it was then: "It now seems unlikely, from the very nature of the growth of intellectual abilities, that such a test can ever be devised."[3] Armed with the best overlapping tests that they could find, however, the University of California team, undeterred, plunged in.

Its researchers fully expected to find, as one of them would put it later, "a general unitary quality of mind"[4] that grew as the child grew, at best in the orderly accruing increments of normal weight gain, at worst in the customary fits and starts of height increase. Instead, they soon found themselves in a world of febrile, fragmentary change. Seen in statistical profile, the preschooler's geography of developing intelligence was neither an unbroken plain, a gently swelling hill, an upward tilting plateau, nor a succession of peaks and valleys that climbed in their accumulation ever higher. Rather it proved to be a curiously ragged terrain of sudden, unexpected pinnacles and leisurely, inexplicable troughs, of rocketing ups and roller-coaster downs. Diverse mental functions in their contour lines converged and diverged, entwined, grew in parallel, and rode each other piggyback. Except that the more complicated was always erected on the scaffolding of the simpler, there appeared to be little rhyme, little reason, no finely fixed pattern of universal import. When plotted sequentially on the same graph, the IQ's of different children over the first few formative years resembled the luxuriant, helter-skelter growth of deepest jungle vine. Here was nothing logarithmic, algebraic, or even purely additive. Here was biology with a vengeance.

In general, the details were straightforward enough. Initially it was discovered that while mental growth the first year was rapid, the rates varied wildly. Sensory and motor functions predominated—what Harry Jerison might have called practice with the tools and materials of basic intelligence. Although they formed the basis for further intellectual development, researchers found, precocity or retardation in them did not necessarily have all that much bearing on what was to come. There was a pronounced shift the second year to "concrete adaptations," the first tentative stroke on the preliminary sketch that would ultimately become Jerison's mental picture of the possible world. Test scores then had no predictive value either. Only when increasingly abstract processes began to come in around age four did relative stability assert itself.

Even then, "relative" was the operative word. Of the forty-eight children followed from birth in the Berkeley Growth Study, only a fifth maintained approximately the same relative status with their peers over the first nine years of testing. Some grew more slowly, others more rapidly; sometimes their scores converged, sometimes they diverged. No consistent trends could be seen. The

187

lack of a pattern was a pattern, researchers noted, that appeared to be "inherent in the processes of mental development."[5]

True, according to a dozen tests taken during their school years, the average individual variation in IQ was no more than an insignificant 6 points, the amount that can be expected routinely if a child is given the same test twice just days apart. But, cautioned the researchers, these were only the "central tendencies," that old bugaboo, Galton's mythic average man again. In reality, at the extremes, wide shifts in intelligence could and did occur, at any age, across a broad array of mental abilities. Indeed, the more than 150 children in the Guidance Study tested annually for sixteen years betrayed in their scores a capacity to fluctuate so staggering it would invalidate any two such tests today. The scores of five children increased or decreased more than 70 points, the categorical difference between mental retardation and giftedness. These tremendous changes were not registered abruptly, in a single year, but gradually, over a long period of time. Thirteen other children lost or gained 30 or more points. A third of the group varied as much as 20, and almost 60 percent fluctuated 15 or more points—the magic number men of differing skin color fight over today.

Physical illness, family tensions, social strain, all appeared reflected in some of the more extreme case histories (although honesty compels the researchers to admit that the same kinds of misfortune were undoubtedly present on occasion in the lives of children who moved from age to age, test to test, without appreciable changes in their levels of intellectual performance.) For example, the IQ of one only-child sank from 133 to 77. She was born when her mother was forty-four, the father thirty-seven. The mother's estimated IQ was 65 to 70. Both went to school until age fourteen. The girl was overindulged by her mother, who babied and fed her into obesity. The mother always complained that her daughter never gave her enough affection.

One boy, described as small-statured, thin, with very poor musculature, had spent only one six-month period in his life free from illness. He had a history of early ear infections and chronic bronchitis, headaches (early glasses) and stomach pains (appendectomy). By age eighteen he had had three operations and three serious accidents. Despite an early strained family situation and below-average test scores in his preschool years, he grew to find his greatest security in intellectual interests and achievements. His IQ increased from the mid 90's to around 160 before falling back down to 135.

A girl afflicted with intermittent, severe eczema and asthma and plaged by overweight, bad vision, economic insecurity, maternal friction, and the scorn (because of her brainy interests) of the racial minority to which she belonged, varied in IQ 44 points—from a well-above-average 121 to a soaring 165—a figure shared by one in an estimated 5,000 people.

Concluded the study psychologists in the face of such towering inconsistencies:

> It should be re-emphasized that [while] the results for the group suggest mental test stability between 6 and 18 years, the observed fluctuations in the scores of individual children indicate the need for the utmost caution in the predictive use of a single test score, or even two such scores. This finding seems of especial importance since many plans for individual children are made on the basis of a single . . . score.[6]

The California study team, unlike the Galtonians before them, were taking Alexander Pope's side with man—any man—instead of men.

What of the predictive uses of IQ scores into adulthood? The studies showed a high degree of consistency between the last adolescent testing and the first adult testing sixteen years later—once more, for the group as a whole. In general, they reported, their subjects had gained roughly one year of mental growth in the interim, principally in vocabulary and information. Only a tenth of it could be attributed to the abstract, nonverbal processes of thinking. A follow-up test ten years later showed a general leveling off in short-term memory and arithmetic, as well as something Sperry and his followers in their concern with the left-hemisphere bias of Western society might have predicted: a drop in all performance tests—those that measure, however imperfectly, the spatial, imagistic specialties we now know to be in the province of the right hemisphere. Not surprisingly, the follow-up

189

study indicated, language remained as strong as ever. Like Old Man River, it just kept rolling along.

The citadels of psychometry in this country, however, have never been without a strong streak of Yankee pragmatism. Tests had to be good for something besides keeping scholars busy and undesirable aliens out. Did the early scores, and those that followed, cast a long shadow anywhere else besides the halls of Academe—in, say, the marketplace?

The University of California studies carefully refrained from any such insinuation. But then, that field of inquiry, a legitimate one, had already been.preempted by one of the giants of psychometry, Lewis Terman. It was Terman's study that was to link intelligence to success in the public mind. And it is the Terman study, begun six years earlier, that is, in the finest traditions of American mercantilism, best remembered.

The Terman Study

The Terman study is a classic of its kind, a monument to human persistence. For all its limitations—and they have come back to haunt us—it remains an unprecedented, unrelenting search-and-discover mission across the previously uncharted territory of intelligence and its social impact. Fifteen hundred mentally "gifted" Californians were first tested in 1922, then methodically traced through the intervening fifty years by a Stanford University research team under Terman's leadership until his death in 1956. Until recently the study slumbered in the archives at Stanford, rousing itself for a dutiful addendum every decade or so, otherwise sleeping the sleep of any scholarly work whose time is past, whose details are interred in the textbooks, whose basic conclusions have become so much a part of our collective unconscious we scarcely know—if we ever knew—where they came from.

Then, starting in 1969, a pair of controversial assertions rocked the world of educational psychology and spread their tremors through the fabric of our society:

• University of California psychologist Arthur Jensen suggested that compensatory education had failed because blacks were genetically inferior in intelligence. Despite massive efforts at amelioration, he pointed out, blacks consistently scored on the average 15 to 20 IQ points less than whites as a group. Catch-up programs of education as tools for achieving economic and social equality, he concluded, were consequently doomed.

• Harvard psychologist Richard Herrnstein declared that by marshaling its intellectual resources to the tasks that most demand them with a system of graduated status and financial rewards, the United States was encouraging a degree of social mobility that would inevitably result in a society of two distinct classes. These, he said, would be "the haves and the have-nots," an ironically engineered mockery of our egalitarian heritage.

Success in life, both men strongly implied, hinged on a high IQ. Where, critics demanded in the ensuing uproar, was their proof? Why, came the reply, in the Terman study.

Said Jensen, "Findings such as [Terman's] establish beyond a doubt that IQ tests measure characteristics that are obviously of considerable importance in our present technological society. To say that the kind of ability measured by intelligence tests is irrelevant or unimportant would be tantamount to repudiating civilization as we know it."[7]

Said Herrnstein, "Whatever the flaws in the study, there can be no reasonable doubt about its main conclusion. An IQ test can be given in an hour or two to a child, and from this infinitesimally small sample of his output, deeply important predictions follow— about schoolwork, occupation, income, satisfaction with life, and even life expectancy. . . . No other single factor matters as much in as many spheres of life."[8]

What exactly was the Terman study, anyway, and what precisely did it say? Did it, as Jensen and Herrnstein suggested, support their respective theories on the failure of compensatory education, the rise of a mental meritocracy? Did it really help prove that blacks as a people were deficient in native intellect, that society was fast metamorphosing into one in which pure brainpower would triumph *über alles*?

Lewis Terman had been a gifted child himself, the product of a one-room Indiana schoolhouse. He had definite ideas about brightness, and the germinal one that took deep root in the early

1920's—about the time he fixed a jaundiced Hoosier eye on the Mexican and Indian children—was that those who displayed excessive amounts of it had been absurdly stigmatized for well over half a century.

"Prior to that time the youthful prodigy was generally regarded with a mixture of admiration, awe and hopeful expectation," he would later write in his epic five-volume report, *Genetic Studies of Genius.* "Then, after 1850 or thereabouts, one finds an increasing number of treatises, written chiefly by doctors and educational theorists, in which the 'precocious' child was classed with the abnormals, depicted as a neurotic and alleged, if he survived at all, to be headed for post-adolescent stupidity or insanity.

"'Early ripe, early rot' was the slogan of those who favored slow maturation. The myth became prevalent that many of the great geniuses were dunces in childhood."[9]

In the appalling absence of evidence for any of this, it became Terman's belief—one equally unbuttressed by facts other than his own observations—that the truth lay to the contrary. Brainy kids would retain their edge as adults. Why not? No physiological factors that he could see militated against it. There was, moreover, apart from that irrational atmosphere of childhood prejudice, no obvious reason why they should not be at least as emotionally sound and physically fit on the average as anyone else. Indeed, if he were right about the power of superior intellect to propel people ahead on all fronts in an industrialized society—and it seemed so, just looking around him—then by and large they should grow to be socially more mature, educationally more advanced, and vocationally more successful. That was all the more reason, if you thought about it, to be healthy in mind and body.

Armed with a grant from the Commonwealth Fund of New York, generous by standards then, a pittance now, Terman set out with his assistants to canvass a quarter-million youngsters in search of those among them intellectually well within the top 1 percent of the state's school population. And thereby he set in motion the IQ hassle that has raged on and off in one form or another to this day.

For financial reasons Terman decided at the outset to limit his search mainly to larger and medium-sized urban areas. Teachers up through the eighth grade were asked to nominate and rank their three brightest students. More shrewdly, in recognition of the fact that under existing California educational policy those who performed most precociously in school were allowed to skip grades and find their own level, the youngest in each class was also included. Later both older and younger pupils were screened and added. The result was an ultimate study group of 1,528 children, 857 boys and 671 girls. The preponderance of males Terman chalked up to their natural aggression in an essentially male-dominated society. On the average their tested IQ overall was 150, some 20 points above the bottom of the range psychologists generally designated as gifted. (The study's title, *Genetic Studies of Genius,* was an egregious misnomer and Terman knew it. In its most mundane interpretation, genius begins where gifted leaves off. But like the farmer who gets his mule to obey by first hitting it on the head with a stick, Terman realized something dramatic was needed to capture the public's attention.)

With a pledge of confidentiality, Terman then secured everyone's cooperation for a barrage of further tests, interviews, and questionnaires—the latter two involving pupils, parents, and teachers alike—designed to evoke the best composite physical, mental, emotional, and social profile possible.

The results were immediately gratifying. The children in his sample tended to be bigger, stronger, faster-maturing 'sexually, more successful all-round in school and, strangely enough, better developed ethically.

As the years went by and the Stanford team watched, queried, tested, and recorded the results on punch cards, the group as a whole abundantly fulfilled Terman's every expectation. Indeed, in the long fullness of their adult lives, its members on the average have far outstripped the population mean in every predicted category of human performance from money made to honors earned. And they have done so with less delinquency, less alcoholism, less mental illness, fewer criminal convictions, and fewer early deaths. There were, of course, a few surprises. For one thing, the number of years most of them stayed in school was totally unrelated to either IQ or level of academic achievement. One Terman subject entered Stanford at age fourteen with only two years of formal

193

schooling behind him. Of the six men who reported the highest income in the group's middle years, only one had finished college. The highest income was earned by a man who never went to college at all.

Many of Terman's subjects are in their sixties and seventies now. They remain, despite advancing years and the nomadic nature of Americans today, faithful correspondents. (Some still exchange chatty Christmas cards with former field workers. During the Second World War, statistical queries were assiduously answered from front-line foxholes.) In 1972 the study observed its golden anniversary with yet another questionnaire, this one probing the problems of aging and retirement, and the changing status that adjustment to both must bring. The results are still being studied, but one thing is certain. Whatever the import of these twilight findings, the Terman group taken as a population has been indisputably outstanding in those accomplishments by which Americans generally judge success.

So Terman was right. Or was he?

Did it follow from the thrust of his study that they had succeeded because of their high IQ? Be careful. If so, it also follows that Jensen and Herrnstein are right in using the study to argue their side of the larger issue today: that in a competitive society it is primarily the IQ that will determine life success.

As it happens, those at Stanford closest to the data simply do not think its correlation between early IQ and later success is all that clear-cut. More to the point, Professors Lee Cronbach and Robert Sears, the study's scientific custodians, feel the Terman data just aren't germane to any of these more volatile social issues. They believe the figures have been woefully misinterpreted and grievously misused in the service of arguments foreign to Terman's intention.

"I don't see any connection," Cronbach says flatly. "The study meant more in the 1920 context than it does now. Terman had in mind the hope that these young people would, over the years, prove to be effective in an all-round way. He did, I think, establish this convincingly, to the point where the question hasn't been raised since. But all he wanted to do was follow a group of bright kids and see what happened."[10]

194

Adds Sears, an authority in child psychology, "It doesn't say anything at all with respect to where the quality being measured came from. Whether they were bright because of certain genetic input or certain home influences is not answered by this study."[11]

What was being measured and where it came from, Sears and Cronbach would agree, are questions that haven't been answered yet, by the Terman study or anything else. To Terman's credit he wasn't trying to answer the nature-nurture question, although almost nothing in his admirers' advocacy implies otherwise. Herrnstein did concede that IQ-based predictions of long-term performance such as Terman's work suggests "are not perfect, for other factors always enter in. . . ."[12] Indeed they do. Terman himself admitted as much when he wrote about one of the tests he employed:

> This is not to say that [it] taps all kinds of intellect one would like to measure. Some aspects of intelligence are so elusive that no tests man has been able to devise have so far enabled us to map them or quantify them. Creative intelligence, for example, or the ability to make new mental constructs out of one's repertoire of informational and conceptual raw material, has been faintly glimpsed but never adequately measured.[13]

Critics today go further. For reasons which a closer look at the Terman study may clarify, they believe the standardized test purporting to measure innate mental skills on a comparative scale may in fact reflect more accurately what it least intends to: exactly those crippling inequities of intellectual opportunity inherent in a stratified society. At the most, critics say, it may mirror a critical interaction between inborn abilities and socioeconomic background whose ingredients can hardly be teased apart, much less separately weighed. In that regard, had Terman known the uses to which his data would be put half a century later, he might have structured his study to avoid two steps in methodology that in today's highly charged social context are all but pernicious errors. As it is, both led him to pick, by current standards, what Sears frankly concedes to be "a poor sample" for the kind of forensic exercises the Terman study is being used to support now.

In the first place, there were few blacks or Mexican-Americans in the schools he chose from. The rising tide of minority migrations to the West Coast—and the specter of core-city degrada- tion—were as yet decades away. (Oakland and Berkeley, for example, were only 3 percent black. Today they are 40 and 50 percent respectively.) There were, in fact, few lower-class kids of any kind. As noted earlier, the population he canvassed, by dol- lars-and-cents design, lacked any rural component, which would have been predominantly poor. And despite compulsory attend- ance laws, in the California of the 1920's lower-class white chil- dren in the larger cities and towns seldom went to school. They were too busy helping their parents. So the sample at the outset was heavily weighted toward the white middle and upper classes. Over 80 percent of the fathers were professionals, semiprofes- sionals, and businessmen, facts which Terman, whose inclination was strongly hereditarian, indirectly recognized in words that would win him bedfellows on the other side of the argument to- day: "No race or nationality has any monopoly on brains. The non-Caucasian representation in our gifted group would certainly have been larger than it was but for handicaps of language, envi- ronment and educational opportunities."[14]

In the second place, Terman further refined the sample away from a telling cross-section by his prime method of preliminary screening, the teacher recommendation. Such an intensely per- sonal method is far from infallible, as anyone with the slightest ap- preciation of human nature knows. (The youngest child in each class did turn out to be the much more fruitful nomination.) Er- rors of commission, of course, would be caught by further testing; no teacher's pet would slip through the net. But what about errors of omission? The nonconforming children, the withdrawn, the ones who failed to affiliate with adult concepts of learning and re- sponded negatively to established values—these would naturally have been the most likely overlooked by teachers anxious to be confirmed by "science" in their professional judgment—and, not incidentally, in their egos. Such children might have tested highly intelligent, it seems fair to speculate, yet years later, because of their renegade temperament, perform significantly lower in a so- ciety beginning to place a premium on corporate teamwork— which would have worked to the detriment of the study's IQ-success relationship.

Sears thinks it is possible this could have happened in a significant number of cases. Cronbach doubts enough were missed to materially change the picture. He does believe, however, that the sample was clearly shaped by the demands of the existing society as well as the specialized nature of the tests. As usual, the tests were geared to the left hemisphere at the expense of the right. Children who later excelled in art and literature were few: those destined to become outstanding in science and engineering, the conventional left-hemisphere professions such as law and medicine, were many. "That may say something about the extent to which the arts are a special talent," Cronbach concedes. "But it also says something about American culture at that time. It wasn't encouraging very many people to go in that direction. The arts were a good way to starve."[15]

(Cronbach's remark also says something about Herrnstein's concept of a mental meritocracy. Where would it find room for a Picasso, who as a right-hemisphere-dominated child had trouble telling the numeral 7 from a drawn nose?)

Finally and most crucially, if such a study is to be appreciated and understood for what it says as well as for what it doesn't, it has to be seen for what it is: not a fascinating story about a group of people but, at bottom, a statistical profile. Vast confusion if not outright mischief can result if it isn't. The gifted child Terman talks about is not flesh-and-blood reality, though it derives from that in the aggregate. It is what psychologists call a reification; a lifeless abstraction treated as if it had concrete existence; a composite figure, Galton's mythic average man given a spurious breath of counterfeit life. Just as in the Growth Studies, mathematics had papered over a world of human differences, spanned a gamut of experience between two extremes. Nothing dramatized the dangers of disregarding this simple fact more than the follow-up substudy Terman's team conducted in 1947. In an attempt to assess more accurately the factors that had made for career success, Terman-appointed judges examined the records and life-styles of some 750 men in a representative subsample to winnow out the 150 most successful (called the A group) and the 150 least successful (called the C group). What differences would they find? The results forever shattered Terman's conviction

197

about IQ as the pure, unassailable fount of societal achievement.

If IQ were indeed the chief determinant of success, the range of differences between the two groups should not have been great. But on the average, the judges found, the differences between the two groups on those indexes to life performance accepted as indicative from the outset—job status, income, education, health, and social adjustment—were striking. They were almost as striking in some categories as the differences between Terman's gifted and the national average.

Eight times as many A's as C's were in the professions or business. Those in the A group earned on the average twice what those in the C's did. Nine out of ten A's had graduated from college; less than four out of ten among the C's. The A's had better health, higher self-confidence, wider interests, more hobbies; the C's unhappier wives, twice as many divorces, greater feelings of inferiority, three to four times the frequency of unemployment and job change.

There was no significant difference in the average IQ's of the two groups. Both retested around 150.

(Arthur Jensen would later argue that if IQ's were equal, other factors would then of course determine the outcome of career competition. He compared the design of the Terman substudy to a footrace between runners who had won qualifying races in almost the same times. Just because they were equally fast did not mean the race was destined to end in a dead heat, said Jensen. The result would now hinge on other variables: temperament, motivation, track conditions, luck, and so on. There would still be those that finished near the front of the pack and those that finished near the rear; there would still be a first-place finisher and a last-place finisher. But that would neither invalidate the results of the earlier races nor diminish the importance of being naturally fast of foot. The race, after all, other things being equal, was ultimately to the swiftest, was it not? Jensen's thesis, while tempting, begs the question. Other things are never equal, in any race or combination of races. The most that can be said is that the race is ultimately to he who, for whatever medley of reasons, finishes first.)

If it was not IQ, then, what accounted for Terman's two radically different sets of life outcomes? Terman decided it must principally be the drive to achieve, plus all-round social adjustment. He all but ignored the presence of corollary data on family background for both groups as children that those concerned with the effects of environment would have found impossible to minimize. Three times as many of the A fathers had graduated from college, more than twice as many were in the professions. (About the same percentage as their sons.) Long before the substudy had even been conceived, moreover, field workers had reported a markedly higher cultural atmosphere in the A parents' homes, more books, musical instruments, art, and so on. Members of the A group had also married "better."[16] That is, their wives had more schooling.

Fascinating too were such telltale tidbits as these: far more A's belonged to social clubs, far more C's to labor unions. In a smaller sampling, proportionately far more A's had served in the navy, 80 percent of them as officers. None of the C's entered the navy as officers, and few the army, but 13 percent won in-service commissions. Most eloquent, perhaps, though meaningless statistically, was how one man from each group later died. The A-group man, a physicist, died from exposure to radioactivity while working on atomic weapons. The C-group man, a welder, died from exposure to fumes while working in a defense plant.

It seems eminently fair to ask: Did the C's lack job stability partly because of "inferior judgment,"[17] as Terman would have it, or because they were intelligent enough to know that a lack of family and class advantages had thwarted the fullest development of their natural talents? Did their marriages collapse more often because of inferior adjustment or because their wives shared past endurance their feelings of deep frustration? Did the A's demonstrate what Terman called "a greater breadth of interests,"[18] or did they just have more money and time to pursue hobbies than the C's, who were busy scratching a living out of postwar America? Were the 97 percent of the A's who told the researchers they liked their work, compared to 75 percent of the C's, better adjusted socially or did they just have better jobs and were smart enough to realize it? In short, did Terman, and those that now speak in his name, bet on the wrong horse?

Even those who know the study most intimately cannot agree.

199

Says Harvard psychologist and motivation expert David McClelland, who devised some of the substudy criteria:

> . . . Neither Professor Terman nor anyone else has as yet brought forward conclusive evidence that it is giftedness per se as he measures it that is responsible for these happier life outcomes. For his gifted children were also drawn very disproportionately from the ranks of the educated, the wealthy and the powerful. This means that they had not only a better chance to acquire the characteristics measured in the test but also to be happier (since they had more money) and also to have access to higher occupations and better social standing.[19]

Sears and Cronbach differ. Sears leans to motivation. Cronbach says,

> It's perfectly clear that once you contrast two groups on such an important social event as going to college, given the America of that generation, any other contrast you bring in is irrelevant. You might have to look a little hard to determine whether their going to college or not was a matter of motivation or ability. Motivation plus ability plus finances plus family encouragement is almost certainly the story.
>
> But I don't want to say there's a social-class contamination. As a first cut at the data this is fair. What made for success? All these different things which happen to have a lot to do with family background. But a more subtle cut might separate these things. For instance, I can't even separate motivation from the test the study began with. Binet defines intelligence as the power to take and maintain a given direction, the power of self-discipline. Well, you see, self-discipline means looking back over your work and catching your mistakes before the examiner, or your boss, does. And that's motivation.[20]

And Terman? In the face of these soaring complexities he felt moved to enunciate a manifesto whose pertinence these past twenty-five years have done nothing to dispel:

> We have seen that intellect and achievement are far from perfectly correlated. Why this is so, what circumstances affect the fruition of human talent, are questions of such transcendent importance that they should be investigated by every method that

promises the slightest reduction of our present ignorance. So little do we know about our available supply of potential genius, the emotional compulsions that give it dynamic quality, or the personality distortions that make it dangerous.[21]

It was a gracious if nettlesome admission from the man who had developed the Army Alpha test and the Stanford-Binet amid the plaudits of his colleagues and with such high hopes for psychometry's future. The words, lofty and sonorous, scarcely reflected his true feelings, as they rarely do with any of us. Sears says laughingly, "Terman was a shy, retiring chap who began by assuming everyone intelligent was just as strongly motivated in life as he was. When he found out that wasn't true, he acted as any man would who was being challenged by his own data.

"He was absolutely infuriated!"[22]

If Terman was distressed by the backlash of his own data, you have to wonder what he would have thought about the later studies done by McClelland and Christopher Jencks. McClelland took the top eight students he had taught in a class twenty years before and compared their careers to those of eight classmates who had barely passed. The two lists were indistinguishable. Both included lawyers, doctors, teachers, and research scientists. The only difference was that those with higher grades got into better law or medical schools, prompting McClelland to observe, "doubtless the C-minus students could not get into even second-rate law and medical schools under the stricter admission . . . standards of today. Is that an advantage for society?"[23]

Neither the amount of education nor grades, he further found, related to vocational success as a factory worker, bank teller, air-traffic controller, or scientist. Only in high status jobs such as stock and bond salesman—where speech, clothes, manner, old school ties, and family connections contribute to success—did a strong correlation exist, in McClelland's opinion a strong clue to what IQ tests are really getting at.

He went on to cite one table in a study of a typical Middle American small town which purported to show the usual strong relationship between social class, IQ, and college-going which leads to occupational success.

201

The traditional interpretation is that more stupid children come from the lower classes because their parents are also stupid, which explains why they are lower class. A higher proportion of children with high IQ go to college because they are more intelligent and more suited to college study. This is as it should be because IQ predicts academic success. The fact that more intelligent people going to college come more often from the upper class follows naturally because the upper classes contain more intelligent people. . . . However, a closer look at the table suggests another interpretation that is equally plausible. . . . It appears to be no more likely for bright children (high IQ) from the lower classes to go to college (despite their high aptitude for it) than for "stupid" children from the upper classes. Why is this? An obvious possibility is that the bright but poor children do not have the money to go to college. . . .[24]

Moreover, when Cronbach concludes that tests are "giving realistic information on the presence of a handicap" he is right, McClelland agrees, but "psychologists should recognize that it is those in power who often decide what is a handicap."[25]

In the middle ages they required knowledge of Latin for the learned professions of law, medicine and theology. . . . Only those young men who could read and write Latin could get into those occupations, and if tests had been given in Latin, I am sure they would have shown that professionals scored higher . . . than men in general, that sons who grew up in families where Latin was used would have an advantage . . . compared to those in poor families where Latin was unknown, and that these men were more likely to get into the professions. But would we conclude we were dealing with a general ability factor?[26]

Finally, along comes Harvard sociologist Christopher Jencks and his associate, Mary Jo Bane, to declare—after heading a task force that examined a computerized mountain of data from all walks of American society—that IQ accounts for no more than 10 percent of the variation in job performance and less than half that in job income. How could such a thing be, when test scores play such an admittedly significant role in determining both school grades and the credentials eventually earned, which in turn affect occupations and earnings?

The answer was simple, really, suggested Jencks and Bane. At

SHOULD OLD IQ BE FORGOT?

each stage there are many exceptions, "and the cumulative result is that exceptions are almost commonplace."[27] What, then, were the factors leading to economic success? Jencks and Bane, though slightly more circumspect, had a breezy answer for that one, too.

> Unfortunately, we do not know enough to identify with much precision the other factors leading to economic success. All we can do is suggest their complexity. First, there is a wide variety of skills that have little or no connection with IQ but have a strong relationship to success in some specialized field. The ability to hit a ball thrown at high speed is extremely valuable, if you happen to be a professional baseball player. The ability to walk along a narrow steel beam 600 feet above the ground without losing your nerve is also very valuable, if you happen to be a construction worker. In addition, many personality traits have substantial cash value in certain contexts. A man who is good at figuring out what his boss wants, or good at getting his subordinates to understand and do what he wants, is at a great premium in almost any large . . . organization . . : Similarly, a person who inspires confidence is likely to do well regardless of whether he is a doctor, a clergyman, a small businessman, or a Mafioso. . . .[28]
>
> Finally [said Jencks and Bane] there is the matter of luck. . . .

You have to wonder what Lewis Terman would have thought about *that*.

203

Chapter 8

Testing Today and Tomorrow

Nothing illuminates the current state of testing better than the stories told by two of its staunchest supporters, Raymond Cattell and Hans Eysenck. According to Cattell, of those who took the two qualifying examinations he designed for Mensa, the international society of high IQ adults, fully three-quarters who passed either one failed the other. Eysenck, a research psychologist who believes the IQ to be both basically inherited and important, reports with mystification a British salesman who bought a town house and seaside villa as well as several cars and sent all his children to college—despite an IQ just under 70. A certified moron, he had spent time in a home for the mentally defective before his wife got him released.

In a laudable attempt at explanation, Eysenck credits luck, extroversion, and other unspecified qualities of temperament for "an unduly large part"[1] of the man's success even as he contends that morons, generally, can do little more than learn useful tasks under supervision. Faced with the equally conflicting results of the Mensa test, Cattell decided it was because he had tested separately his two conceptual kinds of intelligence, fluid and crystallized. That the unlettered, however bright, should fail when tested on crystallized intelligence—that invested in the learning skills of formal education—is no surprise, although it does engender suspicion about what was being tested: ability, achievement, or both. But why the ranks of those passing the test of fluid (*i.e.,* culturally formless) ability should exclude most of those passing the test of the crystallized is something Cattell left unclear. Not that it mattered to Mensa, which decided to use one test and abandon the other.

Psychologists critical of IQ testing are seldom so charitable. "The testing movement in the United States," says Harvard's David McClelland tartly, "has been a success, if one judges by the usual American criteria of size, influence, and profitability. . . . On what assumptions is the success of the movement based? They deserve careful examination before we go on rather blindly promoting [them] as instruments of power over the lives of many Americans."[2]

Princeton's Leon Kamin criticizes the "glamor of scientism surrounding the testing industry that has made it difficult for people to ask a very simple, straight-forward question: 'Where is the evidence that people who do well on this particular test will perform the job in question better than others who don't do as well . . . ?'" Kamin has no doubt of the answer. "I think the evidence shows, on the contrary, that the enormous majority of tests that are in everyday use . . . simply don't predict anything."[3]

Tests do far more harm than merely offering nothing for something, other critics charge. They help create, claims Yale's Edward Zigler, former director of the U.S. Office of Child Development, the mystique of an IQ that can and should be dramatically improved by every stratagem from crib mobiles to early infant reading. The result is a joyless, apprehensive quest by both parent and child for what Zigler terms the "elusive . . . carrot of intellectual superiority."[4] In his view that carrot is a slender hothouse specimen short on nourishment; the result is often only superficial gains at the expense of real and lasting mental development. By what divine wisdom, he demands, do we assert that such an intellectually forced-fed child is superior to the child with artistic ability, to the child with athletic prowess, to the child who is considerate, kind, and a pleasure to be around?[5] The problems of growing up today, he concludes, are due to a deepening crisis of motivation and values that has nothing on earth to do with low IQ scores.

In the face of such heartfelt accusations, defenders of the testing faith are inclined to shrug, concede its limitations, and challenge its detractors to come up with something better—or fall back upon a recitation of the merits of having a high intelligence that assumes a curious kind of face-facts inevitability magically extended to include its present means of testing. "The bright and the dull have always been recognized," says Arthur Jensen. "They would still differ if there were no IQ test.

"Throwing it out will not improve a person's intelligence any more than throwing away the thermometer will cure a patient's fever."[6]

Criticism, however, is not confined to those on the outside looking in. At a conference on testing's problems, S. A. Kendrick, executive director of research and development for the College Entrance Examination board, saw fit to repeat an observation made by another educator almost two decades earlier.

> When a test is designed to predict success in a particular occupation—stenography, for example—it is usually labeled as a stenographic aptitude test. . . . If a test is to be used to predict success at schoolwork generally, why is it not more consistent, more descriptive and less open to misunderstanding to label [it] a test of scholastic aptitude rather than refer to it as an "intelligence test"?
>
> One cannot legitimately say, "the intelligence test shows that certain of our peoples are bright and certain of them are dull. The bright ones succeed well in our schools, so our school is doing a good job with bright pupils. The dull ones are doing poorly, but the tests indicate that they could not be expected to do any better, so we need not worry about them." Such an evaluative use of intelligence tests results is utterly fallacious. One cannot justify securing poor educational results from "poor" students by saying the tests show them to be "poor" students; the tests were specifically constructed to do just this—to label as "poor" those students who do not do well in our schools as now organized.[7]

In his controversial book *Inequality,* Christopher Jencks agrees that IQ scores, whatever they measure, should remain in school where they belong. They measure, he believes, only one rather limited variety of intelligence, the kind schools value. About the most that can be said about students who do well on them is that they tend not only to get good grades but to stay in school longer.

As for the challenge to find alternatives, University of Illinois psychologist McVicker Hunt laments that the pervasive use of intelligence tests so reinforces the concept of the IQ that it undermines all evidence to the contrary. Its power is such, says Hunt, that it can destroy even the motivation for ingenuity in teaching: "The saddest words in education, when applied to student performance, are 'as well as can be expected.' "[8]

Amid the shot and shell of charge and countercharge, no one as yet has matched England's Eysenck for breathtaking pragmatism. "Intelligence tests are not based on any very sound scientific principles, and there is not a great deal of agreement among experts regarding the nature of intelligence," he writes. "On the other hand, intelligence tests, right from the beginning, have been outstandingly successful in their practical application." Because of this, says Eysenck, "psychologists interested in the subject tended to become technologists, eager to exploit and improve these tools, rather than scientists eager to carry out the requisite fundamental research, most of which still remains to be done."[9]

On that point there can be no argument. As for the legitimacy of their application, in a takeoff on E. G. Boring's classically circular definition, one writer decided that "the only thing of which we're absolutely certain is that intelligence tests measure what intelligence tests measure."[10]

Exactly what do intelligence tests do? How are they designed, constructed, validated, and scored? What are the assumptions behind them? What are their goals, their philosophy, their intent? Are the tests intended to evaluate, to diagnose, or to predict? Are they, in sum, legitimate tools, and if so, legitimate for what? All these questions must be asked and answered if their role is to be intelligently determined, much less revised to reflect our growing knowledge of man and his brain.

A good place to begin is to ask a question that undercuts their pretense at being no less scientific than the measurements of weight and height: What ages can they test and what ages can they not? Because of the early fluctuations found by the growth studies, it is generally agreed that tests given before the age of six are largely worthless as predictors of later intelligence. Their diagnostic use in these formative years, moreover, must be limited to detecting the more severe forms of retardation. As to evaluation for its own sake, the results of most preschool tests are too erratic even for that. Not only don't they mesh with each other, they can't be expected to mesh with the results of the same tests given later. Although one study found that three-month-old infants could "think," such flickerings of intellect are too easily confused with the sharper stirrings of sensorimotor development. Concedes Eysenck, "Six, therefore, is perhaps the lowest age at which IQ tests are to be taken at all seriously, and even at that age they should not be taken *very* seriously!"[11]

At the other end of the age scale, all is fresh contradiction. Traditionally, most research has shown that intelligence drops or levels off in man's declining years, though not at the precipitous rate the cross-sectional comparisons across generations indicated. A recent analysis of longitudinal studies in Germany, however, suggests this conclusion may be skewed by elderly people whose mental performance falls as their health fails and death approaches. Of several hundred men and women between the ages of fifty-five and seventy-five whose intelligence was examined at two five-year intervals, those who lived from one study to another were found to have had, on the average, significantly higher scores on their previous test than those who had since died, regardless of their age. This "terminal drop" afflicting those whose health had begun, or was about to begin, its final deterioration, pulled down the group's average. Those willing to be tested, moreover, showed a lower mortality during the second five years than those who refused, possibly because the latter sensed their powers fading. If they keep their health—and perhaps more important, their zest for living—and if the IQ means anything at all, the elderly may not only retain their intelligence but improve it. A recent Santa Clara University report points in that direction. It disclosed that the average IQ of a group tested at intervals since 1931 had risen from an initial score of 111 in childhood to 130 in middle age, long after the IQ is thought to peak.

The reliability of testing throughout adulthood is by no means unquestioned, even by proponents of the IQ. As Eysenck points out, tying the mental and chronological ages together to yield the ratio expressed as IQ would work fine all our lives—if both continued to increase until we died. But most tests are constructed on the assumption that mental age plateaus around age eighteen. Thus, if a person has the mental age of the average eighteen-year-old on his eighteenth birthday, his IQ is 100 (Stern's formula of dividing mental age by chronological age and adding two zeros). But if he took the same test and still had a mental age of eighteen when he was thirty-six, even though his intelligence had not changed, his IQ would then be only half what it was, or a retarded 50. The plunging IQ is strictly a statistical artifact, the consequence of intelligence not being a linear absolute like the incremental minutes, hours, days, months, and years of clock and calendar time.

To get around this, adult intelligence tests base their average IQ not on any ratio between mental and chronological age, but on the average number of correct answers given by the group used in standardizing the test questions for the larger population. The result, confesses Eysenck, is a "kind of make-believe operation"[12] that says if the IQ could be applied, this is the IQ an adult would have. Although the best of the adult tests are praised as clinically helpful, Cattell remains unconvinced. Because of differing experiences after the homogeneous years of common schooling, he thinks any standardized test applied from the age of twenty on is an exercise in "pure illusion."[13]

Our yardstick shorn at either end, we are left with a measurement that is undisputed even among its adherents only in the school years. Even here the validity of the IQ is moot. Admits Eysenck, "we come up right from the beginning against the difficulty that no satisfactory criterion does in fact exist."[14] Furthermore, the concept that a child is endowed from birth with a potential which sets an upper limit to achievement, claims Joanna Ryan of Kings College, Cambridge, is a logical absurdity. Potential, innate or otherwise, cannot be separated from the behavior that expresses it. Intelligent behavior, in turn, is not born in a vacuum, but derives from skills developed in collision with the environment. Efforts to minimize the vagaries of this interaction by testing talents and knowledge assumed common to all, she believes, are doomed by the complex and ubiquitous differences of varied upbringing that invariably out. "The notion of potential ability both as something abstracted from all interactions with the environment and at the same time as something measurable in a person's behavior," she says, "simply does not make sense."[15] No wonder Robert Sears of Stanford frankly refers to his mentor Terman's handiwork, the Stanford-Binet, as a "crude, limited, clumsy instrument."[16] In the light of all we have learned in the last half-century, adds his colleague Cronbach, tests today reflect "sheer obsolescence. Nobody has thought hard."[17]

Most standardized tests in addition, stress ever-increasing competence in such informational skills as reading and writing which, as Cronbach points out, relies on what the child should know and is "really a test of previous achievement."[18] Such an approach, Sears thinks, ends up testing at best little more than half of man's intelligent behavior. Predictably, the half that is tested utilizes mostly the verbal-symbolic-analytical properties of the left hemisphere, not the concrete-spatial-imaging abilities of the right. The Wechsler Intelligence Scale for Children (WISC), perhaps the most widely used test in the United States today, devotes equal space to performance tasks, but here another problem intrudes. As Eysenck observes, exactly the same type of test item can be posed in a verbal, numerical, or perceptual-spatial manner, and a person's success may depend on which.

In any event, the specter of lateralized function haunts the testing process. Which half of the brain is more intelligent? Should intelligence be computed by hemispheric addition, subtraction, division, or multiplication? Who—or what—can possibly tell? Certainly the standardized IQ test cannot. It has difficulty enough with the subtleties and vagaries of the left hemisphere, and ends by relegating most of the right hemisphere's gifts to the more mysterious—and somehow linguistically diminished—realm of "special aptitudes."

Finally, Eysenck believes, intelligent behavior—the hemispheres aside—can be divided in so many different ways that to test each adequately would require, at the rate of one hour per subtest over a forty-hour week, a month of full-time testing for each person. To those who scoff at such sustained testing, Eysenck likes to point out that tests of engines and metals may go on for years. Is man's brain any less ramified in its performance, any more impervious to environmental stress and strain?

As it is, given such wide latitude in the kinds of mental items and how they may be offered, the small samples selected by any two tests can be significantly different. Any one person's two scores, in fact, may vary as much as 10 points either way. To put it more pertinently, the nature of the test itself can spell the difference between being labeled "gifted" with all that it implies socially, or simply "above average."

Even the scores are not what they seem. The ratio between actual age and mental age is retained, granted, but the resulting scale reveals less than it obscures. Eysenck is fond of comparing its workings to how a thermometer measures temperature. The thermometer, however, whether Fahrenheit or centigrade, is what scientists call an *interval* scale. That is, the difference in temperature between 70 and 60 degrees is exactly the same as between 40 and 50. Thermometers are not *ratio* scales like height and weight, which combine intervals and ratios into a more meaningful measurement. Zero degrees is not the absence of temperature as weightlessness is the absence of weight. It is an arbitrary jumping-off point. What's more, while two inches are twice as high as one, a temperature of 100 is not twice as hot as 50. Limited though a thermometer may be, it is farther up the ladder of scaling sophistication than the IQ. The IQ is an *ordinal* scale, a ranking by order only, like the scales for the hardness of minerals and the quality of lumber. In essence, it is not a raw score at all, but the result of putting a raw score through a statistical transformation that yields a numerical symbol of order, like the numbered chit you get at a busy barbershop. Since ordinal scales cannot be used arithmetically, we cannot say that someone with an IQ of 130 is twice as smart as someone with an IQ of 65, or that the difference between IQ's of 50 and 100 is the same as the difference between IQ's of 100 and 150. The popular misconception that IQ measures intelligence the way a ruler measures length, Joanna Ryan emphasizes, grew out of the common psychometric practice of calculating average scores for groups from individual scores.

Even then, the resulting order is somewhat idealized, Eysenck admits, a euphemism for pushing and squeezing until it fits the bell-shaped curve of Galton's normal distribution with as many scores below the average as above. This does not mean, Mendelians would insist, that intelligence has proven to be distributed normally, like height. The normal distribution of IQ scores is simply a consequence of test construction and standardization.

Nor does its scoring system square with the IQ's underpinning

211

philosophy of innate potential, as expressed through mental behavior that becomes stable over time. The late developer is no more a stranger to psychometry than the early bloomer—as the 70 points lost or gained by five persons during the University of California Growth Studies demonstrates. Yet the IQ tends to penalize the late developer by tying mental and chronological ages together in a ratio that confounds quality of intellect with the rate of its development. As Joanna Ryan observes, the IQ makes it almost a psychological impossibility to consider the late developer potentially as intelligent as the early bloomer before the fact. The two ideas—today's score, tomorrow's potential—though not incompatible in spirit, refuse to coexist in the chill shadow of finality cast by the first IQ. In a competitive world, who can calculate the price paid for that in shattered self-esteem and stunted motivation, in missed opportunities and dreams deferred? What can be said is that this unjustifiably sows a fertile field for the worst sort of self-fulfilling prophecy. For test scores too often determine how the slow developer will henceforth be treated educationally— which in turn, since innate potential must be invested in behavior to be tested at all, may have a critical bearing on how he will perform on his next IQ test. If he fails to realize his maturing gifts because of inferior schooling—born of the lesser expectation his initially poorer score has generated in those around him—teacher reaction is likely to be the one that haunts McVicker Hunt: "He did as well as could be expected." The lethal consequence has come full circle, with no one the wiser.

As for the intrinsic value of the scores themselves, assuming they could be left raw and purged of their ordinality, there is paradoxically less to them than meets the eye, and more. In most tests, various kinds of items are bunched together and graduated by age along a scale of increasing difficulty, to be cleared like hurdles from the lowest to the highest. The Stanford-Binet simply totals the number of items got right, regardless of their nature. Thus, the same score can be achieved in countless ways, and tells nothing about individual strengths and weaknesses. The use of a single score masks the fact that Johnny may be a verbal giant but a pygmy at math. The other major standardized test, the WISC, divides the scores of its subtests into two categories, performance and verbal (including arithmetic and other forms of symbol manipulation). But there again, such arbitrary amalgams do violence equally to all three reasons for testing—diagnosis, evaluation, and prediction—by obscuring important individual differences on the subtests. Short of test-maker convenience, there seems little justification for reducing man's intelligence to little more than a license plate or Social Security number.

But if item selection and scoring are fraught with problems, neither approaches the leap of faith in standardization. Since the IQ is designed to express how one child's intelligence compares to that of all others the same age, test items must be standardized. That is, they must be based on the performance of a large sample of people that resembles proportionately the overall population in such variables as urban or rural residence, parent education, occupation, and income. To do this, the subtests must be "normed," in effect, consumer-tested to make sure they yield appropriate results in the total response, which is to say an array of individual scores that nicely fits the bell-shaped curve of normal distribution when statistically adjusted.

Until recently both the Stanford-Binet and the WISC have been one of the last surviving citadels nationally of racial segregation. Their samples included neither blacks nor children from homes where the primary language spoken was other than English, predominantly Spanish. Moreover, both tests traditionally have used the census as their reference point. Since the census tends to miss the poor, the migrant, the single, and the unemployed, the result had been to bias the standardizations in the direction of the white middle class. Its socioeconomic status, of course, is superior by definition, and since socioeconomic status is highly correlated with better test performance, the standardization sample was in reality a cut above the population it supposedly stood for. The result was a built-in contradiction in terms: More than half those tested were destined, through no fault of their own, to have below average IQ's (that is, below the average of the white middle class). The sample was biased; the distribution skewed; the "ruler" warped to begin with.

Under increasing minority pressure, both the Stanford-Binet and the WISC were renormed in the early 1970's to include both

213

blacks and English-speaking Latin Americans in their standardization samples. Then the size of the hidden discrepancy became clearer. Moving the Stanford-Binet average to where it belonged meant a difference during the critical years of fifteen to eighteen of from 6 to 9 points. Correcting the displacement, however, did little to erode the worrisome 15- to 20-point difference in black and white average IQ's, affecting as it did disproportionately those around the average of both groups. The correction did allow large numbers of minority children to escape the stigma of being judged less intelligent than average by a standard that excluded their true peers. But the existence of the new standard tacitly recognized that when their peers were included it dragged the standardization sample down.

While a touchy and continuing problem, the external variables of race and environment have at least been met head-on in standardizing. Wholly evaded from the beginning has been the subtle but equally important chain of internal variables known as personality. Personality affects not only test performance, but the very form of expression intelligence can take. For instance, by their nature as a standardized instrument, most IQ tests deal exclusively in static questions which are *convergent*. That is, they have only one right answer. In contrast, as we know, much of man's thinking in response to the challenges of life is what Guilford characterized as *divergent*. His thinking is more a matter of generating a lot of answers, all of which may be right, then picking from them what appears to be the best, usually while under such delimiting pressures as available time and money. By narrowing the range of response called for, convergent questions reward a uniformity in thinking that pays off nowhere else as much as it does in the classroom.

To be sure, divergent thinking has its perils for the test-maker. If permitted, it is hard to score and harder still to evaluate. Writer James Fixx tells two stories that illustrate this. Asked in a lesson on even numbers if 5 could be divided by 2, one primary pupil replied that it certainly could, the answer was 2½ and 2½. Was he right or wrong? An older student questioned on how to find the height of a building with a barometer ignored atmospheric pressure altogether. Drop it off the building, he answered, time how long it takes to strike the ground, then calculate the distance with the formula for acceleration of a falling object. Or simpler yet, offer to give the owner the barometer if he will tell how tall the building is. Should such a student be given credit or dismissed as an arrogant know-it-all?

In the book *Race and Intelligence* which they edited, British social scientists Ken Richardson, Martin Richards, and David Spears observe that

> high IQ people tend to be good at straightforward logical problems that have one correct answer. They do not do well when dealing with uncertainty, when probabilistic strategies are needed, and they often do even worse when a series of quick judgments of this kind are called for. . . .[19]

Until now, a child's or an adult's immense diversity of cognitive style far outstrips the psychometrist's, they add wryly. The result has been to load the standardization and the test that follows against those whose mentality may be the most revealing, creative, and valuable.

Such a test of such a person, according to Alice Heim of Cambridge, can be traumatic if not crippling. The highly intelligent subject of critical bent can be undermined by a multiple-choice which includes unsound items—"of which, there are, alas, many instances." Seeing two equally defensible answers to a question, she argues, he may deliberately answer the other questions wrong out of sheer frustration or anger. Similarly, she thinks, the obsessional type of person may be incapacitated to the point of failure by the casual instruction not to spend too long on any one question. Mood as well as temperament can powerfully influence test performance, contends Dr. Heim, who objects to any attempt to split intelligence away from personality and consider either in isolation. When depressed, suggests Heim, our behavior tends to be "retarded"; we may be dejected, slow, and underactive; we shall probably attempt fewer items. Things matter less. Conversely, when we are elated and in high spirits, we have greater confidence and a greater willingness to try; we tend to speed up.

Persistence, motivation, anxiety—all can figure significantly in the caliber of test performance, even proponents of the IQ are quick to concede. Testers are less willing, however, to follow the implication of this where it leads: back to the doorstep of a standardization that fails to incorporate psychological variables, either because it technically cannot or philosophically dares not.

Eysenck, for example, freely admits that anxiety can cost the test taker 7 or 8 IQ points. In fact,

> A single test may be spoiled for many different reasons. The child may have a headache, or be below par for some other reason. He may be worried or upset by something that has happened to him or his family. He may have a tummy ache, or his pencils may break; he may have gone to sleep late. There are a thousand and one things, none of which would have a very profound effect on the score, but which if they accumulate could produce quite a marked discrepancy from the child's actual IQ.[20]

Yet a few pages earlier in his book *Know Your Own IQ*, Eysenck feels impelled to a curious defense of the intelligence test against the very kind of sensible observation he later makes:

> If indeed an IQ were determined simultaneously to be intelligence, persistence and anxiety, then the fact that little Johnny had an IQ of 90 could be due to the fact that he was very dull but persistent and little prone to anxiety, or it could be due to the fact that he was very bright but anxious and lacking in persistence. It might be due in fact to any number of interactions of these elements so the information would be very nearly useless in the absence of any knowledge of little Johnny's standing in these three qualities separately. If we wish to know a person's intelligence, persistence and anxiety, then we require three measures, not one, and to criticize a measure of intelligence because it tells us nothing about non-intellectual qualities is not a reasonable criticism.[21]

A reasonable criticism, he seems to be saying, is the kind that considers IQ strictly in isolation from any psychological variables that might influence the information it extracts—in short, in the vacuum that nature abhors.

What, finally, success in life aside, can be said of the IQ's predictive value?

Unlike Terman before him—or Jensen and Herrnstein today—Eysenck has no illusions.

> . . . An item which is a good measure of a child's intelligence at the present *moment* may or may not be a good measure of his *future ability*. If we want to use our intelligence tests as measures of future as well as present ability . . . then surely a great deal of research should be done. . . . As far as I know . . . no effort is being made to improve existing tests along these lines.[22]

Only in predicting the results of schooling does Eysenck relent.

> The results of very large numbers of carefully planned investigations support the conclusion that IQ tests, properly constructed, administered and evaluated, show considerable agreement with the success of the child at school. . . . People with low IQ's do not on the whole do as well in academic and intellectual pursuits; this is as near to an unalterable law as psychology has yet come. . . .[23]

Under the circumstances it is virtually impossible not to agree with Lee Cronbach when he says that existing tests "aren't prepared to do much more than select kids for the kind of education schools offer."[24]•It is difficult too to argue with Richardson, Richards, and Spears when they say in conclusion that:

> We need two things—a description of intelligence and an adequate theory of its mode of development. Psychometrics is unable to investigate the nature of intelligence because it is concerned with the relative ranking of people on criteria derived from the values of a selective educational system. For this tradition intelligence is what the tests test and high intelligence is doing well at school. We cannot use this notion to examine the relationship between intelligence and education because it presupposes a particular connection between the two. It also cannot deal with cognitive diversity in a way which approaches reality because it uses one or a very small number of dimensions of evaluation. [Factor analysis] is irrelevant to the present argument because these factors are properties of the test-taking performance of groups . . . and not of individual children.

217

It may be true that a scientist learns little about a phenomenon unless he can measure or count it, but it is equally clear that there are many things that can be measured and counted without teaching us anything.[25]

It is, in sum, tempting to extend to the whole of IQ testing today the epitaph published in 1972 by Buros Mental Measurements Yearbook—the *Guide Michelin* of psychometrics—for the Stanford-Binet: "Its time is just about over. *Requiescat in pace.* [Rest in peace.]"[26]

Testing Tomorrow

In 1971 the U. S. Supreme Court enjoined a Virginia firm from giving IQ tests to potential janitors. In 1972 a U. S. District court in San Francisco ordered the county's schools to stop using IQ tests as the main criteria for admission to classes for the mentally retarded. The resulting 2-to-1 ratio of blacks over whites, black attorneys successfully argued, constituted a form of racial discrimination. In 1973 four northern California high school seniors asked the state legislature to investigate the cost and value of college entrance exams. That same year prestigious little Bowdoin College in Maine announced that it was pleased with its three-year-old policy of accepting homemade works of art and music with entrance applications in lieu of standardized test scores. Entering students not only felt "emancipated" by the option, Bowdoin reported, but those who exercised it generally got better grades in college than those who didn't.

Despite these isolated breezes of change, however, the testing movement is in no imminent danger of drying up and blowing away. Quite the contrary, at a time when more Americans have been to high school than had been to elementary school three decades ago, the business of testing is bigger and better than ever. Says the College Boards' S. A. Kendrick, "As I look at the prospects for higher education during the next decade or so, I think I see more testing rather than less."[27]

If testing is here to stay, as it appears, what new directions can intelligence testing take? What new methods are being investigated? What new directions should be explored? Supporters and critics of testing alike generally agree that the single-standard, single-scored test based on the concept of intelligence as a global, monolithic, independent entity is on its way out. They are less than unanimous on what should take its place.

As Robert Sears puts it,

> The direction we're heading is to break down general intelligence into components, musicality, ability to assimilate and use auditory input, receiving, recognizing and organizing visual symbols, and so forth. What we sample should not be a question merely of how good or how much, but *for what.*
>
> We'd like to know, for example, that of two kids who test exceptionally well on reading, one has a real bent for philosophic abstraction, the other for precise measurements of scientific function. We also want to know more about motivational characteristics. One kid does well with a pat on the head. Another is closed-in, does well with verbal praise but may not be obvious about it. Then there's what psychologists call locus of control. Is it external or internal? To what does the child attribute his failure or success, himself or outside circumstances? One says "I goofed, I wasn't prepared." The other says "The teacher doesn't like me, the test was too hard," or "I was lucky." These traits are vitally important to motivation.[28]

Lee Cronbach thinks both testing and teaching will have to be alive to these and other issues of personality, as well as be more prescriptive in nature.

> We're going to have to change educational methods so as to work with a person on his own terms. If we do we'll wind up with a very different concept of what the test is supposed to be doing. It's leaning away from prediction and toward prescription. By that I mean prescription of an education *method,* such as we've been using in remedial reading.[29]

Cronbach cites one study in which college psychology students were given a personality test to determine whether they achieved best through conformity or independence. Those whom the test characterized as conformist were then taught by highly organized, instructor-dominated techniques. Those whom it characterized as independent were given maximum latitude in teaching them-

219

selves. The results were dramatically positive for both groups.

Cattell, of course, feels that future measures of both crystallized and fluid intelligence will be necessary for the diagnostic and predictive values of each. While both can help us get at the causes of scholastic success or failure, neither in his opinion is as good as this year's grades in predicting future school performance. Only when a person's life "turns a corner" and he enters career or job training do crystallized and fluid abilities become predictive. Crystallized intelligence may remain steady or even climb, says Cattell, for it increases with age and experience. But fluid intelligence, he believes, falls soon after we enter adulthood, which is why old dogs don't learn new tricks, though they may already know more tricks than the young dog dreams of. Society needs not only to test both types of intelligence, he concludes, but also to refrain from confusing the two while it decides which, if either, it would be wiser to emphasize.

The answer to that is not as obvious as it might seem. The standardization of a crystallized test, Cattell explains, becomes unanchored the moment it is made, and drifts in whatever direction the tide of education happens to take because it is based primarily on what the sample group knows, which is always changing. For instance, a comparison of eleven-year-olds in an English city of 300,000 before the Second World War with eleven-year-olds there thirteen years later showed a definite upward shift on the British Binet—but no trace of a significant difference on a "culture-fair" test of fluid abilities. Similar culture-fair tests have demonstrated virtually no difference in fluid intelligence among Americans, British, Germans, French, Italians, and Taiwanese—although pronounced regional differences, says Cattell, have prompted him to suggest another social blockbuster: a world map of intelligence.

In one sense, then, fluid intelligence is more stable than crystallized. But in another it isn't. Cattell's research indicates that daily changes in fluid capability based on fluctuations in normal physiological efficiency do occur: "Our subjective conviction that we are brighter on some days than we are on others is borne out. . . ." To that variability must be added a simple but complicating fact. Broadly speaking, fluid intelligence, uninvested as it is in the culture, tells us little about the individual's ability at the moment of measurement to cope with the world around him. It is purely a potential, in Cattell's eyes, and must be invested in culture before its pragmatic life value can be assessed. For those reasons, Cattell thinks, any social policy decision to favor one kind of intelligence test at the expense of the other must confront the inescapable conclusion that "the dual IQ becomes indispensable almost anywhere when testing adults."[30]

Another school typified by McVicker Hunt and David McClelland would abandon the omnibus test altogether for *criterion sampling*, or a point-by-point checklist of the various kinds and degrees of competence demanded by specific situations. They differ, however, in their focus. Hunt would apply this to growing up, McClelland to holding down a specific job. To Hunt, a childhood checklist based on sequential stages of intellectual growth, like Piaget's, has enormous appeal. Since most developmental changes Piaget observed are far more stable and dependable than those indicated by the IQ, Hunt would hitch the meaning of performance to the graduated scale rather than rely on comparisons between children. Thus a child's intelligence would be gauged by how far up Piaget's fixed ladder he could climb, regardless of his age.

Two such Piagetian test batteries are now in the works, one by Adrian Pinard at the University of Montreal, the other by University of California psychologist Read Tuddenham. Pinard's has the dual advantage of requiring the child both to point out the answers to nonverbal questions and explain all his solutions. He thereby avoids on the one hand left-hemisphere processing of right-hemisphere problems, and on the other emphasizes and differentiates the quality of a child's reasoning. As Pinard and writer Evelyn Sharp explain, "a child who says that a nail sinks to the bottom of a tank of water 'because it's tired' is obviously in a different stage of mental development from one who says that the nail sinks 'because it is made of iron.'

"Neither explanation is correct, of course, but to equate the two is decidedly unfair."[31]

Pinard has barely scratched the surface in converting Piaget's three decades of experiments to useful test questions, a herculean task that has occupied Tuddenham for over ten years. Although the latter's efforts have paid off in a much broader and more complete array of items, his test suffers from the hemispheric limitations Pinard has avoided, as well as from Tuddenham's own theoretical reservations. An "unchastened differential psychologist" despite a year's study at Piaget's side, Tuddenham remains concerned about the Swiss psychologist's lack of interest in human variability at any age as anything more than minor variations on a more important (for psychology) lifelong theme. He wonders too, paradoxically, if Piaget's method of tailoring a dialogue to a particular child doesn't lose as much in the general sense as it gains in the particular.

What's missing from the Piagetian approach, adds McVicker Hunt, is solid knowledge about what kinds of experience the child needs to climb from one rung of the developmental ladder to another. He suggests criterion sampling should be based on whatever prerequisites in understanding, motivation, and information-processing a child must have to handle a given learning situation. Unfortunately, Hunt fears, the necessary skills on the part of those best equipped to determine such prerequisites—teachers—have been reduced to an intuitive art by the very dearth of systematic information.

David McClelland, for his part, would extend criterion sampling into an area of human intelligence where a detailed knowledge of prerequisites frequently does exist: adult performance in real-life skills. Just as Thurstone looked up from his PMA's to observe that if you wanted to hire an egg-candler you should see how good he is at spotting bad eggs, McClelland likes to point out that if you want to know how well a person can drive a car, give him a driver's test. Testing theorists, he declares

> have got to get out of their offices where they play endless word and paper-and-pencil games and into the field where they actually analyze performance into its components. . . . It requires real sophistication . . . . If someone wants to know who will make a good teacher, they [sic] will have to get videotapes of classrooms . . . and find out how the behaviors of good and poor teachers differ. To pick future businessmen, research scientists, political leaders . . . they will have to make careful behavioral analyses of these outcomes and then find ways of sampling the adaptive behavior in advance.[32]

McClelland's tests would be designed to reflect openly, faithfully, and completely all that was learned. In place of a stability that too often means the test is "simply insensitive to important changes," McClelland would put measures "valid in the sense that scores on them change as the person grows in experience, wisdom and ability. . . ."[33] He freely concedes the dangers of the same excessive fragmentation that struck the "atomic" theorists of intelligence; of ending up with thousands of specific tests for dozens of different occupations; of diluting their overall meaning to meaninglessness. But he is satisfied that a common thread of competencies runs through the fabric of any intelligent behavior, a skein that includes but is not restricted to *communication skills* ("by word, look or gesture"), *patience* ("easily measurable . . . relatively stable over time and can be taught directly") *ego strength* (". . . develops with age and to a higher level in some people than others") and, curiously, *moderate goal setting* (". . . distinctly preferable to setting goals either too high or too low, which leads more often to failure").[34]

Such tests too should involve what McClelland calls *operant* as well as *respondent* behavior.

> One of the greatest weaknesses of nearly all existing tests is that they structure the situation in advance and demand a response of a certain kind. . . . But life outside of tests seldom presents the individual with such clearly defined alternatives . . . life is much more apt to be characterized by operant responses in the sense that the individual spontaneously makes a response in the absence of a very clearly defined stimulus. . . . To use a crude example, a psychologist might assess individual differences in the *capacity* to drink beer, but if he used this measure to predict actual beer consumption over time, the chances are that the relationship would be very low. How much beer a person can drink is not related closely to how much beer he does drink.[35]

By their nature, of course, operant tests tend to stress divergent thinking. However, most tests of divergent thinking that do exist put an unnatural premium on the sheer multiplicity of answers without either rewarding the best or penalizing the worst. Needed are more measures like the airlines scheduling test that McClelland and an associate invented, a thorny slice of simulated life that confronts you with problems in getting from one city to another with a minimum of time, energy, money, and inconvenience. As in real life, several workable possibilities can be devised, but one is the most efficient.

Needed too, McClelland thinks, are measures of operant thought with a high order of "behavioral abstraction" expressed in a wide range of behaviors which factor analysis would probably not show related at all. For instance, the need for personal power, McClelland's experiments have shown, is released through such diverse and apparently unconnected outlets as drinking, gambling, accumulating status symbols, and harboring stifled aggressive impulses. A test that taps the strength of this need and the individual's means of venting it, McClelland suggests, will better predict how he will do in the real world than all the word games of traditional IQ.

By and large though, these new avenues of testing all perpetuate, one way or another, the supremacy of the brain's left hemisphere at the expense of the right. Processing by paper and pencil continues to dominate. Right-hemisphere solutions to nonverbal problems still must be talked about analytically. A balanced evaluation of the brain as an intelligent whole may only be possible if these methods are coupled to those that can test the right hemisphere separately, such as Shepard's imagistic paper-folding—or even Galton's long-forgotten visualization of the breakfast table. In psychology, such adaptive transitions from the experimental to the clinical are not exceptional but typical, as illustrated by how the WISC performance scales grew out of earlier block tests for the deaf and dumb. Even at that, some of the right hemisphere's more specialized abilities seem destined forever to defy simple, accurate, and quick evaluation. Music and art have resisted meaningful quantification for half a century. Nothing appears to work better than simply to give a child a pot of paints or a second-hand violin, sit back, and wait.

Despite or because of these drawbacks and complexities, some researchers persist in pursuing that Holy Grail of the testing movement, an infallible neurological indicator of intelligence untouched by human hands, fates, or prejudices. The latest such discovery of any impact is the Neural Efficiency Analyzer developed by John Ertl, of Ottawa's Center for Cybernetic Studies. (Ertl devised it after he scored an ignominious 77 on a conventional IQ test while getting his PhD in psychology.) It utilizes one of the Drys' best friends, the visually evoked cortical potential, to measure the speed with which information is transmitted to the brain. The time it takes a flash of light to register as a change on the EEG—a variable called "latency"—he reasonably interprets as an index of the brain's information-processing efficiency. A hundred flashes are delivered, the total elapsed time in latencies added up, and an average struck in milliseconds. The lower the average response time, the more efficient the brain—and, claims Ertl, the more intelligent.

Ertl admits the evidence for such a claim is largely medical, basically the inference that can be drawn from the fact that drugs and chemicals known to reduce mental sharpness also depress latency (as they do simple reaction times). He concedes too that speed is only one index, and probably a lesser one, than intellectual power—the slow but profound rumination—which his machine cannot measure.

His many critics are as annoyed by his rush to incorporate and merchandise as they are by what they consider to be the hasty premise behind it. Although several of them have found an intriguing correlation between latency scores and tested IQ—without producing anything like Ertl's star scorer, a belly dancer who speaks ten languages and has a master's degree in political science as well as a reported conventional IQ of 186—they believe the connection's meaning is still far from clear. Recent studies indicate latency times can be influenced by additional variables such as the subject's state of arousal (as can, for that matter, his intelligence). Curiously, the more relaxed a subject is, the less attentive, the higher the apparent relationship to IQ. "It's a neat gadget," confirms one pioneer in the field of cortical potentials, "but it's not yet time to turn it over to the school teachers."[36]

Ay, there is the enduring rub. Who is to say which if any of these new approaches to intelligence testing or its substitutes should be tried on a major scale? Who is to say, the people or the professionals, Its time has come? Eysenck writes,

Much of [the] failure to use these more advanced and power-ful measures of testing lies in the conservatism of teachers and

225

others who were brought up on the traditional IQ test, and in part the reason lies in the fact that the development of such measuring devices is expensive and requires considerable research spread over many years. Society has not shown itself particularly concerned. . . .[37]

Nor, for that matter, McClelland would add, have the test-makers. In an extraordinary Daniel-in-the-Lions'-Den speech two years ago at the Educational Testing Service—a $25,000,000 operation that has 3,000 employees and occupies a three-acre campus in Princeton, New Jersey, but markets no IQ test—McClelland put the challenge squarely in their laps. Only by dropping the term "intelligence" from its vocabulary and embracing a broad profile of achievements that included ego and moral development as well as scholastic competencies, he declared, would the industry of testing "turn from the sentencing procedure it now is into the genuine service it purports to be."[38]

He said he saw almost no chance of that. "I have been arguing for this approach for over twenty years," he told his audience, "and as far as I can see, the testing movement has been affected little by my eloquence."[39]

Part III
INTELLIGENCE AND SOCIETY

Sinners Can Repent
But Stupid Is Forever.
—Sign on a principal's desk

Chapter 9

Nature, Nurture, and Jensen

Intelligence, like every characteristic that makes us each uniquely human, is determined by both our genes and environment. The exact genetic contribution to any and all our traits is complex beyond man's wildest imaginings. Experimental pathologist David Kohne calculates that if we could pass gene pairs under an electron microscope at the rate of one per second, it would take 200 years to identify all the sequences of DNA in one person. As it is, our technology is such that we would be lucky to process ten pairs a day, which means that at the going rate it would take us 100,000 years to decipher any individual's 100,000-gene legacy from the estimated 5,000,000 to 10,000,000 genes that comprise the whole of human heritage. According to geneticist Walter Bodmer, moreover, the number of genetically different sperm or eggs any one human being could in principle produce is many million times the number of people that have ever lived. The myriad influences of the myriad environments existing on our planet, if less quantifiable, are scarcely simpler to sort out, even assuming they could somehow be separated meaningfully from the genes that flourish at their interface like cultured cells on a dish of jellied agar. Asking which of the two is more important when nature in her wisdom unites them, environment or heredity, notes Donald Hebb, is like asking "which contributes more to the area of the field—its length or its breadth?"[1]

Despite its endless complexity, however, heredity no less than environment can be intelligently manipulated to socially desired ends. Thoroughbred horses, blue-ribbon beef, pedigreed pups and prizewinning hybrid tomatoes are proof of that. And yet, possibly because human genetic engineering with its Orwellian over-

228

tones of totalitarian tinkering is so odious, possibly because environmental variables seem so visibly amenable to powerful change with or without our help every day, man's nurture, not his nature, has for generations been the dimension that draws our eyes and action. Alter environment, we had almost come to believe without reservation, and you could with patience and perseverance alter anything. Our genes of course were included. With rare exception, what could they do but fall smartly into line?

Nowhere were the pervasive effects of environment more evident than in one brutal and shameful fact of the American experience, with all its ugly ramifications: racial inequality. And nowhere did it seem that the skills of technocratic management could better be enlisted in the service of national remedy than there, as prescribed by two decades of social policy since the Supreme Court's historic desegregation decision. The income gap between blacks and whites, with all that entails, need not continue inexorably to widen. Black capitalism need not falter, the combined sales of its 100 largest companies be forever eclipsed by any one of half the nation's 500 largest white-controlled corporations. Fully a third of all black families in their rat-infested slums need not labor out their lives in unending poverty, despair, and futility. Action could and would be taken, something done. The environment talisman could be found, and quickly it was: education. Never mind that blacks scored on the average 15 to 20 points lower in IQ than whites. Even if the tests were valid, this was only a small part of the larger problem. It too could be fixed. After all, hadn't the same situation existed between Israeli children of European and Oriental Jews before their stimulating life together in a kibbutz nursery brought them *both* up to an IQ mean of 115, ten points above the European children's previous comparative high? The same thing could happen here. Equalize education. Throw the children of the races together in a healthy mental setting and all blessings would automatically follow: equal IQ, equal opportunity to achieve high socioeconomic status, the eventual acceptance of blacks into the American mainstream. The grand plan was breathtaking in both its simplicity and scope: Give them good, white, middle-class environments—first at school, then at home—and good, white, middle-class things would start to happen.

When they didn't, when the grades of black students fell and racial tensions in the classroom rose, when exasperated white teachers began to label refractory blacks "unteachable" and urban school systems such as Chicago's reported that youngsters of all races entered first grade with above-average potential, then sank below the national mean, a mood of confusion set in. Black "deficits" in education, that sanctioned passport to the promised equality of opportunity, were not responding to the solution of a shared academic environment. The mood of confusion turned to one of frustration when a massive federal study by sociologist James Coleman found that black and white schools which remained segregated were surprisingly not all that different in physical facilities, teacher caliber, and formal instruction. Coleman detonated an even bigger bombshell. Not only was the black scholastic environment virtually the same, nothing in it appeared to affect IQ performance in the least.

Maybe, then, government planners decided, black deficits were not deficits at all, but differences; differences in ways of thinking which IQ tests, admittedly standardized on the white middle class, simply failed to detect. The federal emphasis changed. If black children were going to break from the starting block with an even chance in the race for the best of life, they were going to have to make up for lost time. They were going to have to be equipped with rudiments of the mental skills the larger society valued *before* school. Enter now project Head Start, which in its first eight years would spend two and a half billion dollars in quest of such a goal. And now the frustration turned to anger on both sides. For the gains soon faded like the winter snows or were pitifully small to be so exorbitantly expensive. Whites grumbled that such "glorified baby-sitting" was becoming a bureaucratic boondoggle the likes of welfare. Blacks lashed back with charges of continued tokenism and warned of open warfare in the streets if the long-delayed democratic promise of American life was not at last fulfilled. In the dark of night liberals wondered and educators doubted. What was it going to take to undo three hundred years of slavery?

Then along came Arthur Jensen.

The works of Arthur Jensen have been described as everything from "winds gusting through the capitol at gale force"[2] to "aca-

230

demic manure"[3] spread by "the crown prince of pseudoscientific racism."[4] But the most telling description probably belongs to Thomas Sowell, a onetime economist at the Urban Institute in Washington. Sowell believes Jensen is "easily the most controversial intellectual figure of our time, perhaps the most controversial intellectual since such nineteenth-century giants as Darwin and Marx." He calls Jensen's papers "a thoroughly professional job and clearly a contribution" even as he adds a stunningly visionary afterthought:

"It will [sic] not be the first time that the development of a whole field has been advanced by the work of someone whose own theories ultimately proved to be wrong."[5]

What makes his assessment especially worth noting is the fact that Sowell is both an environmentalist on the issue and a black man. Furthermore, he is one of the few on record of either his race or persuasion, perhaps the only one of both, to find anything redeeming in the thoughts of a scholar who—until he trained his sights on the fulminous question of racial differences in IQ—had not once been criticized for shooting from the hip in a quietly impressive career as an educational psychologist.

By now almost everyone who reads a magazine or skims a newspaper knows that Arthur Jensen is the University of California (Berkeley) professor who dared speak the unspeakable: that underprivileged blacks might have failed the nation's best remedial efforts because they were genetically inferior to whites in higher intelligence. In the mild, scholarly, and circumspect language of social science, Jensen used 123 pages of the winter, 1969, *Harvard Educational Review* to trace out his closely reasoned argument that "compensatory education has been tried, and apparently it has failed."[6] Two-thirds through an otherwise didactic dissertation on the relative roles of heredity and environment in shaping human intellect, Jensen sedately opened fire on one of the most cherished bastions of American social policy. After a sketch of the evidence, he concluded with a skeptical review of existing interventional programs and some sound suggestions for taking new directions to satisfy the thrust of his paper's title, *How Much Can We Boost IQ and Scholastic Achievement?*

But by then almost no one was listening. Goaded by a sharp news sense, hounded by approaching deadlines, reporters had long since fled to their typewriters. There, confronted by the prolix style of the professional scholar—once characterized as "never taking a step without leaving a footnote"—they did what they were trained to do. They distilled and reduced its meticulously qualified central point to Sunday supplement simplicity. Jensen had taken pains to point out that just as American Indians scored higher on average IQ than blacks despite lower socioeconomic standards, U. S.-born Orientals scored higher than whites whatever their SES. In the media's pell-mell rush to print, however, such distinctions were lost. Thus was "jensenism" born.[7] At its best it was a hack hereditarian stance a basement below the elevated reaches of Jensen's germinal argument. At its worst it was the racist's wet dream, a "scientifically approved" back-of-the-hand to black aspirations.

All but overnight Jensen became a "notorious white supremacist,"[8] about as popular among American minorities, campus radicals, and civil libertarians as Adolf Hitler, to whom he was openly compared. Students for a Democratic Society crashed his classes, heckled his lectures, and shut down with nonstop clapping his attempts to give invited speeches elsewhere. Demonstrators at a national convention of education researchers charged the rostrum, ripped up his speech, and hurled it in his face. He was barraged with hate mail, bomb threats, vile sloganeering, and such virulent vituperation on the telephone that the university finally assigned him bodyguards. Despite their zeal, few of those who questioned him showed any signs of having read his paper.

Jensen also had problems with those who might have been expected to read him through, his colleagues. The Society for the Psychological Study of Social Issues, an arm of the American Psychological Association, called his views unwarranted and declared the nature-nurture question unanswerable until social conditions for all races were equal—a Utopian sentiment, one observer noted, that would set back all research on the subject a hundred years. One prominent psychologist publicly accused Jensen of fifty-three major errors or misinterpretations, all of them, suspiciously, antiblack. When challenged to produce his substantiation, it took two years and a request from the APA Committee on Ethical Standards for him to comply. Jensen promptly rebutted all points but one, that arising from a typographical error long since corrected. Another member sent out a blank for the membership to use in expressing itself on the issue multiple-choice fashion. Shot back Jensen, "Since when can empirical questions be answered by a show of hands?"[9]

True, as one of his critics would later remark, "that article was being cited in court cases, in Congress, by members of the Nixon administration, by others who were attempting to turn back programs of school integration and educational improvement for blacks and other minorities."[10] Public debate was therefore essential. But why should its level have been, in the words Berkeley philosophy professor Michael Scriven employed to describe campus reaction everywhere, so "truly appalling"?[11] The answer, Thomas Sowell feels, lay in the fact that Jensen touched "an even rawer nerve" than race because his view "runs counter to a central assumption of the prevailing social philosophy of Western intellectuals for at least the past two centuries," namely, "Locke's faith that each person enters the world as a blank page on which society writes what it will."[12] Jensen's work, Sowell concluded, had undermined the whole hidden structure, reducing many to what William Havender calls "fibrillating impotence."[13]

Today, though all but out of the public eye at last, neither Jensen nor his theory show any sign of disappearing from educational psychology. Indeed, like the scholar he is, Jensen continues to shore up his embattled position. Whatever the engine that drives him, a thirst for new knowledge or the quite human hunger for honest vindication (or both), the spectral shade of his supposed findings continues to haunt us. It haunts us through Congressionally struck-down busing laws, through racial beatings in school-segregated Boston, through bus bombings and burnings in Denver and Michigan. For our own survival as a nation if nothing else, his ideas must finally be understood, once and for all—as much for what they don't say as for what they do, where they may be right as well as where they may be wrong (for nothing about human differences, in the end, is sure). Only then can we intelligently consider what can be done to remedy the ravaging situation in which we find ourselves.

In essence what is Jensen telling us? Here, stripped to its bare bones, is his thinking.

From the genetic standpoint [he begins] races are breeding

233

populations which are relatively isolated from one another by geography, environment, and culture. Indeed, races are themselves classifications based on degrees of similarity and difference in human structure, blood composition, and biochemistry brought about by the presence or absence—in gross terms, frequency—of certain genes. The isolation of these populations from one another over many generations causes such inevitable differences to accumulate in "gene pools," the racial reservoirs of inheritance. These differences are in turn physically expressed through their members in dozens of different ways both extensive and profound.

What, specifically, are the genetic processes involved in creating these racial differences? There are several, but only one process appears the likely evolutionary mechanism for such polygenetic traits, those like height and weight, which are believed determined by large numbers of genes working in concert (probably no less than twenty, no more than 100). That process is natural selection—plagues, famines, wars, mass migration, or the generation-by-generation choice of one kind of mate by another. Here, all the genes which together shape the polygenetic trait are selected simultaneously. What happens then is both technical and complex, but detectable in any genetic analysis of the trait itself. If certain criteria are met (in the severity of the selection pressure, in the heritability of the trait) these genes combine and recombine in successive generations to give a directional thrust to the quality in question.

How do we know that this applies to intelligence? Unlike manifest physical differences, we infer intelligence from behavior. The biological basis of behavioral differences observed between the races remains much more in dispute, although the infant science of ethology (the comparative study of animals and their behavior, preferably in their native habitat) strongly suggests that man's behavior is equally subject to evolutionary change. Since humans have never been bred like prize cattle—outside Hitler's Aryan youth movement, anyway—the bulk of the evidence for intelligence being a polygenetically conditioned trait is necessarily statistical, the conclusions stemming from it both probabilistic and subjective. But these converging lines of evidence, and the weight they lend to the heredity hypothesis when integrated into the polygenetic model [Jensen believes] are both resistant, and superior, to any and all of the ad hoc environmental criticism levied against them.

To begin with, based on genetic analysis of the thought pattern implicit in any individual's test scores, whatever ability IQ measures has the same telltale genetic "architecture" as height. So that ability satisfies the requirements of a polygenetic trait shaped and differentiated by the evolutionary mechanism of natural selection. Both traits, moreover, follow the characteristic bell curve of normal distribution when plotted from census figures for height on the one hand and large samples of standardized test scores on the other—as any such trait should do.

But if intelligence is a polygenetic trait, what kind of natural selection operates to create black-white differences?

In the last few million years the strongest selection pressure in man has been for behavioral traits of increasing intellectual complexity: comparing, analyzing, separating, grasping relationships, classifying, counting, abstracting, conceptualizing, recalling, imagining, and planning. As ethologist Konrad Lorenz points out, and Harry Jerison would surely echo, these mental manipulations must come about from environmental demands acting directly and selectively upon the rich range of behaviors made possible by the increasingly complex nervous functions of our developing cerebrum. Obviously, tilling the soil and inventing new tools would make more of the demand Lorenz had in mind than hunting wild animals and fighting hostile tribes [Jensen thinks]. Other related factors would conspire to intensify that initial advantage. Hunter-warrior societies traditionally travel light in nomadic pursuit of their needs. As a consequence their populations historically tend to be smaller. Farming societies, in contrast, stay in one place, barring crisis, because they can grow what they need, including larger populations. The larger the population, the more the exceptional individuals most likely to make new discoveries, perfect new skills, and innovate the old. Each new invention, furthermore, divides the population into those who can master its use and those who cannot—and tends to select reproductively in favor of those who can.

Though minuscule in its original expression, that favoritism if translated into repeated reproductive preference can increase one gene's frequency a hundredfold in a thousand generations. (The separation of blacks from whites is technically fixed at 2,000 generations.) Under such circumstances the smaller primitive societies could hardly be expected to keep pace with the larger agricultural societies in magnifying the selection forces that propagate the polygenes responsible for higher cognitive abilities. Indeed, that "genetic gap" would be both ongoing and cumulative in its effect—until or unless the primitive society takes the necessary steps to start closing it. Even then, races differ by thousands of critical years in the time since they abandoned hunting and gathering, with many clear-cut gradations as a result in their adaptation to higher forms of civilization. The degree to which they manifest various accepted criteria of intellectual advancement (complexity of language, etc.) rank-orders them much as do standardized IQ tests when applied to representative members of their race reared under similar conditions of civilized life. In sum, as a direct consequence of such cultural lag-time, the lesser of them simply haven't as rich a gene pool for higher intelligence.

Granted, then, that intelligence is a polygenetic trait differentially conditioned in the races through natural selection. But heredity, as we know, is not the whole story. Environment plays a crucial part in its expression. How crucial is the crux. In quantitative terms, if quantitative terms are possible, how much of the difference in any race's tested intelligence on the average can be accounted for by environmental factors?

According to a large number of studies based on quantitative genetics, in the intelligence of the average individual the proportion of the difference due to genes is at least twice that due to environment, and probably more. The similarity of any two individuals' test scores, in fact, can be shown to increase with the closeness of their kinship, from unrelated persons at one end of the scale to identical twins at the other. Broadly put, this is what we mean when we speak of a trait's heritability.

But how do we know the same heritability applies to differences between races as well as individuals? We don't. We suspect this to be true because both differences, race and individual, are quantitative, not qualitative. In other words the relevant genes for intelligence are the same ones in all populations. It is their number, their frequency, that differs.

Even so, how do we know that the relative heritability for each race is the same? Again, strictly speaking, we don't, although the polygenetic theory gives us probabilities in the form of predictions that can be tested. One prediction that suggests the same heritability for both races is Galton's principle of regression to the mean. Children, remember it says, fall somewhere in IQ between their parents' and the population mean. In short, they climb or sink toward the average. If Galton is right, therefore, the IQ of a given child's sibling—its brother or sister—should be just about halfway between the given child's and the population mean. Since blacks on the average score 15 points below whites, if the polygenetic model is correct, the siblings of a white child and a black child perfectly matched for IQ would on the average have different IQs because each would regress toward its own racial mean.

This is exactly what happened, says Jensen, when he studied the scores of all the black and white siblings in the elementary schools of a racially mixed, medium-sized California community whose population was 40 percent black. Both sets of siblings regressed a constant fraction to their respective racial mean, not to the mean of the combined populations.

A knowledge of heritability drawn from the polygenetic model, moreover, places crucial constraints on the magnitude of the average IQ difference between races that can reasonably be accounted for by environmental factors alone (assuming the same heritability for both). Using the polygenetic model, only 6 to 8 points of the difference need be environmentally explained. But if no genetic difference in average IQ is assumed, and all of it is attributed hypothetically to average differences in environment between races, the environmental variance between families within either population would have to be radically different than it demonstrably is. To get such an average difference between races with curves drawn to represent each race's distribution of environmental factors, both curves would have to be pulled into such steep humps that they would bear little resemblance to the reality of the differences experienced by those families they stand for in the aggregate. One would almost have to assume within one country two ranges of environment so dramatically differing in their gradations as to defy belief.

What of that insidious something one research team labeled "malicious allocation,"[14] which Thomas Sowell attempts to capture when he writes that "being black in white America is something more than making a few thousand dollars less or averaging fewer years in school"?[15] Couldn't this intangible bridge the gap left when measurable differences in environment are accounted for?

Jensen thinks not. If such a uniform, consistent factor exists he finds no evidence that it has any effect on IQ. In fact, carefully reviewing the testing evidence, he finds little convincing support for environmental theories all along the line. The notion that average black IQ declines because of inequities in education or teacher treatment simply does not hold up. The full 15-point IQ gap is manifest as early as age five, when children enter school. A review of existing studies reveals the further jolting fact that the average IQ difference between black and white children of middle and upper-income families is even larger—20 points. Indeed, Jensen finds, the high SES black children actually score 2 points lower as a group on the average than low SES whites. The relative environments of the two populations, however matched, simply don't differ enough to explain such an invidious comparison.

As for test or examiner bias, in his own study of several types of tests administered to thousands of black and white children by examiners of both races, Jensen found no significant or systematic effects on the scores of either. Special tests devised to gauge attention, speed, persistence, and effort—all likely parameters of subtle unrest or intimidation in black performance—likewise revealed negligible differences. But Jensen reserves his most far-ranging psychometric critique to accusations that IQ tests themselves are racially slanted. He analyzed the relative performance of the two races at all ages from five to twelve on the widest possible range of tests (verbal, nonverbal, culturally loaded, Piagetian, etc.). For every type of test the pattern of performance was the same, which hardly could have been expected had bias been built in. Both profiles, one way or another, would have been skewed.

There was, however, one enormously significant difference. In all kinds of measures, blacks scored two years younger on the average than whites. Their identical performance profiles, when overlaid, were offset just enough from each other to account for the entire difference. To confirm this, Jensen divided his white sample into two different age groups that overlapped so as to simulate the average two-year difference he had found between blacks and whites. Then he compared the two profiles at every point. The fit was all but perfect. As a group blacks did not on the average perform qualitatively different than whites. The difference was purely quantitative. They simply performed at a different age level.

Nor did Jensen find any convincing evidence that malnutrition or the lack of meaningful mother-child relations during the preschool years figured significantly in the difference. If anything, black mothers when studied proved more likely than white to teach their young children in play. As for nutrition, there was no convincing evidence either way. It was true that expectant ghetto mothers given supplemental nutrients before birth produced children who scored on the average 5 to 8 points higher than children whose mothers had been given placebos. But both groups of children lost 3 points between ages three and four. Since the four-year-old test is the first to contain a g (or general intelligence) loading of any consequence, Jensen argues that the earlier gains evidently induced in the experimental group by supplemental nutrients may very well have been purely psychomotor. Otherwise, he asks, why weren't the gains sustained when the test emphasis shifted from measures of mostly neurological development to those of a more intellectual character? Furthermore, in a deficit study of poor slum families, their diets turned out to be above the recommended national standards. None of them, what's more, showed any of the physical or emotional symptoms normally associated with the extreme malnutrition caused by acute or chronic famines, such as in Biafra or some remote regions of the underdeveloped world. Their severity simply has no parallel in this country, says Jensen, not even among the Mississippi black children discovered eating clay as a dietary supplement a few years ago.

Admittedly, he concluded, much of his evidence was inferential. But in the absence of controlled laboratory breeding experiments, almost all evidence for the heritability of human differences is exactly that: inferential. After all, who would argue that the average difference in stature between Pygmies and Watusis is the result of differing environments? Lacking any compelling environmental theory to explain the black-white IQ gap, and given the fact that genetics is the more important determinant of IQ differences within any race, we would be scientifically amiss [Jensen said] not to seriously consider such a "reasonable hypothesis" a sound basis from which to launch objective research in quest of objective knowledge.

Of such mild stuff is Jensenism made.

Or is it really so mild?

"Anyone not familiar with the standard litany of academic disclaimers," says geneticist Richard Lewontin, referring to Jensen's original HER phrasing of the same conclusion, "will . . . find nothing to disagree with since it says nothing.

"But of course, like all cant, the special language of the social scientist needs to be translated into common English. What Jensen is saying is: 'It is pretty clear, although not absolutely proved, that most of the difference in IQ between blacks and whites is genetical.' "[16]

But is it that clear? And if it is, does that mean what we commonly think it does? Does uttering the awesomely final-sounding word "genetics" slam the door on a dead issue? Does it signify the gap is immutable, foreclose on all efforts we might make to remove it, relieve us of even the responsibility to try? We know this is the meaning of jensenism. But is it the meaning of Jensen?

From the beginning Jensen's thinking has been shot through with Pope's injunction: Do not understand me too quickly. For most of us there is little danger of that. Indeed, writes Thomas Sowell, "The one conclusion that is virtually inescapable from [reading Jensen] is that the whole area of environment and testing is an almost bottomless pit of complexities. It cannot be reduced to the level of Archie Bunker, who could never make it through one paragraph of Jensen's analysis."[17] But if Jensen has had six years to refine and articulate his theory, his more responsible and expert critics have had equal time to grasp it, concoct countertheories, and hone their criticisms to a cutting edge. And although the coals of contention are still heaped high and continue to glow with as much heat as light, the net result of what amounts to an unspoken public moratorium has been to shake down the pros and cons of this disquieting issue into something approaching their true perspective. What, then, do we find?

Outside the bounds of his polygenetic theory itself, there is virtually no proof that Jensen is wrong, and much evidence that he is right. As Harvard bacteriologist Bernard Davis told the National Academy of Sciences:

> . . . Every geneticist knows that when two populations . . . have been separated and exposed to different selective pressures for many generations, they inevitably accumulate many hereditary differences. Behavioral traits in man can hardly be an exception; and even though their genetic component cannot be dissected with precision from environmental influences it is undoubtedly substantial. Hence human races surely differ, to some degree, in the distribution of genetic potential. . . . Our educational system would surely become more effective if we could develop measurements of innate abilities. . . . It would indeed be tragic if studies were inhibited for fear that they might . . . demonstrate some degree of difference . . . [That] should be irrelevant in a society dedicated to providing every individual with the fullest opportunity for developing his capacities.[18]

In opposing Jensen's views with what it frankly calls "every tactic including disruption," argues Eysenck, SDS has given us a

> . . . real whiff of . . . "Left-Fascism" . . . [Efforts to explore the issue are] greeted with scorn by those who already [know] the answers. . . . Of course any putative differences are due to environmental factors. And, of course, anyone who dares to doubt these truths must be a racist, seduced by the establishment into utter intellectual prostitution. . . . And to be sure, if we *know* the truth . . . then the end justifies the means: burn books, boycott publishers and book-sellers, break up meetings,

241

threaten and persecute those who dare disagree with you. . . .
In my view it bodes evil for our society that these attitudes
should be found among students . . . among those who have
been selected specially for their intellectual ability, and who have
been trained . . . in the use of reason. . . . God help the next
generation![19]

Not all the evidence is on Jensen's side, of course, and not all
those who oppose his views have abandoned the voice of reason.
Room remains for honest doubt on several points, particularly in
regard to the validity of the IQ test as a global measure of human
intelligence. Black educators, psychologists, and civil rights
groups have enjoyed their greatest success in this area of discrimination, as we know. Compulsory IQ tests are now banned in
many states, including California, as well as in New York City. But
Jensen holds steadfastly to the position that IQ tests are "one of
the few technological products of psychology that actually
work."[20] As we have seen, a formidable army of his peers does not
agree. Whatever the test measures, they say, it has not been
proved to capture some broad and pervasive entity largely prede-
termined called intelligence. Both sides can muster considerable,
impressive, and conflicting evidence. But the issue, bitterly fought
along disputed borders with inconclusive weapons, remains a
Mexican standoff. If Jensen cannot prove himself unquestionably
right about the IQ's legitimacy, his enemies cannot prove Jensen,
an expert in the statistical limits of its uses, indisputably wrong.

So Jensen stands like a sturdy Viking at the pinnacle of converging lines of evidence, unacknowledged king of the mountain,
daring anyone and everyone to topple him off. Or does he? Can it
be we read him wrong? Let's look more closely at his polygenetic
theory, and at one aspect of his research, his own seminal discovery that has seldom seen the light of popular press. Is it barely
possible that the true impact of his argument is not what—or
where—it seems?

Jensen's grasp of genetics is recognized by his expert critics, although they would certainly hasten to add that heritability is open
to other interpretations. Bear in mind, at any rate, that his conclusions are both probabilistic and subjective, as he has always been

242

the first to point out. Neither Jensen nor any ethologist, it should be obvious, can prove that farming in ancient times took more brains than tracking game, although in the snug harbor of retrospect it may seem probable. More to the point, Jensen concedes at the outset that he cannot prove that heritability as he defines it is the same for both races. Nor does he try. He simply says that while heritability within races cannot establish heritability between races, if the former is high, that increases the likelihood of the latter. And so it does, though by how much no one can say. Thus, he reasons, if white heritability is 80 percent, in the absence of convincing environmental evidence to the contrary, it is probably the same for blacks. Therefore the average difference in IQ between the races can only be about 20 percent environmental.

Even this initial leap is more one of faith than facts. "The fact is," says intelligence researcher John Horn, Cattell's protégé, "that 100 percent of the variance in a trait *within* a group can be due to heredity when all the difference *between* groups is due to environment."[21]

But bear further in mind, Jensen's 80 percent heritability estimate for whites is just that, an estimate. It is based on a survey of studies which relied mainly, shades of Galton, on comparisons of IQ scores for identical twins reared apart. Since identical twins issue from the same egg and have the same genes, any difference in their mental performance once normal test error is discounted must be, by definition, entirely environmental. But identical twin studies have their problems. Most are based on relatively small and diverse samples for such giant generalization—a little over a thousand pairs in all—and Jensen's responsible critics are far from satisfied that the data are all that impeccable. Jensen does a smooth statistical job of meshing the different researchers working at different places in different times and using different investigative procedures. Still, the findings are not free from the suspicion of flaw. Some of the IQ's, for example, are based on unstandardized tests, others on the always-suspect judgment of teachers, and still others on the assessment of the researchers themselves, working with interviews not from the twins but from their parents. By their very nature, moreover, the study samples

243

are social accidents that lack the kind of careful experimental controls that might have thrown their environmental variables into bolder relief. As it is, certain ambiguities are subject to interpretations that yield diametrically opposed conclusions. In sum, though the data behave in Jensen's accomplished hands as if intelligence were a normally distributed polygenetic trait like height— even to jumping nimbly through the statistical hoop of regression to the mean—his critics cannot wholly escape the conviction that his point remains unproven. This is particularly so since there is nothing in genetic theory that requires even that a polygenetic trait have normal distribution, much less that it square conveniently with one known to be built into the testing process itself as a gratuitous if not unreasonable assumption. For that matter, they add, there is nothing that says the same environmental variable need affect any two individuals the same way or to the same degree, much less any two populations.

Finally, as for differences in gene frequencies between races, zoologist Jerry Hirsch calculates that the number of comparisons that could legitimately be made may approach a half million. And that, he stresses, is without varied selection pressures, and in the absence of mutations and recombinations occurring at different places and times and in different frequencies—all of which happen with the kind of unpredictable irregularity that drives the statistician up the wall.

In rebuttal, Jensen merely points to how the converging lines of evidence fit his model. Again, most of this evidence is from tests, which brings us once more back full circle to the IQ. Question that, and his whole edifice of probability buckles and quakes. But in the absence of anything else as solid, it stands.

Suppose, however, we grant him his thesis. Let us agree that Jensen's polygenetic theory is right. What happens then?

Contrary to what his less enlightened foes might fear, the world of educational psychology does not instantly collapse in a helpless heap. For as any geneticist knows, Jensen is saying less than it might seem. Heritability, however much it may contribute to the differences in average intelligence between races, is not a characteristic of traits but of populations. Geneticists would say it describes not intelligence itself but the proportion of the total genetic variance in intelligence that can be attributed to a specific population living within a given environment. In short, it is no airy abstraction that can be cut loose to rise and float free, but a concrete concept pragmatically grounded in the here and now. As such, heritability can never be divorced from its existing environment. In fact, as Jensen's theory extends ethology, heritability depends directly upon the dynamics of the environment to bring out the selection pressures that will eventually alter the critical gene frequencies for intelligence. Otherwise the intellects of both hunters and farmers could, broadly speaking, advance uniformly through the ages and their diverse environments.

Does this mean, then, that if Jensen is right, blacks will just have to wait another 2,000 generations—or given their 300-year apprenticeship to Western civilization, even a fraction of that—for full genetic redress? It does not, for a reason that Jensen himself openly recognizes but, in the opinion of some environmentalists, tends unjustifiably to downgrade. That reason is embodied in yet another factor of man's genetic equation, one they feel equal in importance to heritability. It is called *range of reaction.*

Range of reaction refers to the broadest possible expression of any individual's genetic constitution in collision, one could say, with the broadest possible manifestation of environments. As ethologist Niko Tinbergen puts it, "Living things do not move passively through the physical processes of the environment; they do something against it."[22] What a person inherits is his *genotype,* his genetic constitution. What it "does against" his environment, how it manifests itself, is his *phenotype.* His genotype is immutably fixed by his gene frequencies. We cannot see, hear, touch, taste, or feel it. We can only infer it from his phenotype. Because the range of possible environments his genotype might be called upon to react against is so vast—in theory, anyway—the genotype can have any one of a number of possible phenotypes. Phenotypes can of course differ greatly or little but differ they must, even in identical twins. If seen together, for instance, identical twins do not look absolutely identical. One may be taller or heavier, the other may have different posture or a faintly different caste to his facial fea-

245

tures. When they speak, moreover, they may reveal strikingly different personalities. For as Peter Lindsay and Donald Norman noted earlier, in processing information no two people, however similar their environments, receive identical inputs in identical order and use identical procedures to organize them. Much less do they evolve the same big picture of their experiential world. Unrelated people from unrelated environments, naturally, can be expected to differ even more.

The critical question then becomes—for Jensen's more qualified critics—how much can a specific environment influence for good or ill the *phenotypic expression* of any genotype? If Jensen's polygenetic model of intelligence is correct, how wide is the range of reaction?

Wide enough to more than account for the average 15-to-20-point IQ difference between blacks and whites, cry Jensen's qualified critics in near unison. McVicker Hunt, one of psychology's prime believers in the almost limitless plasticity of phenotypic intelligence, has compiled a cross-cultural study that makes exactly that point. He compared children from middle-class Massachusetts families and lower-class Illinois welfare families with children from Athenian orphanages and day-care centers believed to fairly represent the lower half of the Greek capital's socioeconomic structure. In short, as nearly as could be controlled, the study (an amalgam of three studies, really) compared the same phenotypic range in both cultures. Their relative performance on a Piagetian task, when translated into an IQ scale, indicated that the range of reaction for the two populations a half world apart differed by some 75 points.

Admittedly, the Piagetian task was basically one of the sensorimotor development underlying higher intelligence, rather than of higher intelligence itself. Too, the children were all under age five. But Hunt points out that another researcher, Wayne Dennis, found essentially the same thing when he gave an IQ test to samples of "typical" children ages six to nine living in fifty cultures around the world. So environments when compared across cultures do make a difference in phenotypic expression beyond anything that might have been expected from Jensen's interpretation of his own polygenetic model, Hunt would argue. Indeed, if the bulge due to genetic retardation were eliminated from the lower end of the normal distribution curve, the range of reaction would almost equal in effect that of heritability.

"Clearly," Hunt concludes, "there is dissonance between any argument based on statistics of heritability and [one based on] ranges of reaction."[23] For that reason he and his fellows feel Jensen has been too quick to dismiss Head Start and other compensatory programs as failures.

Jensen could justly claim, in return, that the methods of Hunt and Dennis are at least as open to question as his compilation of the troublesome twin data. But technicalities aside, he feels his opponents are claiming far too much for the range of reaction, especially on the basis of existing environments in this country. After all, he could rightly point out, this is where the issue must be decided, not in Greece or in half a hundred other spots across the globe where the relative range may be dramatically different. To compare them is to compare apples and oranges. As Jensen sees it, given a normal distribution of intelligence with 80 percent heritability—which both his model and the converging lines of evidence do—the range of reaction in the United States is about 30 points at best, from one end of the environmental scale to the other. In any case it is nowhere near 75.

Indeed, Jensen demonstrates that a 30-point range of reaction is sufficient to explain any of the more spectacular environmental successes in psychological literature, including psychologist Rick Heber's celebrated University of Wisconsin "Milwaukee Project." Heber and his staff gave a group of ghetto black children intensive, specialized one-to-one tutoring from birth to age two, and something approaching that from age two to five. Although their mothers had a mean IQ around 80—near-retarded—the children's IQ on the average soared some 20 to 30 points above a control group at the end of the preschool years. This, as both Jensen and Heber have pointed out, does not "refute" either Jensen or heritability as some environmentalists have claimed. Even assuming the same mean IQ of 80 for their fathers as for their mothers, Jensen notes, when the children's normal (upward) regression to the population mean is coupled with the 30-point range of reaction, the increase is adequately accounted for. In short, moving any genotype from one end of the environmental scale to the other will increase its phenotype that much.

Isn't this just another way of saying that environment can make the difference, that we have only to engineer it skillfully and the desired result will follow?

In theory, the range of reaction can be manipulated to eliminate the black-white IQ gap below and around the average by maximizing phenotypic expression of existing black genotypes, yes. But it cannot alter gene frequencies. Genotypes and phenotypes are not the same thing, consequently do not obey the same genetic laws, as we can readily see from the paradox that would occur should we find the means somehow to grant the radical environmentalist his most cherished dream: a universally optimized environment. If that happened, everyone's environment would by definition be equal. And genotypic differences would if anything produce a more profound difference between individuals in manifest IQ than we now have, muddied as it is by environmental variation. If Jensen is right, the same would be true of racial differences. Equalizing environments would intensify, not eliminate, the effects of heredity.

And yet Heber's success and the cross-cultural comparisons of Hunt and Dennis do tell us something useful and important. They tell us that totally new and different environments could in principle close the average IQ gap; could, if new and different enough, mean a brand new educational ballgame with exciting and different rules. For geneticists, Jensen, and his more knowledgeable critics all agree: Existing heritability in no way limits what might be achieved if children of any race or society were reared in more mentally stimulating environments than we now have.

But what do we do to create such effective and radically altered environments? How should they be new, in what way different? Exactly where can they be changed to make them more stimulating mentally?

As Jensen emphasizes, whether planned or accidental, environmental variables involve "many more or less random effects with unknown, unpredictable or (as yet) uncontrollable causes,"[24] which prompt the more conservative to adopt the geneticist's cau-

ENSEN

tionary habit of calling them "nongenetic factors" rather than environmental. After all, anything added to the genetic equation from outside the genes is in the strictest sense environmental. Included are every conceivable phenotypic influence from the womb on: prenatal nutrition, the flow of placental oxygen, physical ease of birth, etc. Probably less than half of the nongenetic factors that influence the phenotypic expression of human intelligence, Jensen estimates, are the direct result of such known and manipulable aspects of life after birth as family income, parent education, health care, and housing. Even the effects of those we have found difficult enough to influence favorably, as programs like Head Start lamentably prove. The problem is further confounded by the fact that what raises the phenotypic expression of one genotype, or of one genotype in one race, is not theoretically bound to do it in another. Perversely, it may actually lower it.

Thus Jensen is guilty of understatement, to put it mildly, when he observes that our knowledge of how the environment conditions IQ is far less complete or definite than most people recognize. McVicker Hunt states the case more succinctly: "It is one thing to say that most of the class and race differences now evident are not biologically inevitable . . . quite another to say that reducing the deficits . . . is easy."[25] According to psychologist Carl Bereiter, one of the world's leading innovators in teaching the disadvantaged, grappling with this challenge "may well be the major policy problem facing public education in our time."[26]

It is here, almost entirely without receiving either attention or credit for it, that Jensen first focused his fire, soon made an important discovery, and now offers sound advice that ironically—because of who he is—will probably continue to be ignored for all the wrong reasons. In fact, it was Jensen's early recognition of this need for diversity that led him to examine more deeply the black-white IQ difference in the first place. As he tells it, one of his graduate students first pulled him from his ivory tower with a question: Why did minority children in Berkeley's classes for the educably mentally retarded, most of them black, appear far brighter than white EMR's on the playground? Jensen went to look and saw that his student was right. Often the minority EMR's were "quite indistinguishable in every way" from children of normal

249

IQ, except in their scholastic performance and IQ scores.[27] Indeed, the middle-class white EMR's seemed more retarded all around.

Were the minority children victims of unfair testing, as would later be claimed? Jensen suspected they were. He decided to find out by devising a test of direct, on-the-spot learning free of the information and skills tapped by the traditional IQ, skills unequally taught across cultures, if critics were right, by a school system inculcated with white middle-class values. As Jensen freely confesses, at that time he "more or less equated"[28] learning ability with intelligence. Sure enough, he found, when tested on a host of practical cognitive acts—short-term retention of anything seen or heard, breadth of memory for such things in multiples, rote learning—black EMR children performed as well as white children of average IQ, some even as well as the white gifted. So did representative samples of all disadvantaged children, who generally scored 10 to 20 points lower than middle-class white children on standard IQ tests.

Initially Jensen thought he had hit upon "the first culture-fair tests that actually worked."[29] But as he probed further, he reports, he found that he was wrong. His direct-learning tests were tapping a valid mental ability, all right, an important one; one that could be made as demanding and difficult as he liked, one that required every bit as much of the child's attention and effort as any other kind of test. But although he found that ability to be an integral part of some subtests on the Stanford-Binet and Wechsler, it had nothing to do with Spearman's *g,* that general factor which to a greater or lesser degree permeates every kind of IQ test whether it be verbal or nonverbal, culturally loaded or culturally neuter.

That factor, Jensen at length concluded, involved something his direct learning tests didn't: the mental manipulation and transformation of inputs in order to arrive at a satisfactory output. This conceptual ability—including as it did discrimination, generalization, abstraction, classification, and judgment—he christened Level II intelligence. None of his minority EMR's, he went on to demonstrate, could score in the average range on any test having a substantial loading of it. Though low SES children, especially blacks, usually surprise by scoring slightly higher on verbal and more obviously culture-loaded items of IQ than expected, on heavily loaded Level II (or *g*) tests they did not. Nor did the otherwise disadvantaged children he tested on Level II exceed their IQ performance.

What, then, could be said of his direct-learning tests? They clearly got at something significant, which Jensen decided to call Level I, or *associative learning ability*, a quality characterized by reception, retention, and recall on cue with a minimum of mental manipulation or transformation.

If Jensen had been the racist his more rabid critics claim, he might have junked his findings right then and there and gone back to his ivory tower to root for more esoteric truffles. Or as others intemperately suggest, he might have held them up as proof positive that most blacks—or minorities or any low-IQ, low-SES child for that matter—were fit only to dig ditches, keep other people's houses, or be the unremitting file clerks of the world. Instead Jensen aimed his findings straight at the ossified heart of American education in a manner that Malcolm X himself would not have faulted. In fact, as Thomas Sowell says, ". . . Jensen's conclusions are almost indistinguishable from those of many liberal and radical critics. . . . Indeed some black 'militant' teaching programs rely on a nonabstract approach similar to what Jensen advocates."[30]

What Jensen wrote and published, in brief, was this:

> . . . if a child does not learn the school subject-matter when taught in a way that depends largely on being average or above average [on Level II] he does not learn at all, so that we find high school students who have failed to learn basic skills which they could easily have learned many years earlier by [other] means. . . . If a child cannot show that he "understands" the meaning of 1 plus 1 equals 2 in some abstract, verbal, cognitive sense, he is, in effect, not allowed to go on to learn 2 plus 2 equals 4. I am reasonably convinced that all the basic scholastic skills can be learned by children with normal Level I learning ability . . . educational researchers must discover and devise teaching methods that capitalize on existing abilities for the acquisition of those basic skills which students will need in order to get good jobs when they leave school. . . . One of the great and relatively untapped reservoirs of mental ability in the disadvan-

taged . . . is the basic ability to learn. . . . If diversity of mental abilities, as of most other human characteristics, is a basic fact of nature, as the evidence indicates, and if the ideal of universal education is to be successfully pursued . . . schools and society must provide a range and diversity . . . just as wide as the range of human abilities.

. . . The ideal of equality in educational opportunity should not be interpreted as uniformity of facilities, instructional techniques, and educational aims for all children. . . . The reality of individual differences thus need not mean educational rewards for some children and frustration and defeat for others.[31]

Where and when did Jensen say this? Some of his critics might be surprised to find it in the concluding paragraphs of his HER paper.

So Jensen early on, all but unnoticed by his detractors, joined the ranks of those discerning psychologists who realize that other races, different people, think differently in important ways that any effective system of education must take into account, IQ or no IQ. But again, how are we to build on these differences, rather than use them indiscriminately to tear each other down?

Before attempting to answer that, let's pause a moment to examine for clues what Jensen found. What do we know about the brain that might explain the phenomenon of Level I thought, an ability that Jensen's factor analysis found an entity in its own right, one he now believes controlled by a distinctly different set of polygenes than Level II? (As the term implies, he first thought one was erected on the other, an idea he has since all but abandoned.) It is the left hemisphere, of course, that manipulates and transforms symbolic input in the abstract, verbal, cognitive sense, that Jensen uses to define Level II. But can a case be made that the straight computerlike input-output of Level I is a right-hemisphere function? Remember, split-brain experiments have shown that the right hemisphere is *perceptive* (receptive) whereas the left hemisphere is *expressive* (linguistic.) The right hemisphere also has the stronger pattern-detecting capacity, and is more relational and associative in its thinking. Together with its ability to recognize and respond to rudimentary language, these attributes make it a likely candidate for Level I function, particularly in the absence of any need to perform complex abstract operations on the input.

Then too, a right-hemisphere locus might explain why the EMR and low-SES children who are black score better on Jensen's direct-learning tests than comparable whites. As he acknowledges, Level II (or *g*) is "only a part of the total spectrum"[32] of mental abilities, but the most strongly emphasized in white middle-class culture because it is so closely related to both scholastic performance and socioeconomic status. If Level II intellect is both polygenetically conditioned through natural selection and reinforced in its phenotypic expression by white middle-class values, as Jensen theorizes, why shouldn't the same dynamics be true of Level I in the black population? If a technological society trains and rewards the left hemisphere disproportionately in one population better fitted for it on the average, wouldn't another population historically excluded (for whatever reason) naturally compensate by developing the other hemisphere, at least in those areas open to it?

Although there is no hard evidence as yet one way or the other, this is what a cursory look at American society today suggests. All but shut out of the mainstream of Big Business and conventional left-hemisphere professions, blacks are overwhelmingly represented in commercial sports, and are on the ascendancy in such right-hemisphere fields of artistic endeavor as music and entertainment. According to a landmark twelve-year study by Ellis Torrance of over 200 pupils in the seventh through twelfth grades, creativity by any parameter he used shows no preference for race or socioeconomic status. Unlike IQ, creativity is and remains relentlessly linked to the right hemisphere. Clearly, then, the right hemisphere in all its manifestations, Jensen's Level I among them or not, offers the most promising avenue for fresh and innovative educational research.

But getting back to the challenge of creating radically new environments to optimize the effects of such innovation, what makes the vital difference between those which have succeeded and those which have failed? What does the Milwaukee Project apparently have that Head Start did not? Can we isolate the germ of its success? Or must it remain tantalizingly out of our reach, one of

Jensen's elusive nongenetic factors destined forever to defy our detection, prediction, comprehension, and control?

At this point we can only guess. For unless Heber and his staff are holding something back, the basic content of their enrichment program differs little from all those that have come and gone with such high hopes and meager lasting success. But one difference does stand out above all others, shining like a beacon in the darkness of modern education: the almost incessant attention paid to all the target children most of their waking hours since birth. Only once before have the annals of psychology recorded anything like such a massively sustained investment of tutorial time and energy with—significantly concomitant—such a dramatic payoff. Thirteen orphaned infants in Iowa, committed through a chain of circumstance to the doting care of institutionalized retarded women who played with them constantly, gained 7 to 58 points in IQ. Only once since has Heber's seeming success been repeated, this time in a slightly different but equally important context: by a remarkably single-minded family which deserted the bustle of English urban life to create above a bleak Welsh mining town the revolutionary learning environment they could find nowhere else. As chronicled by Michael Deakin in a marvelous little book called *The Children On The Hill,* a Jewish schoolteacher from London and his Montessori-trained Italian wife reared prizewinning prodigals in music and math as well as two other creative and imaginative preschool children strictly on their own, with no help from anyone. How did they do it? They did it by surrounding their children with a loving environment free of tension, guilt, and aggression; one full of toys and simple learning aids, often of their own invention, designed to draw out and develop interests as they appeared rather than train abilities traditionally presumed latent.

For those familiar with the Montessori system, there is nothing unusual about this. What was extraordinary was the parents' absolute dedication to the intellectual and psychological needs of their children. Both mother and father, when he was home from his teaching, allowed nothing to interfere with their presence and availability from morning to night. Work around the house as well as their own adult needs were postponed until the children went to bed. They were always and ever totally attentive.

Perhaps this, then, was their secret, and Heber's. As Willie Loman's distraught wife, Linda, cries from the heart to save her life-defeated husband in Arthur Miller's *Death of a Salesman,* "Attention must be paid."[33] If it is, all the money in the world may turn out to be secondary.

Chapter 10

The Intelligent Woman

From early childhood òn, that towering nineteenth-century genius Francis Galton had, as his unremitting tutor and Merlin-in-residence, his sister Adele. Adele was only a few years older and taught him letters as they played; he could point to them all before he could speak. He knew his capitals by the age of one and both his alphabets a half year later. He could read a little book, *Cobwebs to Catch Flies,* when he was two and a half, and could sign his name before he was three. By five he could recite much of Sir Walter Scott's epic 6,000-line poem *Marmion,* and understood it all. "Adele had a wonderful power of teaching and gaining attention without fatiguing," Lewis Terman would write much later. "She taught herself Latin and Greek that she might teach him. She never had him learn by heart, but made him read his lesson, bit by bit, eight times over, when he could say it."[1]

On the day before his fifth birthday, the father-to-be of modern IQ testing wrote the following letter to his sister:

> MY DEAR ADELE,
> I am 4 years old and I can read any English book. I can say all the Latin substantives and adjectives and active verbs besides 52 lines of Latin poetry. I can cast up any sum in addition and can multiply by 2, 3, 4, 5, 6, 7, 8, [9], 10, [11].
> I can also say the pence table. I read French a little and I know the clock.[2]
>
> FRANCIS GALTON

"The only misspelling is the date," the pedant in Terman observed. "The numbers 9 and 11 are bracketed . . . because little Francis, evidently feeling that he had claimed too much, had scratched out one of the numbers with a knife and pasted some paper over the other." By six, under Adele's tutelage, Galton had become thoroughly conversant with *The Iliad* and *The Odyssey*. It seems that Adele also taught Francis a good deal about entomology, and at seven he was knowledgeably collecting both insects and minerals—presumably guided, if not pushed, by her fair hand. But in the long retrospect of history a nagging question persists. As Frank Barron puckishly notes, "these are fascinating facts about young Francis Galton, and certainly we should not be surprised to learn that so brilliant and so favored a youngster became illustrious. But we might wonder, Whatever became of Adele. . . ?"[3]

Adele, alas, vanished forever into the sedate drawing rooms of Victorian London, the earliest victim of her bachelor brother's massive and lifelong gift for myopic self-congratulation. She was not the only woman teacher to have been conveniently forgotten by her most famous male pupil, and by no means the first female whose intelligence was used to further some masculine career, then absorbed into the fabric of man-dominated society without so much as a murmur. With rare exceptions, moreover, women still lack the unquestioned opportunity to exercise their judgment in all phases of the nation's intellectual life with anything approaching the role reserved as a matter of course for men. Not surprisingly, the Carnegie Commission on Higher Education has found that the largest undeveloped reservoir of intelligence in the United States belongs to that clear majority of Americans who are women. Although about half the country's high school graduates are female, reports the commission, the percentage of women in higher education declines progressively the higher up the ladder of academic achievement you go. Only about a third of those with master's and doctor's degrees are women. Only a quarter of college faculty members are women. Only one full professor in ten is a woman. (For that matter, only two of the Carnegie Commission's illustrious nineteen-member board of blue-ribbon experts were not men.)

To be sure, the current resurgence of feminism both inside the Women's Liberation Movement and out is making itself increasingly felt on all fronts—those directly linked to intelligence and those that only subtly reflect the implied inferiority, mental or otherwise, of women. But even the most ardent feminist would agree that in most instances such power and progress have been more apparent than real. More directly to the point of intelligence, University of California psychologist Ravenna Helson took an imaginary look from the "observation platform" atop her own "ivory tower" in Berkeley and saw not a campus in revolutionary ferment but a peaceful community of patriarchal and matriarchal subcultures whose composition was virtually unchanged by the turbulent sixties:

> To the north, there is the law building. Of every ten students going in or out of the door, nine are men. Nearby is the physics building, where the same is the case, and so it is also in engineering, geology, forestry, agriculture, business, the medical school. On the other hand, if we look to the south we see that three of every four students going into the library science building are women, and the same is true of elementary education and home economics. If we put a dime into the telescope on the observation platform and look into these various buildings, we see that many of the buildings to the north have expensive equipment, and that the textbooks and blackboards are full of mathematical equations. The buildings to the south have little mathematics and little expensive equipment, but they do have a door that says "Women" on every floor.[4]

There is something unspoken beneath all this; a hint of why fully half the world's people should be routinely oppressed by the other half. Perhaps it is expressed by the Russian proverb that says, "It is what woman doesn't know that adorns her." But, we must blush to ask, is it really? The question would be ludicrous were it not for the fact that most men still seem to believe—and women to behave as if—a younger Clare Boothe Luce tamed an eternal truth a generation ago when she advised the woman alone to dress like a girl, act like a lady, think like a man, and work like a horse if she wished to survive. All too often in our society, thinking like a man still appears to be woman's sole passport to the executive boardroom (if not bedroom). Thinking like a woman is still best left to housewives who have nothing better to do; or on

258

those rare occasions when men must turn the tables mentally for their own benefit, reserved to swift flights of brainstorming in the cosmetic, fashion, and soapflake industries.

So circumstances justify our asking, Do women really think differently than men as a rule, and if so, how? Are there significant sex differences in native human intellect, and if so, what?

Unfortunately the answers to these intriguing and important questions are obscured by a linkage of factors. For one thing, psychology itself is guilty of an insidious brand of sexism in its basic research. A broad two-year survey of experiments found that all-male samples were used almost a third of the time, for no better reason than the dubious one of availability. To make matters worse, the woman survey team discovered, more frequently than not the results were grandly generalized to both sexes—to wit, this is how people (not just men) are. In less than half of those studies employing males and females had researchers bothered to check for sex differences in their experimental outcomes. Where they did, three-quarters of the time they found them. What kind of science is it, the survey team felt impelled to demand of their profession, that neglects a sharply differentiated half of the population in one experiment out of three (blithely extrapolating to it from the other half), then compounds the omission in the other two experiments out of three by ignoring in their design any possibility of significant difference?

For another thing, as University of California psychologist Read Tuddenham points out, such an emotionally charged issue carries the seeds of its own distortion. As Tuddenham writes in the context of Jensenism,

> . . . when people are passionately concerned to 'prove' the equality of groups—and unfortunately scientists are no more dispassionate than other men—it becomes personally dangerous to do or to report research on group differences, because it threatens the quasi-religious convictions of those who dominate the academic establishment. . . . Sex differences . . . became virtually a taboo topic when people were politically agitated over equal rights for women. . . . Now that equal rights are once more an emotional political issue, we can expect good research on sex differences to go into temporary eclipse.[5]

259

Finally, testing itself may have contributed most to the atmosphere of murkiness that envelopes the sexually divided landscape of intelligence, muting the bold relief in which the comparative abilities of man and woman might otherwise be expected to stand. Shouldn't the tests, for all their limitations and despite their statistical assault against the uniqueness of the individual, give us a reasonably clear silhouette, two fairly well defined profiles to contrast in the aggregate? They should, but the evidence suggests they do not. In a commendably democratic but shortsighted effort to standardize the tests without regard to sex, the test-makers have traditionally thrown out all those items on which either males or females excell overwhelmingly as a sex. In assembling the Stanford-Binet, for example, more than thirty such tests were eliminated. In effect all the rough edges have been knocked off, the arrowhead that might have pointed tellingly this way or that rendered a smooth, round medallion to ornament the brow of society.

Nevertheless there are differences; differences in basic rates of intellectual development; differences in cognitive makeup that persist throughout life; differences whose potential importance, while yet unproven, continue to be dismissed out of hand to our detriment.

To begin with, during the early years girls are much more precocious than boys both physically and mentally. According to Harvard's Jerome Kagan, a leading authority on child development, infant girls are earlier to talk, to detect differences in pictured faces, to exhibit the baby's natural fear of unfamiliar events and surroundings—all signs of superior intelligence at that age. As a rule, Kagan adds, girls not only speak their first word months before boys, they are also first at the preschool level to understand sentences as well as to use negative forms of speech and the passive voice. (At eight months some of them will even jabber back to a "talking" tape recorder, something boys almost never do.) This precocity is probably due to a process of organic maturation called mylenization, or the growth of the fatty sheath which is believed to insulate the nerve fibers of the brain and central nervous system, speeding the spread of their impulses. Mylenization is known to be faster in females; at any rate males eventually do catch up.

There are other early significant differences, if not out-and-out superiorities. Distinct variations in the sexes have been demonstrated in block-building preferences, handedness development, picture drawing, the early use of toys, and attention to detail. At the age of two, for example, twice as many girls as boys fail to build a block train. Two years later three-quarters of the boys are able to build a block gate but less than half the girls; yet by five almost all the girls can build one from a model while four out of ten boys can't. Attentiveness, form perception, and manual skills also differ. Since girls can manipulate objects with finer finger control, moreover, they are earlier to copy writing, dress, and eat neatly. By the time they enter first grade, girls tend to excel in reading, writing, and drawing; boys in number work and Piagetian conservation tasks. In addition their interests seem to vary along sexual lines, both in subject and style, as they grow older and the environment continues to exert its ever-increasing influence. Girls draw people and houses; boys draw vehicles. Before puberty girls' play preferences tend to be diversified and balanced; boys are more likely to become obsessively preoccupied with a single pastime. In general, say child development experts Arnold Gesell and Frances Ilg, the girl's mentality at this age is more fluid, flexible, organized, and conforming. She "has more poise, more folk wisdom, and more interest in matters pertaining to marriage and family."[6] She is certainly, in the sense of being a social creature, the more intelligent.

More significantly in the long run, perhaps, growing girls show less variability in both physical and psychological traits than boys. In other words they go to less extremes, and in fewer numbers, in such matters as height, weight, and—for what it's worth—IQ scores. In short, just as there are far fewer female giants and midgets, there are far fewer certified female geniuses and idiots. Which is important for the unending nature-nurture controversy because, as Kagan says,

> this has strong implications for how boys and girls respond to parent handling. Suppose, to use an analogy, you have two balls of clay. One, representing the girls, is of a relatively even, consistent material; the other, standing for the boys, is more varied. If you squeeze and mold the two balls of clay they will receive the

261

pressure differently. Because the girls are less variable, you can more surely predict the effects of your impress—your handling of the child—than you can with boys.[7]

This may be why cognitive development and social class are more closely related in girls than in boys, Kagan thinks. A girl in America tends to try to live up to the image of feminity consciously modeled by her mother, one of being, as Kagan puts it, popular, sociable, and able to talk to people easily. As a result she is much more likely to adopt family values in life and education than a boy, whose psychology, at least in this area, is less deeply shaped by the more businesslike attitude of his mother, which essentially echoes that of his father: that he strive to develop independence, some sense of responsibility, and a vocational role. In sum, while most boys in the daily absence of their working fathers are allowed if not encouraged by the surrogate parent to grow into men, girls are subtly (and not so subtly) trained by their role-model mothers to be women.

At the other end of the time scale a longitudinal study of mixed twins from ages sixty to ninety indicates that the vicissitudes of aging are less harshly inflicted upon the mentalities of women. The mean scores of women in the group, tested twice at a twenty-year interval, exceeded those of men in almost every area of intelligence. The differences, while not great, were nevertheless significant and enduring, suggesting that intellect declines more rapidly in males than in females.

But it is at the brain's peak of maturity that the relative intelligence of the sexes understandably inspires the most curiosity—and controversy. For years almost every comparative study published showed small but significant differences in verbal abilities favoring women of all ages—and larger, more dramatic differences favoring the spatial abilities of men, especially in their prime. The prevailing social order, such research implied, was one with nature: Women made the best English teachers, men the best engineers. Now, however, psychologist Eleanor Maccoby of Stanford, perhaps the world's foremost authority, has decided after painstakingly reviewing all the evidence that those sex differences found in specific mental attributes may have been overstated. Enduring verbal differences after mylenization, she believes, are minimal at best. As for the supposedly emphatic sex distinction in spatial ability, Maccoby thinks much of it may have resulted from imprecision. What kind of spatial ability? she asks. Recent evidence suggests male superiority may actually be limited to purely visual tasks, since tests of auditory localization and pattern-tracing by touch betray no sex difference. Even then, investigations in several varied cultures have shown that the more independence women have in a society, curiously, the less discrepancy in their spatial scores! Thus the difference, for a complex of reasons, may be environmental, not innate.

But controlled clinical studies are one thing, the great mass of IQ tests quite another. Despite disputed male-female differences, the total IQ as analyzed from the results of seventeen different major studies reflected almost no sex difference. Women may be slightly stronger in one area and men in another, but overall their intellects balance each other out. Yet two of the most popular individual tests employed nationally outside a research setting, for all their efforts to achieve uniformity across sex by jettisoning items biased in one direction or the other, reveal something quite different. Based on the standardization samples themselves, girls had higher IQ's on the Stanford-Binet than boys between the ages of two and a half and five; between five and a half and fifteen, boys did. What's more, on the Wechsler Adult Intelligence Scale (WAIS), males had higher IQ's than females, both full-scale and in nine of the eleven standardized age groups, across a presumably representative population. Males not only surpassed females in spatially dominated performance categories, as expected, they also outscored them in verbal IQ's. Clearly, something was wrong somewhere if the WAIS could not agree with a generation of comparative research on sex differences. David Wechsler conceded that, "There are systematic, but for the most part negligible differences in verbal, performance, and full scale score in favor of the male subject"—to which Dr. Lissy Jarvik, a veteran woman investigator of intelligence at the UCLA Neuropsychiatric Institute snaps: "The difference may be negligible; the trend surely is not!"[8]

Wechsler was so taken by these clear-cut sex differences, Jarvik reports, that he constructed a masculine-feminine index on the basis of the more differentiating items. "A positive MF score signifies a masculine, and a negative score a feminine trend," writes Jarvik. "I leave to [you] the . . . implications of that scale."⁹

If they are biased, these purportedly unbiased tests are obviously helping prop up the lopsided status quo in their own small way by giving an unwarranted edge to men at the expense of women. If they are not, if Maccoby and the controlled studies have erred with their smaller samples, then we must ask where this ostensible male superiority, razor-thin as it is, comes from. In any event one thing is sure. Comparative scores aside, there are demonstrable differences in how the sexes think as well as pronounced variations in the relative contours of their intelligence—some of which, if pursued, shed badly needed light on intelligence and its testing for all of us, regardless of sex, race, or social class.

First and foremost, we must ask, are there any physical differences in the brain or body of man and woman that could account for sex variations in intelligence?

As it happens, there are an enormous number of sex differences that have the potential to affect intelligence, notes Jarvik. Most of them start at puberty, precisely the point where the tested IQ of boys tends to spurt ahead and that of girls to tail or level off. In addition, researchers admit, nobody knows but what anatomical or physiological changes occur in the brains of pubescent teenagers. (Parents would swear on a stack of medical encyclopedias that they must.) There is amply reliable evidence from studies of hormonal defects and sex chromosome abnormalities, moreover, to implicate both the genetic code and the endocrine system in sex-related differences of intelligence. Pediatricians have long known a condition called Turner's syndrome, which results in dwarfed, web-necked females who suffer an extraordinarily poor space and number sense (another area where males usually excel) even when compared to normal women. These females lack one of the sex-determining chromosomes, a startling reversal of the more recently publicized genetic disorder in which uncontrollably aggressive, often criminal males were found to have one too many. Girls with Turner's syndrome tend to be highly verbal and feminine. Boys with the extra sex chromosome tend to approach the physical ideal of masculinity. They are tall, strong, muscular, often very good-looking—and frequently dumb as a post. Exactly what these chromosomal deficiencies or excesses mean—whether sex chromosomes actually carry genes for sexually differentiated styles of intelligence, the recipes for two distinct kinds of pudding, as it were, and too much or too little of a good thing can spoil the mix—remains a genetic mystery. But obviously there is a close connection.

Even more provocative, intelligence in both sexes apparently can be influenced powerfully by the action—or inaction—of sex hormones. In the so-called testicular feminization syndrome, genetically normal males are somehow insensitive at the cell level to their own male sex hormones. In other words, the hormones for unknown reasons fail to do their masculinizing work, which leaves the field to the normal complement of female sex hormones in their body. As a consequence, and despite their normal male chromosomes, such men develop a normal female appearance (including breasts), frequently marry, manifest feminine attitudes—and perform like women on intelligence tests. On the other hand, in the adrenogenital syndrome—characterized by an excess of male sex hormones in the infant's bloodstream for a critical period before birth—girls affected not only grow up to be aggressive tomboys even when their condition is remedied postnatally, they also joined with boys in reported studies to register, on the average, remarkably superior all-round IQ's. In one study of ten adrenogenital girls the mean IQ was 25 points above the population average; six of them were in the gifted range. In another study of seventy adrenogenital boys and girls, seven out of ten tested above average in intelligence. "We cannot yet say definitely that the high levels of [prenatal] male sex hormone are the direct cause of the increased intelligence," writes Dr. John Money of Johns Hopkins, the crack medical psychologist who conducted one of the studies and coauthored the other. At this point, the Women's Liberation Movement peering peckishly over his shoulder, Dr. Money bites the bullet: "Though there is a good chance that this is in fact the case."[10]

Maccoby, for one, demurs—for one of those reasons that make medical research into human intelligence so fascinating and fraught with hazard. In the smaller study the excess of male sex hormone was due to the child's absorption from its mother of an adrenogenically acting synthetic pregnancy hormone given to prevent a threatened miscarriage. To detect and treat the condition successfully requires a sophisticated level of medicine not available to a random sample of the population, Maccoby argues, hence Money's study sample is undoubtedly biased upward on the socioeconomic scale—a point borne out by the fact that six of the nine fathers were college educated. Since parent education is positively related to a child's IQ score, Maccoby contends the performance of Money's group should not have been compared to that of the population at large. The result was bound to be invidious, she believes, because an IQ of 125 "would appear to be a reasonable level to expect"[11] from such a highly selected sample. The same argument might be applied to the larger study. Here the excess of male sex hormones was due to a genetic defect in the child itself. But again, the data may be skewed by the fact that fully a quarter of the sample benefited from an elevated brand of diagnosis and therapy that suggests parents with a higher SES. Further clarifying evidence is offered by Katharina Dalton of England, where national health care might be expected to mute the SES factor to relative insignificance. The children in her study were from mothers in all walks of life who took artificial pregnancy hormones. Dalton looked at school work, rather than IQ tests, and found progressively higher attainment the more hormones the mother had taken. Unfortunately for feminists awaiting the dénouement with bated breath, she failed to analyze her data for sex. Maccoby could stick safely to her guns: "We cannot conclude that male or female hormones increase intellectual performance differentially. No study has yet compared the effects of male and female hormones, upon male and female children, in one design."[12] Still, there seems little room for honest doubt that sex hormones play an important role in shaping our intelligence, one way or another, through their little-understood impact on the central nervous system.

Finally, from the physical standpoint, there is a lingering question of possible sex differences in lateralized function and its underlying physiology. Could it be the brains of men and women are organized, even subtly structured, differently? It could. Several

266

researchers have suggested as much, notably Canada's Doreen Kimura, and Herbert Lansdell of the National Institute of Neurological Diseases and Stroke. From deficit studies involving the surgical removal of cerebral tissue from one hemisphere or the other, Lansdell has tentatively concluded that subtle differences may exist between male and female brains in cerebral localization of cognitive functions. When part of either temporal lobe was removed from adult epileptic patients, Lansdell found they lost language or spatial functions as hemispheric organization would dictate—but women lost more in the verbal area, men more in the spatial. Yet in a word-association test having more to do with how other people think than simple verbal comprehension, men were affected by left hemisphere surgery, women were not. The same discriminatory phenomenon occurred with a test on the objective meaning of proverbs. Since the location of speech had been pinpointed in the left hemisphere of all subjects with the sodium amytal-carotid artery test, Lansdell theorizes that the symbolic-linguistic abilities of the two sexes must somehow differ.

Similarly, another postoperative test on epileptic patients showed that while men suffered losses in artistic aptitude with surgical lesions of the right (or nonlanguage) hemisphere, the performance of the women actually improved—probably because the disruptive tissue had been cut out. In other words, their artistic aptitude was unaffected by surgery in the hemisphere supposedly governing it. Based as it is on a handful of cases, as well as on neurological deficits in the already damaged epileptic brain, Lansdell's work can only be generalized with care. In her work with the healthy brain, on the other hand, Kimura reports a tendency for males to exhibit a right hemisphere superiority in certain visual-spatial tasks. In agreeing with Lansdell that the brains of males and females may be differently organized, Kimura echoes Jerison in speculating that "Most of human evolution must have taken place under conditions where for the male hunting members of society accurate information about both the immediate and the distant environment was of paramount importance. For the females, who presumably stayed closer to home with the other nonhunting members of the group, similar selection processes may not have operated."[13]

267

In reviewing the evidence, Kimura concludes too that brain lateralization occurs earlier in girls, which contributes to their precocity. Given the brain's growing hemispheric specialization for language as the commissures link up and mylenization progresses—Sperry, Kagan, and others think—that could explain both the apparent female superiority in early language and subsequent inferiority in at least the visual aspect of spatial development. ". . . In the nonverbal art forms—music and painting—there are far fewer women than one would expect," writes Kagan. "Perhaps this assymetry in choice of creative mode is the price women pay for their initial left-hemisphere advantage. Perhaps it is woman, not man, who is the intellectual specialist; woman, not man, who insists on interlacing sensory experience with meaning."[14]

At any rate when it comes to lateralization Maccoby is on firmer footing than before when she points out that "unfortunately many studies do not use both sexes and much work remains to be done before we can make even tentative conclusions."[15]

As for actual differences in brain structure, there is scattered if less than compelling evidence to support it. A band of neural tissue at the base of the hemisphere connecting the two egg-shaped halves of the thalmus—the major sensory relay station between the spinal cord and the cerebral cortex—is inexplicably missing in one man in three, but only one woman in four. Male neurological patients found without it by Lansdell on X ray, moreover, did slightly better in nonverbal tasks than those with it. There was, he theorized, just that much less opportunity for interference between the mutually antagonistic hemispheres. The opposite, however, was true of the women he tested. They did worse on nonverbal tasks when the band was missing, which indicated to Lansdell that their brains must be less cleanly lateralized and needed this natural connection more to function with fullest efficiency.

According to several other studies, the hemispheres of the sexes seem to differ too in their relative length, order of mylenization, density of outgoing fibers, and arrangement of blood supply. But the samples were so small, the hypotheses they might inspire so conflicting, that nobody as yet wishes to make much of them. The last word, if there is one, belongs to Harvard's eminent pioneer in the field of brain research, Dr. Norman Geschwind. Noting "gross anatomical differences visible to the naked eye"[16] between the hemispheres in postmortem, Geschwind has predicted sex differences in the normal human brain eventually will be found.

So in sum, a broad spectrum of physical contrasts ranging from genetic to chemical to structural, may exist collectively in sufficient magnitude to forever define and separate intelligence by sex.

But what of personality, of the interlocking matrix of the prevailing masculine culture? Just how important are these pervasive variables?

Judging by a mass of accumulated evidence, they may be every bit as important. Men, for example, are bolder in judgment, take more intellectual risks, and have higher curiosity. Women, in contrast, are more emotional in making decisions and, possibly for that reason, better at solving problems under stress. What Ravenna Helson calls a phallocentric style of thinking in her view distinguishes men: purposive, analytic, forceful, penetrating. Women, on the other hand, are "pregnant" with "an emotionally charged mass of developing ideas"[17] gleaned from reflection and intuitive inner vision, shaped by ingenuity and craft, and protected by a nature that is stubborn, manipulative, and enduring. They make better grades, have intellectual rather than technical interests if gifted as undergraduates, prefer more to map their own courses and set their own pace when gifted, and are less likely to fall into "sterile patterns of academic gamesmanship"[18] at the graduate level. The caricature of the flighty female notwithstanding, their thinking stays remarkably stable. That of men, in comparison, becomes increasingly analytic as their attention span grows and they come through age to control both their youthful restlessness and impulsivity—factors that evidently bother the woman's intellectual performance not at all.

Recognizing all this, declares Helson, the overriding psychological goal of our life and education ought to be "nothing simpler than differentiation and integration of masculine and feminine traits [through] flexibility, patient suffering and recognition of diversity."[19] What our society desperately needs, she believes, is a true psychic androgeny—the happy reconciliation of natural opposites—instead of the not-so-peaceful coexistence of a poorly disguised (even from ourselves) hermaphrodism.

That this simply has not happened—and at whose expense—is

reflected in one area of psychosexual comparison more and more researchers deem most important: self-esteem. In primary school, reports Maccoby, children of both sexes are still committed to the virtues of their own sex. Boys list strength, competence, and having more interesting things to play with as advantages of being a boy, while girls say that girls are nicer, better behaved, and get to wear pretty clothes. (Already, observe, parental and societal values are having their impact.) More significantly for self-image, some psychologists feel, primary girls get better grades, strongly suggesting that they feel every bit as good about themselves as boys do. But as they get older, something strange and ominous occurs: Both boys and girls progressively have a better opinion of boys and a worse opinion of girls. In one recent study, ninth-grade girls, regardless of social class or IQ, rejected the traditional stereotype of wife-and-mother, feminists will be glad to learn, but were not at all positive about women in the professions. In another study college coeds who had A grades generally scored much lower on self-esteem than those who made C's and "tended to gauge their worth in terms of social acceptance by their peers and friends."[20] In five scientific fields, another study showed, full-time female graduate students entered with higher grade-point averages than men but less confidence. They had a lower level of professional participation and thought of themselves as students rather than scientists or scholars. And finally, both men and women interviewed in another study, especially the women, rated men as "more worthwhile" than women.

(One researcher demonstrated women's ingrained contempt for their own kind when he had a group of them rate the scholarship in an essay signed, alternately, "John McKay" and "Joan McKay." Although it was the same paper, the women generally thought John's article was scholarly and Joan's commonplace— the academic equivalent of the feminist jibe that "a woman gets wrinkles but a man's face is lined with character."[21]

Clearly, cultural factors all too familiar to each of us are implicated increasingly as girls grow up. But at what point, and where, do they begin to stigmatize the girl of shining promise? Schools and teachers, parents and home, appear to share the blame for a process that sets in so subtly and spreads so insidiously

270

that we can scarcely tell where an honest appreciation of differences ends and the train of unfairly discriminating action starts. In class girls are rewarded for dependence, friendliness, and conformity; boys (at least to a greater extent) for autonomy, independence, and creativity. Analyzed for content, third-grade readers in one major study depicted the female sex as sociable, kind, and timid, but inactive, unambitious, and uncreative. The fictitious figure nurtured in the story was usually female, the wise oracle male, as were three-quarters of the central characters. Fed a steady diet of such social reinforcement by textbooks and teachers alike, it is no wonder that girls find it harder as they grow to know who, how, and what they really are mentally. On graduation they are more difficult to counsel says an expert, because they tend to be less realistic in appraising their abilities, and often exhibit essentially a zero relationship between their scholastic achievement, intelligence, and aspirations for the future. They have, in short, with all possible tenderness and consideration from the day they first toddled off to kindergarten, been adroitly engineered, with their own willing and unconscious help, to forfeit or fail.

As for home and family—the crucible in which personality is fired, formed, and hardened—one of the most arresting theories on their influence has been advanced by David Lynn, a child-development researcher from the University of California at Davis. Because each sex faces a different set of circumstances in learning how it is supposed to behave, Lynn believes, differing mental attributes are naturally and selectively called forth. Girls learn to be girls by identifying with their mothers. They have before them a warm, living, intricate lesson to be mastered. (Be this and all will be well.) Boys, on the other hand, in the absence of their working fathers, must learn to be boys by groping their way through a thicket of essentially negative and sometimes conflicting clues laid down by the females around them. (Don't do that, it's sissy. But don't do that, either. It's destructive or disruptive.) But do what? They have a problem to be solved.

In solving a problem the situation must be explored and restructured, the goal determined, the guiding principles gleaned from a mass of inferential evidence. Lacking a live model, Lynn thinks, the boy gets his rewards for objectively piecing together

271

from his environment the appropriate masculine role. In learning a lesson, however, exploration, goals, and principles can be largely ignored. It is the given, albeit in all its infinitely arrayed complex detail, that must be absorbed and understood. Thus the girl, unlike the boy, grows up in a close personal relationship that fosters a strong need for affiliation, and is rewarded for her skills in imitation. It is not surprising to Lynn, then, that in learning females often show greater docility, passive acceptance, and dependence. (Additionally, in motor tasks requiring a stimulus response, boys are the more active, girls the more reactive.)

No PhD in comparative psychology is required to know which kind of intelligence modern society most avidly values. By the time women reach college, assuming they haven't already married and dropped out of education, a pervasive pattern of discrimination by style—and therefore sex—is set for life. As Ravenna Helson writes,

> Where men predominate, there are high salaries, a high level of research activity, and emphasis on the inventive, analytical, abstract, quantitative, instrumental and technological. Where women are relatively numerous, there are lower salaries, a lower level of research activity and emphasis upon conservation of knowledge, socialization of the young, and upon appreciating and bringing into relationship the insights, expressions, points of view and ways of life of people in different times and places. . . . "Discrimination against women," states the Newman Task Force [a U.S. Office of Education team investigating university life], "in contrast to that against minorities, is still overt and socially acceptable within the academic community." Among graduate students, women are more likely to be attending school part-time, they have less contact with faculty and fellow students, are taken less seriously by the faculty, and have lower vocational aspirations.[22]

When a leading neuroscientist can conceive the question of women's creativity in terms of whether they could be made into men "in the best sense of the word,"[23] writes Helson—a process the male scientist feared would be agonizing if not impossible—then clearly society is mired in a swampy kind of thinking. Such thinking, as educator Nevitt Sanford says, permeates an academic

272

atmosphere in which "new experiences [between the sexes] are simply organized according to old stereotypes," and women still treated "like girls in a mining camp."[24]

That such prodigious sex-typing, as psychologists call it, has all the unrestrained power of the self-fulfilling prophecy can be seen in the fact that undergraduates agree almost unanimously on the so-called "masculinity" or "femininity" of college courses. They do this despite authoritative pronouncements like Jerome Kagan's that "even if a small proportion of occupations—and it is probably less than 1 percent—is biologically better suited to one sex, most roles in Western society can probably be filled with competence by men or women."[25] Perhaps the students are only calling a spade a bloody spade, but such an attitude on the part of both sexes is hardly conducive to change. Indeed, in their unrelenting obeisance to the sex stereotype outside the halls of ivy, males and females alike do their damndest to ensure its dogged perpetuation. Men, many of them acutely aware of the "feminine" side of their nature, drink to feel powerful, i.e., "masculine," say the studies. Women, their sense of identity undermined by divorce or unwomanly success in the male marketplace, drink to feel "more feminine." Despite renewed attempts all around him to achieve true equality under law, man still has his private bar, bowling team, and hunting lodge, woman her social club, fashion show, and sewing circle. At almost every level of American society the sexes remain as rigidly and resolutely segregated from each other, in one critical way or another, as their great-grandparents were.

Self-image aside, are there biological bases to the psychological differences behind sex-typing? In another exhaustive survey Eleanor Maccoby answers, in effect, yes but no. Her analysis of the evidence indicates, contrary to popular belief, that boys are neither innately more independent nor innately more active. They do appear to be, however, more naturally aggressive, an evolutionary legacy from prehistoric male and female roles. (Just as the adrenogenital syndrome produces tomboyish girls, when male hormones are given to pregnant primates the incidence of rough-and-tumble play among their female offspring shoots up markedly.) Even this, however, in every society from the Kenya warrior's to our own, is fast changing. Girls and women today are more ag-

273

gressive in expressing their anger—if indirectly—more athletic, and more criminally hostile than ever. In the last decade the increase in their rate of violent crime (homicide, assault and robbery) is three times that of men. Athletically, women are more flexible, have better balance than men, and have broken world records and won Olympic championships during every stage of the menstrual cycle. In some noncontact sports less dependent on size and brawn, notably track and swimming, they have shattered many of the old male marks, and their performance now approaches that of men. Indeed, one researcher found virtually no difference in tests of native athletic ability between the sexes until age ten, when, he believes, sex-typing takes over. (Boys even failed to dominate in throwing a baseball when their untrained arm was pitted against that of the girls.) As for linguistic aggression, despite the clichéd sex differences in speech so artfully captured in *New Yorker* cartoons, careful investigation by another researcher turned up few really significant differences in how the sexes talk, profanity included.

In the relative absence of biological underpinnings, then, there is every reason to believe that psychological differences, at least as they affect intellectual performance, could be nullified and sex-typing done away with. The best avenue of experimental approach to this, Maccoby speculates, might lie in training girls to be more independent with an eye toward determining if that would in turn automatically overcome male superiority in spatial-visual tasks. Remember, a rather mysterious indirect correlation appears to exist across cultures. There are no sex differences in spatial abilities among Eskimos, for instance, where sex roles are clear-cut but the status and independence of women is high. Nor are there sex differences in mathematical abilities—another male-dominated area which has a major spatial component in some of its disciplines—among the Swedes, who emphasize sex equality.

In her study of creative women mathematicians, moreover, Ravenna Helson has given us a powerful example of how females who manage to rise above the tyranny of sex-typing can excel in intellectual competition with men. Although less mechanical than most men, Helson's subjects were more mechanical than most women and just as intelligent, creative, egocentric, and sensitive

274

as their male peers. Nor, more significantly, were they any less "feminine" than other women in their thinking. They were strongly introverted and intuitive, and showed only the faintest preference for thought over feeling.

Biology, then, despite suspected differences in the physical correlates of intelligence, needn't be an insurmountable obstacle to relative equality in intellectual achievement. Cultural conditioning remains the more likely key. As Kagan says, "If our society believed that girls should be strong and bold, the cultural patterning we see now would be reversed"[26]—even if the sexes remained enticingly different in their thinking.

Finally and curiously, the power of society to shape the roles of both sexes consciously and unconsciously in pursuit of an assumed biological imperative has led to several kinds of confusing fallout. For one thing, the expression of intelligence in both sexes has been psychologically distorted. Brighter boys were by and large and more timid, anxious, inactive, and nonaggressive— more "feminine"—than their "masculine" peers; brighter girls more active, independent, and competitive—more "masculine"— than their "feminine" peers. The incredible result, charges Lissy Jarvik, is a psychological profile that pictures intellectual performance as incompatible with femininity in girls and masculinity in boys!

In reality, of course, it is the stereotypes that are out of joint. It is time we junked those stereotypes and stopped living by them— or took an honest look at our real attitudes toward intelligence.

For another thing, it obviously follows, the popular notion that men are naturally more left hemisphere in their thinking—more analytical, logical, and rational if not more verbal—and women more right hemisphere—more intuitive, comparative, holistic— may be nothing more than a socially convenient mass delusion. Men may ordinarily use their left hemisphere more as adults, but there may be nothing natural about it if by natural we mean innate, inborn. It may very well be natural if by natural we mean the inevitable outcome of a social system designed to reward disproportionately certain left hemisphere attributes and those who learn to exercise them best while wielding the levers of power— namely men. Women, by the same token, may ordinarily use their right hemisphere more as adults, but that too may be only the foregone result of a social system that leaves to them the right hemisphere abilities it deems least important while reserving recognition in the few arts it values to those whose talents in them have been fostered—again, men. The fascinating and insidious interplay of the two resulting sets of stereotypes—man thinks, woman feels; the left hemisphere is intelligent, the right hemisphere, while artistic, is not—is almost too much to contemplate.

Chapter 11

*The Gifted Child**

The scene is a peaceful oak-shaded elementary school in your neighborhood. The time is tomorrow. Arriving at his office, the principal is astonished to find it barricaded by a band of militant parents. As he blinks in the unaccustomed glare of television lights, they confront him with—can this be happening?—a list of nonnegotiable demands:

• The intelligence of all children must be individually tested and independently evaluated, regardless of teacher recommendations and classroom performance.

• Discrimination against the nonverbal gifted must be reversed.

• Better tests, more research into ways of determining special talents as well as general intelligence, must be developed.

• Above all, an imaginative and comprehensive program of full-time education designed for the gifted must be established with all possible speed, whatever the cost.

"Piecemeal tinkering, eclectic dabbling will no longer do," their prepared press release reads. "The latest ideas, information, techniques, and materials must be massively employed. Even more essential, the program must be staffed by intensely committed teachers secure enough in their profession and safe enough in their jobs to see the gifted for what they are: a challenge, not a threat."

Concludes the press release ominously, "at stake is nothing less than the future of this country."

Such demands, of course, are as inaccessible to instant satisfac-

*Parts of this chapter appeared in *McCall's* magazine.

tion as they are nonnegotiable. The principal pleads for more time, other meetings. Whereupon the parents, fed up by what they see as a bureaucratic stall, join with older students (reform-minded achievers, vengeful dropouts) and volunteers from Mensa to throw a picket line around the school and invade the cafeteria for a teach-in. When they refuse to leave, police are reluctantly summoned, the pickets dispersed, the squatters arrested. The next day they are back, vowing not to allow classes to continue or to pay that part of their taxes destined for education "until the gross inequities victimizing the gifted child are remedied."

This time, however, they are not alone in their anger. Arrayed against them is an even larger and more indignant group of parents, brandishing such signs as "Segregation Is Undemocratic," "Testing—Private Discrimination at Public Expense" and "Equal Opportunity: Cornerstone of Our Republic." The playground has become a battleground for another bitter skirmish in one of the oldest unfinished wars ever to plague American social history, one with its roots plunged deep in our turbulent political past: the war between Jacksonian democracy, with its emphasis on the greatest good for the greatest number, and Jeffersonian democracy, with its concern for the unique needs of the individual. The last refuge of our dying innocence—a truly democratic but equal system of public education—has become the freshest arena for our clashing sensibilities.

As implausible as such a schoolhouse scenario sounds, it is anything but airily hypothetical. The fictive list of demands by parents rests on a solid foundation of facts, feelings, and attitudes. Teachers are notoriously biased in gauging pupil intellect. They tend to pick the clean, the polite, the orderly, the interested—and research indicates they are wrong more often than right. Schoolwork is a woefully inadequate index. The paralyzing sameness of the traditional curriculum panders to the lowest common denominator. It turns the brightest kids off or into chronic losers. Although some nonverbal children when carefully tested have proven gifted, being nonverbal still too often means a one-way ticket to trade school. Even when such children are detected, few schools know what to do with them or are equipped to do it if they did. Schools do continue to handle IQ scores as highly classified infor-

278

mation or a bureaucratic embarrassment. Our frontier canons to the contrary, there is nothing sissified or shameful about exceptionally high intelligence, but the gifted child, assuming he is even recognized, is still shunted to the backrooms of Academe legislatively and treated as an awkward stepbrother of the mentally handicapped. Finally, the best tests generally available, as we have seen, provide only a narrow measure of human mental potential and practically no meaningful indication at all of latent creativity. They reflect, in fact, and only crudely, little more than those skills the schools are set up to teach, a mutually damning indictment. All in all, there is little wonder that lawsuits by parents against schools for failing to do their job, unheard of just a few years ago, are sharply on the upswing.

In sum, these issues are very real, and reflect an even deeper ecological issue that smolders just beneath the surface: If our children are, as we never tire of saying, our most precious resource, how shall we conserve and develop the best that is in them, for our sake as well as theirs?

There is sadly ample evidence that many of our creative and intelligent best are being wasted, as surely as our polluted lakes, oil-smeared beaches, and smog-fouled air. In a 1970 report to Congress, the U. S. Commissioner of Education admitted that federal efforts to aid the gifted and talented were "all but nonexistent."[1] Unfortunately, nothing much has happened since to mitigate against using the present tense in reciting the forlorn figures.

To wit:

As a nation, we spend forty-three times more on the underprivileged and twenty-eight times more on the handicapped. Of an estimated 4,000,000 gifted youngsters of all ages—a pool of potential talent with undreamed-of depths—fewer than one in twenty is even being identified. Of those that are, less than $10 a year is being spent on each. State and local efforts are little better. Although twenty-one states have legislation much of it goes scarcely beyond codified rhetoric. Only ten states have at least one staff worker assigned more than half time. Only four—California, Illinois, Connecticut, and Georgia—budget major monies and none comes close to realizing the full intent of its underlying philosophy. By no stretch of the bureaucratic imagination can any of their programs—a mixed bag of teacher training, limited curriculum enrichment, and special projects—be held up as shining models. Nor is the private sector much help. A dozen independent schools for the academically (left-hemisphere) gifted are in operation, but their numbers of children are negligible, their impact slight. Where are the foundations, those flowing founts of scholastic innovation? Few if any dollars from the $280-plus million granted annually to education—one-third of all foundation philanthropy—trickle down to the gifted.

Perhaps even worse, as nationwide hearings have made evident, there is scant public support for such programs beyond the parents of the designated gifted themselves. As it is, they represent only a fraction of the parents who might be interested if their children were identified—or, to be scrupulously fair, might not be. One in five parents, the Department of Health, Education and Welfare found, either limit their gifted child's vision to high school or fail to communicate educational goals of any kind. Except for California, with its statewide platoon of volunteer organizations, advocates for the gifted compose at best a small and poorly organized lobby. Worse yet, the federal report indicates, their modest accomplishments and aspirations have met with "apathy and even hostility"[2] among teachers, administrators, guidance counselors, and school psychologists. As a consequence the requisite identification process has been at most "piecemeal, sporadic and sometimes nonexistent."[3]

Even where it exists there are frustrations that undermine the most ambitious of efforts. Group intelligence testing, preferable because it is far cheaper for perennially strapped school districts (the best individual IQ tests cost about $75 a child to administer and analyze) is no more reliable than teacher recommendations. And unbelievably, over half the schools surveyed said they had no gifted students at all! How school attitudes and staffing result in such an Alice in Wonderland state of affairs can be seen in the results of an unpublished survey undertaken and filed away without fanfare during the Johnson administration. States with full-time consultants to the gifted, the unreleased study showed, served 40 percent of the country's public school population and reported three-quarters of the designated gifted. Those having no consultants even part-time served a little less than a third of the population but uncovered only 1 percent. Says one of that survey's authors, Connecticut's Dr. William Vassar: "States without full-time programs just don't go out and discover the kids, much less do anything for them. It's like gardening. You can have good soil, but if you don't cultivate it, nothing much is going to grow."[4]

Worst of all, noted the HEW report, the nation's approach to the gifted, limited as it is, is dogged by virtually every administrative and bureaucratic ill that can afflict government enterprise: lack of funds, lack of leadership, lack of trained personnel, lack of public understanding, lack of priority, lack of legislation, appallingly poor diagnosis of the very population it is supposed to serve, too much isolation, too little organization, and a stubborn history of nonintervention and state autonomy in how federal funds should be used. Concluded the commissioner's report with a candor astonishing in a government agency:

"The educational system does not accept the right of an individual to be different from his peers. The general tendency is to pull the person [down] to the average. . . ."[5]

Where, critics might well have asked had such a report ever been made public, is the evidence for such a damning indictment? If the grades of the gifted don't show it, how do we know they are superior in intelligence to others their age? Who says they can do much better than they are doing? What proves they are hurt by the lack of challenging outlets? If they are so bright and creative why can't they make it on their own? Doesn't cream just naturally rise to the top?

Carefully and patiently, one by one, the commissioner's report sought to knock down each argument. In surveys of selected academic subjects, it pointed out, gifted kindergartners given free rein were found to be performing at the second grade level, gifted fourth-graders beyond the seventh, and gifted high school seniors better than college seniors on tests employed for admission to graduate study. So not only were they superior, their superiority grew progressively as they grew older. Another survey showed that over half the gifted consistently worked beneath their capability. So in a conventional atmosphere they were short-changing themselves and society. Thousands of youths in the top intellectu-

281

al bracket, moreover, were dropping out every year, taking with them into the menial (and increasingly limited) job market talents that would never be realized. That could not help but hurt society.

As for the cream rising, one official sourly noted that such a notion must stem from the assumption that human beings "are no more complex than a bottle of milk." The cream of our talent could rise in a warm, supportive atmosphere too often missing from our schools, he adds, but for now it appears "homogenized, if not curdled."[6]

The question of giftedness is compounded not only by questions of who is gifted and why, but how.

Talent has always had what educators call a "social referrent." As Harvard's Richard Herrnstein argues in a more forbidding context, society takes pains to define, develop, and reward those abilities it needs. Galton could classify the eminent of his day into eight professional categories. In Terman's time, law, medicine, teaching, and the growing roll call of social sciences were intellectually paramount. The Sputnik generation of gifted in the late 1950's, given a rocketing push by American-Soviet technological competition, gravitated toward the natural sciences and aerospace engineering. Today, high achievement in hundreds if not thousands of complex fields is not only possible but necessary for modern survival. Success depends not only on the traditionally recognized gifts of abstraction and symbol manipulation but on special qualities of originality, fluency with ideas, intellectual curiosity, independence of thought, and flexibility in forging new concepts. In short, it depends on cognitive creativity. None of this is really new. These abilities have been there all the time, coyly hiding behind the all-enveloping skirts of that global entity traditionally called general intelligence. Those on the leading edge of educational psychology just think about them differently now, in terms of discrete characteristics that can be detected and honed independently. What's more, as we have seen, giftedness of an equally distinctive character is clearly called for in such nonacademic but intellectually demanding disciplines as the creative and performing arts, human relations, group management, government, and politics; in the spiritual leadership of a Gandhi, the mechanical aptitude of a Leonardo, the psychomotor skills of a Jack Nicklaus.

The question is further complicated by the perversely taxing and changeling nature of the child itself. How are we to separate the "Morning Glory," that precocious performer whose talents mysteriously wax and wane before he's grown? How are we to recognize early the "Late Bloomer" whose abilities suddenly flower long after the school has assigned him to the back row of its awareness? How are we to weigh the effects of a miserably deprived home life on one child against the influence of a domineering, ambitious mother on another? How, finally, are we to know him—by testing, and having tested run the risk of freezing forever in the teacher's mind the upper limits of probable accomplishment for a child who may have had an off day (or, not to exaggerate, who may because multiple-choice exams are anathema to his style of thinking, have an off day *every* day)? Or are we to risk trusting him to identify himself with his actions in an educational atmosphere often so pedestrian it causes him to learn to be unintelligent?

And what of those whose gifts are equally precious but so highly specialized—in our society—that they require tailor-made environments? In Brooklyn white parents fight to get their arts-minded youngsters into a public school sandwiched between black and Puerto Rican neighborhoods because topflight musicians and artists teach there. But who discovers and fans the flickering spark of another Casals, another Wyeth, in the bleak backwoods areas, the culture-starved small towns, the ghettos of big cities less endowed than New York?

Who, finally, shall know him if not the teacher? Certainly not the principal who revels in orthodoxy; not the district administrator who prides himself on running a fiscally taut ship; not the school board that must, of hard necessity, look primarily at the bottom line on the balance sheet.

But he is there for those who bother to look. He cannot turn himself on and off at the sound of a bell; he has an amazing gift for total absorption when interested. Periods, schedules, and lock-step lesson plans all interfere with his ferocious, single-minded, insistently egocentric appetite for learning. He spurns close supervision; he can use the library on his own and produce independently. He sees commonplace things in different ways, greater depth. He solves problems through fantasy. He composes songs, poems, and stories at a prodigious rate. He has, in his junior high years, unbounded energy. He is, for all of that, at once adult and childlike. He knows his limitations but when thwarted or bored will deliberately disrupt routine or seek attention by proposing novel possibilities. His self-image is often strong to the point of arrogance. At the same time his sensitivity when he is balked can result in abysmal feelings of inadequacy and worthlessness. He is, in sum, both a promise and a pill. So is his education. What he needs out of school, as expert Ruth Martinson puts it, "is not limited to skills acquisition—the results of which are represented annually to the public to prove that bond issues are justified. It is education based on [his] right . . . to take an active part in the determination of his own learning agenda, to question and to learn from the search for his own answers, and in the process to expand his talents, knowledge, interests and curiosity about his own particular universe."[7]

That kind of education, manifestly, costs more than we as a nation have until now been willing to spend—for the gifted or any child, in faith and understanding as well as money and energy. Schools, after all, it can be legitimately argued, have enough trouble educating the great mass in the middle or raising up the disadvantaged at the bottom in the manner we have always employed. To divert a school's limited resources or further fragment a teacher's energies, especially to the heady requirements of those who by definition are already the most fortunate, seems unthinkable to many. But ducking the issue is at best a copout, at worst a recipe for disaster. Ducking it leads to the Illinois high school senior who learned to read and write Russian on his own (although he had never heard it spoken) and buried himself so deeply in physics he failed the simpler math courses required for graduation. Ducking it leads to the Texas teen-ager who delighted in trigonometry but refused to do boringly simple fractions and was caught, horror of horrors, not smoking a joint or downing an upper but writing her own math textbook in study hall. Ducking it leads to her mother being told variously throughout twelve unhappy years of school that her daughter was retarded; brain damaged; abused; had emotional problems; had a defense mechanism; had a flawed personality because of some nameless mistake made by her parents. Ducking it leads at last to the principal telling them that the psychologist who had found her in the top half of the top bracket on the Stanford-Binet "did not know what he was talking about . . . that [she] was definitely from an unstable home life and would be treated and taught accordingly because he, the principal, was 'fed up.' "[8]

And yet, it rubs rawly against something deep within us to read what a thirteen-year-old California boy had to say about what it means to be gifted in the typical American public school system today:

> Schools have been my adversaries, my antagonists in the quest for enlightenment . . . they are no place for individual thinkers . . . the pressure of conformity . . . does strange things to [them]. Classic symptoms are tiredness, nonattention, chronic boredom, a tendency to daydream, and, worse yet, truancy. I know because I have experienced and done all these things in an attempt to escape from the realities of the dull schools I attended . . . there is little or no chance to be creative in the average public school. The need to create is paramount in man, and it cannot be expected to show itself at regular intervals. Nor can it be turned on or off at the whim of some school administration.
>
> The prime reason for studying is examinations. I do not believe in examinations . . . because they are usually obsessed with examining one's memory for the retention of trivia. I have taken a few tests . . . that represented good judgment on the part of the persons who prepared them. The questions . . . were direct, concise, and exactly to the point; one understood them completely by virtue of their own simplicity. . . . [But] such tests are only a handful compared to hundreds, maybe thousands, I have taken. Personally, I think that examinations should be replaced by informal discussions between student and teacher.
>
> Free learning and conventional classes [can] not coexist. Someone would have to possess the mentality of several supergeniuses, or the adaptability of five chameleons, to weather a school day like that. I still feel [however] that free learning . . . offers the best of all possible worlds: It allows the subject to be fun and interesting and the student to be creative, resourceful, responsible, and, most of all, satisfied.[9]

Historically, special education for the gifted in this country has always been, in one critic's words, like a rocking chair: always in motion, going nowhere. Enrichment flourished in at least a hundred major schools before the Second World War but by the time of Sputnik in the 1950's almost all programs had been suspended for lack of funds and staff. When the Russians put the first satellite aloft, a chorus of woeful voices, led by that of Admiral Hyman Rickover, father of the atomic submarine and an impeccable egghead, mourned it as a stunning blow to our prestige. Only half of the top quarter of our high school graduates went on to earn college diplomas, it was pointed out amid much hand-wringing, less than three in a hundred qualified students got a PhD. Our scholastic standards had sunk so low, we were told, that the United States was in imminent danger of losing the Cold War (the only war we had going at the time) unless they were elevated, our best talents marshaled immediately to the task. The American high school, as one educator describes it, straightaway became "the scene of a national talent hunt comparable in scope and vigor to the search for promising athletes." Our academic best were culled, counseled, force-fed like Strasbourg geese, and sedulously recruited into the college of their choice.

Unhappily for our notions of national honor, the same educator notes, it wasn't long before large numbers of them woke up, wondered what on earth they were doing in science and engineering, and switched majors. The more luckless of those who stayed on went out from the halls of ivy into Bleak House: an aerospace job market that was only an anemic shadow of its former robust self. And still nothing had been done for those who felt more at home with a Stradivarius or a syllabus than a slide rule. In the next decade professional publications on the gifted, more prevalent during the three years after Sputnik than in all the previous thirty, fell off by half. The chair had rocked back.

Today, despite the absence of any immediate compelling sense of national emergency (but wait; like a city bus one will be along shortly) there are signs on the fringe that the academic climate may once more be changing, the rocker getting ready to rock forward again. For one thing, an increasing amount of university study is now reaching down into hundreds of high schools, touching the intellectual lives of thousands of students. For another, early admission to college—at Indiana's DePauw University a select group of high school juniors have been admitted as freshman—is almost standard. More significantly, perhaps, alternative schools have sprung up like wild flowers all across the arid landscape of conventional education. Although their average life span is brief (two years), they not only brighten the corners where they are for a few short seasons, they seditiously bore from within to undermine establishment stodginess. And they have succeeded, on balance, in moving the glacial public school system one silly millimeter closer to what advocates of the gifted and creative regard as the ideal classroom. It is the classroom that features opportunities to ask unexpected questions, pursue offbeat knowledge, play with ideas, do things just for fun. It is the classroom free from the constant threat of competition and evaluation, inhibiting psychological "sets," preconditioned habits of thinking and the canned response. It is the classroom mercifully missing the teacher who finds security in hewing to the gospel of the textbook, in dominating the class by lordly right, in being the Oracle, in keeping things quiet and neat. It is the classroom so fraught with excitement that teachers have to devote staff discussion to strategies for clearing kids out at the end of the day.

The indications of such a revolt against the status quo are small and scattered but concrete. An Illinois industrial town has a class of sixteen second-through-fifth-grade boys all at least six years ahead of their age who meet an hour each week to study science. An hour isn't much but the value of even that brief exchange cannot be dismissed. The kids are so happy they won't leave to play; the teachers are happy because most of the kids used to be bored and troublesome. In one Chicago school the ghetto gifted from the lower grades get a rich range of liberating, organized out-of-school experiences. In Cleveland more than 5,000 of the better students receive special instruction in higher forms of thinking such as analysis and synthesis. Connecticut has a science center with an observatory for staggered use by 8,000 kids on an old Nike missile site; a revamped college campus for retrieving the disadvantaged; a renovated synagogue that caters to pupils from eighteen surrounding school districts adept at creative arts. In Annapolis over 100 kids from twenty-five schools are crisply drilled on the finer points of informal logic. Where programs exist, interest is high. In one Virginia suburb of Washington, D.C., the waiting list is three years long. Where programs don't exist, a subterranean unrest with things as they are is brewing; school

287

boards that haven't had a new member in a decade are being over-turned like fruitbaskets.

In California, programs for the gifted reach over a hundred thousand youngsters at an annual cost of around $8 million. They reach but that's about all. California pays its school districts $50 for each gifted child identified, and currently another $70 a year to finance special instruction for him. Most involve as little as forty minutes a day. To get state money, the school must first certify that the child is indeed gifted; in other words, test him itself. Given the spectacular lack of success with which teachers often put forth candidates, the result can be a most distasteful game of budgetary roulette: If three are tested and one qualifies, it will be over two years before the district breaks even financially on the gamble. No wonder poorer districts have little taste for testing, bother to certify few children, and put what random dollars for the gifted that do sift down into a few extra books for the library. The State Department of Education has been saying for years that it needs a minimum of $240 per child even to approach its goals. As a 'consequence of being chronically on the shorts, the California program—a sophisticated amalgam on paper of counseling, tutoring, seminars, enrichment, correspondence courses, and special classes—limps along like a jumbo jet getting by on what it can squeeze out of the pumps at the corner station.

"There's too much competition for money in special education," one official says of the state's long-standing decision to lump the gifted with the handicapped. "At appropriations time somebody brings a palsied child down the halls of the legislature and the lawmakers practically hand him their billfolds."[10]

The same year the U. S. Commissioner of Education made his gloomy report to Congress, I visited several California classes for the gifted in preparation for a national magazine article. I also made trips to a private school for the gifted in Los Angeles. What I saw, while encouraging, was hardly cause for unbridled optimism. And like the commissioner's statistics, I suspect, little has changed much for the better since.

Eighteen miles south of San Francisco is a pleasant, modernistic structure of long open galleries and polychrome plastic paneling.

In one room, housing seventeen fifth-through-eighth-graders with tested IQ's of 150 and above, there was a breezy bedlam of excited conversation, physical sprawl, incessant movement, and awesome clutter. Teachers of the gifted spend little time on class control. Quipped one, "You just open the door in the morning and get out of their way." The walls were adorned with humorous collages. Punning headline: HE'S NOT DEAD, BEATLE SAYS SPIRITEDLY. Aphorism: HUMOR IS NOTHING BUT GROWN-UP PLAY— MAX EASTMAN.

Few of them looked up as I walked in. They were either busy with their contracts—individual lesson plans mutually arrived at with their teacher—or absorbed in one of their two group projects: a book they were writing about their town and an airline-sponsored competition among schools to see which class could create through the magic of advertising the most authentic-sounding airline. First prize: a flight to Europe. A quartet of boys and girls rehearsed the commercial they had written before running through it in front of their videotape camera, bought with state funds for the gifted.

"Did you know there's a partial eclipse of the sun next month?" a radiant little moonfaced ten-year-old named Janet asked me. "Don't miss it. There won't be another until the year 2017."

"These kids are great," one of their teachers told me when she could catch her breath. "But their parents sometimes need help. Janet's father drills her two hours a night." There was a commotion in the schoolyard. The teacher went out to investigate, then returned. "That was one of ours." She sighed. "Until Danny came in this class he thought he was the biggest brain in the world. His parents, I'm sorry to say, did nothing to discourage him. Now he can't stand to be crossed, even when he's wrong. Another boy just disagreed with him. Danny hit him and broke his glasses."

She nodded toward a handsome Chinese-American boy moving slowly around the room with a friendly smile. "They'll drive themselves if you don't watch them. He's done a year's work in two months. Know what we've made his homework now? To play."

Across the bay and to the north, in Oakland's bleak lowland black belt, lies a low and grimy building of institutional red brick with a dreary outcropping of Quonset prefabs. Behind the windows of one, papered with festive drawings to keep out the slanting afternoon sun, is one of the city's special classes, this one for "high potential IQ's" among underprivileged sixth-graders. Minority kids from Oakland's underbelly, most of whose parents had never finished high school. They have every reason to be different but, except for the strident urgings of one gangly black girl that her girlfriend shadow-boxing a teasing boy "knock him out," they too were sky-high on learning. "What is a gall?" asked one pupil's poster, then defined it. "If I bring a snail," began another, part of a citywide natural science program, "do you think you could keep it alive one month?" The ghetto gifted class had kept it alive two.

Proudly their teacher—a chunky, energetic redhead who was herself a onetime fifteen-year-old college freshman—ticked off their accomplishments: a letter-writing campaign to save the Bay, an oceanographic cruise, class inquiries into piano tuning, lasers, bees, spinning, folksinging, Antarctica, the Soviet Union, urban crisis. "We talk a lot about core city problems," she told me. "They're quick to see the analogies to the underdeveloped everywhere. For instance, we screened a coffee company film about Brazil. It was sheer propaganda and they knew it. They wanted to know where all the poor were." An example of Ruth Martinson's deeper education.

Because ghetto young do not test as well as their suburban counterparts—whatever the reason—the district relies heavily on teacher recommendations. Out of the twenty-two pupils, says the teacher, "three don't belong here. But I refuse to let them be taken out." Contrary to what others might think, she said, their being there didn't hurt the rest and helped them. "I've taught the gifted several years and it's fun," she admitted, "but a few years ago another teacher with a low-IQ math group and I got together and taught them all. As a team. Both classes did fine. You couldn't tell one from the other." She watched several boys run the film strips they had drawn through a slide projector. "When they came in a lot of these kids knew nothing about working on their own. One girl in art just sat there with a blank piece of paper. She was waiting for me to tell her what to draw. By midyear, though, I'd put these kids up against any gifted class in Oakland."

Forty miles down the peninsula and a day later, seven-year-old Kenneth exploded through the "magic door" to his classroom—a curtain of varicolored, floor-length paper streamers—and then remembered its significance: playtime was over, time to calm down. The previous year, Kenneth, son of a chemical engineer and a schoolteacher, had been trapped in a ghetto of the spirit. In medical terms he is hyperkinetic, for complex neurological reasons, feverishly overactive. While not crippling physically, his impairment is severe enough that he cannot master his movements sufficiently to ride a bicycle, handle a pencil, or sit quietly in a chair for very long. One thing, however, he can do surpassingly well. He can think.

In the first grade Kenneth wouldn't do arithmetic and workbooks turned him off. He just daydreamed, "about things more important," he would later tell his teacher. In a class discussion one day about the meaning of Christmas, he blurted, "Christmas is the prism of life. That's when the love we keep to ourselves all year long is refracted out." The other children laughed; Kenneth developed a stammer. On the Stanford-Binet he tested in the high 140's but wouldn't repeat any words less than five syllables or he might have done better. The first grade teacher felt he was just lazy. Perhaps he was. But the district decided he belonged in their class for the underachieving gifted, taught by an imaginative, intelligent young woman who was planning to return to Stanford for her PhD.

Number facts, she found, bored Kenneth. "Why do that?" he would ask. "We've got computers." He was ready for algebra and geometry provided she would spare him repetitive exercises. Dick and Jane bored him too. He had read a book of inorganic chemistry, taught himself Braille and the manual alphabet, and aspired to become a biochemist who would find a cure for blindness. Now, today, given his own choices, Kenneth reads at the junior high level. And when he talks in class he doesn't stammer.

"These kids," his teacher says, "have tremendous capacity for self-direction and evaluation. But they're repelled by structure and drill. They're perfectionists. Sometimes they see their gifts as a threat. Their perceptions are so advanced they feel overwhelmed. They think like twelve-year-olds but function like seven-year-olds." For the first semester she spends most of her time undoing what the regular school system has done the first year. She must build up their self-esteem. "When he first came in"—she pointed out one boy—"he drew a sign on his desk: 'Dumb Sits Here.'" Their gifts, she agreed, can isolate them as effectively as a crippled arm or leg. They have little contact with children their own age at home, and see the classroom as a haven. It is hard to get them outside, and when she does, they tend to congregate by themselves along the far fence. All stay for a creative workshop when the regular school hours end.

Her secret, if it can be called that, is simple. "It's respecting the child. It's listening to him, treating him as an individual. Put these kids back in a highly structured system—we did it once, experimentally—and their behavior reverts to chaos. That's our most serious problem, I think. How can I get them to accept the rigidity, the absurdity, of regular school when they leave here?"

She saw me through the magic door. "They won't line up, so I had to do something to cool them off when they came in. Six of them are hyperkinetics, and the rest have too much on their minds. It bugs the principal. They're not going to learn to stand in line, he says. Well, I don't think that's anything they're going to need—unless there's another depression."

When I first wrote about the Mirman School it was a vest-pocket-sized institution of four full-time teachers and five part-time teachers wedged between an imported typewriter company and a wholesale electronics firm in a rundown commercial section of west Los Angeles. Today it occupies a casual and colorful new $300,000 building high in the dusty Hollywood hills bordering Mulholland Drive, up where the hot dry winds from the San Fernando Valley rattle the basketball backboards and scour the lawns to concrete hardness. The student body has doubled in size to 100 private pupils, ages five through thirteen, no mean feat since its tuition does not come cheaply: $1,600 a year. The school is run and brooded over like a large but dignified family restaurant by Norman Mirman and his wife, Beverly. Norman is tall, spare, and gently donnish. Beverly is warm and voluble, the proverbial Jewish mother running in and out of the half-dozen classrooms push-

292

ing metaphoric bowls of chicken soup. Kids, kids, you should eat, already.

Back in 1962, Norman Mirman, then a teacher of teachers at the UCLA Graduate School of Education, was asked to teach a class that quite blew his scholarly mind: "Teaching Children With Special Problems—Blind, Deaf, Cerebral-Palsied and Gifted." That did it. The Mirmans started a class of nine in their home, moved then to what Beverly fondly calls "the topless district," and finally set out to raise funds six years later for their new school. The fund-raising drive was not your conventional tale of non-profit enterprise and taxfree success. Foundations, philanthropies, and government at all levels were remarkably unresponsive. A personal solicitation of some sixty blue-ribbon sources by the school's most influential father, the vice-president of an international corporation, yielded only about $10,000. In a nation that prides itself on the pursuit of all that money can buy, the Mirmans had a frustrating time selling academic excellence to anybody but the parents as an over-the-counter investment. They finally had to finance it like any other business.

"Do you know what one corporation head told me?" remembers Beverly. " 'You're asking me to cry over millionaires?' " Her husband shook his head. "It's this distorted idea of democracy. You can have coaches for athletes, uniforms for the band, but if you do anything to set apart the gifted you're accused of elitism."[11]

Although the mood of the Mirman school is much like that of the public school classes, it has a more classical core. Art, history, French, science, and music give way in sudden spurts of tangential interest to mythology, literature, English, politics, Jackson Pollock, electronics, and science fiction. But there is nothing undisciplined in their approach—and, some would insist, nothing very free. "We try to teach them to think, to analyze, to evaluate," says Norman, who has the traditionalist's respect for the left hemisphere. They're so glib verbally it's important somebody pin them down.[12] Teachers delight in the small class size, their active role in curriculum development, and the satisfaction of working with bright kids who give good feedback. The parents and children are both elated by an experience that is everything public school is not. In fact the Mirman files are chock-a-block with case histories of how their children were treated before they came there. Together they make up quite a horror story.

David, for instance, is the nine-year-old son of a college physics professor. When he was in public school in the first grade he did so well academically that he was summarily moved to the second. There his pace slowed dramatically. He wouldn't finish workbook assignments. He got into playground fights, frequently blew up in tears at home, and developed a facial tic. His teacher complained that he was incapable of second-grade reading or math and suggested he be put back into first. When David's mother pointed out that he had been accelerated precisely because of his demonstrated abilities, the teacher became defensive. David was then interviewed and tested by the school counselor, who not only praised his intellect and maturity but said he was highly original. David remained in the second grade until the day, says his mother, "he came home seething with anxiety. He had been ordered to write 'I will stand in line properly outside the classroom' three hundred times. It was the first time I had ever refused to have a child of mine do his school assignments."

When his parents enrolled David at Mirman, his old breezy confidence returned and his tic went away. "The nice thing is," he told his mother, "nobody laughs when you give your opinion. Everybody has different ideas. After all, there is no right answer to some questions."[13]

Caleb's parents, on the other hand, always had definite ideas about their son's education. "My wife and I felt learning should be wholly spontaneous," says his father, a young Beverly Hills attorney. "Something you enjoyed. Something you acquired as easily, as naturally, as a suntan."

But public school kindergarten hopelessly disillusioned both Caleb and his parents within a few weeks. Caleb had never had coloring books because his parents believed that they stifled creativity. So in school, when he was told to color a circle, square, or triangle, Caleb complied, but instead of neatly crayoning inside the prescribed lines, Caleb drew wild improvisations of his own. "He knew perfectly well what a circle and a square and triangle were," says his father. "You'd think that was the point of it all. But

294

no, if Caleb didn't color it exactly as he was supposed to, he didn't get a smiling face on his paper. Worse, he got the idea that there was something wrong with him for not getting it."

When his mother asked for a conference, the teacher said Caleb had a "mental problem" and should see a psychologist. The psychologist tested the boy, found his intelligence exceptional, and recommended the Mirman school. Caleb's parents were afraid the competition there might be as destructive as public school conformity, but their fears have proved unfounded. "We like the school's attitude that education is not a series of answers—facts and dates—but a series of questions."

And Caleb? That morning he had announced it was Indian day and—dressed only in feathered headband, daubs of lipstick, and a loincloth made of paper towels—had tried to start off to school. Says his father, "You know he feels good about school if he's willing to go there naked."[14]

But not all case histories are so happy—and for reasons that strike at the heart of the problem that any school or class for the gifted poses for American education: the problem of who is gifted and how. The Mirmans use a cutoff of 130 on the Stanford-Binet as administered by a staff psychologist. The Mirmans rarely see the applicants before they're tested, much less get to know them, so their emotional investment in the outcome is small. There was never, in fifteen years, the heartbreak of rejecting anyone they knew—until Heidi.

Heidi, as we shall call her, was the younger sister of a girl who had been in Mirman school for years. Heidi was bold, saucy, self-assured, utterly grown-up for five, and awesomely articulate. Beverly Mirman adored her. There was never any question in the Mirman's minds, nor in those of Heidi's parents, that when the time came Heidi would enter Mirman school as her sister before her. And yet, when the time did come, Heidi marched in for her test, calm and chipper, talking a mile a minute—and failed by many points. She was in the low 120's, considerably above the average but far below the school's average IQ, which is in the mid-150's. Her parents had her retested by an independent laboratory and again she fell decisively short. The little girl who had become a fixture at the reception desk while waiting for her mother to pick up her sister, who had captivated Beverly Mirman with her remarkable maturity and wit was, according to all the accumulated wisdom of the testing art, too dumb to go to Mirman school.

That experience haunts Beverly Mirman. "I wanted badly to take her but would it have been fair? We accepted a boy once who was two points under the cutoff. He had a devil of a time. But you can't help wondering. What is not making it going to do to Heidi? We never dreamed she wouldn't. It all seems so terribly—unfair."[15]

It does. The whole numbers game does. But the Mirmans and many earnest and capable professionals like them believe you have to draw the line somewhere. Of course the distinction between 131 and 129 is artificial; there can be a difference of five points between tests on any two days that is entirely meaningless. Does that mean, then, that the cutoff should be lowered to 125? And having lowered it, what about 120? Or 115? If you don't draw the line somewhere, you don't draw it anywhere.

If there is an answer, what is it? It lies, perhaps, not in segregating the gifted but in offering, like the best of the alternative schools—like the best of any schools—individualized instruction, differentiated programs. If children gifted or otherwise can be trusted to work largely on their own, guided and occasionally helped by a competent teacher, then a true alliance of Jacksonian and Jeffersonian ideals is possible. Education can be both democratic and elite. The artificial distinction between 131 and 129—and 100—can be done away with. Certainly such an approach would take us far toward solving the problem of how to provide for the wide range of individual differences found in any school population. It would undercut the often perverted use of the tracking system, whereby minorities whose school achievement is well below norms because of social disadvantages are "resegregated"—relegated through ostensibly academic groupings to slow-learner or nonacademic programs where the education is manifestly inferior and dead end. Such efforts are the final irony because the common stimulus for our concern with both the disadvantaged and the gifted is the firm belief that children from low-income, ethnic, and racial minority groups are the nation's largest unmined source of talent. (And unless something is changed, critics would contend, likely to remain so.)

Above all, costly as it might be, such individualization would free us from our greatest dilemma, one well expressed by Illinois education specialist Ernest House writing in *The Elementary Principal:*

> We cannot allow the development of new castes. Neither can we allow the extinction of intellectualism in our schools. . . . Should each individual be developed to his fullest? Even if this means giving him increased advantage over his cohorts and making an unequal situation even more unequal? Should we spend money increasing the intellectual skills of intellectually gifted children when so many others can't read?[16]

Denying the gifted their fullest developmental opportunities, warns Columbia University educator A. Henry Passow, will not in itself upgrade the attainments of the less able. "Such misguided and meaningless egalitarianism," says Passow, "contributes to the development of no one in particular."[17] Yet there always looms the danger that the pursuit of excellence can only be accomplished by a retreat from equality and vice versa, he cautions. The problem is as obvious as it is difficult. Whether it is insoluble only time will tell.

But while the needs of the disadvantaged are starkly visible by their social consequences, the unsatisfied needs of the gifted are more subtle, their weakening effects hidden to all but the most discerning. For example, the staff of a Springfield, Virginia, elementary school held a seminar on the gifted and came up with some rather thoughtful questions and conclusions that suggest the deeper consequences of our neglect. The gifted child, they wrote, "may be a fluent reader, but does he skim difficult material and find he has learned little from it? He may be quick to abstract and generalize, but has he developed the habit of backing his conclusions with solid evidence? Is he learning to approach open-ended questions cautiously, identifying every possible position and its defenses?"[18]

Their conclusions were equally incisive: In the crystallizing absence of a peer congregation, where instruction is aimed at the lowest common denominator, the gifted child is deprived of the chance to struggle for achievement, to triumph over obstacles, to toughen his mental muscles. He is deprived of the need to master his whims, rein in his attention, submit to discipline for the sake of future goals. He is deprived of a basis for realistic self-appraisal and a sensible humility in the presence of talents equal or superior to his own. He is in sum, they decided, in his own way, as deprived as the most impoverished child of the ghetto.

We have been talking about the gifted, and look what has subtly, insidiously, and almost unnoticeably happened: We have ended up talking about the gifts of the left hemisphere, as teachers, educators, and psychologists all but invariably do. Where is the right hemisphere, the artistically gifted, in all this? We know how pitifully inadequate, in most cases, public school facilities and instruction for the needs of the gifted have been and are—and until something dramatic and far-reaching occurs out of the pendulum swing of the hemispheres, will continue to be. But what about a child's later years? What about college?

The most telling commentary, perhaps, can be found in the fate of the National Merit Scholarship Corporation's experimental program to admit artistically and scientifically creative students to college on scholarships. The creative scholarships were financed by grants from the Ford Foundation, the Carnegie Corporation, and the National Science Foundation. Begun in 1961, the program recruited 363 creative students during its seven-year history—or less than one one-hundredth of those selected strictly on academic criteria alone. Then, despite the fact that the creative more than held their own scholastically with the academic scholarship winners—and excelled them on extracurricular achievement—the program was discontinued when the Ford Foundation grant was not renewed.

As sad as that is, it only reflects the prevailing left-hemisphere bias of society, a bias innocently betrayed by the National Merit Scholarship Corporation's president, Edward Smith, in the final paragraph of his letter accompanying the news that it was no more:

"I should add that all students selected were Finalists in the Merit Program. The Finalist designation requires very high academic performance. As a result, the students chosen, however promising with respect to creativity, were chosen from a group that was first screened for extremely high academic potential."[19]

Chapter 12

The "Mentally Retarded" in America

The demure, pretty young woman, her pompadoured hair pulled back into an enormous bow, wears an ornate white dress and sits with a cat curled in her lap, an open book clasped in her hands. Her dark wide eyes are mischievous, almost bold. The impression she gives is of the invincible English governess in the Gothic novel who comes to run the mansion and care for the master's children, and ends by putting everything in its place, including him. In many ways Deborah could have done it, too. At twenty-two, she was an excellent seamstress and musician. She could cook, sew, garden, do beadwork, weave baskets, carve wood, and refinish furniture. She was fond of children and good with them. She learned new tasks quickly, had a good memory for the practical, was observant and ever willing to learn. But having as she did the IQ of a nine-year-old child, Deborah Kallikak never did anything remotely romantic beyond contributing her star-crossed family lineage to the most famous study of familial retardation in American psychology. Nor did she ever go anywhere except across the street to a state institution for adults, where she lives to this day, an eighty-five-year-old woman arthritically confined to a wheelchair.

The idea that Deborah might have been able to make her way in the outside world never entered the head of Henry Goddard, the pious and starchy research director of the Vineland, New Jersey, School for Backward and Feeble-Minded Children, where Deborah—illegitimately born in a poorhouse—grew up. Why, as Goddard pointed out, she could not be depended upon to know money, define abstract terms, remember what she read, or count without using her fingers! How could such a person fail to fall "prey to the designs of evil men or evil women" and "lead a life that would be vicious, immoral, and criminal"?[1]

That Deborah Kallikak would still find it almost impossible to make it in the world today—even as an accomplished domestic when domestics of any skill are as rare as the whooping crane—is a sad measure of how short a distance we have come. For the tragic truth is—their art shows and "Olympic" track-and-field meets to the contrary—our mentally retarded remain for most of us a secret shame, their name a stigma bitten deep as the mark of Cain. So empty has been their lot, so anguished the lives of those who love them, that even doctors still resort to poignant stratagems of feeble rationalization in breaking the news to parents. As one pediatrician confided:

"I tell them, 'You're lucky. One of the saddest things about being a parent is seeing your child grow up. That won't happen to you. You'll have a child all your life.' "[2] And after the parents die, what? Under the circumstances, even the overweening righteousness of a Henry Goddard has seemed until recently a small price to pay for the lifetime attention their plight demands.

But now there is a glimmer of honest hope on the horizon. For recent advances in medical science enable us increasingly to prevent, detect, and correct many of the worst forms of hereditary and congenital retardation. In addition, we now know, fully 85 percent of all retardates show no physiological damage, which means we can start to focus most of our remedial effort on the critical first five years after birth, when mental development is most susceptible to environmental stimulation. Then we can begin at last to sort out true familial retardation from the effects of severe social deprivation that merge with, magnify, and mimic it. More, we can take steps to see that the retarded realize something closer to their full potential. To do that, we can use exciting new techniques of hemispheric compensation which promise literally to bypass mild and apparently localized retardation like Deborah's.

But first, if such a sea change is to be enacted anytime soon it must be matched by something comparable in our heads, if not our hearts. We need to recognize a fundamental truth: "Mentally retarded" is a label applied to the widest range of deficiencies. For

301

of course there are not only degrees of retardation but kinds as well, each of whose deficits illuminates yet another fascinating aspect of human intellect. To know as much about them as we can is to know ourselves better, which is value enough. But equally important, to know as much as we can is to face the mentally retarded and make decisions about their problems intelligently, instead of with mingled fear and revulsion and the futile hope (half-hidden even from ourselves) that they will somehow, with no help from us, simply go away.

What causes mental retardation? There are as many causes as there are kinds and degrees. Our intellect is vulnerable from conception, when our father's genes may be a factor, to the preteen years, when the suddenly manifest side-effects of therapeutic drug overdose or the insidious slow ravages of chronic lead poisoning (sifting down from white paint in old houses) can take an irreversible toll. In between, the budding brain is menaced by everything from incompatible parental blood types to maternal measles and hepatitis; impaired function of the mother's pancreas, liver, or heart; kidney lesions; and twenty-six different viruses that can attack it through the placenta. Long before birth, moreover, abnormal genes can program us for disaster. Our biological inheritance, we know, is contained in our DNA, the long double bedspringlike chains of molecules composed of four distinct kinds of biochemical building blocks. Variously aligned, they sequentially encode all the information needed to manufacture a half million different proteins or enzymes, catalysts which comprise our body cells. Each functions as a tiny self-contained chemistry set to perform its specific job. Geneticist James Bonner once calculated that each of our one million million cells is jampacked with three yards of submicroscopic DNA bearing in meticulous linear code the equivalent of the *Encyclopaedia Britannica.*

As Bonner likes to tell it, each strand of DNA is divided into "chapters" on how to make one particular type of enzyme. These we call genes. The DNA in each cell is made up of several strings of genes, each a "book" of genetic chapters on one organic "topic" or another. This we call a chromosome. Each cell has two sets of chromosomes, one from each parent. In producing the sex cells used in reproduction, the number must be cut in half, so that when egg and sperm unite, the normal chromosome count is restored. In one of every 200 live births, however, this split goes inexplicably awry—a condition characterizing several forms of severe retardation, chief among them Down's syndrome or Mongoloid idiocy.

Hereditary biochemical errors determined by or linked to genes can also create pernicious defects in the action of the enzymes. One of the better known is *phenylketonuria* (PKU), a metabolic flaw in which a mysteriously errant enzyme turns one amino acid essential for infant neural growth into another with different properties. Another such error can cause storage disorders in brain metabolism, disrupting the critical mylenization of neurons. When that happens, brain cells fail to become fully insulated and never develop adequate conductivity. For all the legendary security of the womb, moreover, the fetus is physically prey to a host of negative influences from its mother. Her diabetes can starve its blood of glucose, the brain's main fuel. Her malnutrition if severe enough may rob its brain of the ability to synthesize protein and produce healthy neurons, as well as impede the normal growth of the central nervous system through lack of vitamins. Insufficient maternal thyroid hormones or poor placental oxygen supply can likewise impair the fetal brain's protein-making capacity to the point of outright cretinism. Even the effects of psychogenic drugs such as tranquilizers, if given too liberally to the mother during pregnancy, are now thought to affect the proliferation, migration patterns, and maturation rates of cells in the developing fetal cortex.

During birth, the baby may fare little better. The relationship between birth defects and abnormally strenuous labor and delivery has long been recognized, but evaluated solely in terms of time. Now we suspect that the force of uterine contractions or forceps application may be just as critical. Nor is the immediate post-delivery period without its dicey aspects. All the metabolic magic largely dormant in the newborn must be switched on soon after it is extruded into the hostile world. Environmental temperature and oxygen levels may be vital, and vitally different, for the brain of each infant. Studies show that blood-oxygen saturation at birth

303

can vary between 10 and 90 percent for different newborns, who also manifest remarkably different tolerances for oxygen deprivation. For that matter, too rich a mixture in the incubators of some prematures, we learned only after years of tragic experience, can ravage their retinas and cause permanent blindness.

Nor at that point is the mentally healthy newborn entirely out of the woods. Monkeys raised in isolation can be retarded in their behavior by the reduction of sensory input at critical stages of development, although some catch up later if exposed in time to active monkeys of the opposite sex. Until recently we didn't know if this applied to humans, requiring as the primate experiments did a rigorously restricted environment and deliberate deprivation of maternal influence. Now, however, according to neuropsychologist James Prescott of the National Institute of Child Health and Human Development, there are ominous indications that depriving a child of loving physical contact with its mother can cause functional retardation, even organic damage to the brain. Prescott stresses that such conclusions are tentative. The data need further evaluation. Nevertheless preliminary evidence points not only to drastically depressed dendritic branching of neurons in extreme cases, but also in more moderate instances to inhibited communication between brain cells because of faulty functioning in the neural transmitter substances.

These devastating effects are not limited to those rare, pathetic children chained and shut away for years by cruel or deranged parents. They are found too, says Prescott, wherever children are coldly institutionalized. Such a child becomes passive, then withdrawn, finally with the onset of puberty and its turbulent hormonal changes, violent and aggressive.

So we are never wholly without the hazard of retardation during our brain's developing years, even though our chances of succumbing grow statistically rarer with the passing of time. And most forms we now know enough about to prevent, treat, or at least understand, if not cure. But some types of retardation and their causes continue to defy our comprehension, even as they suggest the brain's enormous complexity and untapped potential.

One such bizarre anomaly—perhaps the most fascinating—is

the idiot savant, so named because, while hopelessly retarded in most aspects of intelligence, he is an absolute whiz in one—usually calculation. Though rare, such "figure freaks" dot the pages of mathematical history. Jedediah Buxton, an unlettered farm laborer, carried a thirty-nine-digit number around in his head for two and one half months while multiplying it by itself at intervals to arrive at the correct square. The celebrated New York retardate twins known only as Charles and George are calendar savants. They cannot multiply 7 times 4, yet they can tell you almost instantly on what day of the week any date fell or will fall for 40,000 years. In one of nature's most paradoxical mismatings, idiot savants share their phenomenal and unexplained talent for rapid-fire figuring with the child prodigy. André Marie Ampère, the French father of electrodynamics, and Karl Friedrich Gauss, the German mathematician, astronomer, and physicist were similarly endowed with Buxton's remarkable ability. So for that matter was Truman Henry Safford of Vermont, a Harvard astronomy professor who at ten demonstrated just what prodigious feats the savant's mathematical mind was capable of. Safford was asked to multiply in his head 365, 365, 365, 365, 365, 365 by 365, 365, 365, 365, 365, 365. As described, it was rather like comedian Avery Schreiber's uproarious depiction on TV of the living computer:

> He flew around the room like a top, pulled his panteloons over the top of his boots, bit his hands, rolled his eyes in their sockets, sometimes smiling and talking, and then seeming to be in agony, until, in not more than one minute, said he: 133, 491, 850, 208, 566, 925, 016, 658, 299, 941, 583, 225.[3]

How in the name of IBM do they do it? The "lightning calculators," as psychology calls them, offer few clues, even to those who are unretarded, but the clues they do offer are forever intriguing. More often than not they have two distinct traits in common. For one thing they are blessed with photographic memories. George and Charles can tell you the weather on any important date for the last twenty years. The trait may be familial. One unimpaired savant's brother, an actuary, had his books burned in a fire but rewrote them in six months from memory. Then again, the savants are obsessively focused. Taken to a stage play in London, one early savant was unmoved by its theatrics but informed his hosts how many words had been uttered by the actors and how many steps had been taken by the dancers.

In other equally significant ways they differ. Some of them resort all but instinctively to square roots, cube roots, factoring, and other tricks and techniques of the mathematician. George, for example, according to a statistical consultant, actually has memorized one full 400-year cycle of the Gregorian calendar, and connects any day and date by subtracting multiples of 400 until he arrives at the cycle he knows. In essence, then, George uses the symbolic manipulations of the left hemisphere. Another equally impressive savant, however, worked by arranging and rearranging marbles, buttons and shot in patterns. Not only were such concrete representations important to him, wrote his English biographer, "he believed that his arithmetical powers were strengthened by the fact that at the time he knew nothing about the symbols for numbers." In brief, his mental materials were imagistic, perhaps related to the pattern-recognizing proclivities of the right hemisphere implicit in the crack chess player's instantaneous grasp and indelible memory of the board at every move. The Dutch psychologist A.D. DeGroot has shown that chess masters have total recall for any formation pregnant with meaning, no matter how extensive the array of pieces. When pieces are scattered at random, however, they remember the exact positions no better than anyone else.

In either case the savant's fascinating gift is worth our study if only on the off-chance we might learn some way to adapt it to our needs. Or have we not with our specialization done it to a lesser degree already? One researcher believes the savant's skill may be nothing more than the natural outgrowth of extreme isolation, whether imposed by a defective brain or the social surrounding. Prisoners in solitary confinement have developed similar talents, he says. And yet is he any closer to solving the savant's riddle than the statistician who seeks to explain George by delimiting his mastery to the memory of *only* 146,000 days and an ability to instantly juggle multiples of 400? Is either of them as close as the Cambridge mathematician who writes,

Blessed with excellent memories for numbers, self-confident, stimulated by the astonishment their performance excited, the odd coppers thus put in their pockets and the praise of their neighbours, they pondered incessantly on numbers and their properties; discovered (or in a few cases were taught) the fundamental arithmetical processes, applied them to problems of every increasing difficulty, and soon acquired a stock of information which shortened their work. Probably constant practice and undivided devotion to mental calculation are essential. . . .[4]

Such lines contain almost a prescription for optimum learning. With few amendments, they would fit every talent from tightrope-walking to the concert piano. They might even be stretched to fit Pullen, the heralded "Genius of Earlswood Asylum" in England, who just may be the only idiot savant in recorded medical history whose unique gift was tactile and kinesthetic. According to writer S. Stansfeld Sargent,

Pullen astonished authorities by producing remarkable crayon drawings, carving expertly in ivory and wood, and constructing ship models so intricate and detailed that they are still displayed in the two large workrooms placed at his disposal in the asylum. His proudest accomplishment was a ten-foot model steamship that took more than three years to complete. Equipped with brass anchors, screws, pulley blocks, copper paddles, 5,585 copper rivets and 13 complete lifeboats, it also contains nearly a million and a quarter wooden pins fixing the planks to the ribs. Pullen made these with a special instrument of his own designing. The cabins are decorated and furnished with chairs, tables, beds and bunks.[5]

Otherwise, adds Sargent, Pullen was sadly deficient. Until the age of seven he did not speak, and then for a long time uttered only the word "muvver." He learned to wash and dress himself and eventually write the names of simple objects, but beyond these childlike accomplishments he failed forever to go. Although his observation, attention, and memory were good, he was considered emotionally unstable, childish and—the psychological understatement of the nineteenth century—"lacking in mental balance." A brain defect of undisclosed nature which left him nearly deaf in childhood, doctors decided, had cut him off from others and made possible his tremendous powers of absorption. Sargent too recognized the enigma a man like Pullen poses. "How much his striking achievements were due to this intense and single-minded preoccupation with mechanical things, and how much was due to innate special abilities," he writes, "it is impossible to say."[6] The same, of course, could probably be said of Edison, Henry Ford, and a host of other machine geniuses.

But all in all, as one medical specialist would later observe, "the importance of the idiot savant lies in our inability to explain him; he stands as a landmark of our own ignorance and . . . exists as a challenge to our capabilities."[7]

One line of evidence may lie in the scarcely more widespread phenomenon of autism, a macabre and challenging condition which finds the child all but locked in a solitary cell made of its own body. The autistic child cannot love. It shows no interest in being cuddled, and even fails to mold its body to those who pick it up. It does not startle. The flash of a strobe light or the point-blank bang of a cymbal meet with equally dreamy indifference. Other times it screams in terror at the fleeting glimpse of a refrigerator or the honk of a passing car. It can parrot with chilling perfection but cannot fashion from words a fitting response. Asked, "Do you want a glass of milk?" it may answer with a mocking, "Do you want a glass of milk?" not just once but for days. Like some stir-crazy con, it will lapse for hours into hypnotically repetitive or sustained behavior such as rocking, humming, shaking its dangling hands in front of its face, grimacing, or staring raptly at a cupped hand or rhythmically flexing elbow. Then, as if some slender thread of reason had snapped, it explodes without warning into an orgy of vicious self-mutilation that, if uninterrupted, can go on for horrifying hours with seeming indifference to pain. No sadist was ever more cruel. Unless restrained by straps—often for most of their young lives—autistics have been known to chew their shoulders to the bone, pound their heads to a bloody, fractured pulp, bite off their fingers, or pull out their nails with their teeth. And yet, perhaps the cruelest cut of all, they are anything but the dregs of the back ward one might suppose. On the contrary, most are hauntingly beautiful children whose facial expression of uncommonly sensitive attunement, fixed as it seems on some inaccessible star, is often described as "strikingly intelligent." If further irony were needed, the first one hundred studied came from socioeconomic backgrounds far surpassing those of the Terman gifted.

For years autistics were thought to be psychiatric casualties from a cold, destructive environment created by aloof parents who simply did not want them. Believing their parents wished them dead, went the theory, they withdrew into the psychic safety of their own inner fortress. ("Autistic" comes from the Greek *autos*, meaning "self.") Though many are frozen at the infant level and do not learn to feed, dress themselves, or control their bowels, others often score far above average on IQ, which lends still further weight to the popular notion that autism is psychosis, not true retardation. But increasingly it appears that parents have suffered a bum rap. The autistic's own body may somehow be guilty. The question is, how and why?

Biological theories vary, but most involve either a perceptual disorder, a defect in the brain's arousal and attention mechanism, or both. In either case, researchers argue, the blizzard of information routinely showering the autistic's senses does not penetrate its brain strongly or systematically enough to be organized into Jerison's neural clumps and stored as meaningful, integrated experience. The autistic, for example, cannot grasp a movie as anything more than a train of totally unrelated fragments. Shown a photograph of boys playing football, it typically describes them as "marching" or "shaking hands." If you step on its toy, it becomes angry at your foot, not at you. As Bernard Rimland, the psychologist founder of the National Society for Autistic Children and himself the father of an autistic child, writes:

> . . . It seems very much as though the material had entered the nervous system on a single track, proceeded to a point of storage without ever having been analyzed or supplemented, then later emerged from storage in virtually its original condition, on a parallel track, as an all-or-nothing response to a subsequent stimulus.[8]

The autistic, moreover, appears incapable of relating one stimulus-response arc (a mother's caress and its own subsequent feeling of comfort) to another (the looming sight of her as she bends to kiss away its tears). Cross-model transfer—what Arthur Koestler calls cross-referencing—simply fails to occur. So, therefore, do the complex mental modeling and manipulation needed to equate in the child's mind its act of crying with its mother's loving appeasement as something to be remembered or anticipated. In Piagetian terms it never succeeds in establishing a set of accurate and reliable constants. Much less does it learn to split itself, the actor, away from the action and go on to internalize the world outside and its manifold relationships. In his book *Infantile Autism*, Rimland likens the autistic brain to one "operated by a clerk rather than a chemist; raw material comes and goes, but the parcels are never opened and their contents are never mixed to form any useful compound."[9]

Since it cannot assemble much less work creatively with the materials of a complex neural mosaic, the big picture in all its subtle, interlocking, ever-shifting detail is beyond it. It cannot add to or amend its master model of a possible reality because it has none. Without that ability, all things and events are interpreted on the simplest scale of sensory stimulation, as degrees and kinds of sensation. To the autistic, people are simply stimulating objects, himself foremost. If it cannot differentiate the outside world from the inside, the actor from the action, then it cannot conceive of itself as an organized, unitary, unique ego. It is merely a stimulus-response machine.

This would account for the autistic child's uncanny ability to ape speech. It can precociously memorize nursery rhymes, foreign lullabies, names of Presidents, in the instance of one seventeen-month-old an aria from *Don Giovanni*—without the faintest flicker of comprehension, which supports Rimland's contention that they "appear to have done all that they could with language—repeat it rather than understand it."[10] In this they are much like the idiot savant. Rimland thinks the idiot savant *is* autistic:

> My theory is that the idiot savant suffers from a laser-like . . . focus . . . which he cannot broaden to allow himself to see the relevance of what he is doing. . . . [He] is like a man watching a football game through a high-powered telescope. He

310

can count the blades of grass along the 50-yard line, but he can't tell you what's going on.[11]

Some learning must take place, however, since the child will often repeat your question about milk the next time it wants a glass. One autistic habitually referred to his grandmother as "Fifty" because he had once heard her called that in a discussion of her age.

The autistic's overbearing single-mindedness could account too, if indirectly, for both its self-stimulating behavior and its self-mutilating rage. How better control an environment ever filled with things new and strange, and therefore potentially hostile and taxing, than by satiating itself with rigidly selected stimuli that are familar, safe, and undemanding on its unavailing powers of mental manipulation? And if by chance the unexpected, the threatening, the awful does intrude, how better avoid the shrieking terror it holds the next time around than to dramatize its fear of anything unexpected by staging an unforgettable scene that will ensure everyone's fanatic efforts to maintain an uncertainty-free environment—which, given the nature of life, is doomed to fail?

But how is this to explain the autistic child's evident immunity to pain, its patent imperviousness on occasion to sight and sound, its manifest absence of sensory startle? Believers in perceptual defect argue that stimulus and response are so locked into a closed loop by the autistic's flawed neurophysiology as to be all but continuous if not identical. Awash in sensation, its brain is perceptually starved. The lack of any mediation by an intervening reservoir of experience, they speculate, could rob the suddenly onsetting new sensation of its startling impact; familiar sights and sounds of their perceptual import; even injury of its deeper pain.

By itself, obviously, such a theory is far from perfect. It cannot account for the fact that some autistics are retarded in development but not in intelligence. This may have as much to do with diagnosis as anything. True autism is still confused with childhood psychosis and other conditions which betray one or more of its symptoms. In a study by Rimland only fifty-five of 445 psychotic children seen by two different doctors got the same diagnosis twice. Dr. Leo Kanner, the psychiatrist who first described autism, estimates that only one in ten diagnosed autistic really is.

311

The alternate theory, that autistics are cursed with laserlike attention is in some respects more persuasive. In the words of UCLA researcher Ivar Lovaas, "if you tell an autistic child to open the door, he may not hear the words at all; he may focus so intensely on the movement of your lips that he will not hear the sound of your voice."[12] Given simultaneous auditory, visual, and tactile clues to a complex stimulus, Lovaas has found, normal children respond uniformly to all three, conventional retardates variously to two or more, autistics only to one. Sealed in its psychic cocoon, the autistic conceivably could ignore everything but that which rivets its attention, even love and excruciating pain. But what detonates such explosions of violence, fear, and verbal mimicry? Only the two theories together, faulty perception and attention, seem to cover all behavioral bases as neatly as medical science would like.

Even then they leave researchers groping for the root cause. Some autistics, we now know, have elevated levels of serotonin, one of the body's busy messenger chemicals. But is this cause, is it effect, or is it essentially beside the point? We don't know. Serotonin is best known for raising our blood pressure; only a scant 1 percent of it is found in the brain. Although it is chemically similar to LSD, its role in normal brain functions remains obscure. Some researchers, on the other hand, suspect parents may be genetically to blame in a way that only heightens the irony of the autistic. Noting a preponderance of victims born into families blessed with high educational status, gifted siblings, and extremely bright parents who are usually professionals, they hypothesize that the autistic may have inherited "too much of a good thing."[13] Such a double dose of whatever makes genetically for superior intelligence, they feel, may leave the autistic's brain, in effect, "overbred," and excessively vulnerable to dangers in their early environment.

Rimland points out that an abnormal number of autistics were born prematurely and received medical oxygen that might have damaged oversensitive neural tissue. Curiously enough, he reports, children blinded by too much oxygen showed such unmistakable signs of autism as head-banging, rocking, and mocking speech. As he and others see it, any of the many immediate,

312

pre- and postnatal traumas enumerated earlier could wreak the same havoc on those genetically predisposed to weakness. But for now, the ultimate answer to the riddle remains locked behind the dreamlike gaze of enchanting children by the thousands.

The last baffling category is usually not classified as retarded at all. It is more often called minimal brain dysfunction (MBD), a behavioral grab bag of attention, perception, and expression deficiencies that in themselves are variously labeled minimal cerebral syndrome, neurosensory disorder, hyperkinesis, perceptual-motor disorder, organic brain syndrome, psychoneurotic inefficiency, cerebral dysfunction, associational deficit pathology, and functional behavioral disorder. Like the inky ejections of the squid, most of these diagnoses mask more than they reveal, even as they mirror the frustrations of medical science. A couple are outright misnomers: There is a lamentable lack of proven organic involvement and precious little pathology. But all have one thing in common. If unchecked, they can block learning and make functional retardates out of children with the highest of IQ's.

Though their symptoms often overlap, MBD children generally can be divided into two basic handicapped groups which may only be marginally related: those who cannot pay sustained attention, and those who either cannot properly speak, read, write, or exotic combinations of these.

The first are the hyperkinetic, or hyperactive, those whirling dervishes whò forever plague the conventional classroom. They are nervous, fidgety, aggressive, excitable, impulsive, antic, clumsy, poorly coordinated, easily distracted, fitfully energetic and—at the risk of redundancy—have short attention spans and cannot concentrate. Frequently they perform as well as the normal on IQ tests, but fall behind in schoolwork because they cannot do their studies as quickly or with comparable absorption and persistence. Usually they are an unmitigated disaster on the playing fields as well. Most, like the autistics, are boys. (Indeed, some researchers now regard autism as an extreme form of MBD). Like the autistic, recent studies indicate, the hyperkinetic may be victimized by a defective arousal and attention mechanism, which probably explains why he responds best to stimulant drugs that speed up his system. Consequently, his restlessness may not be an obvious symptom of hectic overstimulation, as once thought. Rather, paradoxically, it may be an attempt to cope with chronic understimulation by seeking a constantly changing kaleidoscope of novel sensation. Beyond that, research has been relatively inconclusive.

The second MBD group suffers from a constellation of language impairments known collectively as dyslexia. Technically, dyslexia means the inability to read properly. The larger condition is better called alexia, or "word blindness." Alexics are prone to a variety of weird symptoms which are frequently confused with brain damage, educational deprivation, and emotional trauma. Some alexics comprehend letters and words as such but cannot connect them to sounds and meanings. Others can speak and understand but cannot write, read, or spell. Still others have enormous difficulty talking, following verbal instructions, and grasping foreign languages. Many read words from right to left, confuse those that have meaning backward (like "was" and "saw"), mix letters whose directional cast is critical (p and q, d and b), read just as efficiently upside down as right side up, and mirror-write or write equally well—or atrociously—with either hand.

There are strong indications that alexia may be hemispheric in origin. Some years ago, Samuel Orton, one of the pioneer theorists in alexia, concluded that while the two sides of the normal brain work in synchrony, with the "dominant" hemisphere leading like the larger of two meshed gear wheels, the alexic brain was different. Its two hemispheres still competed for dominance and lacked a clear division of labor. The resulting hemispheric confusion he saw as a two-way street—with trouble in either direction. Not only did language get in the way of performance tasks, unruly images impinging from the nonlanguage hemisphere also made the use of language all that more difficult.

Orton, it now appears, was not that far wrong. Although hemispheric specialization defies the doctrine of a single dominant side that Orton accepted, there seems to be no reason why the side specialized for a given function shouldn't predominate in its execution. Either side, then, could provide the cerebral drive wheel as the task demanded. If, however, as Orton speculated, functions in the alexic brain were not as crisply compartmented, both hemispheres would try to lead and, speaking metaphorically if not mechanically, the neural gears would fail to mesh. Analyzing the performance of alexics on intelligence tests, Sperry found support for this in an unnatural dispersion of scores, one that painted a statistical picture of two hemispheres fighting over which would do what task how. In addition, EEG readings taken on alexics by investigators a continent apart showed substantially less than the perfect synchronization of normals—more so even, when the children were resting with their eyes closed. But nowhere was this interference better illustrated than in the left-hander.

Left-handers, like children, are significantly more likely than right-handers to recover their speech after serious injury to the left hemisphere. This is not because their language center is located on the right, though that may be true in some cases. Most of them, remember, have language on the left, just as right-handers do. Yet when speech is lost to injury in the left hemisphere, it is the left-hander who most often regains it. Why?

Unlike right-handers, researchers tentatively decided, left-handers must have the power of language expression on *both* sides. Besides their normal center for expressive language, they retained a superior residual capacity in the opposite hemisphere, not just passive but capable of spontaneously taking over the whole job in time of acute need. To prove it, researchers injected sodium amytal into the carotid artery supplying the left half of the brain with blood. Asked to count aloud after the injection, the right-handed subject complied until the drug took effect and temporarily knocked out the speech center. Then he lapsed into silence. The left-handed subject, however, hesitated only momentarily when the anesthetic hit home, then, requested to do so, went on counting orally out of the right side of his brain while apparently asleep!

Under ordinary conditions, it was soon found, this dual capability was something less than the neurological blessing it might have seemed. Being less clearly lateralized to one side, the language in the left-hander's brain disrupted the normal workings of the non-language hemisphere. On intelligence tests, left-handers scored consistently less on perceptual and performance problems than right-handers of comparable verbal intelligence. What's more, the

315

difference between the left-handers' own verbal and nonverbal scores was as much as three times that of the comparable right-handers. In other words, broadly speaking, their nonlanguage hemispheres were only a third as intelligent in their normal functions as the language scores would naturally have led us to expect.

Exactly as alexic theory would have it, the bilateral development of speech was no boon to their language proficiency either. One remarkable study suggests that even stammering can stem from it. R. K. Jones of Lankanau Hospital in Philadelphia found with the sodium amytal technique that four patients who had stammered from early childhood had speech on both sides. When their brains were operated on for other reasons, their stammering abruptly stopped. From follow-up amytal tests it was obvious that the duplicate speech mechanism had somehow been disconnected in a stroke of surgical serendipity. They now showed speech only on one side. For years, Jones concluded, they had been trying to talk simultaneously out of both!

Stammering aside, surface errors in language expression and perception are only the tip of the MBD iceberg. In extreme cases a deep-reaching delay can occur in yoking left-hemisphere symbols to right-hemisphere images, which in turn seems to impede the brain's routine construction of mental models that can be integrated and manipulated. Both perception and expression are thereby distorted. Thus, in theory, faulty synchronization can stymie creativity and retard learning itself.

Relatively few alexics are impaired to this extreme, of course. We would be quicker to call them retarded if they were. But as minuscule as its fallout may sometimes appear, when aggravated by the stressful demands of modern society, MBD can be as devastating in its human consequences as retardation. For while our mental wards are understandably empty of MBD cases, our juvenile halls are full of them. As Peter Koenig perceptively writes of one such boy in *Psychology Today* —a boy who had climbed the predictable pyramid of truancy, vagrancy, vandalism, petty theft, shoplifting, and assault, and now stood poised on the higher path to a life of hardened crime and eventual prison:

> The authorities have several explanations for Mike's behavior.
> They have diagnosed a looping problem characteristic of dys-

316

lexia, a hyperkinetic problem, perceptual problems and impaired hearing. . . . Labels, like the general label juvenile delinquent, beat back the terror of Mike's life for us, but don't help Mike much.[14]

In its more drastic aspects, the mental retardation picture in America continues to improve. Detection and prevention are now more possible than ever. New tests, new drugs, new ideas in nutrition, all play increasingly important parts in the cycle of detecting, curbing, and regulating conditions early on that can cause more serious retardation. Coating hospital diapers with a chemical sensitive to abnormal urine, for example, now exposes PKU in the newborn. In addition, varied patterns of amplitude and differing kinds of delay in response to evoked cortical potentials give neurology its first really reliable predictor of the baby's central nervous system soundness. Just as insulin prevents diabetes, the mental effects of enzyme deficiency diseases like galactosemia (the body's inability to process milk products) can be minimized by early warning, proper diet, vitamins, and hormones. Interuterine transfusions can eliminate dangerous parental blood incompatibility. Transplants can replace defective infant kidneys, organic factories for errant enzymes that disrupt crucial fat metabolism in the brain. Despite the current romanticism surrounding home delivery, the potentially destructive strain of hard labor can be circumvented by more frequent resort to caesarian section. Should genetic flaws be suspected, fluid containing cells from the growing fetus can be siphoned off by abdominal needle (a relatively safe and simple process called amniocentesis), cultured in the lab like a virus, and examined for both defective genes and an abnormal chromosome count. If either exists, the pregnancy can then be aborted with the consent of the parents. Here prevention hits home with a vengeance. Since it costs an estimated quarter of a million dollars to care for one mongoloid child during its lifetime, abolishing Down's syndrome alone during the next decade would save some $40,000,000,000, and as many headaches.

Though far less dramatic, care and treatment in some areas of retardation continue to progress. Many MBD children require little more than special practice and endless patience. In time some simply grow out of it. As adults they become accomplished mathematicians, scientists, musicians, painters, and writers (even though they may never learn to spell). Thomas Edison, Albert Einstein, Woodrow Wilson, Dwight Eisenhower, Robert Kennedy, and Hans Christian Anderson all had early learning disabilities, as did Leonardo da Vinci. Other retardates need incessant attention—and respond hearteningly when they get it. Housed in institutions whose environments are tailored to provide intensive stimulation, mongoloid children today actually fare better in intelligence than they do at home. Comparative studies of evoked cortical potentials prove their brains function far more efficiently. As for the autistic, both positive and negative behavior modification (hugging and cuddling, spanks and electric shock) are being effectively used with one in three to shape and sharpen their social responses, which then frees them to learn more than anyone used to think possible.

The educable mentally retarded are also being accelerated in their learning, at least experimentally, by treating them not as the younger children they resemble in some of their thought processes, but as chronological age-mates of their normal contemporaries. Both benefit, if to different degrees, from special training in *how* to learn as opposed to being drilled on *what* they are to learn, University of Minnesota psychologist Arthur Taylor has found from experiments. Encouraged to embed items for recall in a common meaningful context, for instance—one affording a storylike train of images in action as conceptualized by Stanford's Roger Bower—children whether normal or retarded generate more relations between items, identify more associations, and remember two to six times as much.

But the brightest ray of hope beams in an area that owes much of its theoretical impetus to the concept of the divided brain. All unknown, its foundation was laid almost a hundred years ago when French neurologist Joseph Déjerine reported the baffling case of a wealthy businessman who had lost his reading ability to severe left-hemisphere stroke. Although blinded to the meaning of printed words, Déjerine's patient could still recognize and comprehend on sight such symbolic values as trademarks, the faces of playing cards, and numbers on the stock exchange. The man's language center was untouched, Déjerine determined by autopsy

318

years later, but his same-side visual cortex was ravaged, as were the neural pathways leading to that of the opposite hemisphere. So how could he understand graphic symbols, lacking as he did direct cerebral connections between what he could see and what he could symbolize?

Thanks to the split-brain experiments, we now know that the right hemisphere not only passively recognizes language, but through any combination of our senses integrates and encodes synesthetic mental images that can indelibly capture anything in the tangible world of concrete objects. Everything understood as such is thus retained in all the psychological richness of a multidimensional design; a neural gestalt; a mental icon. Since they must first physically exist to be infused with meaning, trademarks and playing cards certainly qualify in such essential concreteness. Numbers do too, by extension, Harvard's Norman Geschwind observes, since they have strong tactile and kinesthetic overtones because we learn them by using our fingers.

Viewed hemispherically, then, the brain of Déjerine's patient was simply exercising in the absence of one set of abilities another still remaining to it—or so it seemed. Without really concerning themselves with the theoretic whys and wherefores, many reading clinicians have been pulling out all stops recently to surround the symbolic act of using language with all conceivable perceptual "hooks" (excepting, possibly, smell). With utter pragmatism they are teaching English to those who can't learn phonetically, by such diverse means as pictures (visual images), tactile matrices with raised words of wood and sandpaper (kinesthetic images), and "talking typewriters" that combine the aural, the visual, and the tactile (synesthetic images). One inventive therapist even has her students trace with their tongues difficult letters dipped in syrup, to lock a positive, pleasant taste into a kinesthetic feel for its configuration.

But is this the brain's natural way of assimilating perceptual material for abstraction, or is it being used here to augment a defective function? Does the right hemisphere normally complement the left in exercising the brain's symbolic abilities, or does this therapeutically intensified use of it constitute a stopgap, backup strategy?

319

The issue is unresolved, perhaps operationally beside the point. But Michael Gazzaniga is inclined to think that this is the way the brain naturally works. He is even beginning to believe that the hoary concept of cerebral dominance should be taken out, dusted off, and redefined in terms of which hemisphere provides the one and only "final cognitive path" he is convinced exists regardless of the specialized task involved. Gazzaniga places that path in the right hemisphere, since it not only retains residual language but has the pattern-recognizing capacity to initiate symbol interpretation. His theory does little to clarify matters. But it merits mention because it provides the scaffolding upon which he and associates have erected a fascinating new method of teaching aphasics an artificial right-hemisphere "language," one with inestimable implications for rehabilitating the mentally retarded.

First, the chief experimenter, Andrea Velletri Glass, showed Gazzaniga's global aphasics (all massively damaged in the left hemisphere) pictures of objects, plants, animals, people, and scenes. She then demonstrated, by putting them into piles, that the items depicted could be grouped into such unspoken categories as animate and inanimate, edible and inedible, natural and manmade. Could they do that? She gestured. Although the aphasics were by definition utterly incapable of comprehending or generating language, within a very few trials all proved they could still classify. Or were they perhaps just sorting images by memory, merely imitating her? Next they were given a set of arbitrary paper symbols of varied color, size, and shape originally developed by psychologist David Premack for the purpose of teaching chimpanzees to "talk." The symbols stood for words, each of whose meaning was communicated, one after another, by a simple social transaction. The names of the patient and experimenter, for instance, were taught by hanging a duplicate of each's name symbol around his or her neck.

Once learned, could this set of new and alien symbols be manipulated like real language? It could. Starting with simple but vital cognitive distinctions (same, different) all seven patients within a month had mastered them both in their declarative and interrogative forms. (Wordlessly: Is A the same as B? Wordlessly: A is the same as B.) Before the brief experiment had ended, two patients had reached the relatively advanced stage of constructing and comprehending strings of such symbols aligned in simple "sentences." Gazzaniga, Glass, and Premack concluded that despite their massive language loss, aphasics retain a potential for abstraction and conception through the visual-aural images of the right hemisphere, the perceptual gateway to our brain.

But how do we know the same dynamics naturally apply to the mentally retarded, whose brains by definition have never had a left hemisphere that functioned fully up to par?

Until recently all we knew was that retardates given conventional IQ tests predictably scored lower than normal on measures of the left hemisphere—but unpredictably, that they scored significantly higher than normal on visual-spatial-kinesthetic measures of the right hemisphere. Parenthetically, it would be instructive to see what would happen if we defined retardation in terms of right-hemisphere deficiencies, and threw out a net to include those who are "all thumbs" manually, who "can't draw a straight line," who invariably fail to "see their nose in front of their face" when it comes to deciphering a do-it-yourself diagram. The ranks of the educable "mentally retarded" might be doubled.

But even so, the hemispheric issue was muddied in those studies by the random mixing of brain-injured retardates, whose damage was more specific and scores more varied, with the non-brain-injured, whose deficits were more generalized. Now, however, comes a psychologist named Renée Fuller with the best evidence yet that the right hemisphere can be used to teach language, not just Premack's "monkey language," but standard English—and to imbeciles. Fuller, who is chief of psychological services at Rosewood State hospital in Maryland, taught twenty-six retardates with IQ's ranging from 33 to 69 to read at the third-grade level in one year. They ranged in age from eleven to forty-nine, in diagnosis from MBD to mongolism to familial retardation to microcephaly (pinheadedness). Every previous effort to teach them as much as the alphabet had failed.

The key to her system lies in its name. She calls it the Ball-Stick-Bird Method because the letters of the alphabet are simplified by breaking them up and reconstructing them from three basic forms: a line, a circle, and an angle, all of which can be easily recognized by a two-year-old. To each component she gave a color, and—most important for right-hemisphere processing—the name of a concrete object. The circle became a ball, the line a stick, and the angle a bird. (Déjerine's patient, it might be pointed out, referred to the letter Z as a serpent, P as a buckle, and A as a trestle or stand.) Fuller's patients then manipulated the birds, sticks, and balls mentally to form a letter, the congeries of resulting imagistic letters to form words, and the subsequent flocks of birds, piles of sticks, and bunches of balls to create fast-paced, suspenseful space odysseys of lively interest and graduated difficulty.

Not only did they read, notes Fuller,

> they were able to comprehend stories considerably above their mental age and drew inferences about advanced content. Comprehension and vocabulary tests showed performance that exceeded not only mental-age expectations but pretest scores by many years. Spontaneous verbalization of the patients showed that the newly acquired vocabulary was not a passive acquisition but was actively used. . . .[15]

In short, unlike many normal schoolchildren, they clearly understood what they read. Most important of all, adds Fuller (a PhD who was unable to read until age twelve because of perceptual disabilities), *there was absolutely no correlation between IQ and reading performance.* Some students with IQ's in the 30's learned to read as rapidly with comprehension as others in the 60's. One of her faster learners dropped from 39 to 35 even as her poorest student gained 9 points! Concluded Fuller, "I believed what everybody else believed—that you couldn't do this with anybody with an IQ under 50. . . .[16] Such deficiency in general intelligence should preclude reading success. But our subjects were successful. For this reason our results raise questions about the validity and meaningfulness of [IQ] in the real world."[17]

There can be no denying, of course, that some retarded—happily, the fewest—are so severely damaged that they must be confined all their lives, lives which are often mercifully short and a savage drain to any but the most religious. Even then, all but the worst, through painstaking behavior modification techniques of reward and praise, can now be taught to feed themselves, dress, undress, and go to the toilet—for them, accomplishments as towering as the Himalayas. Others previously doomed to endless days of idle staring have since shown they can learn menial jobs such as packing light bulbs when patiently supervised, and thus achieve at least the dignity of partial independence. These are the "TMR's," the trainable mentally retarded. There are 300,000 of them in the United States alone, most still vocationally undiagnosed, untrained, and unemployed, unfortunately.

But it is the 1,500,000 "EMR's," the educable mentally retarded, who provide the bitterest bone of contention. Society has yet to separate to its satisfaction those it believes intrinsically cannot learn all the mental skills deemed necessary to survive in a basically left-hemisphere-oriented world—like Deborah—from those of innately higher intelligence whose opportunity has been brutally blighted by social conditions beyond their power to rectify. How are we to winnow out the one from the other? And as a practical matter, should we? It is here the dispute is hottest, the prospects for constructive change highest. For the undeniable fact is, both have been too long lumped together and indiscriminately "warehoused like surplus scraps of humanity,"[18] to borrow the biting words of Joseph H. Douglass, executive director of the President's Committee on Mental Retardation.

Assuming we could and should separate them, the culturally deprived would be the natural target of remedial measures that have no place in this chapter. But what of that other swarming multitude on the borderline, the true familial retardates with IQ's between 50 and 70, the "bottom rung on the phylogenetic ladder" which includes more than 80 percent of our mentally retarded? What are we to do about these, many of whom have been locked up or otherwise given dismally short shrift in all that makes for a life worth living, despite intact and functioning right hemispheres?

We could, as indicated in the section on testing, develop better nonverbal instruments for assessing right-hemisphere abilities. Even today, according to Rimland, numerous studies of the educable mentally retarded in this country and England show that after leaving school their performance in real-life jobs does not differ all that markedly from that of their "normal" classmates. This

323

says less about their true abilities, one suspects, than it does about the symbiotic relationship between the standardized IQ test and the traditional structure of our schools. Rimland wants a test that would measure "practical intelligence," an external mental quality he calls "here-and-now" intellect or "with-it-ness"—not the inward focus of abstraction but the outward focus of a "stimulus-tied attention" such as that typified by Jensen's concept of type I intelligence. Rimland almost seems to be championing the synesthetic perception of an aroused, alert, and functioning right hemisphere.

In dealing with the marginally retarded we could also resolutely look the other way and pretend they are not there. The suggestion is far from frivolous. Both Jerome Kagan in Guatemala and Freda Rabelsky in Holland have discovered communities where children by custom are placed in almost total isolation for the supposedly critical first year of their lives—without noticeably lasting effect. In what Kagan describes as a "thirteenth-century pre-Columbian village" of "poor, exploited, alienated, bitter, sick" Indians, he saw children shut up in the darkness of bamboo huts to ward off "the evil eye." Clinically retarded by their second year, they grow out of it to become "gay, alert, active, affective"[19] youngsters who perform better than their American counterparts on intelligence tests by age eleven. Rabelsky reports virtually the same outcome in the stable, middle-class nuclear Dutch families she studied. They bound their children and kept them in a room outside the house with no toys and a minimum of human stimulation. While Kagan's kids were nursed, fondled, and carried around much of the time, James Prescott may be perplexed to learn that Rabelsky's Dutch infants were not. Such findings suggest we might do both ourselves and the mildly retarded, the so-called "slow learners," a favor by refusing to single them out for special education. We might do them an even bigger favor in the long run by ignoring them altogether and trusting to their innate potential when exposed to the bustling society at large.

Finally we could—as Jensen and others have proposed with varying degrees of seriousness—embark on a vigorous national program of sterilization for all retardates who satisfy the dual requirement of being both mentally retarded in IQ and socially incompetent, a behavioral catch-all to snare today's Deborah Kallikak the first time she attempts to make change. In Denmark, a forty-year-old program of government sterilization—a stick-and-carrot operation amounting to what one observer called "voluntary compulsion"—confines retardates of less than 75 IQ to an institution until or unless they succumb to such blandishments as free surgery or, where necessary, criminal pardon. All but 1 percent of Denmark's retardation, the genetic flukes that presently cannot be predicted, has been eradicated as a result. But Denmark, as critics are quick to point out, is a tiny, prosperous nation of about 5,000,000 tightly homogeneous people. The United States on the other hand is huge, populous, ethnically and socially varied, economically stratified to the extreme, and riven with racial strife. Even today, black leaders complain, sterilization is being quietly used in some of the twenty-seven states where it remains on the books, against destitute black women with large families, coerced by threats to cut off their welfare or medical aid. The most just and humane federal law, opponents fear, might suffer the same fate in local implementation. In Denmark, it is worth noting, sterilization is also aimed at the chronically alcoholic, psychotic, criminal, and jobless—depending on who is making the diagnosis, all potential flashpoints of racism if exported to this country.

Whatever we decide to do about the marginally retarded, it is clear that what we are doing now really solves nothing. In consigning the "mentally retarded" to special (usually inferior) education, Jane Mercer found in a study of 800 so-called retardates in a heavily black and Chicano district of southern California, the local public school system could support less than one diagnosis in ten with medical data. The other determinations were made strictly on IQ scores, in almost half the cases above the usual clinical cut-off of 70. In short, they were retarded only because the school system for reasons of its own said they were. Such reasons are often understandable: administration ignorance of the technicalities, crushing recalcitrance on the part of pupils unwilling or unable to learn what the schools wish to teach. Then again, the reasons aren't always so defensible. Urban psychologist Thomas Cottle discovered nine black children in New England who were held back a year as retarded on the basis of scores from nonexistent IQ tests forged on their records by counselors who existed only as fictitious code numbers.

Most questionable of all to Mercer, there were three times as many Mexican-Americans and half again as many blacks in the "retarded" group as their proportions in the community would statistically suggest—but only a little more than half as many Anglos. When Mercer tested her own subsample of low-IQ performers from the same geographic area for their social competence on the basis of their practical adaptive ability—traveling alone, playing sports, shopping—the rate of the ostensibly retarded fell by about half. No wonder more and more minority groups are taking schools to court for what amounts to an infringement of the most sensitive human sort: in truth-in-labeling laws.

If labeling is no solution, neither is the latest trend in treatment in that gray area where minimal brain dysfunction produces functional retardation that can masquerade as the real organic thing. There, we are compounding the problem by confusing bad or unwanted behavior with both. For faced with troublesome children of every stripe, schools across the country have been therapeutically dosing them with amphetamines—"speed," at the very time they lecture against the dangers of drugs—on the grounds that they must be hyperkinetic. Even if they were, the relationship between stimulants and hyperkinesis is foggy at best. For every study that shows school performance is improved, another shows that it isn't. More importantly, as Diane Divoky eloquently writes in *Learning* magazine,

> Does more docile, uniform behavior make for better learning? Are daydreaming and drawing during an arithmetic lesson invariably negative signs? Might not inattentiveness be a healthy sign in that particular classroom? Is it enough that such medication makes black ghetto children act more like polite middle-class children—particularly when no change in academic performance accompanies the change in behavior? Are the learning disabilities these youngsters suffer the consequences of bad homes, poor nutrition, a school environment totally foreign to their lives, or a neurological dysfunction?
> . . . We have, apparently, reached that stage in our development when we know with great certainty how a child should and

326

must behave. Moreover, we have at hand a quick and nonpunitive means of getting him to behave that way. Forget about individual differences. Forget that children have always been difficult and cantankerous and wearing, that living with them has never been a job for the impatient or fragile. Forget that modern life makes enormous demands on the young to conform and to achieve. Forget all that, call the psychologist, call for the doctor, and once you have their help and their drug prescriptions, put up your feet and relax. Because then the controls will all be inside the kids, and they'll behave as programmed.

Right, Mr. Huxley? Right, Mr. Orwell?[20]

Nor, finally, are the austere and understaffed corridors of our institutions any remedy. In their book *Hansels and Gretels*, the brother and sister psychologist team of Benjamin and Dorthea Braginsky contend that the vast majority of institutionalized retardates are not helplessly stupid, as society likes to think. In reality, like Deborah, they are "adept, rational, resourceful and intelligent human beings capable of protecting their own interests."[21] In a study in which half the group was told they would go to a new and "terrible" program if they passed a test, the other half that they would go if they failed, the retardates demonstrated to the Braginskys that they could manipulate their IQ responses to appear "bright" or "dumb" at will. Nine out of ten, moreover, did not believe they were retarded. The critical reaction of their colleagues to the Braginskys' book was less than kind. "Yes, retardates see things differently than staff," sniffed one psychologist in joining the many who felt the Braginskys had overstated their case. "So do graduate students perceive their lot differently than their professors. This doesn't imply that we should do away with universities."[22]

But what, then, are we, like the Braginskys, to make of memorable men like Larry (last name unknown) and Mayo Buckner? Larry had spent all his twenty-odd years in institutions as a diagnosed retardate before psychologist Robert McQueen at Nevada State hospital, noting the absence of gross clinical features and Larry's apparent good coordination, tested him and found his IQ average. As it turned out, Larry had assumed the retardate's flat, drab speech, slack mouth, glazed eyes, and shuffling gait because he thought it was expected of him. Or take Mayo Buckner, who lived for sixty-six years in the Glenwood, Iowa, State School for the mentally retarded and left there finally to die—despite an IQ discovered by a new superintendent (when Mayo was sixty-seven) to be 120, high normal. An enthusiastic and thoughtful reader as well as a skilled printer, Mayo could play eight instruments and score musical compositions for a twenty-five-piece orchestra.

Why in heaven's name was he there? As a child, Mayo could sing before he could talk. By five he could pick out on the family organ any song sung or whistled to him. Like Deborah Kallikak, he excelled in other right-hemisphere functions as well: He liked to sew and to carpenter. But, a sickly and sensitive youngster with bad eyesight and hearing, he offended his mother deeply with several impulsive acts that were ill-considered but hardly retarded. To her everlasting mortification, for example, he sang "Little Brown Jug" in church. She had him committed as an imbecile because of a sinister "prenatal influence": Her having seen during pregnancy a blind piano player who rolled his eyes horribly. So Mayo, like Larry a half century later, wound up in a home for the mentally retarded because his mother did not want him.

As writer Robert Wallace related in a memorable *Life* magazine story, Mayo never blamed her. When he died, his body was taken the seventy-two miles back home to Lenox, Iowa, for burial. The story a Glenwood newspaper had printed about his musical talents years earlier contained a description of him that might have served as his epitaph.

Mayo was, said the story, "a shining example of what a handicapped person, with great determination, can accomplish."[23]

Part IV
INTELLIGENCE AND THE FUTURE

What moves and directs the brain of man will in turn
largely determine the future from here on.
—ROGER SPERRY

Chapter 13

Better Thinking Through Chemistry, Etc.

Less than two decades ago one of our wildest fantasies for the future of human intelligence was expressed in a small polemic gem of a novel called *The Child Buyer*. In it, John Hersey depicted a society in which exceptionally bright children were purchased from their parents by the military-industrial complex. To induce an IQ ten times anything known, the children were "conditioned" in a manner that would have made the Marquis de Sade smile. First, to ensure their single-minded service on behalf of national defense, they were brainwashed of all memory and indoctrinated by multimedia techniques to optimum motivation. Next they were neurosurgically stripped of their "distracting" senses. Then they were data-fed to learning fullness by computer. Finally they were set to work on brain-cracking pieces of a larger corporate problem guaranteed to last them the rest of their natural lives. Hersey's ten-year-old protagonist—a plump and lively holdout against all the forces of family, community, and school—ultimately succumbed to the Child Buyer's blandishments. The reason stands as a parable for our times. His mind was unable to resist the challenge.

Yesterday's fiction, of course, is today's fact. Not a decade later Cleveland neurosurgeon Robert White performed on a rhesus monkey a variation of the operation Hersey had foreseen as one of the grisly fates that befell young brains bought by the Child Buyer. With cauterizing iron and scalpel, White pared and burned away bits and pieces of cranial tissue until nothing was left but a cauliflower of moist pink jelly floating in a vase of hard white calcium. Still intact, still connected to a substitute blood supply and nervous system, the monkey's brain went on pulsing for hours with life, if even a sadist could call it that. Judging from the EEG, reported an attending neurophysiologist, its neural activity was "better than when the brain had a body."[1] Bereft of its senses, he suspected, the monkey could think more quickly. But what kind of thinking, he didn't know. Surgeon White was—and is—optimistic about keeping the human brain alive after death using such techniques. Because nerve tissue does not grow back, he is less than enthusiastic about the chances of clinical brain transplant.

Until recently, we could say with utter confidence that whatever was on its mind, only the brain in such grotesque solitary confinement would ever know. With pen in proxy hand, with ancillary tongue ceaselessly wagging, the normal brain even now can only hint at the unfathomed intricacies of its own cerebration. No brain totally turned inward on itself could hope to do better, could it? Soon, as we will see in this section, even this will no longer be certain. For biology and technology have joined hands in a revolutionary new alliance that aims at momentously more than just the chemical acceleration of our thinking. Indeed, that dream of science fiction may turn out to be the most remote—and pointless—of all. The new biotechnology has as its promised end nothing less than man's control over his own mind, his own environment, his own genes, even his own evolution. It not only plans to outfit our brain with wondrous cybernetic accessories just beginning to be glimpsed; our body itself is up for the most elemental redesigning when the coming generation of biotechnologists, suitably equipped with all the knowledge sure to unfold in the next decades, bolts for the drawing boards.

Nothing attracts their advanced guard more than a stratospheric stepup in intelligence. After all, the philosophic imperative is there. Although the estimated net level of man's intellect has not increased in recorded history, primate researchers Harry and Margaret Harlow were voicing nothing original when they said a dozen years ago that human beings had no more, or little more, than the minimal endowment of brains necessary to achieve modern civilization. Bernard Rimland only echoes the prevailing scientific sentiment that such a mandate exists when he notes that

332

there has been "an enormous increase in demand for literate and sophisticated people. . . . Society faces a major surplus of people with IQ's below 120, and a grave shortage of those with IQ's above 120," writes Rimland, "people trainable as engineers, computer programmers, and physicians."[2]

Ignoring for now the left-hemisphere bias built into that statement, its message is clear. Given their way, the biotechnologists of the future will be able to give us race after race of super-Mensas from the genes up.

Putting aside its inherent moral implications, must such a stupendous mental moonshot have such Frankensteinian overtones?

It needn't. In theory there are plenty of ways to increase our intelligence without intervening genetically and without waiting a thousand lifetimes for the natural forces of evolutionary selection to do it for us. Some are readily apparent, others so transparently obvious we hardly see them. All that follow, including the more bizarre, are possible.

Etc., First

Instead of attempting to change man's intelligence outright by direct neural intervention—a dicey prospect at best—we might better begin by modestly changing his present world to make it more accommodating to the fullest expression of what he has in him. Richard Allen Chase of Johns Hopkins defines this new field as the science of *environmental biology:* "Our ability to manipulate the early environment . . . places in our hands the most powerful single influence we can exercise."[3] But why stop at the child? Chase's definition can be expanded to fit the whole of life. For there is much we can do to enhance intelligence from the moment of conception on.

• *Better Gestation and Birth.* The unborn child, we now know, begins to learn long before it leaves the womb—to suck, drink, use its lungs and limbs; to respond to cold, sound, light, pain, and touch. Bored by repetitive signals, it can even be conditioned to respond with movement to varied ones. One might suppose the United States, being among the wealthiest of nations, would

333

possess the caliber of health care to ensure the best prenatal environment to most of its citizens. But because nearly a fifth of its families live below the poverty line and can hardly afford prenatal attention, the United States today has one of the highest infant mortality rates in the industrialized world. One in fourteen American children, moreover, is delivered physically or mentally handicapped—or both. Millions more are born prematurely, prey to a host of brain-damaging dangers, some with stunted brains that will never catch up. More subtly, in seeking to promote the less complicated birth of a lighter child, many competent obstetricians have for years kept the pregnant woman's weight down. In so doing, many researchers now fear, they have innocently undernourished the growing fetus, retarding overall brain growth as well as critical brain-cell size and division. The singular sensitivity of the growing neuron to its environment has been devastatingly underscored by the work of biochemist Stephen Zamenhof at UCLA. Zamenhof has shown that brain cells in rats, chicks, and rabbits can be stimulated to divide by injecting hormones—or to stop dividing by deliberately inducing malnutrition.

As Zamenhof points out, little attention is being paid to the alarming possibility that lack of sufficient prenatal oxygen and nutrition may be invisibly compromising the birthright of the genotypically gifted. The tragedy of this is that we cannot know. "These people grow up to be entirely normal," says Zamenhof, who fears that such a depressing effect may extend even to the second generation. "And society loves what is normal. But in the end this may prove the greatest loss of all."[4]

It would be pleasing to report that our technology has moved with its customary speed and proficiency to remedy matters, pertaining as they do to the basic quality of our people. Mothers are now allowed to gain more weight for their babies' sake, of course, provided they have an enlightened obstetrician. But only one in ten of the nation's maternity hospitals is fully outfitted with an electronic fetal monitor, which can detect faulty placental oxygen flow in the later stages of labor. Neither have we fully investigated the abdominal decompression suit pioneered by Dr. O.S. Heyns of South Africa. The suit reduces labor and potentially punishing abdominal pressure even as it perfuses the placenta with a bath of added oxygen. Not only does it guard against miscarriage and retardation, contend a growing number of British and South African doctors, it produces a phenotypic expression of intelligence perhaps 10 to 20 IQ points higher (for want of a better measure) than under the old sedated conditions of delivery. Heyns introduced decompression in 1955. Eighteen years later it reached these shores—as a scientific exhibit at a national convention of obstetricians and gynecologists.

• *More "Intelligent" Living.* Natural light, exercise, play, proper diet, more respect for our natural body rhythms, more consideration for the aged—all are critical components in the development of humanity's fullest intelligence. "Light," says endocrinologist Richard Wurtman, "has perhaps several hundred important effects on bodily functions. . . . Only a few dozen . . . are currently known and an even smaller number really understood."[5] From a study of fluorescent lighting in a Florida classroom, photographic expert John Ott suspects that "stress radiation" caused by invisible wavelengths may cause hyperactivity. When he installed whiter, full-spectrum light, Ott reports, nervous fatigue, irritability, lapses of attention, and aimless movement subsided. We know that laboratory animals experimentally reared in the dark or otherwise deprived of normal light and other sensory inputs develop perceptual deficits and anomalies traceable to physical changes in neurons and brain RNA. Disturbing as it is to think about, the human brain boxed into an artificial setting may be losing something too.

On the other hand Dr. Ben Feingold, a San Francisco allergist, has successfully treated hyperactivity by putting his young patients on a diet free of artificial food color and flavoring, synthetics whose presence is menacingly ubiquitous in both commercial foodstuffs and, ironically, child medicines.

Regular exercise, moreover, not only tones up metabolism but also steps up the amount of oxygen a beat of the heart can propel to the brain. This can perk up sluggish cells and improve mental performance, as can adult play, which loosens the bars of conformity and allows the creative urge to float free. A cutback in social drinking can help too. Excessive alcohol both destroys neurons and reduces red blood cells to an oxygen-blocking sludge.

We are learning also that circadian rhythms—those body tempos that obey the twenty-four-hour cycle of the earth's rotation—affect not only lower animals but humans as well. These roller-coaster highs and lows are reflected by the biological "clocks" set in our organs, which in turn influence our ability to react, grip, concentrate, compute, remember, tell time, and resist the common cold. The fateful consequences of "jet lag" for decision-making is only the most manifest example. Less obvious but over the long run more important are the individual differences in these inner clock-sets that make some people mentally sharper at night, others in the day—vital differences our system of education ignores.

"Everybody wants to live for a long time," writes Ruth Winter, "but nobody wants to grow old."[6] We don't yet know what causes aging or if it can be "cured." But apart from the usual nostrums of exercise, outside interests, and proper diet, we do know a few things of value for utilizing the aging intelligence. For one, we know that the destructive effects of advancing years on perception, memory, and cognition can be significantly arrested with oxygen therapy. For another, we know that some of the world's oldest alert inhabitants—those celebrated centenarians who live on the border mountains of Tibet—stop in their labors several times a day from childhood on and sink to the ground for a few minutes, apparently in meditation. We might benefit from the same practice all our lives, if only by reducing the stress of modern society.

Finally, we know that the elderly represent a source of life experience and wisdom unmatched anywhere else. After all, they have devoted a lifetime to acquiring it. To share what they have learned, we have only to ask and to listen—and to call a halt to an early retirement policy that has become senselessly progressive from the standpoint of intelligence ecology.

• *Better Education and Mental Training.* Long before this century ends, predicts Alvin Toffler, the educational system as we know it will be a shambles. Before, the most intelligent way to prepare a

336

child for the future was to "arm him with the skills of the past."[7] But if the signs are right, this will no longer do. For we face an accelerating crisis in job identity the likes of which humanity hasn't known since the Industrial Revolution, if then. Today, says Jerome Bruner, there is less and less opportunity to carry through from the initiation of work on a recognizable problem to its completion, or to see plainly how our own task relates to those performed by others. He believes we can only intelligently change our methods of education if we "revolutionize and revivify the idea"[8] of work.

Even so, education will not wait for a certified space-age methodology and curriculum, though both are surely coming and will hopefully utilize the best of minds and machines. No, the new education is here, now. Its many novel forms deserve—and are getting—books in themselves. They won't be dealt with here. But certain trends are evident. Increasingly, anything goes in the classroom that will extend skills, interests, or knowledge. Included are not only a range of esoterica from belly dancing to dinosaur-building but, heresy of heresies, problem-solving courses which require the pupil to generate and evaluate ideas, test hypotheses, infer consequences, marshal evidence, forecast outcomes, abandon untenable theses, and make probabilistic decisions. In short, they teach students actually to *think* rather than just memorize facts and, as one professor-turned-entrepreneur scathingly puts it, "regurgitate them on command."[9]

In addition, as Urie Bronfenbrenner points out, the walls are coming down between school and community. In Boston a program of off-campus work and study in all walks of adult life draws 90 percent of the high school seniors eligible. In New Jersey, a sixth-grade class hit on an imaginative way of expanding its horizons by filling hundreds of helium-inflated balloons with messages requesting an exchange of information and releasing them to waft down over a four-stage area.

Then too, innovators with bold and fresh ideas for learning are going directly to the people, and vice versa. A pair of Stanford professors, for example, toured California in a series of free public seminars on "conceptual blockbusting"—knotty little practical

337

problems and their solutions designed to illuminate, then dispel, the mental "blocks" that habitually stand in the path of creative problem-solving. William J. J. Gordon's commercially marketed system of Synectics (from the Greek for the joining together of different and apparently irrelevant elements) successfully teaches everyone from engineers to core-city problem kids to unleash and channel their powers of creative imagination by the conscious use of concrete metaphor—in effect, obliquely unlocking the imagery of the right hemisphere. Therapists, psychologists, and teachers increasingly encourage the fullest conscious expression of right-hemisphere intuition and fantasy (one enterprising art instructor had her students paint with their left hands) and are rewarded with better cures, more creativity, and faster learning. New psychological techniques aimed at instilling greater self-esteem and a higher degree of self-direction in the child promise to improve the emotional ground on which intelligence must find root. They work, if only because human attention and expectancy do.

Chemistry

Contrary to the extravagant promise of the planarians, human memory pills or IQ tablets—"a virus to give us algebra or French instead of the flu,"[10] as prophesied in one national magazine— appear no closer than the day McConnell dropped his first flatworm into a blender. To be sure, a team of South African doctors has injected an expectant mother with experimental hormones in an effort to double the baby's eventual IQ. They hope to do it by increasing placental efficiency during the last month of pregnancy, when brain-cell development is highest. But since the intellectual and sensorimotor abilities are confounded in infancy, the effects, if positive, probably won't be known for several years.

Otherwise the evidence remains scattered, fascinating, and inconclusive. Mentally retarded children given traces of the convulsant, strychnine, improved in simple performance tasks, but whether it was because the drug in minute, harmless doses really quickens neural efficiency or because it has a tonic effect on their whole central nervous system remains unclear. Elderly people intravenously fed RNA in yeast form showed some improvement in the alacrity of their memory but hardly a wider recall. In a survey involving stimulants, depressants, and drugs to improve the brain's blood circulation, in fact, a research team concluded that none had unequivocably improved mental functioning. Science, in short, failed to support Clarence Darrow's crusty belief that, "You take all the drunks out of history and you take out almost all the poetry, all the genius. . . . What kind of poem do you think you'd get from a glass of ice water?"[11]

The last word on direct chemical enhancement of intelligence in both hemispheres, for now, belongs to psychiatrist Perry London: "A tranquilizer may, by removing the distracting effects of anxiety, make it easier for someone to concentrate and, therefore, remember. An energizer might also have a beneficial effect by arousing a person so that he could pay better attention. . . . [But] it's hard to imagine exactly what an IQ pill would be, because intelligence is probably not a specific physical event in the brain."[12] The "smart pill," in sum, seems a receding mirage—for man, if not for the flatworm.

Both problem solving and creativity, however, have shown themselves amenable to another line of chemical attack having more to do with perceptual manipulation than with direct stimulation of intelligence. It employs hallucinogens, or psychedelics, and has as its objective an altered state of consciousness in which novel ideas and unique solutions are perceived through a phantasmagoric shift of focus or perspective. Just how these drugs work pharmacologically is far from clear. We know that chemically they resemble some of the neurotransmitters, which enables them to pass the blood-brain barrier, that shielding membrane that filters out most substances harmful to our brain. Once inside, hallucinogenics seem to work by blocking receptor sites, altering or interferring with normal neural transmissions, and inhibiting the firing of cells. Attempts to relate these actions to specific neurophysiological responses, unfortunately, have been far from satisfactory. So complex are the transmitter functions, so shrouded in mystery, that simple interpretations of drug effects on their dynamics are impossible. Their very similarity to the brain's neural juices, however, are highly suggestive. Aldous Huxley once pointed out, for example, that when adrenalin decomposes, it leaves something called adrenochrome, which can produce many of the same hallucinatory symptoms observed in mescalin intoxication.

The creative results from psychedelic drug use, in any event, have been mixed. A group of brainstorming architects given LSD under controlled conditions generated far more and better solutions to a design problem, in the opinion of independent judges, than they did when free of the drug's influence. Various kinds of artists, however, generally have reported a disappointing creative experience while high on hallucinogens, although the perceptual aftermath is often valuable.

Psychedelic drugs, furthermore, appear to have taken us eerily near the mysterious source of our own mentation. In discussing how the mind holds to the unproved but psychically real concept of infinity, for example, Andrew Weil ventures perilously close to what may be the holographic heart of the brain when he writes, " . . . This same infinite regression burst in on every sense channel. . . . My intellect was so affected that every time it produced a thought, it would automatically think about the thought, think about thinking the thought, and so on down the tunnel of mirrors."[13]

Indeed, the research possibilities of psychedelic drugs in plumbing the depths of the living brain can scarcely be exaggerated. According to trained, responsible researchers who have rigorously tested them, the mind runs a gamut of sensation in which consciousness, like a time-lapse photograph of an opening rose, compresses and exhibits in stunningly short order every hemispheric, limbic, and primitive brain function characteristic of human awareness at its most intense. The user experiences intensified and transcendent perception, time distortion, heightened symbols and imagery, profound sexual and religious feelings, showering sensations of novelty, significance and import—"virtually all . . . [involving] the right hemisphere more than the left,"[14] writes Arnold Mandell. The automatic neutral barriers and baffles that normally prevent us from being flooded with stimuli from without, or swamped by excessive awareness of the

ongoing information processing within (notes Louis Jolyon West)
are lowered, causing ideas to tumble over one another chaotically;
gales of intense, dominating emotion to sweep the sensibilities.
Such an immense overload (adds Russ Rueger) can cross wires in
synesthesia. Sound may be seen as color, sights heard as noises.
Every nerve may seem to burn with fire. The conscious faculties
(of the left hemisphere) are too puny to stop and analyze the mad-
dening streams of (right-hemisphere) impressions. Awareness of
visual, nonverbal clues becomes so heightened it sometimes seems
as though minds can be read, as the mystics claim. The auras of
the occult are vividly seen.

At its height, the oceanic sensation of melting into the environment can become so encompassing that the (left-hemisphere) ego
seems to dissolve and give way to a deep feeling of unity with everything in existence. Writes Rueger of this sublime state,

> The user may consider himself God, and yet simultaneously
> feel that he/God is everyone and everything. When confronted
> with other persons, he may experience a total merging of identi-
> ty with them, so that it seems that he can think through their
> minds as well as his own. . . . He might feel that he has tapped
> the ultimate source of reality, which can lead him to believe he
> has seen the "true wisdom," that he has "awakened" for the first
> time in his life, that the "real" world is only an illusion. He might
> feel that he has reached a point of total illumination . . . the
> "white light" . . . in which self and environment flow together
> into the clear essence transcending all form that eastern reli-
> gions call the "Void."[15]

In that state, the mind can soar beyond the void itself, winged
on astral flights that beggar the best of science fiction. In *The Center of the Cyclone,* Dr. John Lilly, inventor of the sensory isolation
tank and a recognized authority on dolphins, describes with the
precision of a scientist and the passion of a poet his own out-of-
the-body expeditions to "other worlds" while suspended in his
tank on a dose of acid. Like Gulliver of old, writes Lilly,

> I moved into universes containing beings much larger than
> myself, so that I was a mote in their sunbeam, a small ant in their
> universe, a single thought in a huge mind, or a small program in

341

a cosmic computer. . . . I was swept, pushed, carried, whirled, and . . . by processes which I could not understand, processes of immense energy, of fantastic light, and of terrifying power, my very being itself was threatened as I was pushed through these vast spaces by these vast entities. Waves of the equivalent of light, of sound, of motion, waves of intense emotion, were carried in dimensions beyond my understanding. . . . I moved into a region of strange life forms, neither above nor below the human level. . . . These beings reminded me of some of the drawings I had seen of Tibetan gods and goddesses, of ancient Greek portrayals of their gods. . . . Some of these forms were constructed of liquid, some were constructed of glowing gases, and some were solid state "organisms." The vast variety of possible life forms in the universe passed before me. . . . I was an observer watching them.[16]

Was it all just the drugged dream of a man once described as a "walking one-man syllabus of Western civilization"?[17] Lilly confesses he doesn't know. At the time each happened, he says, "I knew that this was the truth." But at other times, he adds, "I have not been sure."[18]

Nowhere have the mystic properties of the psychedelic experience and its meaning for human intelligence been more brilliantly documented than in Aldous Huxley's account of his first mescaline trip, *The Doors of Perception.* The wealth of his insights is too prodigious to be enumerated here. But what Huxley foresaw with indelible clarity, although he gives no signs of having known about Sperry's research, was the dichotomy of man's split brain and the significance of that dualism. In the end, the author of *Brave New World*—the grandson and brother of renowned biologists, a man whose illustrious family name is synonymous with urbanity, erudition, culture, and sophistication—was moved to turn his back upon the talent that had won him fame and cast his spiritual lot with the unspeakable gifts of the right hemisphere.

Huxley began his psychedelic odyssey that fateful day with a frank admission: "I have always been a poor [mental] visualizer. Words, even the pregnant words of poets, do not evoke pictures in my mind."[19] From there, as the drug took hold, he went on to describe the pinnacle of "cleansed" perception that could be reached by a man often praised for his exceptional powers of visual understanding. In a vase of flowers Huxley saw "what Adam had seen on the morning of his creation. . . . The Being of Platonic philosophy—except that Plato seems to have made the enormous, the grotesque mistake of . . . identifying it with the mathematical abstraction of the Idea. . . ." Later, gazing at a chair, "not merely gazing at those bamboo legs, but actually being them," Huxley reflected that "the function of the brain and nervous system is to protect us from being overwhelmed and confused . . . by shutting out most of what we should otherwise perceive or remember. . . ."[20]

> To formulate and express the contents of this reduced awareness, man has invented and endlessly elaborated those symbol-systems and implicit philosophies which we call languages [Huxley wrote]. . . . Every individual is . . . [their] beneficiary and . . . victim—beneficiary inasmuch as language gives access to the accumulated records of other people's experience, the victim in so far as it confirms him in the belief that reduced awareness is the only awareness. . . . It bedevils his sense of reality, so that he is all too apt to take his concepts for data, his words for actual things. . . . [21]

For Huxley, a shrewd and sensitive connoisseur of the arts, only the artist's cup was deep enough to hold even a particle of the miraculous stuff that was life itself: "What the rest of us see only under the influence of mescaline, the artist is congenitally equipped to see all the time," he mused. " . . . It is a knowledge of the intrinsic significance of every existent. . . ." Even the artist, he decided, fell down in the end. "I knew that Botticelli—and not Botticelli alone, but many others too—had looked . . . with the same transfigured and transfiguring eyes that had been mine. . . . They had done their best to render it in paint or stone . . . without success." Van Gogh's portrait of a chair, "a *Ding an Sich* [a thing in itself] which the mad painter saw, with a kind of adoring terror, and tried to render on his canvas was no more than "an unusually expressive symbol of the fact. . . ."[22]

As he walked that afternoon in the garden, Huxley further divined the brain's hemispheric duality when he observed that my body seemed to have dissociated itself almost completely from my mind. . . . All that the conscious ego can do is to formulate wishes, which are then carried out by forces which it controls very little and understands not at all. . . . In my present state, awareness was not referred to as ego; it was, so to speak, on its own. This meant that the physiological intelligence controlling the body was also on its own. For the moment that interfering neurotic who, in waking hours, tries to run the show, was blessedly out of the way.[23]

Now, suddenly confronted by a garden chair "which looked like the Last Judgment—or, to be more accurate, by a Last Judgment which, after a long time and with considerable difficulty, I recognized as a chair"[24]—Huxley pictures himself shrinking in dread, like a departed soul in the Tibetan Book of the Dead from the Pure Light of the Void. He felt himself one with the schizophrenic in that

> [His] sickness consists in the inability to take refuge from inner and outer reality (as the sane person habitually does) in the homemade universe of common sense. . . . [He is] unable to shut off the experience . . . which he is not holy enough to live with, which he cannot explain away. . . .[25]

The specter of insanity is one of the reasons why psychedelic experience, for all its clues to human intelligence, should be taken off the streets and put back into the laboratory where it belongs. (In 1966 the U.S. government, in effect, gave the LSD business to the bathtub makers by banning its experimental use in this country. Qualified research has since been partially restored, but is scarcely encouraged.) As Theodore Roszak points out, "there is nothing whatever in common between a man of Huxley's experience and intellectual discipline sampling mescaline, and a fifteen-year-old tripper whiffing airplane glue until his brain turns to oatmeal. In the one case, we have a gifted mind moving sophisticatedly toward cultural synthesis; in the other, we have a giddy child out to 'blow his mind' and bemused to see all the pretty balloons go up. But when all the balloons have gone up and gone pop, what is there left behind but the yearning to see more?"[26]

344

At best, psychedelics have a research worth as fleeting as quicksilver. Richard Alpert, who together with Timothy Leary brought "the sacrament of acid" out of academic bondage at Harvard, later abandoned it and embraced Eastern mysticism as Baba Ram Dass because, as he said, the acid trip was a rocket that took you high enough to see the promised land, but always brought you down again. There were, he decided, no pharmacological shortcuts to the true Nirvana.

Even in the hands of the most perceptive and unbiased, psychedelic drugs may never be more than a compelling curiosity. The reason strikes at the roots of the dilemma that is human consciousness. They are, in the vernacular, dynamite to the one characteristic a competent investigator probing its effects must have: sound critical judgment. That fact is amply illustrated by the story a San Francisco researcher tells about an assistant who joined him for dinner while under the influence of LSD. Excusing himself to wash up, the young man returned a long time later in a state of ecstasy. He had, he blurted, discovered the supreme truth, the universal essence, the ultimate secret of life's mystery. It was right there, in the bathroom, printed above the urinal; a sign. "What did it say?" the researcher asked when he could at last break through the orgiastic babbling.

"It says," replied the assistant, calm and composed at last, *"Flush After Using."*[27]

Biotechnology

Biogeneticists see no reason to wait until people are grown before attempting to improve their intelligence. Why not start before birth, with the stuff of life itself? By inserting the fetal needle of amniocentesis, they expect to do more tomorrow than find chromosome defects and justify abortion. They hope to perform prenatal surgery; bank, repair, and transplant genes. Already millions of mouse cells dissected and reassembled have survived. Technically speaking, genetic transplants wait mainly for James Bonner's vision of a "carrier" to be realized and perfected. As

Bonner sees it, some of our most deadly viruses, because they are made of DNA, when "pruned" of their cancer-causing genes can be safely implanted in a tissue-cultured cell, where they spontaneously merge with the genes around them—say, at some future time with a desired constellation known to be associated with intelligence. Later, extracted by a technique already known, they would bear with them some of the host "IQ" genes, to be transferred again when the virus once more was used to "infect" a recipient line of cells. Such virus-borne genes with their precious properties could be cultured and stored in flasks almost indefinitely.

From genetic engineering it is barely a step to embryonic engineering. Laboratory-fertilized embryos could be mass produced by the hundreds from "preferred" intellectual stock, using hormone injections that stimulate the multiple release of eggs—the so-called fertility drugs. This method of hyperbreeding has been used with dairy cows, but for obvious reasons human conception on such a grand scale has yet to be tried. Just such a union of a second-hand sperm and a surgically removed ripe ovum has, however, been achieved *in vitro* (under glass). The embryo lived fifty-nine days. That it lived at all brings closer to haunting reality the final stage of possible biotechnical intervention in human intelligence before birth: evolutionary engineering.

In a thoughtful and incisive examination of its problems and prospects, science writer Albert Rosenfeld once quoted an experimental biologist as picturing a housewife walking into a "new kind of commissary," shopping down a row of packets not unlike flower-seed packages, and picking her baby by label. "Each packet," wrote Rosenfeld, "would contain a frozen one-day-old embryo, and the label would tell the shopper what color of hair and eyes to expect as well as the probable size and IQ of the child."[28] In predicting the date of this (dubiously) blessed event—by 1980 latest—Rosenfeld's visionary biologist was a bit premature. A bit premature too, perhaps, was his projection of the time when the systematic manipulation of genes themselves would make possible "the production of beings whose specifications can be drawn in advance. . . ."[29] Premature, surely, was a concurrent call by the president of the American Chemical Society for the United States to make creation of life in the laboratory a national goal.

Still, the biogeneticist labors on *in vitro,* and the future he seeks is not always so far-distant. For example, the most frightening and futuristic aspect of evolutionary engineering, most laymen would probably agree, is the concept of cloning. Human cloning refers to propagation by cell "cuttings," a tissue-culture technique that would in theory permit us to run any human being we wished through a Godlike Xerox machine to produce hundreds, even thousands, of exact copies of his total person from a single cell.

Fantastic as it sounds, cloning is old hat in agriculture. Navel orange trees are clones. Dates have been multiplied vegetatively as clones for over 5,000 years. Ever since the days of ancient Egypt, date growers have routinely removed side shoots from the date palm and placed them in the soil, where they take root and produce other date palms. Now the same process has been successfully carried out in frogs. As Bonner describes it, an unfertilized egg is borrowed from the female and its chromosomes inactivated by a beam of ultraviolet light. From a cell of a donor male, a nucleus containing its entire set of chromosomes is scooped out and injected into the egg. The resulting tadpoles are both identical to the donor and normal in every way, including number. But mass production to a degree exponentially outstripping the bovine may be just around the corner. A gene from a South African toad cultured in a strain of common stomach bacteria, E Coli, has since been replicated millions of times over when the bacteria reproduced.

"I am sure," says Bonner, "that successful cloning of the mouse will be announced within the next few years."[30] Nobel prize-winning geneticist Joshua Lederberg has predicted an attempt to clone the first man within a decade. Not far behind, presumably, if the biogeneticists are given their head, will march an army of Einsteins perfect down to the last brainy detail. (Included, one supposes, if the great man himself were still available for replication, would be the tip of the nose that turned a mottled yellow when he was angry.)

As for the fully formed brain, today's biotechnologists have al-

347

ready invaded it with a variety of Brave New World techniques that have touched off a storm of protest. But neither direct nor indirect intervention to enhance intelligence after birth appear at all imminent. Ostensibly as a court of last resort, "psychosurgeons" have quelled chronic violence and other serious behavior disorders by creating small, precise lesions in the limbic lobe with pinpoint surgery, ultrasonic energy, radiation, and electricity. Such tissue destruction appears to block the transmission of "negative" neural impulses from the emotional brain. But it can severely blunt the personality, emotions, and intellect as well. Faced with chilling visions of a totalitarian mind control over those who dare deviate, both courts and the federal government have moved to stop it.

Psychosurgeons have also treated such diverse and deviant behavior as criminal aggression and homosexuality by implanting electrodes in the brain's pleasure center and rewarding the offender with delicious jolts to reinforce preferred alternatives. Conversely, their brother "psychotechnologists" have effectively employed painful electric shock and other "aversion therapies" to combat alcoholism, smoking, bed-wetting and nail-biting. Both kinds of behavior modification—stemming as they do from the work of B. F. Skinner, who used positive reinforcement in teaching pigeons to type and play Ping-Pong—can be classified as learning. In its more positive aspects, behavior modification is now an integral and growing part of American education.

But the most promising avenue of all to new sources of intelligence, an avenue at once the most exciting and the least traveled scientifically, leads through half-mapped territory into what J. E. Bogen has christened "the vast unknown" of the right hemisphere. If split-brain researchers are correct about the conscious and independent nature of the cerebrum's right half, it could well be the seat of the budding technology we know as biofeedback.

Biofeedback operates on the principle that all of the body systems controlled outside our awareness by the autonomic nervous system reflect in their operation precise changes in brain electricity—changes we can intentionally duplicate ever after, if we once know when they are occurring. Duplicate the precise electrical state peculiar to the brain for a desired state of function, and control of that state of function will follow. Just why isn't known. But a flashing light or beeper tone—triggered by an EEG or other electronic instrument sensitive to the onset of electrical signals announcing such internal changes—is sufficient to bring our senses into play and set the process in motion.

Some 2,000 scientists nationwide now at work on its mysteries report that the self-control made possible by learning its principles enables users to treat successfully such serious and/or resistant ailments of no known medical origin as high blood pressure, ulcers, asthma, epilepsy, migraine headache, intractible muscle pain, teeth-grinding and diabetes. Just as stress is increasingly identified as the root of much modern malaise, moreover, so is the boon of bone-deep relaxation some forms of biofeedback make possible now seen as its antidote. If our mind can make us sick, they are saying, it can also make us well. Not only can we learn by doing, we can *do*—and undo—by learning.

In addition, biofeedback is becoming an invaluable aid to further investigating the deepest nature of our intelligence. Using the EEG, David Galin and Robert Ornstein have enjoyed success in teaching experimental subjects to "turn on" one hemisphere or the other with biofeedback techniques. The deliberate, controlled development of both sides of our brain from childhood on may be just around the corner—if, of course, our society is willing to reinforce such a process by broadening and deepening the flow of its rewards to include more right-hemisphere pursuits.

Using a GSR—a galvanic skin-response device—researchers have discovered that our skin is both a "bright mirror of emotion"[31] and, paradoxically, a judge of reality whose allegiance to fact easily exceeds the so-called "objectivity" of the left hemisphere. As biofeedback researcher Barbara Brown notes in her book, *New Mind, New Body,* when exposed to subliminally flashed profanity, the skin "explodes" in a frenzy of electric "talk." In fact, it reacts electrically to any change in its immediate environment, wholly independent of our conscious awareness. Given shocks of supposedly varying intensity, subjects decided orally that they were getting less and less. But their skin was not fooled. Its GSR faithfully reported the truth: All shocks were the same. The skin can even be taught a conditioned response while the subject lies unconscious from a general anesthetic—a conditioned response that won't appear until the subject revives. Our receptive sense of touch, in short, appears intelligently at work even while we sleep.

Nor are our other senses any less tirelessly intelligent. Biofeedback studies also provide evidence that other kinds of sensory impressions can be exhaustively stored without "conscious recognition"—if by conscious we mean the self-consciousness of the left hemisphere, not the environmentally responsive consciousness of the right. As the split-brain experimenters learned, determining consciousness may be a matter of choosing the definition that fits.

Where is the left hemisphere in all this?

We know that subjects who receive all possible information, both verbal and perceptual, learn whatever autonomic nervous system control task is asked of them from biofeedback more quickly than those who don't. We know, too, that once a subject gets "the feel" of what biofeedback expects of him, all the beeps and flashes that helped him learn when he was producing the desired effect can be dispensed with. Now, just knowing what he's to do is enough. Does this mean, then, that the left hemisphere takes control of the autonomic nervous system through the agency of the right hemisphere? Does it mean the self-consciousness of the ego makes of the right hemisphere a sort of servomechanism, even if it has no conscious idea exactly what the right hemisphere does in slavishly carrying out its wishes?

No one yet knows for sure. But by displaying his spinal cord electricity on an oscilloscope, biofeedback researchers have taught a subject to control the electrical activity of a single motor cell in his body. Here, obviously, is no normal expression of the motor nervous system, autonomic or not, but a command performance before the altar of the ego. In Barbara Brown's words, such a feat "uncovered a real, acceptable, measurable effect of the will" on the automatic body processes, even as it "produced the physically identifiable higher intellectual processes of the unconscious."[32] Whatever the ultimate nature of such control, and although she persists in using the traditional terminology of the conscious and unconscious, her comments at several ensuing points have an unmistakable air of the hemispheric:

> The revelations of the skin about inner man have been left unattended, to flow on like a babbling child whose language does not meet the consensus of what society deems language to be. . . . Somewhere between feeling man and laboratory-man, the power and knowledge of his interior self becomes screened off from his operational, reasoning mind. . . . The cultural elite of the East developed the practice of voluntary control of internal functions; the cultural elite of the West harnessed the physical world with tools and machines. . . . Feedback could give Western education something it has lacked since the time of Plato—a holistic education, an education of mind and body together, so that finally the student might be instructed in terms of that ancient but futuristic motto: *mens sana in corpore sano* [A healthy mind in a healthy body].[33]

Many of what we are beginning to suspect as the right hemisphere's deepest intellectual secrets, however, cannot yet be controlled, much less understood or explained, by the left hemisphere. Indeed, the self-consciousness we call our ego is as suspicious of these dimly perceived mental abilities as it is aware of them. It casts a fiercely jaundiced eye—or more properly, a pair of fiercely jaundiced visual fields—at those it bothers to name, among them clairvoyance, telepathy, precognition, teleportation, psychokinesis, and *déjà vu*. There is absolutely nothing in our natural senses or their manmade extensions to prepare us for them. What on earth would allow us to read another person's thoughts, communicate by brain waves, see the future as vividly as we see the past, actually visit faraway places with our minds, move objects with our thoughts, recognize in every atom of our being situations and places we would swear were new to us? Most of these things, the left hemisphere righteously concludes, are in the words Henry Ford used to dismiss religion, "the bunk."

Any and all such phenomena the left hemisphere continues studiously to ignore when it can. It is right, it tells itself, to be skeptical. And so it is. What egocentric left hemisphere would not scoff when Arthur Clarke, the author, mathematician, and space-age seer, declares that the spoken word "blue" has been recovered aurally from an aged painting, the vibrations clearly registered on a crystal pickup? What left hemisphere in its right mind could accept as legitimate the "mental photographs" taken by a Chicago odd-jobs man peering into a Polaroid camera—among them recognizable images of the Chicago skyline and the Washington monument—using an energy to expose the film that photographic experts were powerless to pin down? What logic can explain the signaturelike EEG readings from the "inner pulse" of idiosyncratic feeling every great composer imparts to his music, the distinct and consistently repeatable expression of which neurophysiologist Manfred Clynes claims to have captured through the fingertips of such interpretive talents as pianist Rudolf Serkin and cellist Pablo Casals? What analysis can expose to the clear light of reason that inner conviction of invincible intention, that "cocoon of concentration" a leading golfer confessed envelops him in moments of high competitive pitch, attuning his game to what Zen writer Michael Murphy in his metaphysical sports fantasy *Golf in the Kingdom* calls the "energy streamers" that guide the ball unerringly into the hole on a crucial thirty-foot putt?

In brief, how can the left hemisphere hope to cope normally with the paranormal except to debunk it?

Not all these phenomena may be what they seem to the imagination, of course. The ghosts in the machine, to borrow Arthur Koestler's phrase, may sometimes be as devoid of profound meaning as the flapping shade at the open attic window. And admittedly, as one national news weekly put it, the current boom in psychic phenomena may contain "more charlatans and conjurers, more naifs and gullibles than can be found on the stage and in the audience of ten Ringling Brothers circuses." Many such instances of the paranormal are clearly, in the same publication's coy turn of phrase, "feats of clay."[34] But admittedly too, those "Peeping Toms at the keyhole of eternity," as Koestler characterizes scientists, may in the magazine's metaphor be vainly trying to see through a keyhole "stuffed with ancient biases"[35] against the right hemisphere. In an era when physics either suspects or has confirmed the existence of such quandam heresies as antimatter, black holes in the universe, subatomic particles without mass or

352

charge, and minute entities that travel faster than the speed of light, why, concludes the magazine, should anything be assumed impossible? Indeed, having numbed and dangerously overextended its collective nervous system with electric technology, a society that wants desperately to believe in *something* beyond its failed senses would seem to be facing just the challenge it needs: to redefine what is normal.

For some of these things unaccountably can and do happen. Or at the very least, *something* inexplicable to the left hemisphere happens that our right hemisphere perceptually translates as such; something our technological extensions often dutifully record, then stand helpless to refute. The left hemisphere, however, never ceases to try. Never mind that plants appear to react to prospective pain and pleasure with the same kind of EEG and GSR contours as do humans appropriately stimulated. Or that the chemical which we now believe causes plants to open and close in the presence or absence of sunlight is acetylcholine, one of the brain's vital transmitter substances. Never mind that the Russian-invented Kirlian photography seems to prove that the mystics have been right all along, we *do* give off auras of normally invisible light, auras whose incandescent coronas of color vary with our person, the parts of our body, our conscious and "unconscious" feelings, and our health. Never mind even that the pyramid, when used as a container, not only preserves for thousands of years the bodies of kings, as the ancient Egyptians knew, but also appears to have the power to keep milk fresh and make apples riper, cigarettes milder, wines smoother, coffee less bitter, and razor blades sharper.

Never mind any of this. The left hemisphere, for all its striving for scientific objectivity, ends by making its own leap of faith: Everything must have an explanation.

And so it must. Is there, perhaps, no matter how fabulous, an acceptable left-hemisphere hypothesis that makes at least tentative if, until now, largely untestable sense?

There is, and that self-styled old fantasist, Albert Einstein, found it. Matter, he said, is energy. Both are the same; not even our ego can stand between the two. As a matter of fact, the split-brain concept of two hemispheres, two minds, when held up to

353

the light of modern microbiology comes off crassly conservative. In *The Lives of a Cell,* biologist Lewis Thomas, a scientist sensible enough to be president of the Memorial Sloan-Kettering Cancer Center, declares with utmost seriousness that "a good case can be made for our nonexistence as entities." Our cells, he says, are "shared, rented, occupied" by swarms of microscopic life ceaselessly engaged in minuscule energy transactions all their own. This, Thomas audaciously speculates, may be in its accretion what we presume to call *our* life: "I like to think that they work in my interest, that each breath they draw for me, but perhaps it is they who walk through the local park in the early morning, sensing my senses, listening to my music, thinking my thoughts."[36]

Going beyond that, both we and our minute inhabitants may be at base no more than differing gradients of a universal energy, as Oriental philosophies have for centuries, even millennia, told us. Indeed, going deeper than anything but the speculating mind of religion (or physics) can take us, might it be that we are truly one with everything, merely another refinement in an endlessly flowing cosmic energy field; an energy field strung like a spider's gossamer web across the void; a taut and infinitely variegated web at any point of which the faintest trembling is felt at every other point?

Our minds shrink back from the abyss. Where are the facts? they demand. *Fact:* Matter and energy, Einstein showed, are but two faces of light. *Fact:* Nearly every part of the human body, notes Barbara Brown, generates electricity. Only a fraction of it is ever used: " . . . The rest spills out to be dissipated into the environment. One wonders where all that energy goes."[37] *Fact:* Acupuncture works, according to the Chinese, because needles inserted at strategic points in the sick body unblock or slow to a smooth and orderly flow the normally balanced energy that exists in and around the unhealthy organism. *Fact:* With Kirlian photography, Russian scientists now claim, they have fixed those points on the skin as the selfsame areas of especially luminescence that dazzle like solar flares when penetrated by needle. *Fact:* Those acupuncture points, say the Chinese, are the exits and entries for the primal energy that comes as light from the sun, what

Soviet theoretical physicist V. M. Inyushin calls "bioplasmic energy," whose steady-state vibrations between palpably nothing (energy) and something (matter) may result in what cosmologist Fred Hoyle posits as the continuous creation of expanding matter that is the universe. *Fact:* Low-energy radiation from laser light fed through acupuncture needles, Inyushin reveals, has brought about remission in some brain tumors and the regeneration of normal tissue. *Fact:* American researcher Ross Adey discloses that the topical application of electric fields to the brain can sharpen the response of monkeys to stimuli, increase EEG activity in cats, and distort the human sense of time in a "genuine biological transduction (energy transfer)."[38] *Fact:* In a promising new treatment called cerebral electrotherapy (CET), a mild pulse of electricity sent coursing through the brain has relieved anxiety, insomnia, nervous skin rash, migraine, and tension headaches. It leaves the patient feeling relaxed, alert, clear-headed, and refreshed. *Fact:* Physicists first decided all matter was made of atoms, then of subatomic particles. Now they are moving beyond matter, even beyond energy, to embrace the "bootstrap theory," which says that since the basic unit of life has not been found despite all our exquisite rummaging around, we must conclude that it does not exist except as a law or principle. Sir James Jeans, the British astronomer, appears increasingly to be right. "The universe," he said, "begins to look more and more like a great thought than like a great machine."[39] It is by the bootstrap of this great thought, the new physics would have it, that the universe has literally pulled itself up out of nothing.

Can anything in parapsychology possibly top this?

So: Tantalizing as they are, abstruse left-hemisphere facts get us no further toward the ultimate truth than "inexplicable" right-hemisphere phenomena. But if, just if, both these channels communicate a common intelligence in nature and man, where is Excalibur? What is the all-but-magic means by which we might deliberately dip into these fundamental forces and turn them to our needs?

Our best bet, Stanley Krippner and other parapsychologists agree, appears to be right where we would expect: In the biofeedback of brain waves. Barbara Brown concedes as much on behalf of physiology when she says, "Biofeedback may guide the mind in a journey through inner space, into far-distant spheres of consciousness."[40] But such a journey cannot now be easily understood, much less its itinerary intelligently planned. Surface manifestations of the inner brain in action Brown compares to "the Mariner probe peeking at Mars from a distance of thousands of miles."[41] What's more, the state of EEG instrumentation today is about as primitive as that of blood-typing a generation ago. Then we believed nothing much of import existed beyond the simplest classifications of A, B, O, and AB, positive or negative, because that was all our techniques could clarify. But as they improved, we realized the surface of blood chemistry had barely been scratched. It could tell us whatever we were ready to hear. So it is with human brain waves. The ancient Oriental language of Sanskrit has almost two dozen different names for varying states of consciousness; in the West, the closest we come to this delicate degree of mental shading are the four primary categories of gross brainwave frequency and amplitude: alpha, beta, delta, and theta.

Even here the issue is in many ways murky. Because it is easiest to see on the EEG, alpha is the most familiar. But it is neither the largest wave nor the most frequent. Besides, within its prescribed ranges there is almost an infinite variety of alpha, each with its own set of behavior and personality characteristics. (Men with a lot of alpha tend to be dependent and submissive. People with mixed alpha are often impatient and demanding, those with little alpha overtly hostile and aggressive.) Moreover, any individual's alpha pattern, like the brain's pattern of physical convolutions, is as distinctive as a fingerprint. The situation is further complicated, according to Brown, by the fact that many Westerners automatically turn their eyes upward when they close them. This movement of eye muscles, curiously, is recorded by the EEG as alpha. One enterprising researcher has proved this to be so in a third of those tested by teaching them to send Morse code with barrages of eye-batting alpha.

Nevertheless, personality aside, broad generalizations about the mental behavior involved in each of the large brainwave states are instructive. Beta, the fastest, comes when our normal waking attention is focused outward, say in speech or movement. Delta, the slowest, normally occurs only in deep sleep. Both alpha and theta accompany the inward focus of the ruminating mind; when we are thinking, creating, solving problems, or storing and retrieving information. There are, however, significant differences between the two. Generally, alpha is a serene, calm, alert but relaxed feeling of receptivity, theta the trancelike condition of creative reverie most often experienced just before or after sleep.

(It is a convincing measure of Eastern sophistication in these inner realms that yogis tested under Western laboratory conditions can produce all these states and more, at will—including the delta of deep sleep while fully awake.)

Based on some forty research studies of meditation, both alpha and theta brainwaves are linked to the same physiological phenomena. They are marked by decreased respiration and oxygen consumption, higher electrical skin resistance (less GSR chatter) and greater tolerance for such normally intrusive stimuli as loud noise. In effect, consciousness turns inward. Where alpha leaves off and theta begins isn't always clear or important, except that in this twilight domain some people lose all awareness of time, environment, or both. More important, as alpha slows down and slides over into the slower theta rhythms, "the external universe loses its identity," reports Barbara Brown in a telling evocation of Huxley's mescaline-induced impressions, leaving "the sensation of separation . . . a depersonalization . . . an awareness of the unifying thread of life."[42] The key that unlocks this nether realm of meaning is simplicity itself. In the words of another experimenter, you "turn off the word machine";[43] feel; visualize; image. In sum, you cast yourself headlong down into the splendid deeps of the right hemisphere, and you do it by simply . . . letting . . . go . . . of thinking in all of its symbolic left-hemisphere manifestations.

The dreamlike world of theta has been described by science writer David Rorvik as thronged with " . . . imagery so extraordinarily vivid that it is often indistinguishable from reality; 'experiential hallucinations' that are living breathing experiences complete with sights, sounds, feelings, and even smells and tastes. . . ."[44] These sound very much like John Lilly's astral projections.

Such beguiling imagery, naturally, is the stuff dreams are made of. Dreams may not only be our brain's way of amending our master model of reality. They can also be creative. Indeed, some of man's most original ideas have hatched in the sleeping dark of night. Whole poems, entire plots, have sprung full-blown to the nocturnal minds of such writers as Coleridge (*Kubla Khan*), Robert Lewis Stevenson (*Dr. Jekyll and Mr. Hyde*) and James Michener (*Centennial*). The germinating seeds of analytic geometry were given to Descartes, and new theorems frequently came to mathematician Henri Poincaré as nimbly dancing dream figures. The German chemist Friedrich Kekulé found the pivotal clue to organic chemistry in a dreamed-of snake that seized hold of its own tail—exactly, he realized, as rings of carbon atoms in their own way must do. Elias Howe, inventor of the sewing machine, hit upon his method of connecting the needle to the bobbin in a nightmare. Chased by spear-throwing savages, Howe paused to observe, in that detached way dreams make possible, how their spearheads were attached to the shafts.

Nor does the uncanny power of imagery cease on awakening. Faraday, the father of electromagnetics, mentally visualized the lines of electromagnetic force in the air around him. Using such visualization in a setting of relaxed meditation, patients of an Air Force doctor fought their cancers into remission. Each patient pictured his malignancy in his mind's eye, then visualized it shriveling away under a bombardment of white blood cells unleashed by his body's natural immune system. Unlike many other modern physicians, the Air Force doctor did not keep from his patients any details of their condition. On the contrary, in a move that suggests biofeedback at its best, he encouraged them to look at pictures and X rays of their malignancy, and to read about it. The son of a Baptist minister, the radiologist offered his therapy in a frank framework of self-healing reminiscent of Christian Science. Critics could argue that this made the difference, not imaging. But they would still have to explain self-healing—and the fact that given drugs, radiation, and surgery where necessary like any other cancer victims, his patients fared far better than could have been statistically expected from traditional treatment alone. Jerome Singer cites an instance of successful treatment by imagery thirty-five years ago. Peptic ulcer patients with a prolonged history of distress were able to reduce both their anxiety and symptoms by "mentally visualizing" a pleasant experience whenever they felt an attack coming on. On a mundane level, mental imagery, particularly when alive and well in the child, can be used as readily as the symbols of thought to solve many of life's everyday problems. If your child misplaces something, for instance, he is apt to find it more quickly if he is encouraged to mentally visualize where he saw it last, rather than think where he had it last. Sharpened with regular use, such right-hemisphere skills need not, as Gordon Bower laments, wither away with age.

More esoterically, the power of imaging lies at the heart of almost every experience in the budding field of parapsychology. Parapsychology calls itself "the scientific investigation of unknown natural laws" rather than of abnormal phenomena that appear to violate the earthly order of things. It is, in sum, an attempt by the left hemisphere to comprehend what is more germane to the right. As such, it remains thoroughly grounded in the perceptual world, at least as subjectively experienced. Indeed, psychics report "seeing" the identity or location of hidden objects on "TV screens" in their mind; "hearing" conversations yet to be spoken; "smelling" and "tasting" the atmosphere of a country astrally visited; "feeling" heat from the "energy" their fingers release when psychically bending or breaking otherwise resistant metals. Thoughts are secondary. It is the *sensed* that is uppermost, the seemingly real perceptions that meld together in a *knowing* as palpable as the breath of life itself.

In these captivating if sensitive areas of potential intelligence—populated as they are with as many sly and blatant bunko artists as earnest experts and amateurs—biofeedback is just beginning to break solid scientific ground. The preliminary evidence, nonetheless, is intriguing. Psychologist Charles Tart of the University of California, for example, has designed an ESP experiment which dramatically demonstrates the legitimacy of the phenomenon and the validity of biofeedback as an effective tool in its investigation. The subject was isolated in a steel sensory-deprivation chamber. There he was hooked up to an EEG and a GSR. ESP was not mentioned. Instead, he was told (perhaps prophetically) that he was being tested on "subliminal perception." Tart sat in another room and sent an "ESP message" with his mind every time he was given an electric shock. The subject was instructed to press a telegraph key whenever he thought he was being "subliminally" stimulated. His guesses, as it turned out, were miserably inaccurate—but the recorded changes in his brain-wave pattern and skin "talk," when timed against Tart's randomly scheduled shocks, tallied perfectly. His brain and skin were aware of receiving the ESP "signals"—that is, his environmentally conscious right hemisphere was—even if his self-conscious left hemisphere was not.

Brain-wave biofeedback may even liberate psychic abilities in those who have heretofore shown no signs of it. Using biofeedback principles, for instance, a pair of Stanford Research Institute investigators claim they can teach improved extrasensory perception. In another study, one college student taught to increase his theta by EEG feedback—described as an "intense, sincere" young man reluctant to talk about his experiences—told of "seeing" his roommate inform him of his acceptance for graduate school the day before it actually happened. He also claimed to have "witnessed" beforehand the attempted assassination of Alabama Governor George Wallace.

Nowhere, however, have the mysteries of theta brainwaves and biofeedback been more puissantly joined than on the leading edge of technology's farthest frontier—outer space. Allowed a pause in their minutely synchronized labors of engineering and science, precision-minded astronauts have looked down across the silent, velvety miles at the spinning blue-and-white ball of the earth and been moved—not only to pinnacles of insight, but to streams of theta that scribbled themselves telemetrically on EEG drums back at Houston's Mission Control. One astronaut confessed that he had always tried to operate like a machine in life and had failed; another left the space agency to become a Christian evangelist. But none expressed more eloquently the meaning of their "transcendental experience" than Edgar Mitchell, a hitherto tough-minded MIT doctor of science who has since established an Institute of Noetic (from the Greek for "mind") Sciences in California for the study of psychic phenomena.

"It was an altered state of consciousness," Mitchell said. "Virtually all the philosophies, ideas, truths that were part of my scientific paradigm got tossed right up into the air and fell into a big heap like a bundle of pickup sticks. There was suddenly a very deep gut feeling that *something was different* . . . . [I was] seeing, rather, knowing for sure, that there was a purposefulness of flow, of energy, of time and space in the cosmos."[45]

The ultimate drama of outer space, then, all unknown to the surrogate eye of our television cameras, has been played within the astronaut's brain. Inner space, not outer space, appears to hold the greatest challenge to our intelligence.

361

Chapter 14

Of Mice and Men

Three years ago Dr. Norman Dalkey of UCLA, a philosopher and mathematician turned psychologist and computer engineer, set out to test the intelligence of men, not of man. Dalkey is one of the founders of Delphi, a process used by government and industry to elicit and refine group judgments in making forecasts and decisions. Delphi, of course, is named for the city that in Greek legend was the seat of Apollo's oracle, a font of godly prophecy. The nickname, given to Dalkey's brainchild at the RAND Corporation, had long amused him, for he felt there was nothing oracular about it.

"I even resisted the notion of group thinking," he says. "I considered it individual thinking put together by group process into something more effective than what you could get from each individual."[1] Now, however, a new idea had occurred to him.

Dalkey began by giving a group IQ test for adults to one of his graduate classes. He next constructed a curve of normal distribution, and struck the class average. There was nothing unusual about that. Following this, though, Dalkey did something that test makers but not test givers often do in determining the relative difficulty of the items: He noted the plurality preference of the class on each item as registered in their multiple-choice answers. Dalkey then waded into uncharted waters. He wrote each of those down and added them up to get the group's aggregate answers, their collective knowledge as determined, in effect, by referendum.

To Dalkey, the results were astonishing. The group's score was 30 points above the class average. When he took a subgroup of the class's higher scorers, moreover—those who averaged 110 to 120 IQ—and applied the same method, their collective score was even more impressive. It was 30 points higher than that of its highest member. Dalkey thought at first he had stumbled on nothing more than a statistical artifact. But after further thought and study, he decided he had found "a true indication of cumulative intellectual power."[2]

A leading educational psychologist thinks all Dalkey has discovered is a truism. "You would expect that to happen," he says. "On a multiple-choice question of great difficulty, most of the answers, being guesses, would be spread more or less equally across all possible answers. But the people who really know come down on the right answer, giving you what we call a 'modal hump' there. Naturally the plurality vote would dictate that answer.

"I don't see that it says anything about intelligence. Of course, if Dalkey is saying that two heads are better than one, I can't argue. On matters of information and judgment, two heads are. In fact, the more heads the better. That's why we have town councils and juries."[3]

Dalkey is undaunted, precisely because of that essential agreement. As he sees it, there are two ways of viewing intelligence, what engineers might call the mechanical and the thermodynamic. One group, the psychologists, is concerned with mechanics—the intricacies of the pattern, the flow of every particle. The other group, which Dalkey believes really hasn't identified itself yet and to which he belongs, looks at and treats intelligence as a whole. In problem solving and forecasting, they believe, the thermodynamic approach is more fruitful than the mechanical. "We're not concerned with how an individual knows, but with how much," Dalkey explains, which brings him full circle to his class experiment and Delphi: "It seems to me now that the group process is exactly the same thing drawn large, only richer."[4]

The Pawnee Indians, according to one researcher, were a well-disciplined people who maintained tribal order without any of the power mechanisms modern man considers essential. No plans were ever discussed, no orders issued, no work assignments made.

Chiefs were chosen for humility and sagacity, not chest-thumping aggressiveness. "Whatever social forms existed," reports Gene Weltfish, "were carried within the consciousness of the people."[5]

Alas, today's urban society is different. Given our linguistic bias—and the primitive state of our consciousness—heads must be put together. And when they are, more often than not the result is likely to be a dense, meaty sound rather than the synergistic implosion of compounded intellect. Modern government, for instance—Locke's "standing rule to live by"—is hardly a paragon of combinatory wisdom. More than forty members of the House of Representatives decided not to run for reelection this year in frustration over Congressional ineffectiveness in decision-making. Over 700 bills must be considered every session. Their content is so beyond the ability of the human intellect to absorb, much less master, that members are often reduced to voting blind, in obeisance to a thumbs-up or thumbs-down sign given them by party leaders or legislators with a special interest. Snapped one retiring Oregon Democrat, "How could you possibly know what's in all of them?"[6]

Over all, of course, hangs the issue of unlimited Presidential power in the shadow of Watergate. One-man rule is clearly not the most intelligent answer, however brilliant that man may be. In fact, research suggests, high IQ can often produce as many problems as it solves. The brilliant man can become mired in peripheral issues he alone sees, immerse himself in the game for its own sake, worry about whether he is at work on the right aspect, intelligently fear to act to a point of paralysis. Brilliant or not, he may refuse to surrender any real power of decision-making even as he makes à show of delegating it. As one pundit wrote,

> Lyndon Johnson . . . kept George Ball around . . . as a kind of official dissenter [on Vietnam]. The President would hear him out, congratulate himself for taking the other side into account, and march on in the same direction. . . . You can perhaps bring a President to a roomful of knowledgeable people but you can't make him think differently as a result. . . .[7]

Nor, it need scarcely be said, are Presidential aides when invested with real power immune to the hubris it carries with it. After

Watergate and the debacle of Nixon's inner circle, humorist Russell Baker turned bitterly serious to write their most pertinent epitaph:

> They were people with a lust to know everything. They had a vision of total information. . . . Intelligence. One still senses a vocal genuflection when the word passes over their lips. God may be love, but knowledge is power. . . . Theirs was a faith in Total Intelligence. In their dream of ultimate fulfillment, absolutely everything was knowable. . . . They wanted all the facts about everything. . . . The astounding thing, of course, was that the harder the White House labored to know absolutely everything, the less it knew about the relatively few things that it was its business to know about. . . .[8]

Indeed, although Dalkey's clean-limbed piece of classroom research suggests otherwise, there are, alas, too many real-world indicators that group thinking in government is synergism in reverse: The whole is *less* than the sum of its parts. In his book *Victims of Groupthink,* Yale psychologist Irving Janis confessed himself initially puzzled by the horrendous gaffes perpetrated in recent history by those otherwise highly able and intelligent men assembled around the seats of political power. The answer, he found in examining a series of national fiascos, was a surprising adherence to group norms and pressures toward uniformity, "even when their policy was working badly and had unintended consequences that disturbed the conscience of the members."[9]

In every case, Janis discovered to his horror, that adherence was marked by a set of psychological symptoms disturbing in the extreme to the healthy exercise of human intellect. The group was gripped by an illusion of invulnerability. Its members indulged in collective efforts to rationalize away warnings that they reconsider decisions already made. They had an unflinching belief in their own inherent morality. They denigrated their enemies with stereotyped images of weakness and evil. Any dissenting member felt a direct pressure exerted by all the others in the name of group loyalty. Other members self-censored their own thoughts of possible deviation from any apparent group consensus. There was a shared illusion of satisfying unanimity based on the convenient fallacy that silence meant consent. And finally, self-appointed "mindguards" emerged when needed to shield the group from any information that might have shattered its complacency about the ultimate rightness of its decisions. Under such circumstances, Janis decided, individual intelligence became hermetically sealed off from the larger reality it was supposed to serve.

Neither is the private sector, the world of science, business, and industry, any more reassuring in the ongoing intelligence of its operation. The corporate chain of command, complained a $600,000-a-year General Motors vice-president who quit his job, simply would not let him intelligently do the job of planning that his career had trained him to do. "I was being presented with information that had limited alternatives," he said. "This is totally inconsistent with any thoughtful and creative originality. You could never reflect on and modify a proposal. You couldn't be a planner. . . .

"It was like standing in the boiler room and tending a machine and you were just watching it instead of running it."[10]

Differences in cognitive style, moreover, mitigate against consensual intelligence in the conference room as well as the war room. As Theodore Melnechuck perceptively writes of the intellectual life at a prestigious scientific think tank, " . . . Barriers to communication existed . . . between people with different approaches: Some were interested in structure, some in steady-state function, others in the change of those functioning structures with time. . . ."[11]

All of these, said Melnechuck, were deeply ingrained differences in thinking. Staff members also betrayed differing "trajectories of history." Some thought of life as essentially unchanging, others thought of it as progressing, degenerating, cyclical, or perpetually in conflict. "They based their professional lives on such differences," he said, "and had personality differences consistent with them."[12]

Judging from the tenor of such observations, then, there is more than a tincture of unhappy truth to the comic definition of a camel: a horse designed by a committee. But must this be? Isn't it possible to make intelligent, creative group decisions for the common good untrammeled by conformist pressures or the stresses of idiosyncratic thinking, unswayed by the divergent pulls of conflicting emotion? Failing that, can we find some way to screen out these countervailing elements? Better yet, might we make them work for us, instead of against us, in reaching holistic solutions that embody the best of all that is human?

In a fanciful children's story called *Mrs. Frisby and the Rats of NIMH*, Robert O'Brien tells about a colony of government laboratory rats who filch from their white-coated keepers several secrets of modern life—among them reading and electricity—and use them to escape to the quiet of the country. It would be no more fanciful than the story to suggest that they might have learned what psychologist John Calhoun was up to in behavioral systems research at NIMH (The National Institute of Mental Health) and wisely wanted no part of it.

Calhoun built a "Mouse Utopia" in the gravest interest of science. He created a galvanized steel world the size of a suburban bathroom, with warm communal apartments, feeding stations, free-flowing fountains, and spacious runways. He planted electronic resonators under their belly skins to identify all the mice with distinctive signals. He painted them with color-coded stripes to classify their strongest behavioral tendencies. He surrounded them with electromagnetic portals which endlessly recorded their comings and going on a computer. Then he and his assistants sat back and watched. A million visual and computer observations were logged as the mice turned their utopia into hell on earth by literally breeding themselves to death.

Every sixty days the white mice, originally four pairs, doubled until finally there were 2,200 that overflowed all resources and facilities. But by then, three years later, the colony was doomed by another more insidious phenomenon. Its members had developed a "pathological need for togetherness."[13] At rest, many piled on top of one another until they smothered. Hundreds withdrew into the middle of the cage where they greeted all attempts at social contact with slashing attack. Hordes of others scurried after every passing pair of feet, sniffing and probing. "[They] never learn," Calhoun later reported. "Each day they follow human feet about as if they had never seen them. . . . They are . . . deathly quiet. . . . A pallor of silence hangs over the flaccid flowing mass."[14]

The older ones died. Females passed menopause and stopped producing. Males mounted females but ejaculated outside them. The mice no longer bothered to bury their dead. Every behavior compatible with species survival ceased. Doomsday had come.

What is most sobering for man is not that the mice of NIMH died, but how. Beyond a certain critical point, long before the apparent living space was exhausted, even the much criticized stricture of "zero population growth" could not have saved them. For the mice died, Calhoun believes, not from overpopulation per se but from social pollution. It occurred, according to Calhoun, at that moment in each animal's life which anyone who has been in the military or worked in a large bureaucratic office can recognize: when it could no longer complete an action before it was interrupted. "Only the simplest behaviors, such as eating and drinking, were ever carried to completion," Calhoun reported. "The mice never really learned to mate or fight. They never knew stress. Most matured into passive blobs of protoplasm, physically healthy but socially sterile."[15] Some reacted with such signs of stress as hypertension and arteriosclerosis. But they were the lucky ones. At least they were socially alive. In contrast, "the beautiful ones," as Calhoun sadly calls them, never attempted to cope. Rather than socially withdrawing from the system, they never attempted to enter it.

In the main, Calhoun's experiment confirmed what his earlier research with rats had indicated: Free-ranging rodents exhibit genetically determined, culturally modified behavior (reduced growth, social instability, lowered reproduction, higher infant mortality) which contrives to keep population at a steady-state utilizing about twenty-five times the space they would when caged. If density is artifically increased, both animal and group must forfeit some of their potential if all are to stay healthy—or the strongest will survive at the expense of the rest to ensure species survival. In either case "behavioral sinks" result. Females cease building nests, bear litters on the floor, stop carrying and nursing their young, forget them, and abandon them to die. Males become gregarious social drinkers, hypersexed, homosexual, cannibalistic. Although the colony at its most crowded can be kept as hygienically healthy as most, there is an excess of living bodies, too many interacting elements for the social system's natural capacity. Social pollution sets in. Doomsday is on its way.

But of course Calhoun's rodents, while near enough to man physiologically to merit their use in the one-to-one extrapolations of experimental psychology and pharmacology, are not like men socially—are they? Calhoun fears they are too close for comfort. "A mouse has a genetic template that guides the maturational unfolding of its behavior," he says. "Learning may alter this. Man is basically no different—except that learning, traditions and cultures have much more influence on his behavior than heredity."[16]

Ironically, Calhoun believes, it is this unique quality, his marvelous adaptability, which now confronts us with the gravest threat in our species' brief history. The threat is not essentially one of physical overpopulation, though crowding is its catalyst. Rather, it is a threat of social pollution every bit as real as that of his rodents—and as deadly. Calhoun calls its overriding ingredient a crisis in *conceptual space.* Accustomed as we are to thinking of ideas as limitless, his theory takes some getting used to.

As Calhoun sees it, for his first 2,000,000 years or so on earth man was a relatively stable biological animal, composed ultimately of some 4,500,000 persons fragmented into roughly 150,000 hunter-gatherer bands of about thirty members each. The band contained an estimated twelve adults, a socially viable figure unchanged by subsequent evolution and one that comes down to us today in the jury. Each band roamed an average area fifteen miles in diameter until about 40,000 years ago, preserving the stability of its social contacts by moving to other areas when its territoriality was challenged, or killing and being killed. But as available land was filled, man found he had in effect painted himself into an ecological corner. Like Calhoun's rodents, he had exhausted his social space. It was then, Calhoun theorizes, that man rose up to become truly human by thinking himself out of the evolutionary hole his reproduction had dug. He began by conceiving clear-cut, differing roles—to begin with, one for the male, another for the female. Now the allowable group number of adults could double without disturbing the essential equation. Generating more such ideas, he further saw, would allow human species to escape the constraints of its socially determined physical environment by holding down the number of same social interactions while upping their variety. It would allow him to segment his ever-higher density. By continually elaborating this new kind of space, conceptual space, he could maintain a relatively constant density while increasing his numbers.

Even as this common information pool permitted him to draw rules, codes, and theories for coping with the problems of an ever-growing population, moreover, the product of both—information times population—continued to enhance his intellectual capacity. The stage was set for the metamorphosis of biological man into human man through the development of what Calhoun calls his *social brain.* The ensuing historical enrichment and enlargement of conceptual space stood as nothing less than the evolution of human potential.

Today the "metabolism" of man's conceptual space involves two processes—the systematic linking together of groups into ever-larger organizations, and the storage, transfer, and manipulation of information using such "mental prostheses" (artificial extensions) as books and computers. These processes, Calhoun thinks, have contributed equally to the rapidity and effectiveness with which we "move" through conceptual space by enabling us to freely share experiences that maximize gratification from human contact and interaction. By sustaining such a synergism, man has successfully created an increasingly larger and more complex social brain. This has brought us to the point where manipulating conceptual space occupies a role in our collective lives equal to anything else.

But now, to employ a crude analogy from atomic energy, the mix is reaching a point of critical mass. The eruptive increase in man's numbers has pushed his species to its biological ceiling. At the same time, organizations have swollen in size until further growth in human numbers will no longer contribute to the evolution of our social brain with its concomitant expansion in conceptual space or human potential. When both man's biological numbers and conceptual space reach their symbiotic upper limits, like a runaway reactor humankind will socially explode, Calhoun contends, terminating the "continuing experiment that has been man."[17]

The most sinister sign that the critical mass is approaching, Calhoun feels, is embodied in what psychoanalyst René Spitz characterizes as man's *action cycle*—his train of anticipation, appetite, and consumation. Interrupting the cycle before its natural completion causes us anxiety, just as it does rodents. Worse, since human life is lived in a rough but personally recognized equilibrium between frustration and gratification, says Calhoun, as man's small subgroups are increasingly impinged upon or overrun by a surplus of social contacts, his proportion of frustrating encounters is bound to rise—until it drives him to protectively cut off from meaningful exchanges despite a seeming wealth of interactions.

Frustration and alienation cannot help but occur, Calhoun is convinced, because of the interdependency of man's *psychological mass* and the volatile nature of conceptual space. Psychological mass is a measure of the impact on each individual levied by the increased education and consciousness born of ever-greater human potential, says Calhoun, which in turn results in an ever more critical psychological density for the population. The greater the psychological mass of the person, the greater his effect on every other person. In addition, man's hunger for "mind food"—the very thing that has seduced us into believing it limitless—seems insatiable. Conceptual space *does* appear without boundary, if only because from hard evolutionary experience we wish it so. Writes Calhoun,

> Each passing generation needs more information, more ideas, that will help [man] relate to his fellows and make more effective use of natural resources without destroying them for future generations. Each generation must create more new ideas than did their parents. Just creating the ideas is not enough. Ideas locked away in individual minds, in technical tomes, or bottled up by traditional worshipping of outmoded ways or by cultural barriers, lead to starvation of the mind and spirit just as assuredly as holding grain in graneries feeds no bodies.[18]

That cultural imperative, Calhoun believes, drives each man's ego hard up against the other's. And while technology has until now enabled him to overcome most obstacles to survival in the physical sphere, his ego has never been more vulnerable to inundation by the surrounding psychological mass.

Thus, for the first time in man's brief history on earth, the crisis is dual; one not only of numbers but of ideas, of neither alone but of both dimensions of our social brain as each races toward its outer limit. Long before the much-publicized Malthusian doomsday—the theoretical moment a half-century hence when the current doubling rate of world population if not reversed will cause human numbers to flash to infinity instantaneously—our physical density could reach a point of no return where it would overwhelm our capacity to cope with the menace of wildly multiplying bodies by devising further innovations in conceptual space.

The course of man, Calhoun feels, will be fixed in the next ten or fifteen years. "We are approaching the limits of the cortex to process information necessary to codify concepts," as he puts the problem. "It is a needle we have to pass through. . . . Either we dedicate ourselves to making it through to something beyond, or else we don't make it—and there really is no beyond."[19]

In Calhoun's opinion, any one of several outcomes is foreseeable. Taking the worst first, like his mice of NIMH, we might continue to breed so insanely that our society explodes from social pollution and no young can develop the traits needed for species survival. Then again, like his wild rats with limited.space, we might fall to fighting in a survival-of-the-fittest struggle that would end with a few aristocrats ensuring species continuation by allowing their own and a few creative misfits to survive while ruthlessly subjugating the rest of us to extinction. Or we might get the worst of things under some kind of stopgap control only to let the population seep past Calhoun's calculated global maximum of 9 billion people—thereby decreasing just as measurably the intellectual potential of each person alive. He would become, in Calhoun's haunting phrase, "less aware of less and less." Or the population might be wrestled into stasis. If static, each individual would enter early in life—and be forever frozen into—a "harmonizing niche" which would "maximize predictability," assuring every role vacated would be filled precisely by a similar one. Such people, Calhoun fears, would soon become "the beautiful ones," capable of mindless routine but behind their Cheshire-cat smiles, dead to the creative, immune to the challenging.

Each of the last, he says in understatement, is hardly typical of successful evolution over time: "Stable products rarely last. If they did, dinosaurs or frogs would still predominate."[20]

Is there a saving scenario? There is, says Calhoun. It sounds so stirringly idealistic, and so fraught with peril, that the mind recoils in suspicion and skepticism: "Of all life, we are the only species capable of comprehending the implication of evolution.

"Therefore, we must design and guide its further unfolding. Man must direct his own evolution."[21]

Calhoun served on a jury-sized panel of scientific experts which met for two dozen two-and-one-half-day sessions over a period of twelve years to explore the interlocking issues of population and mental health. The panel concluded, not surprisingly, that the focus of such evolutionary planning had to be relating people to people. But where was man's herculean task of wresting control of his own evolution to begin? Man, they decided, must consciously and deliberately evolve a new consensual *image of reality* to fit his accelerating change of circumstance, something far easier said than done. As Kenneth Boulding observes,

> . . . Our basic image of the world tends to be set in childhood or adolescence; hence most people . . . and this includes most people in positions of power, are operating with images . . . which are already hopelessly obsolete. The question of . . . rapid and effective propagation of [new] images, therefore, is of crucial importance, even one of life and death. . . . [22]

Why, if we are as intelligent as evolution has led us to believe, do we resist the change of image that must precede the shift in values that can rescue our kind from the apocalypse?

We resist, Calhoun would say, because it threatens Boulding's big picture, Jerison's model of a possible world—not piecemeal but at its very foundations and in its entirety. Here again, most of us will not be enchanted to learn, we are not all that different from rodents. Calhoun has trained a single rat to drink alone, then introduced it into the midst of a bunch of rats trained to drink together. The gregarious rats came to "help" the alien drink by standing beside him. He interpreted this as wrong, fiercely attacked, and dragged them away. Although half were wounded so severely they died, none ever retaliated—or adopted his ways. If this sounds unlike man, notes Calhoun, we have only to observe how fiercely he defends every aspect of his own cultural status quo when menaced by the well-intentioned efforts of those on the outside to alter it for his own good. For example, around Calcutta rice is grown in quarter-acre plots separated by low dirt dikes which delineate different ownerships. Rodents living in the dikes destroy a fifth of every crop. Since each landowner holds title to several scattered plots, a practical consolidation of these holdings would—as any rational Westerner could immediately see—reduce the need for dikes and cut crop losses tenfold. But the Indian farmers stubbornly resist. This is the way they have always grown rice, in quarter-acre plots. If this seems inapplicable to less primitive, more "sensible" modern technological societies, Calhoun likes to point out, we have only to realize how tenaciously we cling to the private automobile despite its waste, health pollution, and expense when clearly, public transit—as any Calcutta rice farmer could instantly appreciate—is the more intelligent means of mass transport.

In any event, Calhoun makes clear, if man is to be saved from himself it is men, manifestly, that must be swayed. The only indispensable single presence needed, he thinks, is that of the charismatic leader, especially in the arts, who can "translate the new images into forms which can be appreciated intuitively without regard to their rationality or logical substance."[23] But men, not man, must be willing to anticipate, to learn and relearn, rather than waiting to be taught by an avalanche of irresistibly deadly events which may well constitute the last lesson on earth our species ever gets. In the face of our comparatively short and stormy history, can we?

We can, Calhoun believes, if we are intelligent enough to use our social brain to its fullest potential. To do so, we must begin by seeing ourselves as its neurons, then set about consciously molding more sensitive institutions organically patterned after the components of the biological brain itself—which is, after all, both its intuitive and logical model. Such an advanced social brain needs at the outset an *alerting* system analogous to our biological brain's network of senses, according to Calhoun. The alerting system would scan and develop a "continuing anthology" from the existing universe of concepts, ideas, philosophies, purposes, and functions, while simultaneously screening out all irrelevances. It would also set up communication links, much as Jerison sees language as extended human perception. It would, in addition, like the autonomic nervous system, be ever alive to internal stimulation. The more valuable input it would condense and relay to the next level of the social brain, the *appreciation* system. There sufficiently refined group discriminations would be difficult but not impossible, for as Sir Geoffrey Vickers observes, institutions and societies as well as individuals "learn what to want as well as how to get, what to be as well as what to do."[24]

Confronted with the predicament of achieving consensus in ever-larger organizations, however, Calhoun would shun a single appreciation system in favor of a jury approach. Each of the twelve groups could focus on a major area of human concern, all laced together in an overlapping sequence. He calculates their minimum necessary population by 1984 to be 20,000,000. That would be one in ten of those "creative concerned individuals" he calculates would exist to maintain Teilhard de Chardin's theoretic *noosphere*—that interconnectedness of people capable of generating images of sufficient strength and pervasiveness to elicit acceptance swiftly enough. Calhoun calls this jury of appreciation a *Teilhard* in de Chardin's honor, but confesses that to bring it together will, in classic understatement, "take a concerted effort."[25]

Once assembled, Calhoun is convinced, members of the Teilhard would become units in a mind greater than themselves, and gain the identities and purposes they have so largely lost in complex mass society by a process not unlike the synergism of biological cerebration itself. Like the temperature for which a thermostat is set, its thoughts would rise to match the needs of its surroundings. Through its inner alerting system, moreover, the social brain would take care always to maintain a balance between the values of the individual and those of society, between the freedom of its

375

members and the collective efforts of the Teilhard, especially as they pertain to enhancing the effectiveness of the creative in generating new cultural templates, new images to live by.

Elevating creativity, Calhoun feels, would at once reduce man's aggression and promote a slowdown in population increase. Konrad Lorenz, he points out, has shown that man, unlike more powerful flesh-eaters, lacks a mechanism to inhibit killing his kind; when escape is blocked, his primitive forebears murdered their "enemies," who were other men. Crowding or encroaching precipitated mutual aggression. Now that social cohesion has led to vastly larger groups, the encroachment threat to tangible physical objects, peers, and space has been displaced to behavior, traditions, and values. The "enemy camp" becomes any idea suspected of threatening experience or survival. Creativity thus becomes what the ethologist calls a "releaser for militant enthusiasms," by defusing the threat from altered circumstances or divergent values with the phenomenon of satisfactory discovery. The same dynamic indirectly holds for what Eric Erikson calls the "generativity" of the sex urge. The sex urge, Erikson thinks, is an attempt at self-duplication through producing and rearing children. By promoting survival of one's values and the creation of new ones, man can channel off the power of the sex urge into his "brain children," leaving a relatively steady state of population.

When and if that happens, Calhoun thinks, our social brain will have evolved to the point of saving the species. Positive new additions to conceptual space will be duly perceived, evaluated, integrated into overall social planning and transmitted to the social brain's *motor* systems of a renewed and revitalized "establishment" for appropriate action. We will have then seen in de Chardin's visionary words that "man is building his composite brain before our eyes."[26]

If this does not happen, we will have no one to blame but ourselves, suggests Lord Brain:

> . . . As individuals we are all receptors, capable of supplying the higher centers with information. What information they get, therefore, depends on us. We are also the motor nerves, and what society does is done by us. But we are again, collectively,

ourselves the higher centers, the forebrain, which mediates for the social mind the difficult task of receiving the information, learning from past experience, reacting to it emotionally yet controlling its emotions; above all, looking into the future.[27]

And if we fail?
Then, says Calhoun, "Orwell's *1984* will be a paradise compared to reality."[28]

The scene at any Tavistock conference is in stark contrast to Calhoun's vision of the social brain in action. It is, rather, a textbook study in mindless anarchy. One group rebels against all organizational restraints in the name of a formless independence, then tries to wrest control of the entire conference away from the professional staff. Another invades and occupies the premises of a third, which retaliates by kidnapping the second's elected leader in a vain attempt to extort back its original space—which it hasn't the faintest idea how to use. A fourth hammers out an exhaustive plan of cooperation with its neighbor, appoints an emissary to negotiate, then disowns both him and his mission the moment he is gone.

Inside each group, the situation is no more rational. Its ten or so members sit in a stiff circle with their consultant, a severe and unsmiling sort who rarely addresses any one of them and often does not bother to answer at all. He does nothing to make them feel more comfortable. Rather, like an ill-bred host who has abdicated all responsibility for a party he knows is going badly, he sometimes points out the tactics used by each to dispel uneasiness: introducing themselves, making small talk, rearranging chairs, attacking someone who dares stick his neck out in an effort to get something, anything, constructive going. The growing uneasiness, all of them come to suspect, is part of the conference plan. After four days of such random togetherness, many leave in disgust or bewilderment. "They should give us our money back," muttered one disenchanted participant. "Nothing happened."

On the contrary, exponents of the Group Relations Conferences developed by London's Tavistock Institute would say, *everything* happened. Writes psychologist Margaret Rioch, a frequent conference leader:

377

The elements of our society which produce crime, insanity, riots, wars and the manifold injustices which we deplore, are present in the conference, in each group of nice, intelligent individuals who come full of the best intentions.[29]

Indeed, the Tavistock Conference's very air of aimlessness is engineered to catch, like a spark in a bottle, what every human thinks he wants but really dreads like death itself, that precious something each must truly have before he can ever give any of it away in the successful mass pursuit of life's common goals: freedom. Rioch sounds almost Biblical when she says, "How easily we give up our wills and our minds if someone will take our sins upon him and free us from the terrible burden of responsibility for the choices we make."[30]

Developed by the Centre for Applied Social Research of the Tavistock Institute of Human Relations in London, such conferences spread to this country in 1965. They draw from all disciplines interested in group process, vary in length from four days to two weeks, and offer in a deceptively tranquil residential or academic setting what Rioch describes as "an opportunity . . . to learn new ways of relating to the world." Such ways are never delineated or prescribed outright, much less handed down as cant. Rather, says Rioch, the situation is deliberately kept in flux, in her poetic words, rendered

. . . mutative. Metaphorically speaking, one is pushed swiftly to the edge of a chasm and carried by the forward impulse in a long leap across the abyss to new and undiscovered country on the other side—unless, of course, one falls back into the old country or into the depths.[31]

Unlike encounter or sensitivity training, Rioch explains, the group task is to study the processes going on in the group as a *whole*, especially covertly, with emphasis on the nature of authority and the problems in exercising it.

In every group the underground spring of chronic and enduring human dependency bubbles to the surface almost at once—despite the fact members are told time and again, orally and in writing, that how they learn and what they do is up to them, that no one knows or has planned what will occur, that they are free in every sense of the word to come or go, to learn or not learn, what and how they please. "Members behave strikingly like sheep," remarks Rioch. "With great docility they do what they believe the staff would like them to do; or with terrible locking of horns they refuse to do what they believe is required of them. In either case they place the authority for their behavior outside themselves. . . ."[32]

In the beginning, the stereotyped role of each group member is easily recognized: the fighter, the funnyman, the peacemaker, the sexy one, the shy one, the spokesman. But as the days wear on in the psychic vacuum created by the consultant—who attempts to comment instructively on the unfolding process but refuses to be drawn in—the cultural accretions of a lifetime are peeled away and the raw dynamics of man's first coming together as it might have been—and still is beneath the manicured surface of society today—are often revealed to everyone's astonishment. A woman finds herself crying without knowing why, even without wishing to, as if uncannily, she admits, the group were crying through her. Another member discovers he can do anything with the group he likes; that he almost *is* the group. This realization stimulates in him the grandiose sense of power that typifies the despot. Writes Rioch,

> . . . The sense of being all-powerful and the feeling of being a marionette . . . are essentially two sides of the same coin. . . . An aspect of our lives is revealed in them to which we are usually blind, namely the unity of the individual with the whole.[33]

This does not mean a group mind operating in some mysterious way, she hastens to add, but a system of interrelatedness in which a change in any part means a change in the whole. What's more, it means that for the group to function effectively, each member has to give up something of his own autonomy to that of all, as represented by their spokesman—and that he in turn must recognize that *his* authority is limited by the degree of authority members confer on him. Their reluctance to surrender any of their freedom sabotages the group to a degree matched only by

379

their all-too-frequent willingness to surrender *all* of it. Thus the appointed leader is "in the unenviable position of being in charge of a group of zombies," says Rioch—until, carried away, he commits them too far, too fast, and they, realizing the cost at last, rise up to repudiate him. Like Vickers, Rioch concludes that "responsibility within a system, if it is anywhere, is everywhere."[34]

Nevertheless, she adds,

> I have frequently experienced a phenomenon toward the end which is like a kinesthetic perception inside my skin. . . . It is as if the members had been staring out of a small barred window . . . shaking violently at the bars which may bend but do not break. Behind them at the other end of the room is an open door. They have only to turn around to walk out of their prison. But before they can let go their cramped hold on the bars and be willing to turn away from the precious bit of light they have to comprehend clearly that they really are—and have been from the beginning—free.[35]

That 180-degree turn must be made, Rioch feels, before man can ever truly commit himself to men. Even so, although she doesn't mention it, everyone in the group must confront a corollary danger: that having given up a part of themselves to the good of all, they have together created a whole more powerful than what any has held back. The whole then threatens to subsume what is left.

"The small group," says UCLA psychiatrist Louis Jolyon West, a onetime air force expert on the "cell" method used by the Chinese Communists to collectivize and solidify their rule, "can be more powerful than all the chemicals, electro-stimulation, media and charismatic teachers put together in changing people's thinking.

"It has the power to change physical perceptions. If it says blue, you'll see blue—even if it's yellow."[36]

Nonetheless, if success is genuine, Rioch contends, the reward is ample: "This is not to preach a moral but to state a fact. Human beings are never more fulfilled than when they are united to a whole."[37]

Unfortunately for Calhoun's grand design, such breakthroughs are distressingly rare. They are rarer yet, of course, in large groups, and all but impossible in even larger groups such as a government agency or city population where the relative anonymity is so painful it exercises a pull upon the more aggressive to make themselves known regardless of the cost, and quells the naturally quiet to a deathly, passive, forfeiting silence. What chance is there, then, for Teilhard's twenty million?

Perhaps there is none—until or unless humans change their image of themselves, their intelligence, and their leaders. For according to Rioch,

> The Biblical image of [men as] sheep which have gone astray instead of following their shepherd is not very complimentary to man. The sheep is not generally thought of as intelligent like the fox or wise like the owl . . . but rather as a mindless animal, requiring someone to think for him. . . . The trouble with this simile when applied to human beings, is that the shepherd is another sheep. He may be dressed up in a long cloak and accompanied by a tall staff with a crook on the end of it. . . . But underneath the cloak is one of the sheep, and not, alas, a member of a more intelligent and more far-seeing species. . . . [38]

Might we not fare better if we went on leaving things to those who know, the experts? Isn't it feasible, in fact, that we might stave off disaster altogether if we could skim the cream of their thinking with strategies like Delphi, which separate out much of the milk of human emotion rather than allowing it to curdle and contaminate cerebration?

We know, of course, where anything as elemental as survival of the species is honestly involved, that a totally remote and dispassionate exercise of the intellect is probably not only impossible but ill-advised in the attempt. Intense involvement, short of panic anyway, gets our richest juices going. But we also know that—unlike many of the formerly voguish "brainstorming" techniques which threw people together in a freewheeling format that let them build up one another's mental pressure until they blew their collective minds—Delphi works where sheer information content is the critical component. Brainstorming may build a better mousetrap. But Delphi can tell us best how many mice need to be

381

trapped today, and predict their consequent population tomorrow.

Delphi does this by inviting written responses to specific questions anonymously, collecting and evaluating them, and then reporting the results back to the group, which on the basis of this freshly assimilated knowledge further refines its answer through another round or two of the same silent procedure. By screening out with paper and pencil the kind of tyrannical group pressures inherent in the boardroom or town meeting type of verbal free-for-all, Delphi eliminates extraneous "semantic noise" (pointless conversation), defuses the forces of thoughtless conformity, and elevates the least talkative to the same operational plane as the most garrulous. Nothing of remotely offsetting value is lost by stilling all voices, Delphi studies indicate. Covering the blackboard with volunteered alternatives, as some more structured stratagems do, is no more productive than free and open communication—which can be even less effective than pencil-and-paper exercises because it allows spoken error to seep into generalized group assumptions without leaving any telltale trace on the record. Face-to-face discussion, in fact, can quickly narrow the range of disagreement (a phenomenon known as *convergence* among Delphians) and bring about speedy agreement—on a dead-wrong answer. (Such misses are determined by the experimental use of so-called almanac questions, whose answers don't exist in handy reference form but can be calculated.) Equally surprising, in Delphi experiments to see how added data affects decision-making, it apparently makes no difference if participants are given the same information or each a different piece of it.

"The essential requirement is that every piece get into the act, somehow, without being biased," says Dalkey, "that it have its chance to play a role in determining the answer."[39]

In some 1,000 exercises applying Delphi to forecast problems in industry and government, Dalkey told me early in 1973, the verifications "looked good." Quantifying human value judgments as a prelude to measuring man's social and personal decisions was next on tap for Delphi. Was Delphi, then, Dalkey's demurer to the contrary, about to become an oracle worthy of its name? Was it destined to free man from the Tavistock trap of unwanted freedom? In a form as familiar as the regimen of the Little Red Schoolhouse, had the genesis of Calhoun's visionary social brain really been there all the time?

Early this year, two years after our first conversation, I phoned Dalkey to check on Delphi's progress. Here is the essence of that interview:

Q. Any new developments in Delphi value judgments?

A. The most exciting is something called group decision analysis. We used to think you couldn't construct a group preference given a set of individual preferences. But now we think we've done it. You ask each member to develop his own fixed scale of preferences. Like the hardness scale in engineering, which expresses the relative hardness of anything in terms of where it lies on that scale. If they can come in with their preferences fixed to such a scale, whatever it is, we find it possible by voting to arrive at a group scale, then a preference on it.

Q. Anything else new?

A. Well, we didn't do it, but there's been a fascinating finding in Oregon. A college psychologist found that if you simply add up an incoming freshman's grade-point average achievement test score, and high school rating, it will give you a prediction of his college performance almost twice as accurate as the best estimate of the faculty. So there may be a whole class of predictions which respond better to what I call *nominal* judgment, some simple aggregation of objective information.

Q. Has Delphi done anything yet on group creativity? The only example I know of lately were piano and violin concertos composed by one of Chairman Mao's youth committees. One critic called them "Chinese junk."

A. We need decidedly more powerful group techniques for that. Also a good criterion. That's what almost all standard investigations lack. They investigate the factors that make a difference, but they don't investigate whether that difference makes a difference. The same is true of the so-called cognitive complexity scales. Complexity is an interesting property of the group decision, but no one has yet asked, Is it a better decision? At the moment let's leave creativity open.

383

Q. What about emotion? Is there any danger that your pencil-and-paper technique when applied to life-and-death judgments may cost you a certain productive fever of creative interaction?

A. You may be right. That's one of the things we're going to explore.

Q. Two years ago you told me about a major forecast involving 4,000 top Japanese scientists, engineers and government officials. They were asked what important events were going to occur in Japan by the year 2,000. I'm wondering. Did they foresee the energy crisis, its crippling magnitude for Japan?

A. Just a minute. Let me take a look. I have the report right here. [A long pause]. Nope. Nothing about the energy crisis.

Q. Did other Delphi studies forecast it?

A. Oh yes! Both a tightening of energy and a crunch in the Mid-east.

Q. Did they forecast the price of oil going up this much? Creating a comic-opera situation in which three Arab princes would drop a million dollars in Las Vegas and leave all smiles?

A. I don't think the price of oil got into those forecasts. What got in was the potential for oil being used to blackmail the Western powers.

Q. If it was forecast, why didn't anyone do anything about it?

A. I think the reason is very straightforward and simple. There's no group in the United States or anywhere else that takes the long-range view.

Q. As a philosopher, what do you make of this gap between what people can see coming and their utter inability to do anything about it?

A. People, and that includes policymakers, have time preferences that are steep. Something happening tomorrow is enormously more important than something happening next year, and so on. And then there's the piecemeal way in which decisions are made. There's no mechanism to look at the total picture.

Q. With sufficient power behind it, you think Delphi would solve the problem.

A. That's my impression, my credo. That as soon as the issue is presented in a holistic context, people in power will take the long view.

Q. That's only a belief, isn't it? You have nothing at Delphi to prove that.

A. [Laughing] That's right. I don't.

385

Chapter 15

Machines and Monkeys

This is the year. This is the year that the information capacity of all the world's computers will assume a commanding superiority of fifty to one over all the human brains on the globe. In less than a quarter of a century—barely four electronic generations of machine or artificial intelligence—the single computer has moved from a scarcely slouchy 11,000 arithmetical operations a second to over 200,000,000, or one for almost every man, woman, and child in the country every blink of the eye. In so doing, it has increased millions of times over its ability to take instruction and direction—if not its ability to think—has broadened its range of job skills enormously, and in perfect keeping with the mundane laws of engineering, has shrunk in size from a railroad car to a cigarette carton.

Within five years, if present predictions prove out, a general-purpose microcomputer with its own central processor and internal working memory will be available on a single silicon chip for less than the cost of the cheapest transistor radio. Looking ahead in its explosive technology only as far as we can look back, that single-chip computer will become capable of processing 20,000,000 instructions a second—and sell for less than a dollar. Truly, "electric prostheses" for the brain seem just around society's next corner.

Man and his machines have long since been locked into that advanced state of physiological interdependency biologists call *symbiosis*. And, indeed, both the degree and pace of machine involvement in our lives continues relentlessly to quicken. Alfred Rosenblatt of *Electronics* magazine reports that more than 2,600 robots are now on the job in American plants and factories, brav-

386

ing poisonous atmospheres to handle red-hot or icy-cold parts, spot welding, spray painting, and inserting pistons into cylinders having fit tolerances too tight for shaky human hands. A third-generation German robot named Syntelman (Synchron Tele-Manipulator) welcomed the West German research minister to a Düsseldorf fair two years ago by pouring him a drink, proffering it, taking back the empty glass and bowing, all with the flourish of a trained waiter. Syntelman looks, and roughly moves, like a human. It perceives its environment with a TV camera and is directed by a master pilot sitting in a cockpit several feet or miles away, who drives it with a three-dimensional servosystem of multiple motors. It has two distant Viennese cousins that can answer telephones, open doors, vacuum floors, shake hands, and introduce themselves—unless someone thoughtlessly pulls their wall plug.

Not only do machines work for us, they have recently begun to work on us, and in some instances, in us, invading us physically and making our bodies their home. They not only diagnose our illness, for example, they have made themselves an often permanent part of our treatment and cure. They keep our heart beating, our kidneys flushing and filtering. They enable us to operate artificial limbs by tapping into tiny pulses of surplus electric current from other nerves and muscles. Experimentally installed in blind eye sockets, they shoot via a miniature TV beam impulses to implanted brain electrodes, which can then trigger picture-like patterns of "substitute sight" in the visual cortex.

Now computers promise to weave the machine's symbiotic web ever wider and deeper into human society. Computers are starting to check out groceries, detect forgeries, and ferret out fraudulent income tax returns. Computers size up construction jobs and allocate their costs in man-hours and materials. Computers operate high-speed rapid transit systems without human train drivers, conductors, or ticket sellers. Computers manage the breeding of beef cattle by the hundreds of thousands from the calf up, all but untouched by human hands. Computers run tellerless banks, do rudimentary psychotherapy, and counsel college students on career choices from thousands of occupations. Computers have balanced the entire ecology of wildlife environments, telling loggers how much debris to leave in streams for fish habitats and farmers

387

how far to drop their level for irrigation when fish are spawning. One scholarly computer is conducting historical research into the lives of the 1,300 men who served on some 60,000 committees of the Massachusetts colonial legislature just before the American Revolution, seeking in their infinite, brain-defeating detail fresh clues as to what made it happen. Another computer, a binary Jimmy the Greek, has made a career out of handicapping how the Supreme Court will vote on various issues. It has been 97 percent accurate, including the historic 8-0 vote on the Watergate tapes. An on-board computer is being designed for the next generation of American automobiles. It is expected to measure and regulate fuel flow in keeping with weather and road conditions, while keeping an eye on how the car is functioning and warning the driver when things go wrong. If that sounds like a large order, one computer ran the Marxist economy of Allende's Chile. Computers, purists may be horrified to learn, are even helping children compose music, create animated cartoons and write stories and, poems. And, oh, yes—computers are grading intelligence tests.

As we have seen, from working for us it is only a step to working with us, as the inexorable process of man/machine symbiosis swings into ever-higher gear. Delphi planners, for example, have aimed their sights at global decision-making via a worldwide network of twenty computer terminals that now exist, linked by satellite. Such a system, if perfected, could make real the fictional "world brain" of H. G. Wells, an international linkage of experts on everything who would compile, update, and make available to all a "global encyclopedia" of computerized knowledge. Eventually the computer could be refined to ask intelligent questions, computer scientist Michael Arbib believes. When that happens, he thinks, it will by the very nature of the response it gets start to shape human solutions more in its cybernetic image, which in turn will begin to change our ways of organizing. "How can you have plans that are not couched in terms of the organization which must implement them?" asks Stafford Beer in his paper *The Liberty Machine*. "But . . . if the organization is no longer well adapted to the environment, how then can the plans be relevant . . . ?"[1]

Beer's Liberty Machine would be a "Mission Control" on earth, a worldwide network of operations rooms to monitor data on such socially pertinent problems as pollution levels, crime rates, production quotas, educational achievements, and food prices. When distilled, such information would be used to make world projections as a basis for instant decisions. Unlike man, argues Arbib, the cybernetic World Brain would encourage the making of vital decisions from an unprecedented flow of free information (presumably by the concerted human neurons in Calhoun's Teilhardian social brain) rather than from the prejudices and narrow self-interest of some small group of politicians long since prisoners of their own finite little minds with no hope of pardon.

Currently Delphi's network is the farthest cry from the Wells-Arbib-Beer prototype. Its present role is only to aggregate answers. But soon, Norman Dalkey hopes, it will be used to inject new information into the decision-making process. Eventually he envisions an ultrasophisticated computer "moderator" that could orchestrate the various inputs of experts around the globe to maximize the quality of consensus; a giant traffic controller for flying thoughts; perhaps even a mighty Wurlitzer that could compose from the brightest brains of the many a symphonic synthesis of idea and emotion, great music from all parts of the mind.

It might even be done wordlessly, by silent cerebration faster than the tongue can talk. Does such an idea sound farfetched? Scientsts at UCLA and Stanford Research Institute have been working for three years with computerized feedback systems that can literally read minds and do their bidding. As demonstrated at SRI, subjects hooked up to a cap of electrodes which transmit their brain waves to a computer can direct it by thoughts alone to move an electronically screened dot up, down, left, right, slow, and fast. The computer does this by storing in its memory bank each subject's evoked cortical potential patterns for all these commands. It is even learning to store and recognize the unique signaturelike "templates" or patterns for rudimentary spoken, or unspoken, language. The SRI scientist—Lawrence Pinneo, a neurophysiologist and electronics engineer—wants next to electronically "insert" messages into brains, as a prelude to pure thought-communication between people via instantaneous computer "translation."

But more, much more, is to come. Polled by Delphi during a

National Science Foundation study for the Institute of Electrical and Electronic Engineers, two dozen of the world's leading computer experts were unanimous in their opinion that almost all of the practical applications discussed here—and more—will be developed by the year 2000 or shortly thereafter, if they haven't been already. Included, they predict, will be such felicitous devices as a robot chauffeur, a weather analysis system, computer-controlled artificial organs, insightful models of every dynamism from large economies to individual biologies, systems to model the workings of human creativity and value selection, and a "General Factotum" (all-purpose automaton). Included too, they fear, may be such "products potentially dangerous to society"[2] as automated systems of inquiry, intelligence, and identification, with all their sinister intimations of police-state censorship, spying, and suppression. Most significantly, experts agree that computing systems "exhibiting intelligence at adult human level"[3] will be a reality in fifty years.

Not surprisingly, therefore, they concluded that the computer's impact on society in the near future will be tremendous—and from a humanistic standpoint, potentially ominous to the extreme. They foresee, for instance, "a decreased need by most persons for direct contact or interaction with other human beings." Intelligent machines of the future, quite possibly, may supply "not only intellectual stimulation or instruction, but also domestic and health care, social conversation, entertainment, companionship, and even physical gratification." With the possible erosion or elimination of uniquely human activities which typically distinguish man from other animals or machines, they continue, might come a profoundly wrenching psychological dislocation as people "begin to wonder whether there are human capabilities which are truly unique."[4] That sense of dislocation will only intensify as machines increasingly take over mundane labors more cheaply and efficiently, displacing human workers.

At the upper levels of society, the automation of government, law, education, and health care could concentrate responsibility for decision-making far more than it already has in the hands of a powerful technocratic elite. Under such circumstances, the creation of robot "trade-off" rules governing such moral considerations as whether a computerized chauffeur should self-wreck to avoid killing an animal seem petty indeed, though they are the stuff that life's emergencies are made of. Other kinds of ethics and judgments, suggests the IEEE study, will also have to be machine-tooled. Thoughtful experts already question both the automated career counseling systems and such therapy robots as MIT's Eliza. Might not the computer program be biased against certain careers, be unaware of the potentialities of others? And is it not risky to trust an individual who might be on the edge of insanity to a machine that substitutes for the depth and richness of the living therapist a simplistic feedback strategy pegged to a limited and utterly unfeeling program of word patterns and phrases?

These perplexing moral questions may have to be answered sooner than we think. For the computer in all its many and numerically growing manifestations is moving even now and ever faster out of the laboratory and into the mainstreets of our lives—as witness the thirty-one-year-old California computer programmer who was fined and placed on probation for pirating a $5,000 program belonging to a rival firm. For crime is a touchstone to what we value.

Like the lesser machines that preceded it, moreover, the computer is beginning to work *on* us. Connected telemetrically to electrodes implanted in the brain, it can now monitor the ongoing brain-wave states of schizophrenics, epileptics, and autistics, constantly comparing them to "normal" patterns stored in its memory in an effort to correlate episodes of abnormal behavior with gross variations in the brain's electricity. So far such computerized invasions of the mind are strictly diagnostic. But can it be long before they, like their predecessors, begin to work *in* us, responding to and ultimately influencing if not controlling our behavior?

Jose Delgado performed a negative version of just such an intervention several years ago at Yale, on a monkey named Paddy. Each time the computer picked up electrical impulses coming from the area of Paddy's brain generating aggressiveness and excitement, it punished him with a swift jolt of electricity to the area associated with pain and fear. Within two hours Paddy's aggressive impulses were down by half. In a few days they had all but vanished. So had his appetite, energy, and initiative.

Michael Crichton foresees the potentially disastrous results of

391

even positive human application in his not-so-futuristic novel *The Terminal Man*. His protagonist, a computer scientist named Harry Benson, suffers seizures of psychomotor epilepsy which cause him to murderously assault innocent people. An "emotional pacemaker" of pleasure-stimulating electrodes is implanted in him together with a miniaturized computer which monitors his brain via biofeedback. Every time the computer detects a brain-wave change characteristic of impending epileptic onslaught, it automatically aborts it by triggering a burst of soothing stimulation. Unfortunately, the medical team hasn't reckoned with the real-life work of James Olds, the psychologist who discovered several years ago that a rat given the power to stimulate his pleasure center electrically will do so nonstop, twenty-four hours a day, until it drops of exhaustion. Harry Benson's brain goes on just such a neural binge, touching off epileptic brain-wave patterns in exchange for jolts of pleasure in ever-quickening arcs of stimulus and response until attack becomes so incessant that pleasure cannot be marshaled and is overriden in uncontrollable paroxysms of violence.

"The human brain is obsolete . . . the Machines are . . . taking over,"[5] cries Harry Benson early in his ordeal as the medical team—a compassionate woman psychiatrist excepted—coldly and methodically goes about creating the first inner man-machine interface because it can; because it *must;* because it must *because* it can.

The power of such motivation already goads artificial intelligence. As one of Crichton's medical scientists muses realistically, a third-generation digital computer would cost several million dollars, draw enormous power, consume vast space, yet still have only the same number of circuits as the ant. To make one with the capacity of a human brain would require a huge skyscraper, demand energy equivalent to that in a city of a half million. The next generation of computers will be engineered from human nerve cells, thousands of billions of them grown to specification, altered artificially, and packed into six cubic feet with a minimum of heat production and waste—by far the most intelligent entity on the planet. Perhaps, if Crichton were a prophet, it could be transplanted to the human head—an organic prosthesis, a bionic brain, for Cyborg, the half-man, half-machine creature of futuristic mythology.

MACHINES AND MONKEYS

Long before that, of course, someone in authority might call a
halt, guided by the sensibility expressed in Albert Rosenfeld's
view of the computerized brain:

> When this kind of brain-computer hookup is imagined, it is
> usually to envision the computer as remotely controlling and di-
> recting the brain—or a dozen brains, or a hundred. There is no
> reason why it could not work the other way around . . . with
> the computer serving as a vast storehouse of readily accessible
> information. . . .

Even Rosenfeld cannot resist adding:

> . . . A man may be made to remember things that never hap-
> pened to him at all. If memory does indeed consist of electro-
> chemical changes in the structure of certain molecules in the
> brain cells, there is no theoretical reason why, when it becomes
> possible to alter these structures, experiences of any kind cannot
> be implanted at will. The brain thus influenced would never
> know the difference.[6]

And as Alvin Toffler writes with undisguised enthusiasm,

> It may be that the biological component of the super-comput-
> ers of the future may be massed human brains. The possibility of
> enhancing human [and machine] intelligence by linking them
> together organically offers enormous and exciting possibilities
> [such as] the feasibility of a system in which human thoughts are
> fed automatically into the storage unit of a computer to form the
> basis for machine decision-making. . . .[7]

In any case, Michael Crichton's philosophic view of such science
fiction-turned-fact is even more menacing than that of his alter-
ego, Harry Benson: "We are turning men into machines and machines into men."[8]

But are we? If such an exchange is indeed in serious progress,
machines to date are getting by far the worst of it (if by worst we
mean the least of it). For the computer, despite is marvelous and
rapid advancement, remains utterly incapable of the remotest
spark of that divine fire that makes man unique: It cannot truly
think. In fact, there is little a child can do mentally that is not
beyond it. As Arbib likes to point out, the function of a single hu-

393

man neuron is so fantastically complex that it would take an entire computer working around the clock to keep track of it. Massed by the billions, neurons, in computer terminology, are continuously programmed by the environment to express their intrinsic information-processing capacity with a wondrous natural spontaneity and flexibility. As environmental stimulation changes, so does the brain's response. The computer, in contrast, must be preprogrammed (and by the human brain), much of it in what are called overlapping *subroutines*—stereotyped behavior as rigid as the lowly frog's strike response to a flitting fly. It enjoys (tolerates? is locked into?) a Pygmalion-Galatea relationship with man, its god and creator. (To paraphrase Professor Higgins in Shaw's acid updating of the Greek myth when his guttersnipe Galatea rises against him, "You hussy, there isn't an idea in your head I haven't put there!" But Shaw's rebellious flower girl Eliza is flesh and blood—and brain—not paper tape and electronic circuitry.)

To be sure, the computer's tandem speed and thoroughness, when hitched to a high degree of human invention and imagination, often allow it to overcome the built-in limitations of its subservience to man. Arthur Samuel, for example, successfully programmed a computer to play championship checkers. In less than a dozen hours of playing time, it took Samuel to the cleaners after being given only the rules of the game, a sense of direction, and a redundant and incomplete checklist of parameters which were thought to have something to do with checker skills but whose exact contributions were unknown and unweighted. That didn't matter. By comparing millions of permutations every second, the computer blitzed all comers. At that it had learned some game theory, which was not as exhaustive as one might think. As Samuel calculated, if checker moves were explored at the rate of three per nanosecond (one billionth of a second) it would take 10^{21} centuries to exhaust every ramification.

Such astronomical number-mongering aside, the world is a touch more complicated than checkers, and in the IEEE's National Science Foundation study a research team stopped just short of endorsing the sardonic assessment of Hubert Dreyfuss: that artificial intelligence is like the man who, having climbed a tree, announces he is just that much more ready to fly to the moon. (As an example of just how formidable life can be when limited to the computer's own specialty, Lewis Thomas coyly proposes that it be set the task of acquiring a complete file of information on the *Myxotricha paradoxa,* a protozoa which inhabits the digestive tract of Australian termites. Such a job, Thomas estimates, could be done in not more than, oh, ten years.)

Among other things mental, the study reported, machine intelligence is most notably deficient in perception, distilling knowledge from information, and generalizing the result into wisdom. The computer, for example, can scarcely recognize—except by its exhaustive if instantaneous trial-and-error matching—what it is programmed to perceive. In contrast, the child can easily select from its mental models of all living, moving things in the world the image of a pet cat. "If we want a machine to recognize a cat," says Nobel Laureate Dennis Gabor, "we ought [to be able] to give it a whole book, with photographs of cats of all sorts, all sizes, in all positions. Machines at present cannot abstract either the whiskers or the ears."[9] Computer pattern-recognition, in fact, is nothing of the kind. It is something altogether different, called *scene analysis.* In other words, the computer doesn't truly grasp the contour holistically, as the right-hemisphere-dominated left visual fields would do, it scans and itemizes the details as the left-hemisphere-dominated right visual fields would do. To each of these details it assigns an identifying code number; the whole is represented by the total numerical array.

The restrictions imposed by such a grave sensory limitation can be appreciated in the meticulous description by John McCarthy, principal investigator in the Stanford Artificial Intelligence Project, of how a computerized robot goes about locating a cube-shaped block in a rectangular field with its TV-camera eye:

> It accomplishes this by starting at the bottom of the picture and examining each horizontal line a point at a time until it finds a light spot. Then it looks in a little circle around this point until it finds a dark-to-light transition which is presumably a point on the edge of a cube. Taking this point as a center, it strikes another circle and finds another dark-to-light transition. Continuing this process, it traces around the outline of the cube until it comes back to its starting point. This gives it about 100 points on

the edge of the cube. The next step is to fit these points into straight lines and compute the intersections of these lines which correspond to the visible corners of the cube. Unless the cube is lined up with the line of sight from the camera, there will be six edges and six vertices . . . (i.e. the visual configuration of a cube).[10]

Dreyfuss' remark about the moon comes immediately to mind—with no need of programming—when McCarthy adds that "it is through this process that we envisage computers performing such tasks as driving cars and automatically constructing houses,"[11] or taking microscopic slides, core samples, snapshots, or engineering surveys as a fully manipulative and ambulatory automated robot biological lab on Mars. For comparatively speaking, artificial intelligence has yet only climbed a tree.

Nor can the computer today passively understand, much less actively employ, anything more than the most rudimentary elements of the extended perception that is speech. Access to its mysteries is vital, most computer scientists believe, if artificial intelligence is ever to achieve universality, much less earn the right to its name. Currently, computerized voice typewriters can provide reliable phonetic transcription for no more than 500 purely arbitrary words, if spoken one at a time or confined to a limited domain of meaning. Computerized order takers can do likewise. But a computer psychiatrist capable of unraveling an ego fixation, even a computer arbiter capable of resolving simpler labor-management disputes, must await a genuine understanding of linguistic meaning down to the last nuance. It may have to wait indefinitely, for reasons that are complex and many. According to IBM computer experts, language ensnares the computer in a mesh of the obvious: It (language) is not under the programmer's control, it embodies a confusing split of the visual and phonetic, it can be pronounced in many different ways, its symbols are as random in length as words and sentences, and its imperfect segmentation and rules of classification invite errors of insertion, deletion, and substitution. All these barriers must somehow be vaulted before the airline pilot of the future can tell his cockpit computer, "Take this aircraft to Memphis at an altitude of twenty-nine thousand feet, a speed of seven-hundred fifty ground miles per hour."

Or as McCarthy puts it,

The "ear" of the computer is a microphone. The changes in air pressure produced by our speech are recorded by the computer 20,000 times per second. . . . Depending on the shape of the mouth . . . this wave form takes different shapes. Phoneticians have, in fact, classified the sounds we produce according to the shape of our vocal tract. There are about 40 such different sounds (phonemes) in English. When one utters a sentence consisting of several sounds, the computer must first find the boundaries between the sounds before it can decide what the individual sounds are. This is a difficult process since the shape of the vocal tract is continually changing and there is no clear-cut point in time in which we stop saying one sound and start saying another. . . .[12]

Programmed as they are to respond in set fashion to key words, moreover, experimental computer "therapists" like Eliza, notes Terry Winograd of MIT in *Psychology Today,* operate on the most straightforward principles of feedback. They do not "build up a picture of what the patient is saying."[13] For that matter, a simple statement like "Tommy had just been given a new set of blocks. He was opening the box when he saw Jimmy coming in" relies for its root meaning on a casual coupling of inference and context that can throw Eliza into a most unladylike tizzy. Who was opening the box? *He,* the computer would reply if programmed to do so using its customary strategies. What was in the box? Nothing would suffice•it to answer, lacking as Eliza does the most human quality of linking the two sentences together in a natural assumption of their relatedness. Concludes Winograd, "A sentence does not 'convey' meaning the way a truck conveys cargo, complete and packaged. It is more like a blueprint that allows the hearer to reconstruct the meaning from his own knowledge."[14]

What makes the computer even more of a disappointment to Kenneth Boulding is its inability to acquire, represent, structure, and retrieve solid blocks of knowledge out of raw information. However imperfect the natural process, a human being can abstract, can put into the brain and get back out from everything stored there what it needs at the moment. Thus, argues Boulding,

The crucial element in social systems is not information but knowledge. All a computer does is process information. Knowledge, on the other hand, is attained much more by the loss of in-

397

formation than by the gain of it. In fact, that's what organization is about.[15]

Organization, Boulding goes on to say, is "a hierarchy of wastebaskets"[16] which prevents information overload, in the human head as well as in society at large. Computers, of course, for all practical purposes are immune to such overload. But true wisdom—which he sees as the process of forming intelligent images of the world and its future—is not a matter of "piling information on information" but of "sifting, filtering and organizing information."[17] In this process, without programmer help, the most sophisticated computer is no more adept than the most backward child. Accordingly, for all its wonderful thoroughness, Boulding, unlike Arbib, believes the computer is incapable of anything approaching true sagacity:

> . . . There has been a negative fallout from the computer—in the sense that if it produces illusions of certainty, it can lead to worse decisions. . . . The world is uncertain. And decision-making in uncertainty is very different from decision-making in certainty. In uncertainty you postpone things and you muddle through and don't commit yourself. In certainty you zero in. This is fine. It's orthodox decision theory. But you often zero in on disaster. . . .[18]

Furthermore, an incisive examination of robot epistemology (the philosophy of the nature and origin of knowledge), such as H. A. Ernst's for IBM, turns up a wealth of discouraging findings. The net result of most research to date has been an unimpressive line of "systematic robots"—systematic, Ernst explains, being "when you have to admit the whole is less than its parts."[19] Typical is the statement of one research team that its program was "already too complex to lay bare the minimal structure of [our robot] yet it is far too simple to be interesting or convincing."[20] Not only are organic information processing and mechanical information processing two very different things at present, Ernst decided, "we do not understand the difference."[21] Its own epistemological structure, he says, "is always out of the view and reach of the robot itself," put there as it is by the designer, and usually "it is not clear

398

how learning could take place if one wanted it to."[22] In one rare instance where a robot was programmed in a simple if tedious way that would allow it to form hypotheses about its own learning, notes Ernst, it could not record only those that were useful but every one—so as not to waste its time rediscovering those that had already been discarded. A mouse running a maze at least has the option of discard.

In general, Ernst found, the robots were as goal-oriented, as committed to product at the expense of process, as the most ego-driven technocrat.

> . . . The basic direction of experimental inquiry is: first, how efficiently is the robot pursuing its goal . . . second, how can the epistemological structure be reprogrammed to make the robot even more efficient. . . . Most authors consider "learning" to be of the essence. Learning in this context is the experimental acquisition of the specific, "allowed" items of knowledge. . . . If the speed of goal attainment of the robot increases with age, it is considered to be sufficient justification for the introduction of learning. . . . No author has evaluated what learning contributes to the epistemological structure of his robot. . . . It appears that learning is merely tacked on and contributes nothing of interest. . . .[23]

Under the circumstances, concluded Ernst, it could hardly be argued that robot epistemology "has led to howling success or profound insights." Most robots do simpleton tasks in environments so restricted they "would cause any human to become insane within them in a short while."[24]

What's more, although computer scientists themselves don't say so, despite the rise of the teaching machine, the computer doesn't get all that high a mark in disseminating information, either. Programmers and B. F. Skinner must share the blame for that. By consistently rewarding all correct answers and minimizing the frustration of errors, says psychologist Herbert Terrace of Columbia, teaching machines subvert what self-esteem researcher Stanley Coopersmith calls one of the essential growing-up processes of childhood: learning how to fail. Terrace reports that pigeons trained in such an errorless way "go to pieces" when the rules are changed. And in real life, both would agree, the rules not only can be changed but are always erratic at best—as Christopher Jencks discovered when assessing the element of luck.

Indeed, concede computer scientists, "real world environments"[25] may be an all but insurmountable obstacle to the exercise of true artificial intelligence. "To what extent," wonders Ernst, "is a robot confronting a real world when the room contains two sizes of blocks, sufficiently illuminated so that they can be perfectly resolved . . . ? [Moreover] robot projects must contend with the noises introduced by mechanical contraptions that cannot move without joggling their TV eyes. . . ."[26] For once put on-line, the newborn computer has much to learn, more, perhaps, than man can ever possibly teach it. As repositories of that learning, adds another IBM scientist, real world environments are "so difficult that any system proposed to deal with them is almost certainly doomed to defeat unless it is able to take advantage of all [prior] knowledge and all of the intuition, insight, experience, heuristics [random learning discoveries], ingenuity, and downright dirty tricks that can be mustered."[27]

For all their touted memory and information-processing capacity, in sum, the world's estimated 150,000 computers put together are so inferior to a child's fundamental intellect that Sir James Lighthill of Cambridge, surveying the field for the Science Research Council of Britain, concluded frankly that artificial intelligence may be a waste of time. As another study put it, man is "slow, sloppy and brilliant," machines "rapid, rigorous but stupid."[28]

Both judgments may be premature, however, given the speed at which the world's aggregate cybernetic brain can improve itself by programmer feedback even as we sleep. For there are signs that the computer, having moved in less than a decade from simulating a network of interconnected neurons to playing a passable game of chess with man's help, verges at last on learning how to learn—and on its own. In so doing, Arbib suggests, it borders on confirming a thing or two about our own brain as well—particularly the importance of the imagistic right hemisphere. For although programmed in a straightforward, symbolic, left-hemisphere manner, computers today nevertheless are beginning to work not solely by logic but also by analogy and imagistic spatial arrays more common to right-hemisphere intelligence. This

400

cross-modal breakthrough, if it is that, could mean that the computer no longer need rely on the endlessly recapitulative form of past machine perception having the purely passive character of a simple classifier, in Arbib's words. Rather, its perceptions, like man's, could be cumulative, self-correcting—and imagistic. They would, in sum, satisfy Arbib's "slide-box" metaphor of the brain's dynamic extraction mechanism for delving into, and pulling out from, long-term memory what it needs to amend its images of an immediate reality without tediously running through everything on file and analyzing its every detail. It could genuinely recognize patterns, not scan the scene.

Animated cartoons, explains Arbib, employ a slide-box technique to avoid the arduous necessity of redrawing everything in each frame. The background is drawn once. The body of the central character, say, is drawn once also—on a transparent slide that, like the background, can be used repeatedly. Then the moving parts—arms, legs, facial features—are drawn on other slides in various alignments as needed. All three elements—the background, the object of focus, and its moving parts—can be expeditiously assembled to order in the slide box for photographing with a minimum of duplication. This, in effect, is what Arbib feels any intelligence, human or artificial, must do: assemble in the slide box of its consciousness (or cybernetic equivalent) an image of present reality by overlaying the model of the already known (as stored in long-term memory) with the freshly perceived (as brought to attention by short-term memory). The result is Jerison's mental model of a possible world, ever susceptible to amendment.

We know that a relatively crude flexibility can be programmed into the computer, though hardly enough to merit the remotest comparison to the human brain. But is it possible that the computer can "learn" to amend its own programmed responses in the sense of finding, with its blinding speed of search, strategies to break the trap of its stereotypes and set up a slide box of its own?

Strong hints that this may be the case can be found in computer chess, whose experimental role in artificial intelligence a Russian scientist has compared to that of the fruit fly in genetics. Computers have been playing chess since 1950 with ever-increasing sophistication. In the beginning, the computer, for all its quickness

401

at scanning and comparing, could look ahead only four half-moves—two full moves for each side—in a laggardly eight minutes. In other words, it could consider hypothetically a range of possible moves, its opponent's possible replies, its possible responses to these, and its opponent's possible responses to those. Even then, its range of look-ahead was limited to seven alternatives at each player's move, or 2,401 moves by both players in all. The average number of moves available to each player at each turn is thirty, or a staggeringly exponential total for four moves of 810,000. To give some idea of their mental skill, chess masters can easily look ahead more than three turns by each player—six in all—and explore every valuable ramification therein. They can do so because they have learned how to select only the most promising moves and countermoves for mental examination.

Currently, computer chess programmers Albert Zobrist and Frederic Carlson, Jr., reported in *Scientific American,* the new generation of the original chess-playing programs can look ahead five half-moves on the average, in special instances as many as eight. With this broadened range, they can assess a half-million options. Impressive as that may sound, Zobrist and Carlson caution, it scarcely skims the surface of this ancient game in all its intricacies. In all of history, they calculate, men have played fewer than 10^{15} chess games, or a quadrillion (a thousand trillion), no mean figure in itself. But the number of possible ways of moving pieces is more like 10^{125}, or a trillion trillion, enough to beggar even the brain.

Together with senior chess master Charles Kalme, a University of California mathematician, however, Zobrist and Carlson have now set out to shave the probabilities in their favor. They have designed a new approach that enables the computer, like the human player, to generalize from particular mistakes and "accept advice" from the master, Kalme. Using the sixty-four squares of the chessboard and the twelve types of chess pieces as the components of its language, Kalme has "described" to the computer some fifty patterns that occur most frequently in human play—in much the relational manner that human language and spatial perception employ to apprehend the outside physical world. The machine is further equipped to scan the board at any move, search it for any of Kalme's patterns stored in its electronic memory, and record

402

"snapshots" of them. Each pattern found contains in code all options Kalme deems reasonable for a look-ahead that typically ranges from five to ten half-moves, and examines about 10,000 possible moves in fifteen seconds. In addition, each pattern is weighed in value according to Kalme's "advice." The computer can create, weigh, and store some 1,500 snapshots—mosaical fragments whose patterns comprise the big picture—in six seconds.

Using these snapshots, the computer in two more seconds selects and ranks preliminarily the ten best moves. Then, still consulting the snapshots, it explores the ramifications of each move and finally selects the one it will make from a consensus of the various values given all the stored patterns involved. Its game is novice but sound, often clever and aggressive. Within five years, its programmers believe, it will be ready to challenge Britain's international master, David Levy, who has bet a thousand pounds that no computer can defeat him in a ten-game series before August, 1978. (On hearing of this, Russia's Mikhail Botvinnik reportedly told Levy, "I feel very sorry for your money."[29])

But more important than whether the computer will ever do to Levy in chess what it did to Samuel in checkers, is whether Godel's rule applies to its intelligence. Could a program designed by Bobby Fischer ever beat the Bobby Fischer that designed it? Perhaps it could, argue Zobrist and Carlson, if only because of what makes it a computer:

> Even without active learning . . . the computer has some powerful advantages. Because of its memory capacity a computer could be set up to accept huge volumes of advice from teams of experts. In time the computer could know more than any one individual. Because of its tremendous speed the computer can see nontrivial consequences of even trivial advice. Furthermore, the computer is not subject to lapses of memory or concentration; it will not be bothered by poor lighting or brood over a blunder. Once advice is given, the computer will not forget it and will never fail to apply it.[30]

More important yet, in devising their unique computer language, Zobrist and Carlson may have found the key to unlocking

403

what amounts to the computer's right hemisphere. As they point out, the world's greatest players have often tried to describe their techniques in books and articles without, however, creating many grand masters along the way. ". . . It is possible that a significant portion of human chess technique cannot be expressed in words," they write. ". . . It is not just a question of whether one can have thoughts without words but of whether one can have thoughts of much greater content than the words one can find to express them. It is possible that "chess thought depends heavily on spatial perception and that the perceptual processes involved are so subtle and rapid that only the final outcome reaches conscious expression. . . ."[31]

Some computer scientists, they go on to say, claim computer languages have enabled them to think thoughts that could not be expressed in words. "With our chess language," they add, "it may be possible to communicate directly to a computer chess strategies that heretofore have been passed from master to master by means of example or inference.

"Psychologists have evidence that the chessboard is perceived in 'chunks,' or combinations of pieces. . . . We feel that the patterns in our program operate as chunk-detectors and that our entire approach should be of interest to psychologists as a model of human chess perception."[32]

Arbib acknowledges that the burden of Godel's rule is that no machine which is exactly like a human being can ever be built. But, he notes, ". . . common sense says we would never want to build such a machine since we build machines to help us, not to be us."[33]

McCarthy, on the other hand, feels that "two or three brilliant ideas"[34] could lead computer logic to make the leap to true intelligence and all that would follow. When and if that happens, he believes, the question of man-machine equality will be as short-lived as it will be moot. Or as Arthur Clarke crisply puts it, the truly intelligent machine "may be the last invention man is permitted to make."[35] At that, the IEEE report indicates, the machines would then find themselves faced with the same enduring frustration that confronts us all: the exasperating inconstancy of man:

404

. . . Society would be faced with the embarrassing problem of revealing the inconsistencies inherent . . . in human beings. We know that there are many situations in which some people are considered "more equal" than others. For example, white collar fraud involving theft from a company is frequently dealt with less severely than blue collar theft from the same company. Appearance and attitudes often affect judgements, as do family connections or personal acquaintances. Although the adversely affected segment of the public seems to be willing to tolerate such inequities, due to ignorance, lack of power, or indifference, one doubts whether the same passive behavior would occur if an attempt were made to incorporate explicitly the present defects of society into an automated arbitration system.[36]

Monkeys

Koko, a three-year-old pet gorilla, goes to Stanford. She is studying North American sign language for the deaf and mute. A quick learner, she can already signal to her owner when she wants to go out, when she wants food, and when she wants drink. But to researchers in the fascinating new field of intelligent primate language, Koko is clearly just a know-nothing freshman. There are a dozen chimpanzees scattered from Santa Barbara, California, to Atlanta that can converse in one of three languages, only one of them employing conventional hand signs. Taken together, their combined achievements in a few short years suggest that the higher apes have an imagistic capacity for sophisticated communication analogous to the ability displayed by the Gazzaniga-Glass stroke victims. At present there is only one fundamental difference. The chimps are better at it.

In addition to sign language, chimpanzees have demonstrated that they can learn to use a computer typewriter or plastic symbols to do almost all the primary things with their specialized iconic speech that a young child does with his. Through either laboratory-controlled Skinnerian techniques of behavioral reinforcement or warm, incessantly devoted, environmentally rich human contact reminiscent of *The House on the Hill*—only their language is "spoken" in their presence—the chimps have steadily

405

and amid mounting excitement broadened their intelligent world, and that of their teachers.

Repeatedly, they have shown that they can:

• Absorb, generalize, combine, and invent an extensive system of names for objects in their environment. Some have vocabularies of over 150 words which they can use to communicate intelligently in simple, cryptic, but easily understood sentences. They learn, moreover, in much the same explosive manner as the child. In mastering sign language, for instance, one has acquired four signs after seven months of training, eighty-five after three years, and double that after four. Nor are they merely passive receptors. Taught the sign for *open* in connection with doors, another now uses it to refer to containers, drawers, the refrigerator, and water faucets. They make up their own terms, too. Given *cold box* for refrigerator, one in asking that it be open preferred *open food drink* instead. Given the word *duck*, it substituted *water bird*. Another called a cut watermelon *drink*, then *candy drink*, finally *fruit drink*. They easily generalize color from one object to another, as well as categorical terms such as *same* and *different*. When cut or bruised, it learns to sign the word for *pain*.

• Use their words to distinguish agents, actions, and concepts. The chimpanzee responds with alacrity when requested by its trainer to *groom* him, picking through his hair in the finest social fashion of the simian. It in turn knows to ask *him* for a movie or recorded concert when bored. As for concepts, one chimpanzee given the sign *dirty* to describe feces, adeptly transferred it to a macaque monkey which gave it a bad time—and then to teachers who refused to honor its wishes.

• Appreciate their use in the Piagetian sense when referring to things that are not there. The trainers of one who hated dogs signaled her as a joke that there was a big dog outside. Instantly the chimp bristled, became agitated and nervous, as if in danger of attack.

• Translate one language into another. One chimp that had demonstrated a recognition of spoken English for several objects speedily learned their sign language equivalents without the objects being anywhere in sight, an impressive cross-modal transfer.

• Understand, construct, and modify formal language semantically. Schooled in the imagistic, immediate language of manual signs, chimpanzees have nevertheless displayed an instinctive knowledge of psycholinguistic deep structure comparable to that of a child. They have done equally well when trained with plastic symbols and a computer keyboard to assemble sequential sentences that are semantically correct. They can use not only words and sentences, but the interrogative, class conceptions, negation, pluralization, conjunction, quantifiers, and the conditional. Tested on their meaning with difficult discrimination tasks, they have scored 80 to 90 percent. More, they are not above taking the initiative in attempting to modify their language themselves. One chimpanzee persistently refuses to use the copula, the linguistic link between a subject and its predicate, usually "is" or "are." *Banana yellow* makes as much sense to it as *banana is yellow,* although it has been taught that the latter is correct and the former is not. (The Russians would be sympathetic. They have no copula either.)

Chimpanzees do make mistakes—and throw temper tantrums when they do. One raised with humans had seen a fellow chimp only once in her life. When she met another, she labeled it *bug.* In transferring a word to another object, furthermore, their logic is sometimes oblique if not unapt. One, for example, applied the sign for *flower* not only to all flowers but to the redolence of a tobacco pouch and cooking food as well. When she spontaneously transferred signs from objects to pictures of something similar, she was given pictured replicas of the objects themselves in hopes that the chimpanzee, alone of all animals, could abstract from the graphic image. (It is, after all, the only primate that appears to have the self-concept necessary to recognize its own face in the mirror. Other animals see only another animal.) But the chimp, in a sense, failed. It recognized a photo of a cat 90 percent of the time, but a photo of a replica of a cat only 60 percent of the time. The rest of the time she signed it *baby,* a word given her both for baby and doll. It was as if the word to her meant miniaturization or artificial replication.

But children make mistakes, too. Offsetting those of the chimpanzee is the fact—of monumental importance to the issue of underlying intelligence—that it has let its trainer know that *it* knows, unlike the computer, when it is engaged in the wondrous act of formal learning. Shown a new object, one chimpanzee went to her console and said, *Tim, give Lana name of this.* When the trainer complied, Lana proceeded to use the newly learned label to ask him for it. That kind of act clearly supports the research psychologist who says, "Lana's skills are clearly related to human skills. . . . We have to admit that this is a language ability. . . . We've obviously always underestimated the intellectual ability of chimpanzees. . . ."[37]

The chimpanzee uses its language to converse primarily with its human teachers, but it can also use it to communicate, though as yet only in rough and casual fashion with other chimpanzees. Indicating a faucet, one signed to another who was competing with her for fruit, *go drink.* Similarly, she signed *come hug* to younger animals whenever they exhibited distress. And it tries to *teach* other animals. Given a pet kitten, one set it down in front of her, held up an object, signed *what that,* and then, the perfect pedagogue, signed the answer.

Indeed, anyone watching on those occasions when the chimpanzee with the pet cat holds him like a baby and signals *hurt hurt* when he accidentally cuts himself, or later snatches him up from the litter box and races to put him on her toilet seat—can heartily empathize with New York *Times* reporter Boyce Rensberger who recently interviewed such a chimp.

> After each exchange, Lucy and I would stare into each other's eyes for a few seconds. I don't know how she felt, but I was nervous. I was participating in something extraordinary. I was conversing in my own language with a member of another species of intelligent beings. What was she thinking about me? What should I say to her?
>
> Lucy is only eight years old, and because chimpanzees live to be 50 or 60, she is really still a child. What will she know and say ten years from now? Will she be able to tell us what life is like for a chimpanzee? What does she think?[38]

Soviet scientists who have tested dolphins say they are as intelligent as the average six- or seven-year-old child. Arthur Clarke speculates that we might be able to increase the intelligence of domestic animals or evolve wholly new ones with much higher IQ's than any existing now. Should we do it, and if so, why?

We could, of course, put them to work. But if that happened, they might eventually come to be more talented than we. And who knows, if man succeeded in destroying himself or his effectiveness as a species through nuclear war or ecological catastrophe, the apes might through human default have to take over the controls of spaceship earth and evolve into the dominant form of intelligent life on the planet.

If such a scenario sounds vaguely familiar, it should. Pierre Boullé explored its most far-out ramifications in his novel *Planet of the Apes,* which spawned the fabulously successful movie series of the same and similar names.

Naturally, those millions in the audience never took Boullé seriously, even in the deepest, most intuitive, most consensual recesses of the right hemisphere. Did they?

409

Chapter 16

Life with the Multimind

In *The Best and the Brightest,* a disturbing chronicle of the men and decisions that got us into the longest and most fruitless war in our history, David Halberstam wrote:

> The mind was mathematical, analytical, bringing order and reason out of chaos. . . . Always reason. And reason supported by facts, by statistics—he could prove his rationality with facts. . . . He was marvelous with charts and statistics. Once, sitting . . . for eight hours watching hundreds and hundreds of slides . . . he finally said . . . "Stop the projector. This slide, number 869, contradicts slide 11." Slide 11 was flashed back and he was right, they did contradict each other. Everyone was impressed, and many a little frightened. No wonder his reputation grew; others were in awe. . . . When it turned out the computer had not fed back the right answers and had underestimated those funny little far-off men in their raggedy pajamas, he would be stricken with a profound sense of failure, and he would be, at least briefly, a shattered man. . . .
>
> . . . He was intelligent, forceful, courageous, decent, everything in fact, but wise. . . . He was, there is no kinder or gentler word for it, a fool.[1]

Halberstam was describing one of the top officials in the Kennedy and Johnson administrations, a man often called the principal architect of the Vietnam war. But more than that, some would insist, whether intended or not, Halberstam was describing a mind dominated by the left hemisphere—the mind whose rigid insistence on the value of abstraction and symbolic thinking to the exclusion of almost every other attribute has brought us to where, as one scholar phrases it, "the possibility of a complete and apoca-

410

lyptic end of civilization cannot be dismissed as a morbid fantasy."[2]

Until now and foremost for the last three hundred years, these critics would say, the left hemisphere has been in careening control of Western man's destiny. It has exultantly and with lightning speed erected upon the back of the Industrial Revolution the most technologically advanced society the world has ever seen—while systematically exercising the kind of lobotomized mentality that, despite its pragmatic effectiveness, ends by knowing "the price of everything and the value of nothing," as Oscar Wilde once characterized the cynic. Cervantes, if one of his many translators is to be believed, must have had that sort of morally dangerous lopsidedness in mind when he spoke through one of his lesser characters to counsel the Don Quixote in all of us, "Beware, gentle Knight. There is no greater monster than reason."[3]

But now—almost anyone from the least perceptive social observer to the most isolated backwoods misanthrope would have to agree—if this has been so, something momentously new has been added to the old equation. We have only to glance at our newspapers and TV screens, or peep outside our doors, to see. A fresh and curious kind of craziness is in the smoggy air; it pervades society everywhere. The sale of Ouija boards, I Ching books, and Tarot cards is booming. Colleges are offering degrees in witchcraft, and a student has been graduated from one of the nation's leading universities with a bona fide degree in white magic. In London an emergency telephone is set up to handle calls from people plagued with supernatural happenings. A noted New York attorney tells a national law convention that astrologers will one day be called into court as expert witnesses and is not hooted from the podium. A California psychiatrist throws away his couch, installs the latest brainwave reading equipment, hangs out his shingle as a *meta*psychiatrist. Closer to earth, a forty-nine-year-old former principal drops out to become a free-lance, nickel-and-dime storyteller. Fifteen hundred Georgia students streak en masse, prompting a psychotherapist to announce that nudeness is good for you. A West Coast park district puts up road signs to warn motorists of crossing newts. A "wrapping artist" fresh from cocooning a considerable stretch of Australian coast with nylon discloses plans to run a twenty-two-mile-long, eighteen-foot-high curtain across a California county to the Pacific, while in New York City a compulsive Parisian aerialist sneaks out on a high wire strung between the 135-story towers of the World Trade Center because he was "happy, happy, happy"—and is sentenced by the judge to perform in Central Park. A fifteen-year-old Indian guru who cannot read ("I will give you peace, that's it, that's the whole deal")[4] is hit in the face with a cream pie thrown by a Detroit man who wanted to "prove him mortal." A handwriting analyst reports he makes $90,000 a year; the Boy Scouts of America, racked by membership roll-padding scandals, struggles under a $500,000 deficit to avert bankruptcy. A reading expert laments the constant interjection of "you know" in the speech of youth as expressing the benighted if revolutionary notion that "ideas have to be somehow *felt* rather than accurately stated in words,"[5] even as a Hollywood glamor girl shares with the public her own private recipe for self-therapy:

> You close your eyes and . . . just go inside [your head], and 'when you feel you're inside, you look for an opening. . . . You go through that and then you go down a kind of tunnel. You come out, then you look for your guide. It's just far out, it really is. I asked one figure if he was my guide, and he turned into something else. Then I asked him and he said, "Yes." Then I tell him who I want to visit. . . . My guide takes me to visit him. . . . [A] lot of good things have been happening to me since I've been doing it. Somehow it helps—just in terms of connecting with what's around you.[6]

Not to be outdone, politics too, have turned topsy-turvy, in a world where the comic-opera influence of Arab oil has precipitated among nations almost what psychologists would call a "rite of inversion," a situation in which the low have been raised up and the high have been brought low. Some political events are right out of a Marx Brothers movie. The prime minister of Thailand resigns because of *krengchai*, a desire ". . . not to cause anyone trouble, inconvenience or embarrassment,"[7] which so mortifies his foes they ask him to stay on, which of course he does for the same reason. Equally novel, a despotic Greek military regime

412

steps down of its own accord without a shot being fired after seven repressive years and asks the country's civilian politicians, including its exiled enemies, to put aside their differences and form a new government "for the good of the country"[8]—an implausible scenario that might have been written by Woody Allen on one of his wilder impulses. Another war breaks out between India and Pakistan along their common border, only this one is not fought with bullets and bayonets but with competing television programs between two rival stations. The Indians win—a larger share of the Pakistani audience on the strength of their channel's superior entertainment. The Pakistani government trembles.

Nor is the hitherto hardheaded bastion of science any longer immune to the contagious new fever that grips and convulses us. A hiply-attired psychopharmacologist from Baltimore's prestigious Johns Hopkins University rouses himself periodically from what appears to be a meditative trance in the midst of his invited address to expound on his theme that "Aristotelian yes-no cerebration," not subjective, contemplative "Platonic thinking," has made the modern world the magnificent mess it is. No one at the well-attended conference on "inner space," held in Washington by the National Museum of History and Technology and cosponsored by the Smithsonian Institution, so much as bats an eyelash, even when another speaker suggests they are there because of a "crisis of consciousness," a "breakdown of the general consensus about what is real and what is not."[9] The equally reputable American Association for the Advancement of Science opens both its arms and its annual program—if not its sanctions—to the cataclysmic speculations of Immanuel Velikovsky, the eclectic maverick who insists not only on the legitimacy but the primacy of myth and legend in the organic prehistory of the natural world. At Big Sur's Esalen Institute, flagship of the growing Human Potential Movement, an anthropologist, a neurosurgeon, a biophysicist, an Oriental philosopher, a gestalt therapist, a research psychologist in psychic phenomena, and a couple of mathematicians meet to discuss, work with, and ultimately chant as a mantra in perfect seriousness an arithmetic calculus invented to express Boolean algebra.

Boolean algebra is a highly abstruse mathematical system de-

413

signed to make workable the contradictions inherent in some forms of logic, such as that typified by the sentence "this statement is false." It is an integral part of the ineffable logic employed by computers to send spaceships to the moon, but the mixed bag of intellectual pilgrims to Esalen have a goal at once more immediate and distant than that. They are there because a book about the calculus has persuaded them that it can be used to help comprehend, mathematically and logically as well as experientially, the profound paradoxes of living life on earth. Even cold evolutionary certainty, in California anyway, has given way to the insistence of a faction including serious scientists and calling itself "Creationist" that the miracle of Eden be given equal time in elementary education.

And why should it not? Haven't Dutch radio astronomers reported in outer space an object so unbelievably vast that light traveling 186,000 miles a second, they calculate, would take 18,500,000 years to cross it? In an era menaced by everything from an incipient new Ice Age (perhaps as little as a million years away) to the common aerosol can propellant (it may burn holes in the atmosphere's upper ozone layer which shields us from the sun's lethal ultraviolet radiation) can anything be said to be impossible?

Yet some things surely are. It is the way we look at them that has changed.

The air, in fact, is clamorous with change, much of it human and mental, little of it anticipated by the innumerable panels of experts who spent countless hours during the last two decades forecasting what the future would be like in the largely material and utilitarian terms of endless technological progress. Rarely if ever did they pause to consider the truly awesome possibility that nonstop technology might, through man's seemingly bottomless ability to adapt to ever new environments, bring about an evolutionary change where it should have been most expected but was not: in the internal state of our heads; in the biological intelligence we need to survive; in our everyday consciousness. Evolution cannot work that fast, we thought. Changes in man's brain are a matter of millennia, not of generations.

Indeed, apologists for the left hemisphere offer a much more

414

ominous (and less flattering) explanation: Information overload, *future shock.* Alvin Toffler suggests that our mind's "master file" of "kinetic images" (Boulding's mosaical Big Picture?) is being altered, torn up, replaced, and thrown away in bits and pieces at such a frenzied rate under the accelerating bombardment of the "knowledge explosion" that the ability of our nerve ends to cope threatens to short-circuit. If we think of our life as a channel through which experience flows, he wrote prophetically five years ago, we can see that the accelerating rate of change in the world today drastically alters the flow of situations through it. Before, we could cope by mentally chopping experience up into a set of dependable components. In theatrical terms, it had a cast of characters, familiar props and settings, a context of ideas and information, a predictable life span Now it is as if the whole world were crowding onto the stage at once, rehearsing all its plays simultaneously, demanding we take roles in each of them, shifting scenery so fast we lose our cues and cannot decide which line should be uttered or which attitude struck next. Familiar situations alter in flavor, a steadily expanding stream of new ones beats against our brain demanding entry, acceptance, and assimilation.

Even though we are usually unaware of it, Toffler writes, every time we perceive novelty in our environment, a massive *orientation response* is triggered in our body by the brain's attention and arousal system: Pupils dilate, photochemical changes occur in the retina, hearing becomes more acute, muscle tone rises, palms sweat, brain-wave patterns alter, breathing and heart rates quicken, blood rushes to our head, fingers and toes grow cold as veins and arteries constrict to help marshal the blood where it may be needed. If prolonged by the persistence of stimuli so strange, new, threatening, or swift-changing as to be all but unassimilable, Toffler goes on, the nervous system's orientation response is soon succeeded by the endocrine system's more profound *adaptive reaction.* Hormones are pumped into the body's organs to accelerate metabolism, which raises blood pressure and turns fat and protein into energy. The body, in brief, is responding to that bane of modern living: stress.

Stress is a natural and inescapable part of living, of course, as is the body's orientation response and adaptive reaction to it. To

415

eliminate either side of the equation—stimulus or response— would be to eliminate change, growth, self-development, matura- tion, ultimately life itself, as Toffler points out.

But now change is roaring through society so fast, so broadly, and with such ever-gathering speed, Toffler argues, that millions are suffering from acute and chronic overstimulation, from "the dizzying disorientation brought on by the premature arrival of the future . . . culture shock in one's own society."[10] No wonder we have begun to seek refuge, if not revelation, outside the confines of conventional thought, the Tofflers of this world would say. It is altogether permissible to idle our mental engines a mo- ment, considering the uphill climb ahead. But beware that, if pro- longed, it might end not with enlarged or replenished awareness but with a destructive antiintellectualism.

Proponents of alternative life-styles, on the other hand, see in today's rampant cultural flux and confusion something else alto- gether. They see a richly subversive legacy from the late lamented counterculture. As Charles Reich, its Boswell, interprets it, the seeds of a seditious, irreversible change in our national conscious- ness were planted with the student revolution in the late 1960's. Then it was, wrote Reich in *The Greening of America,* that draft re- sisters and other youthful demonstrators first found common cause in a single startling realization: that what they interpreted as society's refusal to hear, to act, even to honor their complaints with an intelligent response, constituted a massive assault upon their sensibilities. It was nothing less, said Reich, than a rape of their consciousness.

By resorting to every conceivable visual, emotional, and symbol- ic stratagem to piece the "seamless web" of entrenched society with shafts of insight, Reich claimed, the students counterat- tacked—after the first extended flurry of forensics, in what could be called a war of the hemispheres:

> A group of students at New York City College appeared dur- ing an R.O.T.C. drill and proceeded to ape each exercise— crawling on the ground when the R.O.T.C. crawled, carrying each other on their shoulders when the R.O.T.C. did that. In Berkeley students produced a "Mill-In" in the administrative offices—a mass coming and going that disrupted work while im- plying the meaninglessness nature of bureaucratic busyness.

416

. . . Demonstrators . . . might walk into a solemn and talky faculty meeting and loudly sell popcorn and hot dogs in an effort to break into the heavy flow of rationality and "freak out" their audience, saying, in effect, "you have been stuck in the same kind of thinking too long."[11]

In short, as an unknown French student would later write on the walls of Paris University, "Imagination is Seizing Power."[12] It was the first revolution in centuries, a Harvard government expert observed, that didn't have material progress as its purpose. It championed an antithetical society, one prizing those very virtues the left-hemisphere-dominated culture appeared least to value, namely those of the right hemisphere.

The long-term result of the student revolution and its aftermath is less certain. The counterculture is dead and gone now, of course, absorbed and digested with nary a significant trace by the system it sought futilely to revitalize. Or so the opinion makers would have us believe. But in view of the incessant turmoil around us, is it? Critics like Reich think not. "The only way to resist an alien idea," declares Philip Slater, "is to ignore it."[13] If it has disappeared, they would agree, it has disappeared like McConnell's enlightened flatworms into the ravenous maw of their naïve brethren—bearing a message that becomes an organic part of the host. In Reich's words, that message is this:

The price of survival is an appropriate consciousness . . . to go along with the revolution of science and technology that has already occurred. The chaos we are now experiencing is the inevitable and predictable consequence of our failure to rise to this necessity. . . . The creation of a new consciousness is the most urgent of America's real needs.[14]

Thus it is, to those familiar with the more dramatic implications of lateralized cerebral function, that the brain almost seems to be moving—boldly at this instant, imperceptibly at that—to right itself; moving from word and symbol to image and feeling, from the sequential and logical and abstract to the total and insightful and concrete; moving in fits and starts to balance the two hemispheres, to restore through all the tumult and shouting a saving equilibrium.

417

Faced with the growing outcries against a rampant "irrationality," historian-sociologist Robert Nisbet felt moved to adopt a different perspective: ". . . I don't think anybody is consciously pursuing irrationality. I think the antirationalists are users of reason, users of the mind in ways that are less conventionalized. They are suggesting that there is a form of knowledge that cannot be had by ordinary induction, deduction, empirical study or measuring. . . ."[15] Thus it might be argued that the steady ten-year decline of verbal and math scores on the Scholastic Aptitude Tests of college-bound high school seniors is not a symptom of educational failure but a profound sign of just such a hemispheric revolution in thinking.

Granting for the sake of argument both the validity of this view and the subterranean viability of the counterculture, where did the impetus for this new consciousness come from? Surely it did not spring full-blown from the headband of some hip Zarathustra. Did it come about consciously (through the left hemisphere) or "unconsciously" (through the right hemisphere) or both?

Beyond citing the catalyzing conflict between the promise of left-hemisphere technology and its peril, between society as it is and as it ideally could be, Reich for one is distinctly at a loss to answer. His fellow critics of the establishment are equally hard put to say. In *The Making of a Counter Culture*, Theodore Roszak, for all his penetrating insight, can do little more than point a mildly congratulatory finger at Spockian permissiveness in child rearing as having prepared the fertile ground. Philip Slater may be closer to the truth of its origins when he credits the culture at large with a spontaneous fail-safe mechanism he calls *social eversion*. Social eversion is a psychological extension of Kenneth Boulding's *break boundary*, a phenomenon in which a structure, system, or medium suddenly turns into its opposite by being pushed to the extreme, the natural phenomenon Teilhard de Chardin refers to when he writes,

> In every domain, when anything exceeds a certain measurement, it suddenly changes its aspect, condition or nature. The curve doubles back, the surface contracts to a point, the solid disintegrates, the liquid boils, the germ cell divides, intuition suddenly bursts on the piled up facts. . . .[16]

418

Such a phenomenon mentally, mingling as it does Toffler's fears and Slater's hopes, can perhaps be seen in a clinical context as far back as the Mount Zion study in the Haight-Ashbury. Noted one report on the mentality of the study subjects,

> . . . The majority . . . showed a marked lack of critical judgment in evaluating their own or other people's ideas. They tend to accept without scrutiny the most bizarre ideas as being potentially valid. They may show their regard for the importance of thought by acknowledging an idea as "Mind Blowing" or by referring to thoughts on which they have "flashed," but they rarely carry these thoughts through to rational conclusion. In short, they honor intelligence, but disparage and fail to engage in sustained intellectual activity. Their inability to persevere in analytic and ordered thinking may be one of the sources of this disparagement of purely intellectual pursuits.[17]

According to the report, they also found it hard to pay attention, to choose between correct and incorrect alternatives, to give an abstract answer without spoiling it with a personalized afterthought. Perhaps more extraordinary, they displayed a marked tendency to what psychologists call "over-inclusiveness," a remarkable oceanic acceptance of anything cognitively generated, reflecting "an enormous need to establish relations among ideas and [perceptions] no matter how strained the [result]."[18] Most unusual of all, they not only excelled at Freud's opprobrious primary process thinking, they did so without obvious self-criticism or anxiety. Indeed, they seemed hardly aware of anything out of the ordinary in their thought processes at any time. When asked on Rorschach tests to be "less imaginative" and to describe only what they had actually *seen* in the ink blots, they typically failed to understand such a distinction. Despite these and other psychosocial symptoms of "impaired ego function," researchers found little evidence of classic mental illness. Instead, the Street People's functioning and experience struck the Mount Zion team not as psychotic but as "uniquely primitive."[19] Within what one psychologist called their "cosmic consciousness"[20] you could almost glimpse Andrew Weil's stoned thinking struggling to be born.

But again, where did such cosmic confusion originate? The use of drugs, almost suicidally heavy in some instances, played an undeniable role. But as Weil points out, drugs and stoned thinking, while highly correlated, are not mutually inclusive. Nor did the Street People's apprehensive performances on the dread IQ tests reflect any generalized disruption of their intellect. Although their scores were erratic and exceptionally scattered across the various subtests—too high in this area to be so low in that—the mean IQ was 19 points above the population average, or in the bright normal to superior range. In the opinion of one of the study psychologists, Stephen Pittel, if this erraticism reflected anything it was their chronic frustration and impatience with the fruits of the left hemisphere. They wanted to know more, to know deeper. "Their impairments were not so much absolute as relative to the task they have undertaken," he adds. "After all, what intellect would not be strained and bent in trying to understand the riddles of existence and resolve the problems of our crazy times?"[21]

As Kenneth Keniston notes, technological society has driven many of the young to drugs with its pressures for cognitive performance while at the same time overstimulating them to the brink of psychological numbness.

Still and all, the question haunts us. How did such a raging primitivism originate in the homes of the most affluent and technologically progressive society the world has ever known?

The answer, if one can be found, may lie in the prophecies of another maverick who correctly foresaw over a decade ago at least in part which way the human brain was headed and has been writing and lecturing about it ever since: Canada's Marshall McLuhan. In his discursive critiques on our ever-growing armada of communications media and technologies, McLuhan has never stopped asserting that the modern world at its most aberrant has not taken leave of its senses. Rather, he insists, it is always, painfully, persistently engaged in adapting them to each new extension of our perceptions. Like Jerison, McLuhan assumes that language came into being to extend our conscious perceptual world through human consensus. But McLuhan goes further: Just as every machine is an "outering"[22] of some body process or appendage—the printing press of speech, the automobile of our feet—every basic media or technology exists to "store or expedite information"[23] with the goal of consensus in mind.

420

As McLuhan sees it, what we call "consciousness" is simply a ratio or proportion among the sensuous components of experience, the perceptual inputs of our senses and their mental models. Of these he assigns a critical primacy to the sense of touch, including the kinesthetic and somesthetic elements of inner feeling, which he sees as a kind of neural "clearing house." There the senses interplay and are translated into one another continuously, for the purpose of presenting to the mind a unified image. This image of a unified ratio among the senses, he likes to stress, was long held to be a mark of our *ratio*nality.

"Our very word 'grasp' or 'apprehension' points to the process of getting at one thing through another," he writes in *Understanding Media*. ". . . 'keeping in touch' or 'getting in touch' is a . . . fruitful meeting of the senses, sight translated into sound and sound into movement and taste and smell. . . ."[24] The Greeks had the notion of a consensus or . . . 'common sense.' . . ." Perhaps, McLuhan is moved to suggest in the first of his imaginative assaults on orthodoxy, touch is not merely touch, either externally or internally, but "the very life of things in the . . . mind."[25] (For that matter, consensus comes from the Latin for "to feel together.")

Every new technology in man's history, McLuhan goes on, even as it acts to extend one or more of his senses alters inexorably the ratio and proportion of all. "Steadily and without any resistance,[26] however imperfectly, the critical relationships of the senses are changed and a new equilibrium created. If the technology is primarily visual (like print), the "ear in the brain" will add its own internal soundtrack in an effort at "perceptual closure" to complete the unified image, McLuhan thinks. If it is primarily aural (like radio), the "eye in the brain" will attempt mentally to visualize what is missing. Because the materials of these relentless transformations are the very perceptions that might otherwise detect them, says McLuhan, "I am in the position of Louis Pasteur telling doctors that their greatest enemy was quite invisible. . . ."[27]

The most significant and lasting casualty of nearly 2,500 years of uninterrupted mechanical technologies, he contends, has been the sense we could least afford to lose: our precious "common sense," that neural clearing house of direct and uncompensated perception, the ubiquitous sense of touch. The alphabet, clocks, money, the printing press, photography, the movies, automobiles—all in McLuhan's eyes have conspired to "explode" our integrative sense of touch and replace it with a highly intensified sense of the visual. To be sure, the eye has a stunning capacity to record and relay to the brain what it sees. Our visual system alone, with its 125,000,000 light-sensitive cells, can transmit almost 4,500,000 bits of data every second, nine times more than all our other senses put together. But since the eye cannot unify, McLuhan feels that we have lost more than we have gained. Indeed, he declares, our mechanical technologies have "brought us near to a state of disintegration by putting us out of touch with ourselves."[28]

As noted earlier, for McLuhan the lethal process of self-alienation in Western civilized man began with the phonetic alphabet—ironically, our most successful attempt at further extending the extended perception that is speech. The phonetic alphabet not only enthroned the visual aspect of language at the expense of its other sensual components, it "smoothed" the "sinuosities and obtusities" of communicated primitive experience into the uniformities of visual order we still think of as the mark of rationality.

> Only alphabetic cultures have ever mastered connected lineal sequences as pervasive forms of psychic and social organization. The breaking up of every kind of experience into uniform units in order to produce faster action and change of form (applied knowledge) has been the secret of western power over man and nature alike.[29]

Money and the clock did likewise. As McLuhan writes, money, like language, talks. And in so doing, it inevitably speeds up human exchange. Indeed, in a highly literate, fragmented society, time is money. Similarly, the modern clock in his view is "a machine that produces uniform seconds, minutes and hours on an assembly-line pattern."[30] Great cultural changes occurred in the West, continues McLuhan, when it was found possible by the alphabetlike application of visual, abstract, uniform units to fix time as duration, as "something that happens between two points."[31] From such a puissant if unspoken concept, he charges, flows noth-

422

ing less than the image of a "numerically quantified and mechanically powered universe."[32] The abstract units of mechanical time gradually pervade all our sense-life, splitting it away from the unique increments of private experience, accommodating the routines of working, eating and sleeping to the clock rather than the rhythmic needs of the human organism. In the end, clocks not only coordinate and accelerate the pace of human meeting, he concludes, they drag man out of the natural world of seasonal fluctuations as effectively as the alphabet released him from "the magical resonance of the spoken word."[33]

In much the same manner, the mechanical technologies of the printing press, the photograph, the motion picture, and the automobile have worked the principles of continuity, uniformity, and repeatability into the woof and warp of Western society. Printing, as McLuhan points out, was the first complete mechanization of a handicraft. It segmented the hand's skilled movement into a series of discrete steps "as repeatable as the wheel is rotary."[34] This led both to typography's 500-year domination of our culture and to the complementary development of photography, which put back into the recording of experience easily duplicated hints of the wealth of gesture alphabetic language had excluded. Movies in turn rolled up "the real world on a spool,"[35] frame by frame. In quickening repeatability until it mimicked the continuous flow of life, cinema pushed mechanical technology's principles to a point of reversal suggesting Boulding's break boundary, Slater's social eversion. The automobile and its assembly line, of course, became the penultimate expression of the mechanical technology.

Through it all, McLuhan maintains, modern man remained blissfully unaware of what was happening to him—ignorant of how such technologies were subtly shaping his psyche; influencing his perceptions; machine-tailoring his brain in their own image. He failed to realize that intensification of his isolated, stripped-down visual faculty conferred not only the fragmenting, divisive power of analytic function, but also the chronic and dangerous weakness of viewing all things as continuous and connected. He failed to see that the strictly visual organization of work and space would lead to an excessive explicitness, centralism, and specialization that left life increasingly cheap and sterile in terms of human relations, while enriching it materially. He failed to grasp that losing the habit of using all his senses at once—and ultimately, losing the ability—would in the end be both a gift and a curse: the gift of being able to act without reacting (indispensable to empirical science) and the curse of personal detachment and noninvolvement in an alienated society of "men homogenously trained to be individuals."[36]

And it all started, McLuhan would have us believe, with something as innocent-seeming as the alphabet.

> Certainly the lineal structuring of rational life by phonetic literacy has involved us in an interlocking set of consistencies that are striking. . . . Consciousness is regarded as the mark of a rational being, yet there is nothing lineal or sequential about the total field of awareness that exists at any moment. . . . Consciousness is not a verbal process, yet during all our centuries of phonetic literacy we have favored the chain of inference as the mark of logic and reason. . . . In western literate society it is still plausible and acceptable to say that something "follows" from something, as if there were some cause at work that makes such a sequence. It was David Hume who, in the eighteenth century, demonstrated that there is no causality indicated in any sequence, natural or logical. The sequential is merely additive, not causitive. Hume's argument, said Immanuel Kant, "awoke me from my dogmatic slumber." Neither Hume nor Kant, however, detected the hidden cause of our western bias toward sequence as "logic" in the all-pervasive technology of the alphabet. . . .[37]

Now, however, in equally deceptive stages and only during the lifetime of the oldest living man, has something McLuhan regards as even more revolutionary to the brain come upon the scene: electric technology. As embodied by the telegraph, telephone, radio, television, and computer, electric technology is in McLuhan's opinion the antithesis of mechanical technology in its mental impact. If the one is detached, fragmentary, and disinterested, the other is all-inclusive and involving in depth. If one is centralized, hierarchical, and concerned with meaning and product, the other is diffuse, democratic, and concerned with process and effect. If mechanical technology is uniform, standardized, intervaled, and continuous (and thus familiar), electric technology is "sudden, counter, original, spare . . . strange,"[38] and simultaneous. If mechanical technology is explosive, electric technology is implosive. If mechanical technology heralded the Machine Age, electric technology ushers in the Iconic Age, or the age of the compressed mosaic image.

As McLuhan sees it, by imposing unvisualizable relationships on everything it touches at instant speed, electric technology, unlike mechanical technology, extends not one sense but rather the entire central nervous system, including the brain. In its operation, he explains, electricity is only incidentally visual and auditory. Primarily and profoundly it is tactile and organic, "endowing each object with a kind of unified sensibility."[39] In so doing, he claims, it deposes the supremely visual and brings back the "mosaic world" of "equilibrium and stasis (balance of forces)."[40] Thus, in extension, man's full sensorium is made whole again. Even more dramatically, McLuhan argues, consciousness is thereby extended on a world scale, without any verbalization whatever ". . . It [becomes] strikingly the age of consciousness of the unconscious."[41]

The telegraph, telephone, and radio have all had a part in the electric revolution that has slyly seized and rearranged our senses, dissolving in their intensive polarity the top-down bonds of delegated authority and the chain-of-command lineal pyramid. But it is television, with its low iconic definition and high human involvement, that affords the most recent and devastating extension of our central nervous system. Says McLuhan,

> The TV image requires each instant that we "close" the spaces in [its mosaic] mesh by a convulsive sensuous participation that is profoundly kinetic and tactile. . . . TV will not work as background. It engages you. The viewer is the screen. He is bombarded with light impulses. . . . The TV image is visually low in data . . . not a photo in any sense, but a ceaselessly forming contour of things limned by the scanning-finger. The resulting plastic contour appears by light *through* not light *on* and the image so formed has the quality of sculpture and icon. . . .[42]

Television has by its very nature replaced the book in the minds of our children.

Children . . . average about six and a half inches from the printed page. . . . [They] are striving to carry over to the printed page the all-involving sensory mandate of the TV image. . . . They pore, they probe, they slow down and involve themselves in depth. . . . They bring to print all their senses, and print rejects them.[43]

Nor does TV reinforce any other lineality in living.

Gone are the stag line, the party line, the receiving line. . . . TV [has] sent Americans questing for every sort of oddment and quaintness in objects from out of their storied past . . . new wine . . . food . . . a new sensitivity to the dance, plastic arts, and architecture as well as the small car. . . . The uniform and repeatable now must yield to the uniquely askew, a fact that is increasingly the despair and confusion of our entire standardized economy. . . . The mosaic can be seen as dancing can, but it is not structured visually . . . for the mosaic is not uniform, continuous or repetitive. It is discontinuous, askew, and nonlineal . . . where [it] encounters a literate culture, it necessarily thickens the sense mix. . . .[44]

The result, McLuhan insists, has been the beginning of a profound change in consciousness from childhood on, one that has absolutely nothing to do with product and everything to do with process.

Pervaded by the mosaic TV image, the TV child encounters the world in a spirit antithetic to literacy. . . . Young people who have experienced a decade of TV have naturally imbibed an urge toward involvement in depth that makes all the remote visualized goals of [our] usual culture seem not only unreal but irrelevant, and not only irrelevant but anemic. . . . The TV child expects involvement. . . . The current assumption that . . . programming is the factor that influences outlook and action is derived from the book medium, with its sharp cleavage between form and content. . . .[45]

Concluded McLuhan a year before the 1965 student revolution burst upon us, trailing the counterculture behind it:

It would be misleading to say that TV will retribalize . . . America. . . . But TV . . . for good or ill . . . has ex-

426

erted a unifying synesthetic force on the sense-life, such as [we] have lacked for centuries. . . . Synesthesia, or unified sense and imaginative life, has long seemed an unattainable dream to western poets, painters and artists . . . yet [the massive electrical extensions] of our central nervous systems have enveloped western man in a daily session of synesthesia.[46]

Today, of course, as McLuhan predicted, the effects of an accelerating electric technology are all around us—and increasingly chaotic. Money is replaced by the credit card, the sheer movement of information—automated, electronic, programmed knowledge. Decentralized, we chaff under clocktime. A single set of skills no longer suffices since, as technological acceleration "approaches the speed of light",[47] the specialist stands condemned to "the sterility and inanity that echo in the archaic form of the departing mechanical age."[48] As McLuhan forecast, "so great is the change in American lives, resulting from the loss of loyalty to the consumer package in entertainment and commerce, that every enterprise has been shaken thoroughly. . . ."[49]

Acceleration alters even the concept of intelligence—though we remain steadfastly, even stubbornly, unaware of it. "It is in our IQ testing that we have produced the greatest flood of misbegotten standards," McLuhan declares. "Unaware of our typographic cultural bias, our testers assume that uniform and continuous habits are a sign of intelligence.

"We have confused reason with literacy, and rationalism with a single technology. Thus in the electric age man seems to the conventional west to become irrational . . . [Indeed], we find ourselves at a loss to define the 'rational', if only because we never noticed whence it came in the first place." On the contrary, just as "data classification yields to pattern recognition"[50] as the prime instrument of the intellect, discovery must replace instruction as the prime instrument of learning in an age when, as André Malraux concedes, narration has been superseded by the image.

Indeed, if we but have the wits to comprehend it, says McLuhan, we teeter on the brink of a staggering promise.

> The world of public interaction has the same inclusive scope of integral interplay that has hitherto characterized only our private nervous systems. . . . To have such power by extension of

427

their own bodies, men [first had to] explode the inner unity of their beings into explicit fragments. Today, in the age of implosion, we are playing the ancient explosion backward, as on film. We can watch the pieces of man's being coming together again. [Now] we are haunted by the need for an outer consensus . . . that would raise our communal lives to the level of a worldwide integration. . . . Man can now look back at two or three thousand years of . . . mechanization with full awareness of the mechanical as an interlude between two great organic periods of culture. In 1911 the Italian sculptor Boccioni said, "we are primitives of an unknown culture." . . . Today we appear to be poised between two ages—one of detribalization and one of retribalization.[51]

All the conservatism in the world, McLuhan is convinced, will not stop the oceanic sweep of electric technology: It is "within the gates, and we are numb, deaf, blind and mute. . . ."[52] Unfortunately, he goes on, such debilities mask from us the imperative need to understand precisely how these assailing new media change our perception. When the magic spell of any one of them is fresh, McLuhan believes, the sense that it extends is numbed as if by shock, or "we could not endure the leverage it exerts upon us."[53] Perhaps, then, when it is seen from the vantage point of ten years later, futurists like Toffler are correct to speak of what afflicts us as information overload, to suggest that we might very well be verging on a universal nervous breakdown. Even Toffler may be optimistic. Perhaps in extending our entire nervous system electrically, including the brain, we have overextended ourselves at last and fatally numbed our senses right to the razor edge of oblivion. Perhaps this time the shock is too great and the patient will not recover, something McLuhan failed to foresee.

Then again, mercifully, there may exist a natural escape hatch, one tacitly recognized not only by the counterculture but, indirectly and all unknowing, by McLuhan himself. For all but buried in his visionary text lies a damning admission that could be its undoing and our hope of salvation: "All media exist to invest our lives with artificial perception and arbitrary values."[54] Leaving aside for now what constitutes genuine perception—and how human values can ever be anything but arbitrary—saving questions remain. Artificial perception at best goes beyond our senses, at

428

worst fails to square with what they tell us to be true. At best it extends our model of a possible reality beyond our unaided senses; at worst it may offer them a model that is suspect if not false. Viewed that way, can technology—mechanical or electric—ever extend perception in such a way as to satisfy our hunger for true experience, or does it fail to carry with it the deep emotional component which would guarantee that?

When our three children were not much younger they used to look up from the TV set and ask with utter seriousness if what they were watching was "really happening," was it "really real?"—as if their senses, even electrically engaged to the fullest as McLuhan would have it, could not be trusted to render from the barrage of electrons that bathed them a reliable test of reality. Antithetically, this may be what the garish swirl of the light show, the infernal shriek and twang of rock music, the psychologically "noisy" assault on consciousness of psychedelic drugs is all about: a desperate, only half-perceived attempt to wake up our technologically blunted, media-numbed natural senses (at the ultimate risk of flogging them to death).

Perhaps then, what we are witnessing raging around us is not the Western mind's final fever or even another deep extension trauma that will pass like all the others, allowing us once more to adjust and make the intolerable tolerable. Rather, it may be an impassioned, yearning, stumbling, at times panicky—and in the strictest primitive sense, probably doomed—flight to return to the pure, unfettered, unextended perception of our own five body senses; to a life of inner consensus; to life that is holistic and experiential.

All the ramifications of the great debate brewing between the opponents of technology and its true believers, between those who favor flight and those who favor fight, between those who would stop the modern world and get off and those who would ride it out, can only be suggested in these pages. But before moving on, let us pause to give electric technology its curious due. If McLuhan is right, it did awaken our right hemisphere from a sleep as deep as death. As Charles Reich wrote of the student revolution in an appropriate if slightly different context, "it is as if some unseen divider, a glass partition, a plastic coating, a separating curtain . . . had been removed"⁵⁵ from one whole side of our brain.

Now that Slater's social eversion has evidently occurred, now that Boulding's boundary is broken and our consciousness is changing, the world seems increasingly no longer the place it was. Meaningless work is out, welfare cheating is in. Heterosexuality is out, homosexuality and bisexuality are in. Civic pride is out, vandalism is in. Tolerance and civility are out, urban violence and terror are in. Self-discipline is out, unlimited freedom—the left hemisphere calls it license—is in. Do your own thing, at your expense or anybody else's. Who cares? Cool it. But wait a minute. Can these last dreary, demonic, and dionysian excesses, these final few affronts to good taste, morality, common sense, and higher sensibilities by the spoiled child, street thug, and psychosexual voluptuary in all of us really be the work of anything deserving to be called intelligence? Of course it isn't. Such acts are by no stretch of the imagination or exercise of logic symptomatic of a higher intellect. They are clearly destructive to both the self and society, the antithesis of what evolution has taught us intelligence is. How, then, are we to explain them, inextricably intermingled as they appear to be with the functions of both hemispheres?

It may be no exaggeration to say that all the thinking that gets us into trouble, whether left hemisphere in origin or right, is a measure of our cerebral susceptibility to the dark hungers, blind drives, and raw passions of the surviving animal nature deep within us. Paul MacLean, chief of the National Institute of Mental Health's Laboratory of Brain Evolution and Behavior, thinks the brain is *triune,* that is, three in one, and he isn't even talking about the hemispheres. MacLean is referring to the cerebrum plus two deeper brain structures, the reptilian survival brain of our oldest ancestors at the very core, and its limbic overlay, the emotional drive wheel of our self- and species preservation.

In MacLean's view, the two lower brains no less than the highest behave as biological computers, each with its own special form of subjectivity and intelligence, its own sense of time and space, its own memory and motor functions. The reptilian brain, he believes, plays a crucial role in such genetically informed behavior as establishing territory, finding shelter, hunting, homing, mating, forming social hierarchies, and selecting leaders. It further gives us, he thinks, a predisposition to imitation in social situations and makes us slave to precedent. "It would be interesting to know," he says, "to what extent it contributes to man's superstitions, ceremonial rituals, religious convictions, legal actions and political persuasions."[56]

The limbic system, our emotional brain, generates in response to the environment feelings that are both protective and aggrandizing; feelings of desire, anger, fear, sorrow, joy and affection. It overrides ancestral memories with the force of current awareness and substitutes what we "know in our gut" for the conventional accumulated wisdom of society. Most important of all, he believes, there is unimpeachable evidence that the limbic brain is uniquely qualified biologically to unite internal and external experience, to fuse the inner individual and the outer reality in creating vivid feelings of what is real, true, and important.

These feelings are often all out of context with and proportion to—as well as quite independent of—our cerebral hemispheres. There is ample clinical evidence, moreover, that the aura triggered when an epileptic seizure strikes the limbic cortex produces exactly that unassailable sensation of what is real and true. In its more severe form the seizure can generate feelings of 'an eerie depersonalization, grotesquely distorted perceptions not unlike those of psychosis or extreme psychedelic drug use. But most striking about the limbic seizure is what MacLean likes to quote from Dostoevsky's description of his own epileptic aura in *The Idiot:* "[It was] a sensation of existence in the most intense degree . . . thoughts occur very clear and bright to me . . . as if this is what the world is all about . . . the absolute truth."[57]

Writing in *The Neurosciences: Second Study Program,* MacLean warns movingly against the dangers of disregarding the coercive power of the lower brains in the name of a lofty, insular cerebral objectivity:

It is traditional to regard the exact sciences as completely objective. The cultivation of this attitude is illustrated by a statement of Einstein quoted by C. P. Snow (1967): "Perception of this world by thought, leaving out everything subjective became . . . my supreme aim." Bertrand Russell (1921) maintained that introspective data are scientifically inappropriate for investigation because they do not obey physical laws. . . . The irony of all such attitudes is that every behavior selected for study, every observation and interpretation, requires subjective processing by an introspective observer. Logically, there is no way of circumventing this or the more disturbing conclusion that the cold, hard facts of science, like the firm pavement underfoot, are all derivatives of a soft brain. No measurement or computation obtained by the hardware of the exact sciences enters our comprehension without undergoing subjective transformation by the software of the brain. . . .[58]

MacLean then follows with a statement that ought to be required reading for everyone, professional or layman, involved or not in the prolonged and lacerating dispute over the nature of intelligence and its proper testing.

[Emotion] appears to have the paradoxical capacity to find equal support for opposite sides of any question. It is particularly curious that in scientific discourse, as in politics, the emotions seem capable of standing on any platform. . . . Although seldom commented on, it is equally bewildering that [science] is able to live comfortably for years, and sometimes centuries, with beliefs that a new generation discovers to be false. . . . As E. G. Boring (1964) emphasized, in paraphrasing a comment of Max Planck: "Important theories, marked for death by the discovery of contradictory evidence, seldom die before their authors."[59]

Regardless of whether MacLean's arresting thesis will itself someday be so marked, our emotions will indomitably exist as long as we do, giving their color, shape, and texture to our thinking whether we wish it or not. And nothing in the triune brain does anything to resolve the dilemma of consciousness raised by the emerging natures of our two cerebral hemispheres. Indeed, they only fragment our mentality further. How do we reconcile all these disparate, impinging, autonomous, overlapping, interrelated, complementary, and antagonistic parts with that "most compelling of intuitions," as Jerison calls it, Bogen's "subjective feeling possessed by each of us that we are one?"[60]

Obviously we do not. Perhaps this is what Arthur Koestler is getting at when he says that the human brain has not linked up in a *balanced* way, is still suffering from what R. D. Laing calls a one-hundred-thousand-year "species freak-out."[61] Perhaps this is what D. H. Lawrence meant when he wrote, "We are divided in ourselves against ourselves. And that is the meaning of the cross symbol."[62] Our language is replete with faintly disguised apprehensions that this may be so. We speak of the insane as mentally "unbalanced" (as if the rest of us were otherwise) and reserve for our most unyielding and universal mental illness the word "schizophrenia" (from *schizo:* "split," *phrenia:* "mind." Psychiatrists, however, when they use labels at all today, prefer an even more telling definiton in the light of MacLean's triune concept: "fragmented mind").

The full range of our mental aberrations may be one symptom of that freak-out, the inner symptom. The outer symptom may be the deliberate violence, cruelty, and destructiveness Erich Fromm calls "malignant" aggression, to distinguish it from the instinctive, built-in impulse to fight or flee when our basic interests are threatened. No wonder the criminal definition of insanity is such a legalistic mess. We are clearly and always of two minds about the roots of our own unique savagery against one another. As Nickolaas Tinbergen points out, man is the only animal that is guilty of mass murder, the only misfit in his own society. But which, then, we are impelled to ask, is worse—the irrational violence of a Charles Whitman who shoots and kills fourteen people at ghastly random from a University of Texas clock tower, or the rational violence of an undeclared war in which more explosives are dropped on one tiny agrarian Asian nation than fell in all of World War Two? We call Whitman's crime an act of mindless violence, yet he had a rapidly blooming tumor pressing on the amygdala, an area of the limbic brain that can instantly provoke us to spasms of aggression if electrically stimulated in the laboratory. So Whitman's hideous act was not mindless at all. It was as firmly grounded in the mind as neurophysiology can make it. At the same time, the air war in Vietnam was defended as logical, rational, reasonable, a mindful act undertaken in defense of our troops. Carrier pilots returning from interdiction missions on which they killed everything that

433

moved in the demilitarized zone told television reporters they were "just doing their job." Yet we grew angry in the hot light of world revulsion or uneasy in the chill shadow of the Nuremberg trials when we were asked how could sanity justify such genocide?

Our emotions, then, cannot be divorced from our intellect. What feeling wants to do, thought generally will find a reason for But the split-brain may give this bromide a new and more menacing meaning: either hemisphere, it appears, in its own way can accommodate. Laing's species freak-out, assuming that's what our more violent behavior is, will find sanction for its atrocities in the coldly rational left hemisphere as well as in the flexible, spontaneous, hedonistic right. It can allow us to commit, with the permission of our hemispheres if not their active connivance, the bureaucratic by-the-timetable butchery of Buchenwald as well as the unspeakably bloody and indiscriminate mayhem of My Lai.

And in the end all will stand rationalized, as Leon Festinger postulates in his theory of cognitive dissonance. Namely, when two inconsistent beliefs are held, and the conflict between them becomes too much to bear, one or both will be changed to make a better fit—even if the end result makes little objective sense. This was perfectly borne out by the sentence two Berkeley researchers composed to express their consensus finding in a street poll of what people thought about My Lai: *It never happened, and besides, they deserved it.*

Emotions can work both ways, of course, for the moral good as well as ill—a point beautifully illustrated in a story editor Norman Cousins tells.

> As sometimes happens in a deadlocked discussion involving money or politics, the impasse may be broken by a simple appeal to moral principal. Until that point, however, people [tend] to hang back from raising or identifying the moral factor. In such cases, it is almost as though the rules of the game call for people to be hard-nosed and "realistic," whatever that means, and they feel awkward and embarrassed about being the first to call attention to the moral issue. Once the matter is brought into the open, however, people have no difficulty in seeing it and almost seem relieved to have it discussed. I remember how, in the negotiations ten years ago for the release of Joseph Cardinal Slipyj, Archbishop of the Ukrainian Rite Orthodox church, who had

434

been interned in a Soviet prison for seventeen years, Premier Nikita Khrushchev spent twenty minutes reviewing the intricate, harsh political background of his case. Having finished this recital of *realpolitik* he sat back in his seat and asked, "Why should I release this man?" I said, as directly as I could, that it was probably the right thing to do. Mr. Khrushchev at first seemed a little startled, as though I had suddenly changed the rules of the game; then his entire expression relaxed, and he nodded and said, "Yes, of course." Two weeks later the archbishop was freed.[63]

So: We are living with a many-faceted brain, a multimind that tells us intelligence is not some static unity to be captured by one test, but a broad and changing natural adaptation for survival at its highest. It is a multimind that puts its intelligence to work in myriad ways; in cultivating a garden as well as a taste for rare books; in putting together an old car as well as a new corporation; in mending a broken water pipe as well as a broken head or heart. It is, most assuredly, in the light of what we have seen, no monolith, but a teeming world inside our heads of words and images, emotion and instinct, that collide and richochet, ebb and flow, crest and subside, bubble and are still—a simmering stew of restless biochemical energy, God's own neural light show. Better we admit that than go on talking and testing as if our brain were a pristine architecture of separate rooms where thought and feeling and aptitude and instinct are antiseptically set apart and can be kept apart—if we but set our minds to it.

Sperry's split-brain experiments, moreover, have shown our cerebral hemispheres to be so mutually antagonistic that he speculates they may even—mind-blowing thought—compete for brain space in our ongoing evolution. Perhaps, then, when men like developmental neuropsychologist James Prescott call for eventual "elimination of the difference between the conscious and the unconscious"[64] to achieve a unified brain, they may be grasping at a psychic impossibility. Perhaps we cannot truly have a functional parity of both. Perhaps we must always choose, consciously or not, one at the ultimate expense of the other.

Many men look at the changes swirling around us and say that this is a time of transformation. But, logic asks, how do we know this is the salvationary transformation that more and more men seek? Perhaps it is only a momentary aberration, a primitive fear reaction, a temporary loss of resolve in the face of the difficult days ahead. Perhaps the transformation really begins with an objective, clear-headed analysis of what social philosopher Ernest Becker called the "stark picture of the human condition without false consolations."[65] Perhaps it goes on from there to systematically build upon the social structure as it exists, with no romantic illusions about a dawning new human potential and without sweeping away in a blindly destructive right-hemisphere temper tantrum everything the left hemisphere has erected. We may even, the ego whispers to us, have to find the courage to admit to ourselves that this is *all* there is, that there may *be* no transformation, just more or less of the same. Perhaps, then, we should stop shouting in public for the wave of the future to please stand up and identify itself, and get on with the rational planning of it where we can.

Reason, logic, objectivity, analysis, ego, rationality—these are the hallmarks of the left-hemisphere-dominated mind, retort the transformationists. Its credo of ever-progressive technologies for always-brighter tomorrows, they say, no longer applies. We know it—sensibly, instinctively, intuitively, in our gut. No longer can we depend on the mystique of the reliably recurring technological breakthrough. We must stop the juggernaut and get off, at some green and leafy level of tribalism on a more human scale.

Thus the great debate that is shaping up is a dialogue, really, between the two sides of the human brain. Such a debate, of course, must discount the obvious fact that those who champion the right hemisphere (if only in the interest of a saving balance) have to meet their opponents on the left hemisphere's own turf if they are to win the day. They must put aside the paints, clays, musical tones, balletic movements, mystic icons, and perceptual senses of the right hemisphere and accept the surrogate assistance of their linguistic left. They must rely on the fire of poetic hyperbole and metaphor to thaw the ice jam of contending logic, analysis, and reason. The irony of this attempt is not lost upon them. As Phlip Slater writes, "I am engaged . . . in a rather ironic enterprise: attempting to encourage people I do not know, through a linear abstract medium, to alter their orientation to the world in a way that should induce them to reject my effort as mechanical and invalid."[66]

How the great debate will turn out, no one can know. But sooner than we can say, every thought, every word, every act—by everyone on earth—will be a decisive taking of sides in their global accumulation. The shape of society, through its systems of reward and reinforcement, will be changed in ways we cannot know.

If this is true and we know it, what do we do next? Need we do anything at all? If Boulding's boundary is broken, what options have we?

We have the one option we have always had. We can reject or embrace the enduring paradox: The mind is a multiplicity of parts whose various functions cannot always be separated, but must never be confused if we are to understand the deepest nature of our intelligence. For our best hope of the future lies neither wholly in the left hemisphere—where we have in the main for so long been—nor wholly in the right—where some would zealously have us go. Nor does it lie in sinking back to the primitive, assuming that were possible. It lies—instinct, logic, and insight all tell us—as those who work with clay know from the throwing lore of the potting wheel, in getting centered. It lies in ending Laing's hundred-thousand-year species freak-out; in linking up in Koestler's balanced way.

If we can do this, if we can keep our heads and put our minds to it, a new Renaissance may be coming.

NOTES

Shortened titles are generally used after the first reference. See Bibliography for publication dates of periodicals, papers, speeches, and miscellany referred to in Notes.

PROLOGUE

1. Personal interview.
2. Personal interview.
3. Personal interview.
4. Wiener, *Ex-Prodigy*, p. 136.
5. Sperry, "Science and the Problem of Values," *Perspectives in Biology and Medicine*, p. 117.
6. *Ibid.*, p. 115.

CHAPTER ONE

1. Speech, San Francisco State University, April 27, 1972.
2. Galambos, "Brain Correlates of Learning (Introduction)," *The Neurosciences: First Study Program*, p. 642.
3. Craik, "When Memory Fades . . .", p. 428.
4. Lindsay and Norman, *Human Information Processing*, pp. 310–11.
5. Personal communication, Georges Ungar, January 22, 1973.
6. Pietsch, "Shufflebrain," p. 43.
7. McConnell, "A Tape Recorder Theory of Memory," speech, May 2, 1963.
8. Sperry, "How a Developing Brain Gets Itself Properly Wired for Adaptive Function," *The Biopsychology of Development*, p. 31.
9. Stewart, "Comments on the Chemistry of Scotophobin," p. 209.
10. McConnell, "The Biochemistry of Memory," *Das Medizinische Prisma*, p. 19.
11. Pietsch, "Shufflebrain," p. 46.
12. *Ibid.*, p. 48.
13. *Ibid.*
14. Asimov, "I Can't Believe I Saw the Whole Thing," p. 31.

15. *Ibid.*, p. 32.
16. Hyden, "Biochemical and Molecular Aspects of Learning and Memory," *Proceedings of the American Philosophical Society*, p. 326.

CHAPTER TWO

1. Bogen, "The Other Side of the Brain," II, p. 153.
2. *Ibid.*
3. *Ibid.*
4. *Ibid.*, p. 145.
5. *Ibid.*, p. 135.
6. *Ibid.*, p. 154.
7. Gardner, "The Shattered Mind," *Psychology Today—Book Club News*, p. 3.
8. Gazzaniga, *The Bisected Brain*, p. 126.
9. Sperry, "Hemispheric Deconnection and Unity in Conscious Awareness," *American Psychologist*, p. 728.
10. Sperry, "Lateral Specialization of Cerebral Function in the Surgically Separated Hemispheres," *The Psychophysiology of Thinking*, p. 212.
11. Ornstein, "Right and Left Thinking," *Psychology Today*, p. 92.
12. Levy, Trevarthen, and Sperry, "Perception of Bilateral Chimeric Figures Following Hemispheric Deconnexion," *Brain*, p. 64.
13. Sperry, *The Psychophysiology of Thinking*, p. 216.
14. *Ibid.*, p. 218.
15. *Ibid.*, p. 215.
16. Sperry, *The Biopsychology of Development*, p. 35.
17. Bogen, "The Other Side of the Brain," I, *Bulletin of the Los Angeles Neurological Society*, p. 105.
18. Bogen, "Other Side of the Brain, II, p. 149.
19. San Francisco *Sunday Examiner & Chronicle*, "Sophisticate or Not, We Need Both Ears," December 22, 1974.
20. Sperry, *The Psychophysiology of Thinking*, p. 221.
21. Gazzaniga, "One Brain—Two Minds," *American Scientist*, p. 312.
22. Bogen, "Other Side of the Brain," II, p. 156.
23. Sperry, "Hemispheric Deconnection, p. 733.
24. Sperry, "Lateral Specialization," p. 209.
25. Bogen, "Other Side of the Brain, p. 138.

CHAPTER THREE

1. Keller, *The Story of My Life*, pp. 34–35.
2. *Ibid.*
3. Jerison, *Evolution of the Brain and Intelligence*, p. 23 (in ms.).
4. *Ibid.*, p. 30.
5. *Ibid.*, p. 37.

NOTES

6. McLuhan, *Understanding Media*, p. 158.
7. Jerison, Marketing Questionnaire for *Evolution of the Brain and Intelligence*, p. 2.
8. Singer, "The Vicissitudes of Imagery in Research and Clinical Use," *Contemporary Psychoanalysis*, p. 169.
9. *Ibid.*. pp. 169–70.
10. "The Freud/Jung Letters," *Psychology Today*, p. 41.
11. Singer, "Vicissitudes of Imagery," p. 165.
12. *Citizen Kane*, p. 155.
13. Bower, "Analysis of a Mnemonic Device," *American Scientist*, p. 500.
14. *Ibid.*, p. 502.
15. *Ibid.*
16. Cooper and Shepard, "Chronometric Studies of the Rotation of Mental Images, *Symposium on Visual Information Processing*, p. 1.
17. *Ibid.*, p. 67.
18. *Ibid.*, p. 86.
19. Shepard and Chipman, "Second-Order Isomorphisms of Internal Representations: Shapes of States," *Cognitive Psychology*, p. 2.
20. Bower, "Analysis," p. 507.
21. Cooper and Shepard, "Chronometric Studies", p. 99
22. Bower, "Analysis," p. 510.
23. Luria, *Mind of the Mnemonist*, p. 83.
24. *Ibid.*., p. 28.
25. *Ibid.*, p. 36.
26. *Ibid.*, viii.
27. Luria, *Mind*, pp. 96–97.
28. Faure, *Spear in the Sand*, pp. 116–17.
29. *Ibid.*, p. 216.
30. *Ibid.*, p. 220.
31. Bower, "Analysis," p. 510.
32. Hiller, "Robert Coles, the People's Voice," *Human Behavior*, p. 21.
33. Bower, *op. cit.*, "Analysis," p. 510.
34. Lenneberg, "On Explaining Language," *Science*, p. 640.
35. Unpublished.
36. Rock, "The Perception of Disoriented Figures," *Scientific American*, p. 78.
37. Walcutt, "Road to Freedom: Disciplined Reading," *Learning*, p. 64.
38. McLuhan, *Understanding Media*, p. 79.
39. *Ibid.*, pp. 84–88.
40. *Ibid.*, pp. 15, 80.

CHAPTER FOUR

1. Dillard, *Pilgrim at Tinker Creek*, p. 26.
2. *Ibid.*, p. 19.

441

3. *Ibid.*
4. Weil, *The Natural Mind,* p. 160.
5. Personal interview.
6. Duckworth, "Piaget Takes a Teacher's Look," *Learning,* pp. 22–26.
7. Skinner, "On 'Having' a Poem," *Saturday Review* (of the arts), p. 34.
8. Skinner, *Beyond Freedom and Dignity,* pp. 89–90.
9. Chomsky, "Language and the Mind," *Psychology Today,* p. 50.
10. Hebb, Lambert, and Tucker, "A DMZ in the Language War," *Psychology Today,* p. 55.
11. *Ibid.*
12. Lindsay and Norman, pp. 431–32.
13. *Ibid.,* p. 432.
14. *Ibid.,* p. 433.
15. Sharp and Pinard, "I.Q. and Point of View," *Psychology Today,* pp. 66–67.
16. San Francisco Chronicle, "Simenon to Quit Writing," February 8, 1973.
17. Bogen, "Other Side of the Brain," II, p. 160.
18. *Ibid.,* p. 161.
19. Brown, *New Mind, New Body,* p. 54.
20. "Freud/Jung Letters," p. 87.
21. Jung, *Man and His Symbols* , p. 82.
22. Bogen, "Other Side of the Brain," III, p. 201.
23. Weil, *Natural Mind,* p. 118.
24. San Francisco Chronicle, "What You Experience for Yourself is the Truth. Something Only Believed Is a Lie," December 12, 1974.
25. MacLean, "The Internal-External Bonds of the Memory Process," *The Journal of Nervous and Mental Disease,* p. 47.
26. English, "TA's Disney World," *Psychology Today,* p. 49.
27. *Ibid.,* p. 49.
28. MacKinnon, "The Nature and Nurture of Creative Talent," *American Psychologist,* p. 484.
29. Barron, *Creative Person and Creative Process,* p. 37.
30. MacKinnon, "Nature and Nurture," p. 487.
31. *Ibid.,* p. 494.
32. Barron, *Creative Person,* p. 24.
33. *Ibid.,* p. 11.
34. MacKinnon, "Nature and Nurture," p. 491.
35. Clark, *Einstein—The Life and Times,* p. 87.
36. Bogen, "Other Side of the Brain," II, p. 199.
37. Barron, *Creative Person,* p. 68.
38. *Ibid.,* p. 77.
39. *Ibid.,* p. 75.
40. MacKinnon, "Nature and Nurture," p. 488.
41. Dellas and Gaier, "Identification of Creativity," *Psychological Bulletin,* p. 64.
42. *Ibid.,* p. 64.
43. Barron, *Creative Person,* p. 176.

NOTES

44. Holt, "The Cuteness Syndrome," *MS*, p. 79.
45. Barron, *Creative Person*, p. 165.
46. Holt, "Cuteness Syndrome," p. 79.
47. Barron, *Creative Person*, p. 168.
48. *Ibid.*
49. *Ibid.*, p. 146.
50. *Ibid.*, p. 177.
51. *Ibid.*, p. 176.
52. Personal communication, May 28, 1975.
53. Eugène Delacroix, *Journal de Eugène Delacroix*, II, p. 74.
54. Campbell, "Transcendence Is as American as Ralph Waldo Emerson," *Psychology Today*, p. 43.
55. McLuhan, *Understanding Media*, p. 66.

CHAPTER FIVE

1. Evarts, "Brain Mechanisms in Movement," *Scientific American*, p. 99.
2. Bower, "Analysis," p. 506.
3. Sperry, personal communication, October 2, 1973.
4. Bogen, personal communication, October 13, 1973.
5. Gazzaniga, personal communication, November 1, 1973.
6. W. Timothy Gallwey, *The Inner Game of Tennis*, p. 31.
7. *Ibid.*, p. 84.
8. *Ibid.*, p. 20.
9. *Ibid.*, pp. 54–55.
10. *Ibid.*, pp. 122–23.
11. *Ibid.*, p. 129.
12. *Ibid.*
13. McLuhan, *Understanding Media*, p. 237.
14. Bogen "Other Side of the Brain," III, p. 199.
15. Kuehl, "Thomas Harris," *Book-of-the-Month Club News*, p. 1.
16. Singer, "Vicissitudes," p. 165.
17. Huxley, *The Doors of Perception*, pp. 73–74.
18. *Ibid.*, pp. 74–77.
19. Saal, "Balanchine: Past? Future? Now!", *Newsweek*, p. 96.
20. Craft, *Stravinsky: Retrospectives and Conclusions*, p. 25.
21. Morgenstern, *Composers on Music* , p. 87.
22. *Ibid.*, p. 245.
23. *Ibid.*, p. 307.
24. *Ibid.*, p. 139.
25. Craft, *Stravinsky*, p. 48.
26. *Ibid.*, pp. 25, 82.
27. Haskell, *Balletomania*, p. 52.
28. Morgenstern, *Composers*, p. 245.

29. *Ibid.*, p. 481.
30. Moore, *Training an Actor*, pp. 14–15, 22–23, 30, 35.
31. Shahn, *The Shape of Content*, pp. 31–32.
32. *Ibid.*, pp. 44–45, 47–48, 49.
33. Hale, *The World of Rodin*, p. 88.
34. Morgenstern, *Composers*, p. 87.
35. Copland, *Music and Imagination*, p. 12.
36. *Ibid.*, p. 15.
37. Morgenstern, *Composers*, p. 442.
38. Craft, *Stravinsky*, p. 45.
39. Nureyev, *Nureyev*, p. 124.
40. Nijinsky, *Nijinsky*, p. 30.
41. *Ibid.*, p. 113.
42. *Ibid.*, p. 226.
43. Haskell, *Balletomania*, pp. 153–54.
44. *Ibid.*, pp. 245–46.
45. Nijinsky, *Nijinsky*, pp. 425–26.
46. Morgenstern, *Composers*, p. 149.
47. *Ibid.*, pp. 373–74.
48. *Ibid.*, pp. 149, 156.
49. Craft, *Stravinsky*, p. 47.
50. Van Gogh, *Van Gogh's Diary*, pp. 26, 108.
51. Copland, *Music*, pp. 41–43.
52. *Ibid.*, p. 49.
53. Shahn, *Shape*, p. 50.
54. *Ibid.*, pp. 38–39, 49, 51, 95, 106, 110.
55. Copland, *Music*, p. 12.
56. *Ibid.*, p. 14.
57. Morgenstern, *Composers*, p. 156.
58. *Ibid.*, p. 148.
59. Craft, *Stravinsky*, p. 91.
60. Lord, *A Giacometti Portrait*, p. 30.
61. *Ibid.*, p. 44.
62. Nijinsky, *Nijinsky*, p. 186.
63. Copland, *Music*, p. 43.
64. Haskell, *Balletomania*, p. 180.
65. Moore, *Training*, pp. 56–57.
66. Shahn, *Shape*, pp. 34–35.
67. *Ibid.*, p. 35.
68. Morgenstern, *Composers*, p. 309.
69. Nijinsky, *Nijinsky*, p. 288.
70. Lord, *Giacometti*, pp. 22–24.
71. Moore, *Training*, p. 62.
72. Haskell, *Balletomania*, p. 86.
73. Moore, *Training*, p. 28.

74. Hale, *World*, pp. 15, 44.
75. *Ibid.*, p. 93.
76. Bernstein, *The Joy of Music*, p. 29.
77. Copland, *Music*, p. 17.
78. *Ibid.*, p. 41.
79. Morgenstern, *Composers*, pp. 294–95.
80. Van Gogh, *Diary*, p. 104.
81. Hale, *World*, p. 69.
82. Copland, *Music*, p. 66.
83. Morgenstern, *Composers*, p. 307.
84. Bernstein, *Joy*, pp. 11–12.
85. *Ibid.*, pp. 13, 29.
86. Bowers, *The New Scriabin*, xiv.
87. *Ibid.*, p. 112.
88. *Ibid.*, p. 35–36.
89. *Ibid.*, p. 62.
90. *Ibid.*, p. 118.
91. *Ibid.*, p. 92.
92. *Ibid.*, p. 72.
93. *Ibid.*, p. 97.
94. *Ibid.*, p. 102.
95. McLanathan, "Leonardo da Vinci," unnumbered.
96. *Ibid.*
97. *Ibid.*
98. Personal communication, Pedretti, September 2, 1973.
99. McLanathan, "Leonardo."

CHAPTER SIX

1. Hirsch, *Human Intelligence*, p. 11.
2. Kamin, "Heredity, Intelligence, Politics and Psychology," speech.
3. Hunt, *Human Intelligence*, p. 33.
4. Galton, *Hereditary Genius*, p. 328.
5. Darlington, *The Facts of Life*, p. 254.
6. Galton, *Hereditary Genius*, p. 12.
7. Halacy, *Man and Memory*, p. 71.
8. Hirsch, *Human Intelligence*, p. 11.
9. *Ibid.*, pp. 11–12.
10. Pearson, *Bernard Shaw: His Life and Personality*, p. 304.
11. Darlington, *Facts*, p. 288.
12. Galton, *Human Faculty*, p. 216.
13. Galton, *Natural Inheritance*, p. 8.
14. *Ibid.*, p. 9.
15. Sargent, *Great Psychologists*, p. 71.

16. Darlington, *Facts*, p. 190.
17. *Ibid.*, p. 191.
18. *Ibid.*, p. 193.
19. Burt, "Inheritance of General Intelligence," *American Psychologist*, p. 176.
20. *Ibid.*, p. 178.
21. Hirsch, *Human Intelligence*, pp. 12–13.
22. Kamin, "Heredity," p. 1.
23. *Ibid.*, pp. 1–2.
24. *Ibid.*, p. 2.
25. Goddard, *The Kallikak Family*, p. 67.
26. Kamin, "Heredity," p. 3.
27. *Ibid.*, p. 5.
28. Kendrick, "An Old Problem Revisited," speech, p. 26.
29. Kamin, "Heredity," p. 5.
30. *Ibid.*, p. 6.
31. *Ibid.*, p. 7.
32. Richardson and Spears, *Race and Intelligence*, p. 179.
33. Koenig, "Man and the Universal Equation," a profile of R. B. Cattell, *Psychology Today*, p. 43.
34. Horn, *Human Intelligence*, p. 54.
35. Cattell, "Are I. Q. Tests Intelligent?," *Readings in Psychology Today*, p. 339.
36. *Ibid.*, p. 336.
37. Burt (Introduction), *The Act of Creation*, by Arthur Koestler, p. 14.
38. White, *Second Tree from the Corner*, p. 173.
39. Burt, *Act*, p. 19.
40. Sargent, *Great Psychologists*, p. 257.
41. *Ibid.*, p. 258.

CHAPTER SEVEN

1. Jones *et al.*, *The Course of Human Development*, p. 15.
2. *Ibid.*
3. *Ibid.*, p. 106.
4. *Ibid.*, p. 104.
5. *Ibid.*, p. 111.
6. *Ibid.*, p. 123.
7. Jensen *et al.*, "Intelligence and Heredity," *Saturday Evening Post*, p. 9.
8. Herrnstein, "I.Q.," *The Atlantic*, pp. 53–54.
9. Terman, *Genetic Studies of Genius*, IV, p. 1.
10. Fincher, "The Terman Study Is 50 Years Old." *Human Behavior*, pp. 11–12.
11. *Ibid.*, p. 14.
12. Herrnstein, "I.Q.," p. 54.
13. Terman, *Genetic Studies*, IV, pp. 128–29.
14. *Ibid.*, pp. 14–15.

15. Fincher, "Terman Study," p. 13.
16. Terman, *Genetic Studies,* IV, p. 339.
17. *Ibid.,* p. 351.
18. *Ibid.,* pp. 326–27.
19. McClelland *et al.,* "Intelligence and Heredity," *Saturday Evening Post,* p. 154.
20. Fincher, "Terman Study," p. 14.
21. Terman, *Genetic Studies,* IV, p. 352.
22. Fincher, "Terman Study," p. 15.
23. McClelland, "Testing for Competence Rather Than for 'Intelligence,'" *American Psychologist,* p. 2.
24. *Ibid.,* pp. 5–6.
25. *Ibid.,* p. 6.
26. *Ibid.*
27. Bane and Jencks, "Five Myths About Your I.Q.," *Harper's,* p. 32.
28. *Ibid.,* pp. 32–33.

CHAPTER EIGHT

1. Eysenck, *Know Your Own I.Q.,* p. 1.
2. McClelland, "Testing," p. 1.
3. Kamin, "The Misuse of I.Q. Testing," *Change,* p. 43.
4. Zigler, "On Growing Up, Learning and Living," *Human Behavior,* p. 66.
5. *Ibid.,* p. 66.
6. Jensen, "The Case for I.Q. Tests," *The Humanist,* p. 14.
7. Kendrick, "An Old Problem," p. 27.
8. Hunt, "Psychological Assessment in Education and Social Class," *Missouri Conference,* p. 22.
9. Eysenck, *Know Your Own I.Q.,* p.8.
10. Fixx, *Games for the Superintelligent,* p. 120.
11. Eysenck, *Know Your Own I.Q.,* p. 16.
12. *Ibid.,* pp. 19–20.
13. Cattell, "Are I.Q. Tests Intelligent," p. 342.
14. Eysenck, *Know Your Own I.Q.,* p. 20.
15. Ryan, *Race and Intelligence,* p. 42.
16. Personal interview.
17. Personal interview.
18. *Ibid.*
19. Richardson and Spears, *Race and Intelligence,* p. 182.
20. Eysenck, *Know Your Own I.Q.,* p. 30.
21. *Ibid.,* pp. 22–23.
22. Eysenck, *Know Your Own I.Q.,* p. 18
23. *Ibid.,* pp. 20, 24.
24. Personal interview.
25. Richardson and Spears, *Race and Intelligence,* p. 180.

26. Buros, *1972 Mental Measurements Yearbook,* p. 428.
27. Kendrick, "An Old Problem," p. 30.
28. Personal interview.
29. Personal interview.
30. Cattell, "Are IQ Tests Intelligent?" pp. 340, 342.
31. Sharp and Pinard, "I.Q.," p. 65.
32. McClelland, "Testing," pp. 7–8.
33. *Ibid.,* p. 8.
34. *Ibid.,* p. 10.
35. *Ibid.,* p. 11.
36. Asher, "John Ertl's Neural Efficiency Analyzer—Bias-Free Test, or Just a 'Neat Gadget'?," *APA Monitor,* March, 1973.
37. Eysenck, *Know Your Own I.Q.,* p. 34.
38. McClelland, "Testing," p. 13.
39. *Ibid.,* p. 12.

CHAPTER NINE

1. Hebb, Lambert, and Tucker, "DMZ", p. 56.
2. Neary, "Jensenism: Variations on a Racial Theme,", *Life,* p. 58d.
3. Rice, "The High Cost of Thinking the Unthinkable, *Psychology Today,* p. 91.
4. Pamphlet, *Students for a Democratic Society,* "Jensenism: A Closer Look," p. 16.
5. Sowell, "The Great I.Q. Controversy," *Change,* p. 33.
6. Jensen, *Genetics and Education,* p. 69.
7. Edson, "Jensenism. n. The Theory that I.Q. is Largely Determined by the Genes," *New York Times Magazine,* p. 10.
8. Rice, "High Cost," p. 91.
9. *Ibid.,* p. 90.
10. Raven, "The Jensen Controversy (Continued)," *Psychology Today,* p. 104.
11. Scriven, "The Values of the Academy," *Review of Educational Research,* p. 544.
12. Sowell, "I.Q. Controversy," p. 34.
13. Havender, "A Comment on Arthur Jensen's Critics," p. 1.
14. Light and Smith, "Social Allocation Models of Intelligence; A Methodological Inquiry," *Harvard Educational Review,* p. 15.
15. Sowell, "I.Q. Controversy," p. 35.
16. Lewontin, "Race and Intelligence," *Bulletin of the Atomic Scientists,* p. 7.
17. Sowell, "I.Q. Controversy," p. 35.
18. Davis, "Letter to the President," *National Academy of Sciences,* July 7, 1970.
19. Eysenck, "The Dangers of the New Zealots," *Encounter,* pp. 88–89.
20. Jensen, "Ethical Issues of Behavioral Science Research: On the Heritability of Intellectual Abilities," Western Psychological Association Symposium, p. 9.
21. Horn, *ibid.,* p. 16.

NOTES

22. Hall, "The Amount of Strain Now Imposed on the Individual May Well Overstretch Man's Capabilities to Adjust," *Psychology Today*, p. 66.
23. Hunt, "Heredity, Environment, and Class or Ethnic Differences," *1972 Invitational Conference on Testing Problems*, p. 11.
24. Jensen, "Heritability and Teachability," *Emerging Issues In Education*, p. 60.
25. Hunt, "Heredity," p. 15.
26. Jensen, *Genetics and Education*, p. 60.
27. *Ibid.*, p. 6.
28. *Ibid.*
29. *Ibid.*, p. 7.
30. Sowell, "I.Q. Controversy," p. 36.
31. Jensen, *Genetics and Education*, pp. 201–3.
32. Jensen, "Improving the Assessment of Intelligence," Western Psychological Association Symposium on "The Theory of Intelligence," p. 1.
33. Miller, *Death of a Salesman*, p. 154.

CHAPTER TEN

1. Barron, *Creative Lesson and Creative Process*, p, 50.
2. Sargent, *Great Psychologists*, p. 54.
3. Barron, *op. cit.*, p. 51.
4. Helson, "Comments on the Paper by Nathan Kogan," *Graduate Record Exam Conference*, Montreal, p. 1.
5. Personal communication, March 2, 1973.
6. Jarvik, "Human Intelligence: Sex Differences," UCLA Psychiatry Symposium, Perspectives on the nature of intelligence, p. 19.
7. Kagan, "Real Differences Between the Sexes." *Parents' Magazine*, p. 62.
8. Jarvik, "Human Intelligence," p. 13.
9. *Ibid.*, p. 12.
10. Money, "Pre-Natal Hormones and Intelligence: A Possible Relationship," *Impact of Science on Society*, pp. 285–86.
11. Jacklin and Maccoby, "Sex Differences in Intellectual Abilities: A Reassessment and a Look at Some New Explanations," *American Educational Research Association*, p. 8.
12. *Ibid.*
13. Kimura, "The Asymmetry of the Human Brain," *Scientific American*, p. 78.
14. Kagan, "The Emergence of Sex Differences," *University of Chicago School Review*, pp. 222–23.
15. Jacklin and Maccoby, "Sex Differences," p. 12.
16. Geschwind, "Language and the Brain," *Scientific American*, p. 83.
17. Helson, "The Changing Image of the Career Woman," *Journal of Social Issues*, p. 43.
18. Helson, "Comments," p. 2.
19. *Ibid.*, p. 6.

449

20. "Self-Esteem, Male and Female," by the editors, *Human Behavior*, p. 40.
21. San Francisco *Sunday Examiner and Chronicle*, "Erasing a Double Standard," by Rasa Gustaitis, June 16, 1974.
22. Helson, "Comments," pp. 1, 3.
23. Helson, "Women Mathematicians and the Creative Personality," *Journal of Consulting and Clinical Psychology*, p. 219.
24. Helson, "Comments," p. 4.
25. Kagan, "Emergence," p. 217.
26. Kagan "Real Differences," p. 63.

CHAPTER ELEVEN

1. Marland, S. P., "Education of the Gifted and Talented, *Report to the Congress of the United States by the U.S. Commissioner of Education*, p. 4.
2. *Ibid.*, p. 3.
3. *Ibid.*, p. 23.
4. Personal interview.
5. Marland, "Education," p. 316.
6. Lyon, "Talent Down the Drain," Special Issue on the Gifted and Talented, *American Education*, p. 14.
7. Martinson, "The Gifted and Talented: Whose Responsibility?," *The Elementary School Principal*, p. 48.
8. Burns, "Letter from a Parent," *ibid.*, p. 33.
9. Merritt, "Slow Frustration: A Student's Comments," *ibid.*, p. 79.
10. Personal interview.
11. Personal interview.
12. Personal interview.
13. Personal interview.
14. Personal interview.
15. Personal interview.
16. House, Special Issue on the Education of the Gifted and Talented, *The Elementary School Principal*, pp. 60–61.
17. Passow, *ibid.*, p. 31.
18. Bernstein, Goff, Cates, and McKay, *ibid.*, p. 90.
19. Personal communication.

CHAPTER TWELVE

1. Goddard, *Kallikak Family*, p. 12.
2. Personal interview.
3. Hamblin, "They Are 'Idiot Savants'—Wizards of the Calendar," *Life*, p. 110.
4. Ball, *Mathematical Recreation and Essays*, p. 378.
5. Sargent, *Great Psychologists*, p. 47.
6. *Ibid.*, p. 48.

NOTES

7. Holstein, "Discussion on Identical Twins—'Idiot Savants'—Calendar Calculators," *American Journal of Psychiatry*, p. 1078.
8. Rimland, *Infantile Autism*, p. 85.
9. *Ibid.*, p. 85.
10. *Ibid.*, p. 81.
11. Rimland, Letter to the editors, *Life*, April 8, 1966.
12. Chance, "After You Hit a Child, You Can't Just Get Up and Leave Him; You Are Hooked to That Kid," *Psychology Today*, p. 79.
13. Rimland, *Infantile Autism*, p. 129.
14. Koenig, "Boy in Trouble: Milestones in a Labyrinth," *Psychology Today*, p. 51.
15. Fuller, "Reading Need Not Be I.Q.-Bound," *The Bulletin*, p. 12.
16. "If Anyone Can Read, What Happens to I.Q.?," by the editors of Newsline, *Psychology Today*, (Reprint, page unnumbered).
17. Fuller, "Intelligence and the Fuller Reading System," American Psychological Association 80th Annual Meeting, p. 30.
18. Douglass, "Guest Editorial: A 'New Thrust' Approach to Mental Retardation," *American Journal of Mental Deficiency*, p. 145.
19. Kagan, "Do the First Two Years Matter?," *Saturday Review*, p. 41.
20. Divoky, "Toward a Nation of Sedated Children," *Learning*, pp. 11–13.
21. Braginsky, Benjamin M. and Dorothea D., "The Mentally Retarded: Society's Hansels and Gretels," *Psychology Today*, p. 24.
22. Rosen, letter to the editor on "The Mentally Retarded: Society's Hansels and Gretels," *Psychology Today*, p. 12.
23. Wallace, "A Lifetime Thrown Away by a Mistake 59 Years Ago," *Life*, p. 132.

CHAPTER THIRTEEN

1. Toffler, *Future Shock*, p. 214.
2. Rimland, "Nutrition and Related Approaches to Improving Human Potential," *51st Annual Meeting of the American Dietetic Association*, abstract of prepared delivered speech.
3. Chase, "Behavioral Biology and Environmental Design," *Psychopathology*, p. 176.
4. Personal interview.
5. Wurtman, "Biological Considerations in Lighting Environment," *Progressive Architecture*, p. 79.
6. Winter, "Ageless Aging," *Family Health*, p. 31.
7. Toffler, *op cit.*, p. 399.
8. Bruner, "Continuity of Learning," *Saturday Review*, p. 21.
9. Crutchfield, "Nurturing the Cognitive Skills of Productive Thinking," *1969 Yearbook of the Association for Supervision and Curriculum Development*, p. 3.
10. Rosenfeld, "Will Man Direct His Own Evolution?" *Life*, p. 108.
11. *Clarence Darrow*, television drama, September 4, 1974.
12. Kent, "Your Mind: How It Can Make You Healthy, How It Can Be Used Against You," *Vogue*, p. 95.

13. Weil, "Natural Mind," p. 157.
14. Mandell and Geyer, "The Euphoro-Hallucinogens," *The Comprehensive Textbook of Psychiatry*, p. 31.
15. Rueger, "Postscript to a Bum Trip," *Human Behavior*, p. 65.
16. Lilly, *Center of the Cyclone*, pp. 48–49.
17. *Ibid.*, book jacket.
18. *Ibid.*, p. 58.
19. Huxley, *Doors of Perception*, p. 15.
20. *Ibid.*, pp. 17, 22, 23.
21. *Ibid.*, p. 23.
22. *Ibid.*, pp. 28–29, 33–34.
23. *Ibid.*, pp. 52–53.
24. *Ibid.*, p. 55
25. *Ibid.*, p. 56.
26. Roszak, *ibid.*, *The Making of a Counter Culture*, pp. 159–60.
27. Personal interview.
28. Rosenfeld, "Will Man Direct His Own Evolution," p. 98.
29. *Ibid.*, p. 100.
30. Bonner, "Beyond Man's Genetic Lottery," Symposium on *The Next Billion Years*, p. 14.
31. Brown, *New Mind*, p. 53.
32. *Ibid.*, p. 83.
33. *Ibid.*, pp. 56, 83, 90, 111.
34. "Boom Times on the Psychic Frontier," *Time*, p. 66.
35. *Ibid.*, p. 65.
36. Lewis Thomas, *The Lives of a Cell*, as reviewed in the San Francisco *Sunday Examiner & Chronicle*, August 25, 1974.
37. Brown, *New Mind*, p. 102.
38. "Do Electric Fields Affect Behavior?," Newsline, *Psychology Today*, p. 89.
39. Oates, "New Heaven and Earth," *Saturday Review*, p. 54.
40. Brown, *New Mind*, p. 111.
41. *Ibid.*, p. 105.
42. *Ibid.*, p. 108.
43. Brown, "A Progress Report on Biofeedback," San Francisco *Sunday Examiner and Chronicle*, June 23, 1974.
44. Rørvik, "The Theta Experience," *Saturday Review*, p. 49.
45. Van Nuys, "The Consciousness of Edgar Mitchell," *Human Behavior*, p. 26.

CHAPTER FOURTEEN

1. Personal interview.
2. Personal interview.
3. Personal interview.
4. Personal interview.

NOTES

5. Weltfish, *The Lost Universe*, p. 6.
6. "Frustration: 41 Congressmen to Quit," San Francisco *Sunday Examiner and Chronicle*, April 21, 1974.
7. Barber, "The Presidency After Watergate," *World and Saturday Review*, p. 18.
8. Baker, "Hooked on Knowing It All," San Francisco *Sunday Examiner and Chronicle*, August 5, 1973.
9. Janis, "The Groupthink Follies," San Francisco *Sunday Examiner and Chronicle*, June 17, 1973.
10. Von Hoffman, "The View From The Top," San Francisco *Sunday Examiner and Chronicle*, September 23, 1973.
11. Personal communication, December 22, 1972.
12. *Ibid.*
13. Pines, "How the Social Organization of Animal Communities Can Lead to a Population Crisis Which Destroys Them," *National Institute of Mental Health Mental Health Program Reports—5*, p. 167.
14. Huth, "Population Growth," *Congressional Record*, S4399.
15. *Ibid.*
16. Wigotsky, editor, "Meta-Designer Faces the Future (Calhoun)" *Design News*, reprint, National Institute of Mental Health.
17. Calhoun, "Control of Population: Numbers," *Annals of the New York Academy of Sciences*, p. 151.
18. Calhoun, "Promotion of Man," *Global Systems Dynamics*, p. 57.
19. Pines, "How the Social Organization," p. 171.
20. Calhoun, "The Positive Animal: Increased Human Potential Enhances Stability of the Total Ecosystem and Preserves Evolution," *M.E.S.*, p. 4.
21. *Ibid.*, p. 1.
22. Calhoun, "Promotion of Man," p. 48.
23. *Ibid.*, p. 54.
24. *Ibid.*, p. 50.
25. *Ibid.*, p. 53.
26. Calhoun, "Psycho-Ecological Aspects of Population," *Environmental Essays on the Planet as a Home*, p. 126.
27. *Ibid.*, pp. 125–26.
28. Calhoun, "Promotion," p. 57.
29. Rioch, "All We Like Sheep—(Isaiah 53:6)," *Psychiatry*, p. 266.
30. *Ibid.*, pp. 264–65.
31. *Ibid.*
32. *Ibid.*
33. *Ibid.*, p. 268.
34. *Ibid.*
35. *Ibid.*, p. 271.
36. Personal interview.
37. Rioch, "All We Like Sheep," p. 272.
38. *Ibid.*, p. 258.
39. Personal interview.

CHAPTER FIFTEEN

1. Arbib, "Man-Machine Symbiosis and the Evolution of Human Freedom," *The American Scholar*, p. 46.
2. "Forecasting and Assessing the Impact of Artificial Intelligence on Society," *Proceedings, International Joint Conference on Artificial Intelligence*, p. 11.
3. *Ibid.*, p. 14.
4. *Ibid.*, p. 13.
5. Crichton, *The Terminal Man*, p. 88.
6. Rosenfeld, "Will Man direct His Own Evolution?," p. 108.
7. Toffler, *op. cit.*, p. 213.
8. Feldman, "Projections of the Terminal Man," *Human Behavior*, p. 69.
9. Personal communication.
10. "How Intelligent Can a Computer Be?," *1967 Stanford University Financial Report*, p. 9.
11. *Ibid.*, p. 10.
12. *Ibid.*, p. 11.
13. Winograd, "When Will Computers Understand People?," *Psychology Today*, p. 75.
14. *Ibid.*
15. Glasgow, "Aristocrats Have Always Been Sons of Bitches," *Psychology Today*, p. 63.
16. *Ibid.*
17. *Ibid.*
18. *Ibid.*, p. 64.
19. Ernst, "Computer-Controlled Robots," *IBM Research report*, pp. 4–6.
20. *Ibid.*, p. 7.
21. *Ibid.*, p. 8.
22. *Ibid.*, pp. 14, 17.
23. *Ibid.*, p. 17.
24. *Ibid.*
25. *Ibid.*, p. 4.
26. *Ibid.*, p. 6.
27. Bagley, "A Paradigm for Artificial Intelligence," *IBM Research Report*, p. 1.
28. Gibson, "Do You Know Your Own Levels of Smart?," *Family Weekly*, p. 23.
29. Zobrist and Carlson, "An Advice-Taking Chess Computer," *Scientific American*, p. 100.
30. *Ibid.*
31. *Ibid.*, p. 101.
32. *Ibid.*
33. Arbib, "Models of the Brain," *Science Journal*, p. 7.
34. Petit, "Quest for a Brainy Robot," San Francisco *Chronicle*, February 4, 1974.
35. Stein, "A Look at the Future: Horror or Happiness?", San Francisco *Chronicle*, April 18, 1972.

36. "Forecasting and Assessing," p. 11.
37. Rensberger, "The Chimp Wants to Know," San Francisco *Sunday Examiner and Chronicle,* December 22, 1974.
38. Rensberger, "An Understanding," San Francisco *Sunday Examiner and Chronicle,* June 9. 1974.

CHAPTER SIXTEEN

1. Halberstam, *The Best and the Brightest,* pp. 213–18, 250.
2. Price, "Purists and Politicians," *Science,* p. 31.
3. Whitemore, *The Adventures of Don Quixote* (screenplay), from Cervantes, *Don Quixote de la Mancha.*
4. *Majaraj-Ji, Lord of the Universe* (film).
5. Walcutt, "Road to Freedom," p. 64.
6. "Faye Dunaway Is Into a New Kind of Self-Analysis," *Family Weekly,* November 18, 1973.
7. San Francisco *Chronicle,* "'Krengchai' Runs the Government," July 18, 1974.
8. San Francisco *Sunday Examiner and Chronicle,* "The Military Junta Falls in Athens," July 28, 1974.
9. San Francisco *Sunday Examiner and Chronicle,* "It was No Meeting of the Minds," February 25, 1973.
10. Toffler, *op. cit.,* p. 11.
11. Reich, *The Greening of America,* p. 354.
12. Roszak, *The Making of a Counter Culture,* p. 22.
13. Slater, *Earthwalk,* p. 72.
14. Reich, *Greening,* pp. 381–82.
15. Glasgow, "The Obsessive Concern with Self," *Psychology Today,* p. 44.
16. Oates, "New Heaven and Earth," *Saturday Review,* p. 52.
17. Calef, *et al.,* "Impairments of Ego Function in Psychedelic Drug Users," *Berkeley Center for Drug Studies,* pp. 3–4.
18. *Ibid.,* p. 4.
19. *Ibid.,* p. 10.
20. West and Allen, "The Green Rebellion," *Sooner Magazine,* p. 6.
21. Personal communication, October 10, 1973.
22. McLuhan, *Understanding Media,* p. 152.
23. *Ibid.,* p. 158.
24. *Ibid.,* p. 60.
25. *Ibid.,* p. 108.
26. *Ibid.,* p. 18.
27. *Ibid.*
28. *Ibid.,* p. 108.
29. *Ibid.,* p. 85.
30. *Ibid.,* p. 146.
31. *Ibid.,* p. 145.

32. *Ibid.*, p. 146.
33. *Ibid.*, p. 155.
34. *Ibid.*, p. 152.
35. *Ibid.*, p. 182.
36. *Ibid.*, p. 177.
37. *Ibid.*, pp. 84–85.
38. *Ibid.*, p. 334.
39. *Ibid.*, p. 249.
40. *Ibid.*, p. 294.
41. *Ibid.*, p. 47.
42. *Ibid.*, pp. 312–14.
43. *Ibid.*, p. 308.
44. *Ibid.*, pp. 315, 321–23, 334–35.
45. *Ibid.*, pp. 314, 334–35.
46. *Ibid.*, p. 315.
47. *Ibid.*, p. 351.
48. *Ibid.*, pp. 249–50.
49. *Ibid.*, pp. 321–22.
50. *Ibid.*, pp. vii, 15, 17, 118.
51. *Ibid.*, pp. 108, 152, 186, 248, 344.
52. *Ibid.*, p. 17.
53. *Ibid.*, p. 302.
54. *Ibid.*, p. 199.
55. Reich, *Greening*, p. 274.
56. MacLean, "The Triune Brain, Emotion and Scientific Bias," *The Neurosciences: Second Study Program*, p. 339.
57. *Ibid.*, p. 342.
58. *Ibid.*, pp. 336–37.
59. *Ibid.*, p. 337.
60. Bogen, "Other Side of the Brain," II, p. 156.
61. Digges, "We're in a Grotesque Endemic State of Psychosis. But It Will Pass," *Human Behavior*, p. 22.
62. Aspen, Review of "Depression and the Body," *Psychology Today*, p. 124.
63. Cousins, "The Improbable Triumvirate," *World and Saturday Review*, p. 14.
64. Boynton, "James Prescott: Touching," *Intellectual Digest*, p. 10.
65. Keen, "A Conversation with Ernest Becker," *Psychology Today*, p. 78.
66. Slater, "Earthwalk," p. 194.

BIBLIOGRAPHY

BOOKS

AARONSON, BERNARD and HUMPHRY OSMOND. *Psychedelics: The Use and Implications of Hallucinogenic Drugs.* Doubleday, 1970.

ALTMAN, JOSEPH. *The Organic Foundations of Animal Behavior.* M.I.T. Press, 1967–68.

ARBIB, MICHAEL A. "Cognition—A Cybernetic Approach," in *Cognition: A Multiple View,* Paul L. Garvin, ed. Spartan Books, 1970.

ASIMOV, ISAAC. *The Human Brain.* Signet Books, New American Library, 1963.

BALL, W. W. ROUSE. *Mathematical Recreations and Essays.* Macmillan and Company, 1947.

BARONDES, SAMUEL H., and LARRY R. SQUIRE. "Time and the Biology of Memory," in *Clinical Neurosurgery.* Williams and Wilkins, 1972.

BARRON, FRANK. *Creative Person and Creative Process.* Holt, 1969.

BATESON, GREGORY. *Steps to an Ecology of the Mind.* Chandler Publishing Company, 1972.

BEER, STAFFORD. "The Liberty Machine," in *Cybernetics, Artificial Intelligence and Ecology,* H. W. Robinson and D. E. Knight, eds. Spartan Books, 1972.

BERGSON, HENRI L. *Creative Evolution.* Greenwood, 1946.

BERNSTEIN, LEONARD. *The Joy of Music.* Simon, 1959.

BLAU, ABRAM. *The Master Hand.* American Orthopsychiatric Association, 1946.

BOAZ, FRANZ. *Mind of Primitive Man.* Free Press, 1965.

BOGEN, J. E., R. W. SPERRY, and P. J. VOGEL. "Addendum: Commissural Section and Propagation of Seizures," in *Basic Mechanisms of the Epilepsies.* Little, Brown and Company, 1969.

BOULDING, KENNETH. *The Image.* University of Michigan Press, 1956.

BOULLE, PIERRE. *Planet of the Apes,* Vanguard Press, 1963.

BOWERS, FAUBIAN. *The New Scriabin: Enigma and Answers.* St. Martin's, 1973.

457

BIBLIOGRAPHY

BRAGINSKY, BENJAMIN and DORTHEA. *Hansels and Gretels*. Harper, Row & World, 1971.

BROWN, BARBARA. *New Mind, New Body*. Harper & Row, 1974.

BUROS, OSCAR K. *The 1940 Mental Measurements Yearbook*. Gryphon Press, 1940.

_____. *The 1972 Mental Measurements Yearbook*. Gryphon Press, 1972.

CALHOUN, JOHN B. "Psycho-Ecological Aspects of Population," in *Environmental Essays on the Planet as a Home*. Houghton Mifflin Company, 1971.

CAMPBELL, H. J. *The Pleasure Areas*. Delacorte Press, 1974.

CATTELL, RAYMOND BERNARD. "Are I.Q. Tests Intelligent?" in *Readings in Psychology Today*. Communications/Research/Machines, Inc., 1969.

CERVANTES, MIGUEL DE. *Don Quixote de la Mancha*, J. M. Cohen translation. Penguin Books, 1950, as adapted for television by Hugh Whitemore in *The Adventures of Don Quixote*, produced for the Columbia Broadcasting System by Universal Television and BBC TV for showing on April 23, 1973.

CHASE, RICHARD S. "Behavioral Biology and Environmental Design," in *Psychopathology*. John Wiley & Sons, 1972.

CLARK, RONALD W. *Einstein, The Life and Times*. World Publishing Company, 1971.

COLE, MICHAEL, JOHN GAY, JOSEPH A. GLICK, DONALD W. SHARP. *The Cultural Context of Learning and Thinking*. Basic Books, 1971.

COLEMAN, JAMES S. *Equality of Educational Opportunity*. Study for the U.S. Commission on Civil Rights. Government Printing Office, 1966.

COOPER, L.A., and R. N. SHEPARD. "The Time Required to Prepare for a Rotated Stimulus," in *Visual Information Processing*, W. G. Chase, ed. Academic Press, 1973.

COPLAND, AARON. *Music and Imagination*. Harvard University Press, 1953.

CRAFT, ROBERT. *Stravinsky: Retrospectives and Conclusion*. A. A. Knopf, 1969.

CRICHTON, MICHAEL. *The Terminal Man*. Knopf, 1972.

CRUTCHFIELD, RICHARD S. "Nurturing the Cognitive Skills of Productive Thinking," in *The Yearbook of the Association for Supervision and Curriculum Development*, 1969.

DARLINGTON, C. D. *The Evolution of Man and Society*. Simon and Schuster, 1969.

_____. *The Facts of Life*. Allen & Unwin, 1953.

"*Day Facilities for the Mentally Retarded*." Data prepared by the Division of

Mental Retardation, Rehabilitation Services Administration, Social and Rehabilitation Service. Government Printing Office, 1968–69.

DEAKIN, MICHAEL. *The Children on the Hill.* Bobbs-Merrill, 1972.

DE GROOT, ADRIANUS DINGMAN. *Thought and Choice in Chess.* Mouton, 1965.

DELGADO, JOSÉ M. R. *Physical Control of the Mind.* Harper Colophon Books, 1971.

DE ROOP, ROBERT S. *The New Prometheans.* Delacorte, 1972.

DILLARD, ANNIE. *Pilgrim at Tinker Creek.* Harper Magazine Press, 1974.

ECKSTEIN, GUSTAV. *The Body Has a Head.* Harper & Row, 1970.

EHRMAN, LEE, GILBERT OMENN, and ERNST CASPARI. *Genetics, Environment and Behavior.* Academic Press, 1972.

EWEN, DAVID. *George Gershwin.* Prentice-Hall, 1970.

EYSENCK, H. J. *Know Your Own I.Q.* Penguin Books, Ltd., 1962.

FAST, JULIUS. *Body Language.* Pocket Books, 1971.

FAURE, RAOUL. *Spear in the Sand.* Harper, 1946.

FISHER, LEONARD J. *Give Your Baby a Chance.* Compass Publications, Hong Kong, 1968.

FIXX, JAMES F. *Games for the Superintelligent.* Doubleday, 1972.

GALAMBOS, ROBERT. "Brain Correlates of Learning (Introduction)" in *The Neurosciences: First Study Program,* Quarton, Melnechuk & Schmitt, eds. Rockefeller University Press, 1967.

GALLWEY, W. TIMOTHY. *The Inner Game of Tennis.* Random House, 1974.

GALTON, FRANCIS. *Art of Travel, or Shifts and Contrivances Available in Wild Countries.* (1872). Stackpole Books, 1971.

————. *Hereditary Genius.* Macmillan (1869), 1914.

————. *Human Faculty.* Macmillan, 1883.

————. *Natural Inheritance.* Macmillan, 1889.

GARDNER, HOWARD. *The Shattered Mind.* Knopf, 1975.

GARY, ROMAIN. *The Gasp.* Putnam, 1973.

GAZZANIGA, MICHAEL S. *The Bisected Brain.* Appleton-Century-Crofts, 1971.

GODDARD, HENRY H. *The Kallikak Family.* Macmillan, 1923.

GOERTZEL, VICTOR, and MILDRED G. *Cradles of Eminence.* Little, 1962.

GORDON WILLIAM J. J. *Synectics.* Harper & Row, 1961.

HALACY, D. S., JR. *Man and Memory.* Harper & Row, 1970.

HALBERSTAM, DAVID. *The Best and the Brightest.* Random House, 1972.

HALE, WILLIAM HARLAN, and THE EDITORS OF TIME-LIFE BOOKS. *The World of Rodin.* Time-Life Books, 1969.

BIBLIOGRAPHY

HAMILTON, BRUTUS. *The Worlds of Brutus Hamilton,* Lawrence Baack, ed. Published by *Track & Field News,* 1975.

HASKELL, ARNOLD L. *Balletomania.* Simon and Schuster, 1934.

HERRNSTEIN, RICHARD. *I.Q. in the Meritocracy.* Atlantic Monthly Press, 1973.

HERSEY, JOHN. *The Child Buyer.* Alfred Knopf, 1960.

HOGBEN, LANCELOT. *Statistical Theory.* Norton, 1968.

HOLT, JOHN. *Escape from Childhood.* Dutton, 1974.

HUNT, J. MCVICKER, ed. *Human Intelligence.* E. P. Dutton and Co., 1972.

HUXLEY, ALDOUS. *The Doors of Perception.* Harper & Row, 1963.

JACOBSON, NILS-OLOF. *Leben nach dem Tod* (Life After Death). Econ Publishers, 1972.

JANIS, IRVING. *Victims of Groupthink.* Houghton Mifflin, 1973.

JENCKS, CHRISTOPHER. *Inequality.* Basic Books, 1972.

JENSEN, ARTHUR. *Genetics and Education.* Harper & Row, 1972.

———. "Heritability and Teachability." From *Emerging Issues in Education,* J. E. Bruno, ed. D. C. Heath & Co, 1972.

———. "The Race Sex X Ability Interaction." From *Intelligence: Genetic & Environmental Influences,* Robert Cancro, ed. Grune & Stratton, 1971.

JERISON, HARRY J. A marketing questionnaire for *Evolution of the Brain and Intelligence.* Academic Press, 1973.

———. *Evolution of the Brain and Intelligence.* Academic Press, 1973.

JONES, MARY COVER, NANCY BAYLEY, and JEAN WALKER MACFARLANE, and MARJORIE HONZIK. *The Course of Human Development.* Xerox College Publishing, 1971.

JUNG, CARL G. *Man and His Symbols.* Dell, 1968.

KELLER, HELEN. *The Story of My Life.* Houghton Mifflin, 1928.

KOESTLER, ARTHUR. *The Act of Creation.* Hutchinson, 1964.

———. *The Ghost in the Machine.* Macmillan, 1968.

LANSDELL, HERBERT. "Comments on Brain Mechanisms Suggested by Studies of Parietal Lobes, by Henry Hecaen," in *Brain Mechanisms Underlying Speech and Language,* F. L. Darley, ed. Grune & Stratton, 1967.

LILLY, JOHN. *The Center of the Cyclone.* Julian Press, 1972.

LINDSAY, PETER H., and DONALD A. NORMAN. *Human Information Processing.* Academic Press, 1972.

LONDON, PERRY. *Behavior Control.* Harper & Row, 1969.

LORD, JAMES. *A Giacometti Portrait.* Museum of Modern Art (publishers), 1965.

LOVAAS, O. IVAR, and ROBERT L. KOEGEL. "Behavior Therapy with

Autistic Children," in *The Seventy-Second Yearbook,* Part I, *of The National Society for the Study of Education.* Behavior Modification (Publishers), 1973.

LOWEN, ALEXANDER. *The Betrayal of the Body.* Collier Books, 1967.

LUCE, GAY GAER. *Body Time.* Bantam, 1973.

LURIA, A. R. *The Mind of the Mnemonist.* Avon Discus Books, 1968.

MACCOBY, ELEANOR, and CAROL NAGY JACKLIN. *The Psychology of Sex Differences.* Stanford University Press, 1974.

MACLEAN, PAUL D. "The Paranoid Streak in Man," in *Beyond Reductionism.* Hutchinson and Company, 1969.

————. "The Triune Brain, Emotion, and Scientific Bias," in *The Neurosciences: Second Study Program,* F. O. Schmitt, ed. Rockefeller University Press, 1970.

MANDELL, ARNOLD J., and MARK A. GEYER. "The Euphoro-Hallucinogens," in *The Comprehensive Textbook of Psychiatry,* Freedman, Kaplan and Sadock, eds. Williams and Wilkins, 1974.

MANKIEWICZ, HERMAN J., and ORSON WELLES. *Citizen Kane.* The shooting script, July 16, 1940.

MARSDEN, HALSEY M. "Crowding and Animal Behavior," in *Environment and the Social Sciences: Perspectives and Applications,* J. F. Wohlwill and D. H. Carson, eds. American Psychological Association, 1972.

MCCONNELL, JAMES V., and JESSIE M. SHELBY. "Memory Transfer Experiments in Invertebrates," in *Molecular Mechanisms in Memory and Learning.* Plenum Press, 1970.

MCLUHAN, MARSHALL. *Understanding Media.* McGraw, 1964.

MCNEILL, DAVID. *The Acquisition of Language.* Harper & Row, 1970.

MILLER, ARTHUR. *Death of a Salesman,* in *New Voices in The American Theater,* Bennett Cerf, ed. Modern Library, Random House, 1955.

MONEY, JOHN. "Determinants of Human Sexual Identity and Behavior," in *Progress in Group and Family Therapy,* C. G. Sager and H. S. Kaplan, eds. Bruner/Mazel Publishers, 1972.

————, and ANKE A. EHRHARDT. "Gender Dimorphic Behavior and Fetal Sex Hormones," in *Recent Progress in Hormone Research,* E. B. Astwood, ed. Academic Press, 1972.

————. "Intellect, Brain and Biologic Age: Introduction," in *Human Growth: Body Composition, Cell Growth, Energy and Intelligence,* D. B. Cheek, ed. Lea & Febiger, 1968.

MOORE, SONIA. *The Stanislavski System.* Viking, 1965.

————. *Training an Actor.* Viking, 1968.

MOREHEAD, DONALD M. "A Piagetian Approach to Language Training," in *Language Perspectives, Acquisition, Retardation and Intervention*, Richard L. Schiefelbusch and Lyle L. Lloyd, eds. University Park Press, 1974.

_____. "The Study of Linguistically Defective Children," in *Measurement in Hearing, Speech and Language*, L. Sadanand Singh, ed. University Park Press, 1975.

MORGENSTERN, SAM. *Composers on Music*. Pantheon, 1956.

MUNTHE, AXEL. *The Story of San Michele*. Murray, 1929.

MURPHY, MICHAEL. *Golf in the Kingdom*. Viking, 1972.

MUSSEN, PAUL, MARK R. ROSENZWEIG, *et al. Psychology: An Introduction*. D. C. Heath, 1973.

NIJINSKY, ROMOLA. *Nijinsky*. Simon and Schuster, 1934.

NUREYEV, RUDOLPH. *Nureyev: An Autobiography*. Dutton, 1963.

O'BRIEN, ROBERT C. *Mrs. Frisby and the Rats of NIMH*. Atheneum, 1971.

OLTON, ROBERT M., and RICHARD S. CRUTCHFIELD. "Developing the Skills of Productive Thinking," in *Trends and Issues in Developmental Psychology*. Holt, Rinehart, Winston, 1969.

ORNSTEIN, ROBERT E. *The Psychology of Consciousness*. W. H. Freeman and Company, 1972.

PEARSON, HESKETH. *Bernard Shaw: His Life and Personality*. Oxford University Press, 1942.

PERLS, FREDERICK S. *Gestalt Therapy Verbatim*. Real People Press, 1969.

PIAGET, JEAN, and BARBEL INHELDER. *Memory and Intelligence*. Basic Books, 1973.

PICK, HERBERT L., JR., and ANNE D. PICK. "Sensory and Perceptual Development," in *Carmichael's Manual of Child Psychology*, Paul Mussen, ed. Vol. 1. John Wiley, 1970.

PINES, MAYA. *The Brain-Changers*. Harcourt Brace Jovanovich, 1973.

QUARTON, GARDNER C., THEODORE MELNECHUK, and FRANCIS O. SCHMITT. *The Neurosciences: First Study Program*. Rockefeller University Press, 1967.

RADIN, PAUL. *Primitive Man as a Philosopher*. Appleton, 1927.

REGAN, DAVID. *Evoked Potentials in Psychology, Sensory Physiology and Clinical Medicine*. John Wiley, 1972.

REICH, CHARLES A. *The Greening of America*. Bantam Books, 1971.

RICHARDSON, KEN, and DAVID SPEARS, eds. *Race and Intelligence*. Penguin Books, 1972.

RIMLAND, BERNARD. *Infantile Autism*. Appleton-Century-Crofts, 1964.

ROMBAUER, I. S., and M. R. BECKER. *The Joy of Cooking*. Bobbs-Merrill, New York, 1953.

BIBLIOGRAPHY

ROSLANSKY, JOHN D., ed. *The Human Mind.* Fleet Academic Editions, 1967.

ROSZAK, BETTY, ed. *Masculine Feminine: Readings in Sexual Mythology and the Liberation of Woman.* Harper & Row, 1970.

ROSZAK, THEODORE. *The Making of a Counter Culture.* Anchor Books, Doubleday, 1969.

———. *Where the Wasteland Ends.* Doubleday, 1972.

RUESCH, JURGEN, and WELDON KEES. *Nonverbal Communication.* University of California Press, 1956.

SARGENT, S. STANSFELD. *Great Psychologists.* Barnes & Noble, 1944.

SCHMITT, FRANCIS O., ed. *The Neurosciences: Second Study Program.* Rockefeller University Press, 1970.

SHAHN, BEN. *The Shape of Content.* Harvard University Press, 1957.

SKINNER, B. F. *Beyond Freedom and Dignity.* Knopf, 1971.

SLATER, PHILIP. *Earthwalk.* Doubleday, 1974.

———. *The Pursuit of Loneliness.* Beacon Press, 1970.

SPEARMAN, CHARLES. *The Nature of Intelligence.* Macmillan, 1927.

SPERRY, R. W. "Cerebral Dominance in Perception," in *Early Experience in Visual Information Processing in Perceptual and Reading Disorders,* F. A. Young and D. B. Lindsley, eds. National Academy of Science, 1970.

———. "How a Developing Brain Gets Itself Properly Wired for Adaptive Function," in *The Biopsychology of Development,* Tobach, Shaw and Aronson, eds. Academic Press, 1971.

———. "Lateral Specialization of Cerebral Function in the Surgically Separated Hemispheres," in *The Psychophysiology of Thinking.* Academic Press, 1973.

———. "Mental Phenomena as Causal Determinants," in *Mind and Brain: Philosophical and Scientific Approaches to the Single "World Knot."* Globus, Maxwell and Sarodnik, eds. Plenum, 1974.

———. "Perception in the Absence of the Neocortical Commissures." From *Perception and its Disorders.* The Association for Research in Nervous and Mental Disease, 1970.

———. "Split-Brain Approach to Learning Problems," in *The Neurosciences: First Study Program,* Quarton, Melnechuk, Schmitt. Rockefeller University Press, 1967.

STAFFORD, PETER, and BONNIE GOLIGHTLY. *LSD: The Problem-Solving Psychedelic.* Award, 1967.

STEIGER, BRAD. *The Psychic Feats of Olaf Jonsson.* Popular Library, 1971.

TERMAN, LEWIS. *Genetic Studies of Genius.* Stanford University Press, 1926–59. 5 vols.

BIBLIOGRAPHY

———, and M. A. MERRILL. *The Stanford-Binet Intelligence Scale*. Houghton Mifflin, 1960.

THOMAS, LEWIS. *The Lives of a Cell*. Viking, 1974.

THORNDIKE, ROBERT L. *Stanford-Binet Intelligence Scale—Norm Tables*. Houghton Mifflin, 1972.

TOFFLER, ALVIN. *Future Shock*. Bantam Books, 1971.

TORRANCE, E. P. *Rewarding Creative Behavior*. Prentice-Hall, 1965.

TURNBULL, COLIN. *The Forest People*. Simon and Schuster, 1961.

VAN GOGH, VINCENT. *Van Gogh's Diary*, as compiled by the New York Graphic Society. Morrow, 1970.

VON SENDEN, MARIUS. *Space and Sight*. Methuen & Co., 1960.

WASHBURN, S. L. "The Evolution of Human Behavior," in *The Uniqueness of Man*, John D. Roslansky, ed. North-Holland, 1968.

WEIL, ANDREW. *The Natural Mind*. Houghton Mifflin, 1973.

WELTFISH, GENE. *The Lost Universe*. Ballantine, 1965.

WHITE, CARROLL T., and M. RUSSELL HARTER. "Intermittency in Reaction Time and Perception and Evoked Response Correlates of Image Quality." From *Acta Psychologica 3. Attention and Performance II*, W. G. Koster, ed. North-Holland, 1969.

———. "The Visual Evoked Response and Patterned Stimuli," in *Advances in Psychobiology*, G. Newton and Austin H. Riesen, eds. John Wiley, 1974.

WHITE, E. B. *Second Tree from the Corner*. Harper, 1935.

WIENER, NORBERT. *Ex-Prodigy*. M. I. T. Press, 1953.

WING, C. W., JR., and M. A. WALLACH. *College Admissions and the Psychology of Talent*. Holt, Rinehart and Winston, 1971.

———. *The Talented Student*. Holt, Rinehart and Winston, 1969.

ZAMENHOF, STEPHEN, EDITH VAN MARTHENS, and LUDMILLA GRAUEL. "Studies on Some Factors Influencing Prenatal Brain Development," in *Regulation of Organ and Tissue Growth*. Academic Press, 1972.

ZIMBARDO, PHILIP G., and FLOYD L. RUCH. *Psychology and Life*. Scott, Foresman, 1975.

ARTICLES

ALEXANDER, DUANE, ANKE A. EHRHARDT, and JOHN MONEY. "Defective Figure Drawing, Geometric and Human, in Turner's Syndrome." *The Journal of Nervous and Mental Disease,* Vol. 152., No. 2 (1966).

ALLEN, ALLEN D. "Does Matter Exist?" *Foundations of Physics* (December, 1973).

ALLPORT, GORDON W., and THOMAS E. PETTIGREW. "Cultural Influence on the Perception of Movement: The Trapezoidal Illusion Among Zulus." *The Journal of Abnormal and Social Psychology* (July, 1957).

American Education, Special Issue on the Gifted and Talented (October, 1972).

ANDERSON, JACK. "My Lai 'Just Like Killing Animals.'" San Francisco *Chronicle* (August 2, 1973).

"Arab Princes Drop $1 Million in Vegas." San Francisco *Chronicle* (December 14, 1974).

ARBIB, MICHAEL A. "Brains, Computers, and Systems Theory." *IEEE Student Journal* (January, 1970). Published by the Institute for Electrical and Electronic Engineers.

_____. "Complex Systems: The Case for a Marriage of Science and Intuition." *The American Scholar* (Winter, 1972–73).

_____. "Man-Machine Symbiosis and the Evolution of Human Freedom." *The American Scholar* (Winter, 1973–74).

_____. "Models of the Brain," *Science Journal* (May, 1967).

_____. "Toward an Automatic Theory of Brains." *Communications of the Association for Computing Machinery, Inc.* (July, 1972).

AREHART-TREICHEL, JEAN. "Computers and Nature." San Francisco *Sunday Examiner and Chronicle* (December 2, 1973).

ARMOR, DAVID J. "The Evidence of Busing." *Public Interest* (Summer, 1972).

ARONSON, ELLIOT. "The Rationalizing Animal." *Psychology Today* (May, 1973).

465

ASHER, JULES. "John Ertl's Neural Efficiency Analyzer—Bias-Free Test or Just a 'Neat Gadget'?" *APA* [American Psychological Association] *Monitor* (March, 1973).

ASIMOV, ISAAC. "I Can't Believe I Saw the Whole Thing." *Saturday Review* (September 2, 1972).

ASPEN, RICHARD. "Depression and the Body." A review of the book by Alexander Lowen in *Psychology Today* (December, 1973).

BAKER, RUSSELL. "Hooked on Knowing It All." San Francisco *Sunday Examiner and Chronicle* (August 5, 1973).

BANE, MARY JO, and CHRISTOPHER JENCKS. "Five Myths About Your I.Q." *Harper's* (April, 1973).

————. "The Schools and Equal Opportunity." *Saturday Review* (of education) (September 16, 1972).

BARBER, JOHN DAVID. "The Presidency After Watergate." *World and Saturday Review* (July 31, 1973).

BARBER, THEODORE X., and WILLIAM B. MEEKER. "Out of Sight, Out of Mind." *Human Behavior* (August, 1974).

BARNEY, WALTER. "Who Is G. Spencer Brown and Where Is That Marvelous Music Coming From?" *Pacific Sun* (September 6–12, 1973).

BARONDES, SAMUEL. "Memory Transfer." A review of *Chemical Transfer of Learned Information* by Ejnar J. Fjerdingstad, North-Holland, Amsterdam and New York, publishers, 1971. *Science* (May 12, 1971).

BAYLEY, NANCY, LEANNE RHODES, BILL GOOCH, and MARILYN MARCUS. "Environmental Factors in the Development of Institutionalized Children." *Exceptional Infant*, Vol. 2, Studies in Abnormalities (1971).

BELCHER, JERRY. "Scouts Having Financial Problems, Too." San Francisco *Sunday Examiner and Chronicle.* (June 16, 1974).

BELL, JIM. "Our President, the Southpaw." San Francisco *Sunday Examiner and Chronicle* (October 20, 1974).

BEREITER, CARL. "The Future of Individual Differences." *Harvard Educational Review* (1969).

BERMAN, SUSAN. "They Are My Sisters, Too." San Francisco *Sunday Examiner and Chronicle, California Living Magazine* (March 31, 1974).

BESS, DONOVAN. "Attack on College Entrance Tests." San Francisco *Chronicle* (March 31, 1973).

BINDRIM, PAUL. "Running Naked Is Good for You." San Francisco *Examiner and Chronicle* (April 7, 1974).

"Biofeedback—Teaching Your Body to Heal Itself." *Family Health* (February, 1974).

"Biological Imperatives." An article about John Money. *Time* (January 8, 1972).

466

BIBLIOGRAPHY

BITTERMAN, M. E. "The Evolution of Intelligence." *Scientific American* (January, 1965).

BLAKEMORE, COLIN, and DONALD E. MITCHELL. "Environmental Modification of the Visual Cortex and the Neural Basis of Learning and Memory." *Nature* (February 16, 1973).

_____. "Why We See What We See." *New Scientist and Science Journal* (September 16, 1971).

BLAKESEE, SANDRA. "How Babies Learn to Talk." San Francisco *Chronicle* (April 24, 1973).

BOGEN, J. E, and M. S. GAZZANIGA. "Cerebral Commissurotomy in Man, Minor Hemisphere Dominance for Certain Visuospatial Functions." *Journal of Neurosurgery*, Vol XXIII, No. 4 (1965).

BOGEN, JOSEPH E. "The Other Side of the Brain—I: Dysgraphia and Dyscopia Following Cerebral Commissurotomy." *Bulletin of the Los Angeles Neurological Society* (April, 1969).

_____. "The Other Side of the Brain—II: An Appositional Mind." *Bulletin of the Los Angeles Neurological Society* (July, 1969).

_____. "The Other Side of the Brain—III: The Corpus Callosum and Creativity." *Bulletin of the Los Angeles Neurological Society* (October, 1969).

BOGEN, JOSEPH E., R. DeZURE, W. H. TENHOUTEN, and J. F. MARSH. "The Other Side of the Brain—IV: The A/P Ratio." *Bulletin of the Los Angeles Neurological Society* (April, 1972).

BOLEN, JEAN SHINODA. "Meditation and Psychotherapy in the Treatment of Cancer." *Psychic Magazine.* (July–August, 1973).

"Boom Time on the Psychic Frontier." *Time* (March 4, 1974).

BOULDING, KENNETH. "Aristocrats Have Always Been Sons of Bitches." Interview with Robert W. Glasgow in *Psychology Today* (January, 1973).

"Boys vs. Girls." *Human Behavior* (March, 1973).

BOWDEN, JUDITH, HERMAN H. SPITZ, and JOHN J. WINTERS, JR. "Follow Up of One Retarded Couple's Marriage. *Mental Retardation* (December, 1971).

BOWER, GORDON H. "Analysis of a Mnemonic Device." *American Scientist* (September/October, 1970).

_____. "How to . . . Uh . . . Remember." *Psychology Today* (October, 1973).

BOYNTON, BARBARA. "Work in Progress—James Prescott: Touching." Interview in *Intellectual Digest* (March, 1974).

BRAGINSKY, DORTHEA D. and BENJAMIN M. "The Mentally Retarded: Society's Hansels and Gretels." *Psychology Today* (March, 1974).

467

BIBLIOGRAPHY

"Brain, The." A series by the editors. *Life* (October 1, 22, November 12, 26, 1971).

BRAZZIEL, WILLIAM F. "A Letter from the South." A commentary on Jensen's paper. *Harvard Educational Review* (1969).

BRIER, ROYCE. "About Geniuses and Industry." San Francisco *Chronicle* (September 21, 1972).

BRODY, JANE. "Best-Kept Brains." San Francisco *Sunday Examiner and Chronicle* (November 19, 1972).

BRONFENBRENNER, URIE. "Tear Down the Walls." Interview by Natalie Davis Spingarn in *Scholastic Teacher* (October, 1973).

BROOKS, MEL. "An Act of Self-Preservation." Interview by Charles Champlin in San Francisco *Chronicle* (June 23, 1974).

BROPHY, JERE E., and THOMAS L. GOOD. "Teacher Expectations: Beyond the Pygmalian Controversy." *Phi Delta Kappan* (December, 1973).

BROWN, ELEANOR. "A Progress Report on Biofeedback." San Francisco *Sunday Examiner and Chronicle* (June 23, 1974).

BROZAN, NADINE. "The Dark Side of Women's Liberation." San Francisco *Chronicle*. (July 13, 1974).

BRUCK, CONNIE. "The Sports Experience: Women's Consciousness-Raising Division." *Human Behavior* (August, 1974).

BRUNER, JEROME. "Continuity of Learning." *Saturday Review* (March, 1973).

BURT, CYRIL. "Inheritance of General Intelligence." *American Psychologist* (March, 1972).

CALDER, NIGEL. "When the Next Ice Age Comes Don't Say We Didn't Warn You." San Francisco *Sunday Examiner and Chronicle* (December 22, 1974).

CALHOUN, JOHN B. "Control of Population: Numbers." *Annals of the New York Academy of Sciences* (June 7, 1971).

———. "Death Squared: The Explosive Growth and Demise of a Mouse Population." Proceedings, *Royal Society of Medicine,* Vol. 66 (1973).

———. "Engineering and the Urban Crisis—Part 3: Urban Congestion." *Design News* (September 15, 1970).

———. "Population Density and Social Pathology." *Scientific American* (February, 1962).

———. "The Positive Animal: Increased Human Potentiality Enhances Stability of the Total Ecosystem and Preserves Evolution." *M.E.S.* (September, 1971).

———. "Promotion of Man." Global Systems Dynamics International Symposium, Charlottesville, 1969.

———, and THOMAS HUTH. "Population Growth." Written testimony in the *Congressional Record,* Vol. 117, No. 47 (April 1, 1971).

BIBLIOGRAPHY

CAMPBELL, COLIN. "Transcendence Is as American as Ralph Waldo Emerson." *Psychology Today* (April, 1974).

CARDINALI, DANIEL P., FRANCES LEVIN, and RICHARD J. WURTMAN. "Control of the Rat Pineal Gland by Light Spectra." *Proceedings of the National Academy of Sciences* (August, 1972).

CARROLL, JERRY. "Heavenly Bodies in the Courtroom." San Francisco *Chronicle* (August 6, 1974).

CHAMPION, DALE. "Safe Place for Newts." San Francisco *Chronicle* (December 13, 1974).

"Checkout Computers for the 1984 Supermarket." San Francisco *Chronicle* (October 1, 1974).

"Child Can Get Bored in the Womb." San Francisco *Chronicle* (November 5, 1974).

"Chile Now Run by a Computer." San Francisco *Chronicle* (January 15, 1973).

"Chimp to Study 'Language' at Stanford." *The Independent-Journal* by United Press International (October 4, 1974).

CHOMSKY, NOAM. "Language and the Mind." *Psychology Today* (February, 1968).

CHOROVER, STEPHAN L. "Big Brother and Psychotechnology." *Psychology Today* (October, 1973).

———. "The Pacification of the Brain." *Psychology Today* (May, 1974).

CLARK, GEOFFREY M., STEPHEN ZAMENHOF, EDITH VAN MARTHENS, LUDMILLA GRAUEL, and LAWRENCE KRUGER. "The Effect of Prenatal Malnutrition on Dimensions of Cerebral Cortex." *Brain Research*, No. 54 (1973).

CLARKE, ARTHUR. "A Look at the Future: Horror or Happiness." Interview by Ruthe Stein in San Francisco *Chronicle*, April 18, 1972.

CLARKE, LOUISE. "The World of the Dyslexic Child." *Family Health* (October, 1974).

CLYNES, MANFRED. "The Pure Pulse of Musical Genius." *Psychology Today* (July, 1974).

CODDINGTON, LEW. "A Psychiatrist With New Ways." *The Independent Journal* (July 30, 1974).

COHEN, DAVID B. "To Sleep, Perchance to Recall A Dream: 'Repression Is Not the Demon Who Conceals and Hoards Our Forgotten Dreams.'" *Psychology Today* (May, 1974).

COLE, J. "Laterality in the Use of the Hand, Foot, and Eye in Monkeys." *Journal of Comparative Physiology and Psychology*, Vol. 50 (1957).

COLEMAN, PAUL D. and AUSTIN H. RIESEN. "Environmental Effects on Cortical Dendritic Fields." *Journal of Anatomy* (March, 1968).

COMMANDAY, ROBERT. "The Collective Composition's Inscrutable Mys-

BIBLIOGRAPHY

tery." San Francisco *Sunday Examiner and Chronicle* (July 29, 1973).

————. "Sophisticate or Not, We Need Both Ears." San Francisco *Examiner and Chronicle* (December 22, 1974).

"Computer 'Supervises' Construction." *P G & E Progress* (December 1974). Published by Pacific Gas & Electric Co.

"Computers Helping with Career Choice." *The Independent-Journal* (October 22, 1974).

CONSIDINE, BOB. "Rule of the Robot Is Getting Close." San Francisco *Sunday Examiner and Chronicle* (August 5, 1973).

"Control of Life." *Life* (September 10, 17, 24, October 1, 1965).

COON, CARLETON S. "Some Problems of Human Variability and Natural Selection in Climate and Culture." *The American Naturalist* (September–October, 1955).

"Correspondence: Political, Technical, and Theoretical Comments," on Jensen's Paper. *Harvard Educational Review* (Summer, 1969).

COTTLE, THOMAS. "Big City Busing and the Golden Opportunity." *The Urban Review* (September–October, 1972).

————. "If B. J. Harris' I.Q. Score Was Faked—Why? And How Many More Might There Be?" *Learning* (November, 1974).

"Court Limits Psychosurgery." San Francisco *Chronicle* (July 11, 1973).

COUSINS, NORMAN. "The Improbable Triumvirate." *World and Saturday Review* (July 31, 1973).

CRAIK, F. I. M. "Primary Memory." *British Medical Bulletin (On Cognitive Psychology)*, Vol. 27, No. 3 (1971).

CRAIK, FERGUS. "When Memory Fades. . . ." *New Scientist* (February 24, 1972).

CRONBACH, LEE J. "Heredity, Environment, and Educational Policy." A Commentary on Jensen's Paper. *Harvard Educational Review* (1969).

CROW, JAMES F. "Genetic Theories and Influences: Comments on the Value of Diversity." A Commentary on Jensen's Paper. *Harvard Educational Review* (Spring, 1969).

CURTIS, L. R. "A Caesarean to Avoid Brain Damage." San Francisco *Chronicle*.

DALKEY, NORMAN. "Analysis from a Group Opinion Study." *Futures* (December, 1969).

————. "An Experimental Study of Group Opinion—The Delphi Method." *Futures* (September, 1969).

DALTON, KATHARINA. "Ante-Natal Progesteron and Intelligence." *British Journal of Psychiatry*, No. 114 (1968).

DANIELS, NORMAN. "The Smart White Man's Burden." *Harper's* (October, 1973).

470

BIBLIOGRAPHY

DANNER, FRED W., and ARTHUR M. TAYLOR. "Integrated Picture and Relational Imagery Training in Children's Learning." *Journal of Experimental Child Psychology,* No. 16. (1973).

DELLAS, MARIE, and EUGENE L. GAIER. "Identification of Creativity: The Individual." *Psychological Bulletin,* Vol. 73, No. 1 (1970).

DEUTSCH, MARTIN. "The Jensen Controversy (Continued)." *Psychology Today* (July, 1974).

DIAMOND, EDWIN. "Can Exercise Improve Your Brain Power?" *The Reader's Digest* (May, 1973).

DIVOKY, DIANE. "Education's Latest Victim: The 'LD' Kid." *Learning* (October, 1974).

———. "Toward a Nation of Sedated Children." *Learning* (March, 1973).

"Do Electric Fields Affect Behavior?" *Psychology Today* (Newsline) (March, 1974).

"Do You Know Your Own Levels of Smart?" *Family Weekly* (June 2, 1974).

DOBZHANSKY, THEODOSIUS. "Differences Are Not Defects." *Psychology Today* (December, 1973).

DOLINAR, LOUIS. "Public Education for the Handicapped." *Learning* (March, 1973).

DOUGLASS, JOSEPH H. "Guest Editorial: A 'New Thrust' Approach to Mental Retardation." *American Journal of Mental Deficiency,* Vol. 76, No. 2 (1971).

DOUST, DUDLEY. "Tony Jacklin—Mystical Perception in Sport." London *Sunday Times* (November 4, 1973).

DREWES, CAROLINE. "His Story of Reviving a Lost Art." San Francisco *Sunday Examiner and Chronicle* (August 4, 1974).

———. "Why She Teaches Adults to Play." San Francisco *Sunday Examiner and Chronicle* (November 17, 1974).

DUCKWORTH, ELEANOR. "Piaget Takes a Teacher's Look. *Learning* (October, 1973).

"Dutch Find Universe's Biggest Thing." San Francisco *Chronicle* (October 18, 1974).

EDSON, LEE. "Jensenism. n. The Theory That I.Q. Is Largely Determined By the Genes." *New York Times Magazine* (August 31, 1969).

"Eighteen Sterilizations Under Duress." San Francisco *Chronicle* (July 23, 1973).

Elementary School Principal. Special issue on the Education of the Gifted and Talented (February, 1972).

471

BIBLIOGRAPHY

ELIOT, JUNE. "A Medical Specialist Who Treats Learning Disabilities." *Oakland Monteclarion* (October 30, 1974).

ELKIND, DAVID. "Infant Intelligence." *American Journal of Diseases of Children* (August, 1973).

———. "Piagetian and Psychometric Conceptions of Intelligence." A Commentary on Jensen's Paper. *Harvard Educational Review* (1969).

ELLIS, ALBERT. "The No Cop-Out Therapy." *Psychology Today* (July, 1973).

ENGLISH, FANITA. "TA's Disney World." *Psychology Today* (April, 1973).

ERHARDT, ANKE A., and JOHN MONEY. "Progestin-Induced Hermaphroditism: I.Q. and Psychosexual Identity in a Study of Ten Girls." *The Journal of Sex Research* (February, 1967).

ERTL, JOHN. "Good-bye, I.Q., Hello E.I. (Ertl Index)." Interview by the editors of *Phi Delta Kappan* (October, 1972).

EVANS, CHRISTOPHER. "Evans Dream Theory." Interview by Barbara Boynton in *Intellectual Digest* (October, 1973).

———. "The Scientology Cult." *Intellectual Digest* (May, 1974).

EVARTS, EDWARD V. "Brain Mechanisms in Movement." *Scientific American* (July, 1973)

"Eye Abnormalities and Brain Damage: A Threat to Children with Astigmatism." *The University of California Bulletin* (January 28, 1974).

EYSENCK, H. J. "The Dangers of the New Zealots." *Encounter* (December, 1972).

FANTINI, MARIO D. "Free the Children: Radical Reform and the Free School Movement, by Allen Graubard." *Saturday Review (Reviews)* (June, 1973).

"Faye Dunaway Is Into a New Kind of Self-Analysis." *Family Weekly* (November 18, 1973).

FEINBERG, LAWRENCE W. "Busing Study Stirs Anger." Washington *Post* (June 11, 1972).

FELDMAN, SILVIA. "Projects of the Terminal Man." *Human Behavior* (February, 1974).

FINCHER, JACK. "The Terman Study Is Fifty Years Old: Happy Birthday and Pass the Ammunition." *Human Behavior* (March, 1973).

———. "Why Are We Afraid of These Children?" *McCall's* (June 8, 1970).

"Finger-Tip Halo's of Kirlian Photography." *Medical World News* (October 26, 1973).

FINNERTY, FRANK A., and SHIRLEY M. LINDE. "The Stress Connection." *Family Health* (November, 1974).

472

BIBLIOGRAPHY

"Fire in the Middle." San Francisco *Sunday Examiner and Chronicle* (June 16, 1974).

"Fish Can Drink Like a Man." San Francisco *Sunday Examiner and Chronicle* (March 25, 1973).

FLEMING, JOYCE DUDLEY. "The State of the Ape." *Psychology Today* (January, 1974).

FLINT, JERRY M. "What Are the Cars in Detroit's 'New' Future?" *Family Weekly* (July 28, 1974).

"Fluctuating Cold Defenses." San Francisco *Chronicle* (January 20, 1973).

FRANKENSTEIN, ALFRED. "Christo's Big Wrap-Up in Sonoma." San Francisco *Sunday Examiner and Chronicle* (August 4, 1974).

FRENCH, JOSEPH L. "Characteristics of High-Ability Dropouts." *The Bulletin of the National Association of Secondary School Principals* (February, 1974).

FROMM, ERICH. "Man Would as Soon Flee as Fight." *Psychology Today* (August, 1973).

FULLER, RENÉE. "Reading Need Not Be I.Q. Bound." *The Bulletin* (June, 1972).

———. "Severely Retarded People Can Learn to Read." *Psychology Today* (October, 1974).

"Furor over Sterilization." San Francisco *Sunday Examiner and Chronicle* (July 29, 1973).

GALIN, DAVID. "Getting the Sides Together." Interview by Rebecca Larsen in Marin County, California, *Independent-Journal* (March 13, 1974).

———. "Learning to Use Both Halves of Your Brain." Interview by Steve McNamara in *Pacific Sun* (April 4–10, 1974).

GALSTON, ARTHUR W. "A Basic Unity of Life." *Natural History* (February, 1973).

———. "The Language of the Leaves." *Natural History* (January, 1973).

GARCIA, JOHN. "I.Q.: The Conspiracy." *Psychology Today* (September, 1972).

GARDNER, HOWARD. "The Forgotten Lesson of Monsieur C." *Psychology Today* (August, 1973).

GARRITY, WANDA. "The Pressure to Succeed." San Francisco *Sunday Examiner and Chronicle* (December 3, 1972).

GAZZANIGA, MICHAEL S. "Brain Theory and Minimal Brain Dysfunction." *Annals of the New York Academy of Sciences* (February 28, 1972).

———. "One Brain—Two Minds?" *American Scientist* (May–June, 1972).

BIBLIOGRAPHY

————. "The Split Brain in Man." *Scientific American* (August, 1967).

GESCHWIND, NORMAN. "Language and the Brain." *Scientific American* (April, 1972).

————. "The Organization of Language in the Brain." *Science* (November 27, 1970).

"Getting Bacteria to Manufacture Genes." San Francisco *Chronicle* (May 21, 1974).

GIBSON, JOHN E. "Do You Understand the Dark World of Dreams?" *Family Week* (August 11, 1974).

GLASS, ANDREA VELLETRI, MICHAEL S. GAZZANIGA, and DAVID PREMACK. "Artificial Language Training in Global Aphasia." *Neuropsychologia*, Vol. 11 (1973).

"Good Time for Some Magia." San Francisco *Sunday Examiner and Chronicle* (July 28, 1974).

GOODGLASS, HAROLD and F. A. QUADFASEL. "Language Laterality in Left-Handed Aphasics." *Brain*, Vol. 77 (1954).

GORDON, WILLIAM J. J. "On Being Explicit About Creative Process." *The Journal of Creative Behavior*, Vol. 6, No. 4 (1972).

————. "Use of Metaphor Increases Creative Learning Efficiency." *Trend* (Spring, 1972).

GORELICK, MOLLY C. "A Single Course in Sex." Interview by Eloisa Garcia Etchegoyhen de Lorenzo in *Human Behavior*, March, 1973.

"Guru Loses Face to a Pie." San Francisco *Chronicle* (August 8, 1973).

GUSTAITIS, RASA. "Erasing a Double Standard." San Francisco *Sunday Examiner and Chronicle* (June 16, 1974).

HAMBLIN, DORA JANE. "They are 'Idiot Savants'—Wizards of the Calendar." *Life* (March 18, 1966).

"Handwriting Test on Job Applicants." San Francisco *Sunday Examiner and Chronicle* (July 29, 1974).

HANLEY, J., D. O. WALTER, J. M. RHODES, and W. R. ADEY. "Chimpanzee Performance: Computer Analysis of Electroencephalograms." *Nature* (November 30, 1968).

————, W. R. RICKLES, P. H. CRANDALL, and R. D. WALTER. "Automatic Recognition of EEG Correlates of Behavior in a Chronic Schizophrenic Patient." *American Journal of Psychiatry* (June, 1972).

HARRIS, T. GEORGE. "Input: Arguments Worth Having." *Psychology Today* (February, 1974).

————. "I.Q. Abuse." *Psychology Today* (September, 1972).

HARTER, RUSSELL. "Effects of Contour Sharpness and Check-Size on Visually Evoked Cortical Potentials." *Vision Research*, Vol. 8 (1968).

474

BIBLIOGRAPHY

HEATH, ROBERT G. "Electroencephalographic Studies in Isolation-Raised Monkeys with Behavioral Impairment." *Diseases of the Nervous System* (March, 1972).

———. "Pleasure and Brain Activity in Man." *Journal of Nervous and Mental Disease,* Vol. 154, No. 1 (1972).

HEBB, D. O., W. E. LAMBERT, and G. RICHARD TUCKER. "A DMZ in the Language War." *Psychology Today* (April, 1973).

HELLIER, MICHAEL. "The Message Is the Medium." San Francisco *Sunday Examiner and Chronicle* (October 6, 1974).

HELSON, RAVENNA. "The Changing Image of the Career Woman." *Journal of Social Issues,* Vol. 28, No. 2 (1972).

———. "Women Mathematicians and the Creative Personality." *Journal of Consulting and Clinical Psychology,* Vol. 36, No. 2 (1971).

HERRINGTON, R. N., and P. SCHNEIDAU. "The Effect of Imagery on the Waveshape of the Visual Evoked Response." *Experientia,* No. 24 (1968).

HERRNSTEIN, RICHARD. "I.Q." *Atlantic* (September, 1971).

———. "On Challenging and Orthodoxy." *Commentary* (April, 1973).

HILLERMAN, TONY. "Robert Coles, the People's Voice." *Human Behavior* (December, 1973).

HOLLAND, JOHN L. "The Selection of Students for Special Scholarships." *Journal of Higher Education* (January, 1964).

HOLT, JOHN. "The Cuteness Syndrome." *Ms.* (March 1, 1974).

"Hormones Aimed at Higher I.Q." Marin County, California, *Independent-Journal.*

HORWITZ, WILLIAM A., W. EDWARDS DEMING, and ROBERT F. WINTER. "A Further Account of the Idiot Savants, Experts with the Calendar." *American Journal of Psychiatry,* Vol. 123, No. 3 (September, 1969).

———, CLARICE KESTENBAUM, ETHEL PERSON, and LISSY JARVIK. "Identical Twins—'Idiot Savants'—Calendar Calculators." *American Journal of Psychiatry,* Vol. 121 (1965).

"How the IRS Picks Returns to Audit." San Francisco *Chronicle* (April, 9, 1974).

HUNT, EARL. "What Kind of Computer Is Man?" *Cognitive Psychology* (January, 1971).

HUNT, J. MCVICKER. "Has Compensatory Education Failed? Has It Been Attempted?" A Commentary on Jensen's Paper. *Harvard Educational Review* (1969).

HUTH, THOMAS. "The Last Mouse—A Fable?" San Francisco *Sunday Examiner and Chronicle* (March 4, 1973).

475

BIBLIOGRAPHY

HYDEN, HOLGER. "Biochemical and Molecular Aspects of Learning and Memory. *Proceedings of the American Philosophical Society* (April 21, 1967).

"If Anyone Can Read, What Happens to I.Q.?" *Psychology Today* (January, 1973).

"Improving the Ecology of Unborn Babies." Chicago *Tribune* (March 19, 1972).

"Inside the Brain." By the editors of *Time* (January 14, 1974).

"Intelligence and Heredity." *Saturday Evening Post* (Summer, 1972).

IRVING, CARL. "Who's Going to Care for the Retarded?" San Francisco *Sunday Examiner and Chronicle* (February 25, 1973).

"It Was No Meeting of the Minds." San Francisco *Sunday Examiner and Chronicle* (February 25, 1973).

JACKLIN, CAROL NAGY, and ELEANOR R. MACCOBY. "Sex Differences in Intellectual Abilities: A Reassessment and a Look at Some New Explanations." *AREA* (April, 1972).

JACOBSON, LAURIE. "Feedback on Biofeedback." *Human Behavior* (July, 1974).

JANIS, IRVING L. "The Groupthink Follies." San Francisco *Sunday Examiner and Chronicle* (June 17, 1973).

JARVIK, MURRAY E., ELLEN R. GRITZ, and NINA G. SCHNEIDER. "Drugs and Memory Disorders in Human Aging." *Behavioral Biology*, No. 7, Abstract No. 1–43R (1972).

JENSEN, ARTHUR R. "The Case for I.Q. Tests." *The Humanist* (January–February, 1972).

————. "Correspondence: Political, Technical, and Theoretical Comments" on Jensen's paper. Assembled by the editors of *Harvard Educational Review* (Summer, 1969).

————."The Differences Are Real." *Psychology Today* (December, 1973).

————."The Effect of Race of Examiner on the Mental Test Scores of White and Black Pupils." *Journal of Educational Measurement*, Vol. 11, No. 1 (Spring, 1974).

————, and JANET FREDERIKSEN. "Free Recall of Categorized and Uncategorized Lists: A Test of the Jensen Hypothesis." *Journal of Educational Psychology*, Vol. 65, No. 3 (1973).

————."The Heritability of Intelligence." *Engineering and Science* (April, 1970).

————."Interaction of Level I and Level II Abilities With Race and Socioeconomic Status." *Journal of Educational Psychology*, Vol. 66, No. 1 (1974).

476

———. "Jensen on Hirsch on 'Jensenism.'" *Educational Researcher,* No. 1 (1972).

———. "Kinship Correlations Reported by Sir Cyril Burt." *Behavior Genetics,* Vol. 4, No. 1 (1974).

———. "Let's Understand Skodak and Skeels Finally." *Educational Psychologist,* Vol. 10, No. 1 (1973).

———. "Level I and Level II Abilities in Three Ethnic Groups." *American Educational Research Journal,* Vol. 10, No. 4 (Fall, 1973).

———. "Race and the Genetics of Intelligence: A Reply to Lewontin." *Bulletin of the Atomic Scientists* (May, 1970).

———. "Race Put-down." A review of "Race and Intelligence," edited by Richardson, Spears, and Richards. *New Society* (February, 1972).

———. "Reducing the Heredity-Environment Uncertainty." *Harvard Educational Review* (1969).

———. A review of "Genetic Diversity and Human Equality," by Theodosius Dobzhansky. *Perspectives in Biology and Medicine* (Spring, 1974).

———. "Understanding Readiness: An Occasional Paper; Avoiding Psychological 'Turn-off' to School Learning." *Challenge* (November–December, 1972).

JOHN, E. ROY. "Switchboard Versus Statistical Theories of Learning and Memory." *Science* (September 8, 1972).

———, PHYLLIS CHESLER, FRANK BARTLETT, and IRA VICTOR. "Observation Learning in Cats." *Science* (March 29, 1968).

JONAS, GERALD. "Manfred Clynes and the Science of Sentics." *Saturday Review* (May 13, 1972).

JONES, R. K. "Observations on Stammering After Localized Cerebral Injury." *Journal of Neurology,* No. 29 (1966).

"Justice on High." San Francisco *Chronicle* (August 7, 1974).

KAGAN, JEROME. "Do the First Two Years Matter?" *Saturday Review* (April, 1973).

———. "The Emergence of Sex Differences." *University of Chicago School Review* (February, 1972).

———. "Inadequate Evidence and Illogical Conclusions." A commentary on Jensen's paper. *Harvard Educational Review* (1969).

———. "Real Differences Between the Sexes: What Baby Boys and Girls Are Teaching Us." *Parents Magazine* (September, 1973).

KAMIN, LEON. "The Misuse of I.Q. Testing." Interview by John Egerton in *Change,* October, 1973.

KANIGEL, ROB. "A Disillusionment with Project One." San Francisco *Sunday Examiner and Chronicle* (April 15, 1973).

477

BIBLIOGRAPHY

KATZ, PHYLLIS J. "A Metaphorical Approach to Education." *Better Schools* (September–October, 1972).

KEEN, SAM. "A Conversation With Ernest Becker." *Psychology Today* (April, 1974).

KIMURA, DOREEN. "The Asymmetry of the Human Brain." *Scientific American* (March, 1973).

KOENIG, PETER. "They Just Changed the Rules on How to Get Ahead." *Psychology Today* (June, 1974).

KRAMER, CHERIS. "Wishy-Washy Mommy Talk." *Psychology Today* (June, 1974).

KRIPPNER, STANLEY. "Foundlings, Environment, and I.Q." A review of "Children of the Creche" by Wayne Dennis. *Psychology Today* (February, 1974).

―――. "Parapsychology Is an Idea Whose Time Has Come." *Psychology Today* (October, 1973).

KUEHL, LINDA. "A Conversation with James A. Michener." *Book-of-the-Month Club News* (September, 1974).

―――. "A Conversation with Tom Harris." *Book-of-the-Month Club News* (December, 1974).

KUMBULA, TENDAYI. "Computer to Help Solve Mysteries of U.S. Past." Los Angeles *Times* (February 19, 1973).

LA FONTAINE, LOUISE, and GERALD E. BENJAMIN. "Idiot Savants: Another View." *Mental Retardation* (December, 1971).

LAING, R. D. "We're in a Grotesque Endemic State of Psychosis. But It Will Pass." Interview by Dudley Digges in *Human Behavior* (March, 1973).

LANSDELL, HERBERT. "Effect of Neurosurgery on the Ability to Identify Popular Word Associations." *Journal of Abnormal Psychology*, Vol. 81, No. 3 (1973).

―――, and J. CLAYTON DAVIE. "Mass Intermedia: Possible Relation to Intelligence." *Neuropsychologia*, Vol. 10 (1972).

―――. "A Sex Difference in Effect of Temporal-Lobe Neurosurgery on Design Preference." *Nature* (June 2, 1962).

―――. "Sex Differences in Hemispheric Asymmetries of the Human Brain." *Nature* (August 1, 1964).

―――. "The Use of Factor Scales From the Wechsler-Bellevue Scale of Intelligence in Assessing Patients with Temporal Lobe Removals." *Cortex*, Vol. IV (1968).

LARENZ, KEITH. "'Krengchai' Runs the Government." San Francisco *Chronicle* (July 18, 1974).

LAZARUS, ARNOLD A. "Basic ID." *Psychology Today* (March, 1974).

478

BIBLIOGRAPHY

"Lefthand Troubles." San Francisco *Sunday Examiner and Chronicle* (December 3, 1972).

LENNEBERG, ERIC H. "On Explaining Language." *Science* (May 9, 1969).

LERNER, WAYNE M., and JAMES V. HINRICHSEN. "Study Behaviors and Their Relationship to Test Anxiety and Academic Performance." *Psychological Reports,* Vol. 30 (1972).

LE SHAN, LAWRENCE. "ESP," from *The Medium, the Mystic, and the Physicist,* Viking Press, Inc. *Intellectual Digest* (May, 1974).

"Lessons for Lana." *Time* (March 4, 1974).

LEVIN, HENRY M. "The Social Science Objectivity Gap." A review of "Inequality" by Christopher Jencks. *Saturday Review* (November 11, 1972).

LEVINE, PAUL H. "Transcendental Meditation and the Science of Creative Intelligence." *Phi Delta Kappan* (December, 1972).

LEVY, JERRE, COLWYN TREVARTHEN, and R. W. SPERRY. "Perception of Bilateral Chimeric Figures Following Hemispheric Deconnexion." *Brain,* Vol. 95 (1972).

LEWIS, MICHAEL, and HARRY McGURK. "Evaluation of Infant Intelligence." *Science* (December, 1972).

LEWONTIN, RICHARD C. "Further Remarks on Race and the Genetics of Intelligence." *Bulletin of the Atomic Scientists* (May, 1970).

———. "Race and Intelligence." *Bulletin of the Atomic Scientists* (March, 1970).

LIGHT, RICHARD J., and PAUL V. SMITH. "Social Allocation Models of Intelligence: A Methodological Inquiry." *Harvard Educational Review* (1969).

LONDON, PERRY. "Your Mind—How It Can Make You Healthy, How It Can Be Used Against You." Interview by Leticia Kent in *Vogue* (October 15, 1972).

"The Lonely Life of the Mentally Retarded Adult." *Psychology Today* (August, 1973).

LOVAAS, IVAR. "After You Hit a Child, You Can't Just Get Up and Leave Him; You Are Hooked to That Kid." A conversation with Paul Chance, *Psychology Today,* January, 1974.

———, LITROWNIK and RONALD MANN. "Response Latencies to Auditory Stimuli in Autistic Children Engaged in Self-Stimulating Behavior." *Behavior Research and Therapy,* Vol. 9 (1971).

———, LAURA SCHREIBMAN, ROBERT KOEGEL, and RICHARD REHM. "Selective Responding by Autistic Children to Multiple Sensory Input." *Journal of Abnormal Psychology,* Vol. 77, No. 3 (1971).

———, and LAURA SCHREIBMAN. "Stimulus Overselectivity of Autistic

Children in a Two Stimulus Situation." *Behavior Research and Therapy,* Vol. 9 (1971).

LYNN, DAVID B. "Determinants of Intellectual Growth in Women." *University of Chicago School Review* (February, 1972).

LYON, HAROLD C., JR. "The Other Minority." *Learning* (January, 1974).

MACKINNON, DONALD W. "The Nature and Nurture of Creative Talent." *American Psychologist* (July, 1962).

MACLEAN, PAUL D. "The Brain in Relation to Empathy and Medical Education." *Journal of Nervous and Mental Disease,* Vol. 144, No. 5 (1967).

―――. "The Brain's Generation Gap: Some Implications." *Zygon* (June, 1973).

―――. "Cerebal Evolution and Emotional Processes: New Findings on the Striatal Complex." *Annals of the New York Academy of Sciences* (August 25, 1972).

―――. "Contrasting Functions of Limbic and Neocortical Systems of the Brain and Their Relevance to Psychophysiological Aspects of Medicine." *American Journal of Medicine,* Vol. XXII, No. 4 (1958).

―――. "The Internal-External Bonds of the Memory Process." *Journal of Nervous and Mental Disease,* Vol. 149, No. 1 (1969).

―――. "Man and His Animal Brains." *Modern Medicine* (February 3, 1964).

―――. "New Findings Relevant to the Evolution of Psychosexual Functions of the Brain." *Journal of Nervous and Mental Disease,* Vol. 135, No. 4 (1962).

"Making a Savant." *Human Behavior* (March–April, 1972).

"Malraux: The End of a Civilization." *Time* (April 8, 1974).

MARCUS, ADRIANNE. "Worlds in Collision: The Struggle at the Science Convention." *Pacific Sun* (March 7–13, 1974).

MARCUS, MARILYN MASAMED. "The Evoked Cortical Response: A Technique for Assessing Development." *California Mental Health Research Digest,* Vol. 8, No. 2 (1970).

MASSOPUST, L.C., JR., R. J. WHITE, L. R. WOLIN, M. S. ALBIN, D. YASHON, and N. TASLITZ. "Electrical Activity of the Isolated Macaque Brain." *Experimental Neurology* (October, 1968).

MCCLEARY, ELLIOTT. "Keeping Tabs on Baby's Birth." *Family Health* (February, 1974).

MCCLELLAND, DAVID. "Testing for Competence Rather Than for Intelligence." *American Psychologist* (January, 1973).

MCGAFFIN, WILLIAM. "Frustration: 41 Congressmen to Quit." San Francisco *Sunday Examiner and Chronicle* (April 21, 1974).

480

BIBLIOGRAPHY

McGAUGH, JAMES L. "Analysis of Memory Transfer and Enhancement." *Proceedings of the American Philosophical Society* (April 21, 1967).

McGUIRE, WILLIAM. "You Have Not Been Injured by My Neurosis." *Psychology Today* (February, 1974).

McKILLIPS, DREW. "'Crime of the Future'—$5,000 Fine." San Francisco *Chronicle* (December 12, 1972).

———. "New Restrictions on I.Q. Tests for Blacks." San Francisco *Chronicle* (November 28, 1974).

McQUEEN, ROBERT. "Larry: Case History of a Mistake." *Saturday Review* (September 12, 1970).

MELNIK, NORMAN. "Mother's Poor Diet Could Damage Children's Minds." San Francisco *Sunday Examiner & Chronicle* (April 14, 1974).

———. "New Black I.Q. Tests Criticized." San Francisco *Examiner* (May 5, 1974).

MERCER, JANE R. "I.Q.: The Lethal Label." *Psychology Today* (September, 1972).

MESKIN, BONNIE B., and JEROME L. SINGER. "Daydreaming, Reflective Thought and Laterality of Eye Movements." *Journal of Personality*, Vol. 30, No. 1 (1974).

"The Military Junta Falls in Athens." San Francisco *Sunday Examiner and Chronicle* (July 28, 1974).

MILLER, JAMES P. "The Brain Machines Are Here." *Human Behavior* (August, 1974).

'Mind-Reading Computer." *Time* (July 1, 1974).

'Miniature Computers. . . ." San Francisco *Sunday Examiner and Chronicle* (March 30, 1975).

MOAN, CHARLES E., and ROBERT G. HEATH. "Septal Stimulation for the Initiation of Heterosexual Behavior in a Homosexual Male." *Journal of Behavior Therapy and Experimental Psychiatry*, Vol. 3 (1972).

MONEY, JOHN. "Differentiation of Gender Identity and Gender Role." *Psychiatric Annals* (December, 1971).

———. "Fetal Hormones and the Brain: Effect on Sexual Dimorphism of Behavior—A Review." *Archives of Sexual Behavior*, Vol. 1, No. 3 (1971).

———, JOAN G. HAMPSON, and JOHN L. HAMPSON. "Imprinting and the Establishment of Gender Role." *AMA Archives of Neurology and Psychiatry* (March, 1957).

———. "Pre-natal Hormones and Intelligence: A Possible Relationship." *Impact of Science on Society*, Vol. XXI, No. 4 (1971).

MOORE, ALICIA HILLS. "In the Wake of Starvation, a Wound Food Cannot Heal." *Life* (January 24, 1969).

BIBLIOGRAPHY

MOSKOWITZ, RON. "Black I.Q. School Case May Spread Across U.S." San Francisco *Chronicle* (June 24, 1974).

———. "An Untapped Source of Brilliance." San Francisco *Chronicle* (September 18, 1973).

MOSS, THELMA, and KENDALL JOHNSON. "The Body as Energy Field." *Harper's* (January, 1973).

MOYER, K. E. "The Physiology of Violence." *Psychology Today* (July, 1973).

"Mr. & Mrs. Robot." *Family Weekly*.

MURPHY, MICHAEL. "I Experience a Kind of Clarity." Conversation with John Brodie, *Intellectual Digest*, January, 1973.

NEARY, JOHN. "Jensenism—Variations on a Racial Theme." *Life* (June 12, 1970).

"New Hint That Autism Is Physical." San Francisco *Chronicle* (April 24, 1973).

NICHOLS, ROBERT C. A Review of Arthur Jensen's *Genetics and Education. Educational Studies*, Vol. 5, No. ½ (1974).

NISBET, ROBERT. "The Obsessive Concern with Self." Conversation with Robert W. Glasgow, *Psychology Today* (December, 1973).

"No Test Scores a Success." San Francisco *Examiner* (May 7, 1973).

NURCOMBE, BARRY. "Precausal and Paracausal Thinking: Concept of Causality in Aboriginal Children." *Australian and New Zealand Journal of Psychiatry*, No. 4 (1970).

OATES, JOYCE CAROL. "New Heaven and Earth." *Saturday Review* (November 4, 1972).

O'DONNELL, PATRICK A. "A Re-Evaluation of Research of Lateral Expression." *Journal of Learning Disabilities* (July, 1970).

OPTON, EDWARD M., Jr., and ROBERT DUCKLES. "Mental Gymnastics on My Lai." *New Republic* (February 21, 1970).

ORNSTEIN, ROBERT. "Right and Left Thinking." *Psychology Today* (May, 1973).

OTTERBURN-HALL, WILLIAM. "A Mathematical Genius in Sarong and Bare-Toed Sandals." San Francisco *Examiner* (March 25, 1973).

OYLE, IRVING. "Mind over Mind." San Francisco *Examiner* (October 25, 1973).

PAGE, ELLIS B. "Miracle in Milwaukee: Raising the I.Q." *Educational Researcher*, No. 10 (1972).

PERLMAN, DAVID. "Brain Disease Chemistry." San Francisco *Chronicle* (November 13, 1974).

———. "A 'Global Brain' for Mankind." San Francisco *Chronicle* (August 28, 1974).

482

BIBLIOGRAPHY

_____. "New Warning on Food Additives." San Francisco *Chronicle* (June 27, 1973).

_____. "Psychiatrists Warn of Growing Black Anger." San Francisco *Chronicle* (February 3, 1973).

_____. "Unraveling a Medical Mystery." San Francisco *Chronicle* (October 26, 1974).

_____. "The Way Bacteria Think" San Francisco *Chronicle* (March 25, 1975).

PETAL, MARVIN. "The Machine That Forgers Can't Fool." San Francisco *Sunday Examiner and Chronicle* (June 30, 1974).

PETERSON, GEORGE M., and J. V. DEVINE. "Transfers in Handedness in the Rat Resulting from Small Cortical Lesions After Limited Forced Practice." *Journal of Comparative and Physiological Psychology*, Vol. 56, No. 4 (1973).

PETIT, CHARLES. "Brain Waves May Tell What's on Your Mind." San Francisco *Chronicle* (February 5, 1974).

_____. "Computer Reads Minds." San Francisco *Chronicle* (June 28, 1974).

_____. "Nutrition and Brain Damage." San Francisco *Chronicle* (October 30, 1972).

_____. "PKU Victims' New Hope." San Francisco *Chronicle* (September 10, 1973).

_____. "Quest for a Brainy Robot." San Francisco *Chronicle* (February 4, 1971).

PIETSCH, PAUL. "Shufflebrain." *Harper's* (May, 1972).

PINARD, ADRIAN, and EVELYN SHARP. "I.Q. and Point of View." *Psychology Today* (June, 1972).

PITTEL, STEPHEN M., et al. "Developmental Factors in Adolescent Drug Use." *Journal of the American Academy of Child Psychiatry* (October, 1971).

PIXA, BEA. "How Your Dreams May Help You." San Francisco *Sunday Examiner and Chronicle* (November 24, 1974).

_____. "The New Exploration of the Brain." San Francisco *Sunday Examiner and Chronicle* (March 10, 1974).

_____. "Psychiatrist Who Employs Mysticism." San Francisco *Sunday Examiner and Chronicle* (July 21, 1974).

PRICE, DON K. "Purists and Politicians." *Science* (January 3, 1969).

PULASKI, MARY ANN SPENCER. "The Rich Rewards of Make-Believe." *Psychology Today* (January, 1974).

RABINOWITCH, EUGENE. "Jenson vs. Lewontin (A Comment)." *Bulletin of the Atomic Scientists* (May, 1970).

483

"Raising Cattle by Computer." *Time* (March 18, 1974).

"A Rand Study on Blindness." San Francisco *Chronicle* (June 3, 1974).

RASCH, ELLEN, H. SWIFT, A. H. RIESEN, and CHOW K. LIANG. "Altered Structure and Composition of Retinal Cells in Dark-Reared Mammals." *Experimental Cell Research,* No. 25 (1961).

RASPBERRY, WILLIAM. "Skill Test of Blacks." Washington *Post* (September 6, 1974).

RAVEN, BERTRAND H. "The Jensen Controversy (Continued)." *Psychology Today* (June, 1974).

"Re-Routing the Rage of Autism's Child." *Human Behavior* (November, 1973).

RENSBERGER, BOYCE. "The Chimp Says He's Ready." San Francisco *Sunday Examiner and Chronicle* (June 9, 1974).

————. "The Chimp Wants to Know." San Francisco *Sunday Examiner and Chronicle* (December 22, 1974).

————. "An Understanding." Interview with a "talking" chimp. San Francisco *Sunday Examiner and Chronicle* (June 9, 1974).

RICE, BERKELEY. "The High Cost of Thinking the Unthinkable." *Psychology Today* (December, 1973).

RIMLAND, BERNARD. "The Differentiation of Childhood Psychoses: An Analysis of Checklist for 2,218 Psychotic Children." *Journal of Autism and Childhood Schizophrenia,* Vol. 1, No. 2 (1971).

————. "Recent Research on Infantile Autism." *Journal of Operational Psychiatry,* Vol. 3 (1972).

RIOCH, MARGARET J. "All We Like Sheep—(Isaiah 53:6)." *Psychiatry* (August, 1971).

RIST, RAY C. "Student Social Class and Teacher Expectations: The Self-Fulfilling Prophecy in Ghetto Education." *Harvard Educational Review* (1970).

"Robot Named Syntelman." San Francisco *Sunday Examiner and Chronicle* (February 24, 1974).

ROBINSON, DONALD W. "An Interview with Christopher Jencks." *Phi Delta Kappan* (December, 1972).

ROCK, IRVIN. "The Perception of Disoriented Figures." *Scientific American* (January, 1974).

ROHWER, WILLIAM D., JR. "Learning, Race, and School Success." *Review of Educational Research* (June, 1971).

RØRVIK, DAVID M. "Present Shock." *Esquire* (October, 1972).

————. "The Theta Experience." *Saturday Review* (May, 1973).

ROSEN, MARVIN. "The Mentally Retarded: Society's Hansels and Gretels." *Psychology Today* (June, 1974).

BIBLIOGRAPHY

ROSENFELD, ALBERT. "Will Man Direct His Own Evolution?" *Life* (October 1, 1965).

ROSENTHAL, ROBERT. "The Pygmalion Effect Lives." *Psychology Today* (September, 1973).

RUEGER, RUSS. "Postscript to a Bum Trip." *Human Behavior* (November, 1973).

SAAL, HUBERT. "Balanchine: Past? Future? Now!" *Newsweek* (November 19, 1973).

SAGE, WAYNE. "Autism's Child." *Human Behavior* (February, 1974).

SANDAY, PEGGY R. "An Alternative Interpretation of the Relationship Between Heredity, Race, Environment, and I.Q." *Phi Delta Kappan* (December, 1972).

SCARR-SALAPATEK, SANDRA. "Race, Social Class, and I.Q." *Science* (December 24, 1971).

SCHAFER, W. P., and MARILYN M. MARCUS. "Self-Stimulation Alters Human Sensory Brain Responses." *Science* (July 13, 1974).

"Scholars Look at Make-Believe." San Francisco *Chronicle* (May 29, 1974).

"Scientists Warn on Freon Research." San Francisco *Chronicle* (December 13, 1974).

"Scientology: An Open Letter to S. I. Hayakawa and the San Francisco Examiner." San Francisco *Chronicle* (April 22, 1975).

SCRIVEN, MICHAEL. "The Values of the Academy (Moral Issues for American Education and Educational Research Arising From the Jensen Case.)" *Review of Educational Research* (October, 1970).

SEAGOE, MAY V. "Terman and the Gifted." *National Elementary Principal* (February, 1972).

SEAMON, JOHN G. "Imagery Codes and Human Information Retrieval." *Journal of Experimental Psychology*, Vol. 96, No. 2 (1972).

SEARCHY, JAY. "Women's Demands on Athletic Equality." San Francisco *Chronicle* (September 3, 1974).

"Self-Esteem, Male and Female." *Human Behavior* (March, 1973).

"Senator Denies He's the Dumbest." San Francisco *Chronicle* (May 24, 1974).

"Sensory Evoked Response—A New Measure of Intelligence." *Psychology Today* (September, 1973).

"The Sexist Scenario in Class." *Human Behavior* (January, 1974).

"The Shattered Mind" by Howard Gardner. Reviewed by the editors, *Psychology Today Book Club News* (January, 1975).

SHEPARD, ROGER N., and GREGORY W. CERMAK. "Perceptual-Cognitive

485

Exploration of a Toroidal Set of Free-Form Stimuli." *Cognitive Psychology* (May, 1973).

———, and CHRISTINE FENG. "A Chronometric Study of Mental Paper Folding." *Cognitive Psychology* (April, 1973).

———, and JACQUELINE METZLER. "Mental Rotation of Three-Dimensional Objects." *Science* (February 19, 1971).

———, and SUSAN CHIPMAN. "Second-Order Isomorphisms of Internal Representations: Shapes of States." *Cognitive Psychology* (January, 1970).

"Show of Paintings by Mentally Retarded Adults." San Francisco *Chronicle* (October 16, 1972).

"Simenon to Quit Writing." San Francisco *Chronicle* (February 8, 1973).

SIMON, HERBERT A. "How Big Is a Chunk?" *Science* (February 8, 1974).

Singer, Jerome L. "The Vicissitudes of Imagery in Research and Clinical Use." *Contemporary Psychoanalysis* (Spring, 1971).

SKINNER, B. F. "On 'Having' a Poem." *Saturday Review* (July 15, 1972).

SLACK, CHARLES W., and WARREN V. SLACK. "Good! We Are Listening to You Talk About Your Sadness." *Psychology Today* (January, 1974).

SMITH, CECIL. "How Many Larrys Are There Living in Our World?" San Francisco *Sunday Examiner and Chronicle* (April 21, 1974).

SNOW, RICHARD E. "Unfinished Pygmalion." *Contemporary Psychology* (April, 1969).

SOWELL, THOMAS. "The Great I.Q. Controversy." *Change* (May, 1973).

SPERRY, R. W. "Hemisphere Deconnection and Unity in Conscious Awareness." *American Psychologist* (October, 1968).

———, and JERRE LEVY. "Minor Hemisphere Function in the Human Commissurotomy Patient." *ACTA Cient Venezolana,* ·Vol. 22, No. 2 (1971).

———. "A Modified Concept of Consciousness." *Psychological Review*, Vol. 76, No. 6 (1969).

———. "Science and the Problems of Values." *Perspectives in Biology and Medicine* (Autumn, 1972).

SPRAGGETT, ALLEN. "Some Day When You Get Check-up You May Ask, How's My Aura?" Marin County, California, *Independent-Journal.*

SPRING, CARL, LAURENCE GREENBERG, JIMMY SCOTT, and JOHN HOPWOOD. "Electrodermal Activity in Hyperactive Boys Who Are Methylphenidate Responders." *Psychophysiology* (July, 1974).

———. "Reaction Time and Effect of Ritalin on Children with Learning Problems." *Perceptual and Motor Skills*, No. 36 (1973).

SQUIRE, LARRY R., and SAMUEL H. BARONDES. "Variable Decay of Memory and Its Recovery in Cycloheximide-Treated Mice." *Proceedings of the National Academy of Sciences* (June, 1972).

486

BIBLIOGRAPHY

"Starving the Brain." *Human Behavior* (December, 1973).

"State Probe of Hospital for Retarded." San Francisco *Chronicle* (October 26, 1974).

STEIN, RUTHE. "Are Men Better Athletes?" San Francisco *Chronicle* (September 18, 1974).

_____. "Man and His Inner Clocks." San Francisco *Chronicle* (March 8, 1973).

STEINEM, GLORIA. "Changing Gloria Also Sees Change." Interview by Joan Lisetor in Marin County, California, *Independent-Journal* (October 10, 1974).

STENN, P. G., E. L. HAIBER, W. VOGEL, and D. M. BROVERMAN. "Testosterone Effects upon Photic Stimulation of the Electroencephalogram (EEG) and Mental Performance of Humans." *Perceptual and Motor Skills*, No. 34 (1972).

STERBA, JAMES P. "Nudity's on the Upswing." San Francisco *Sunday Examiner and Chronicle* (September 15, 1974).

STEVENS, WILLIAM K. "The Justices Number—Computer Predictions of Supreme Court Votes." San Francisco *Sunday Examiner and Chronicle* (August 18, 1974).

STEWART, WALTER W., with rebuttal by G. UNGAR, D. M. DESIDERIO, and W. PARR. "Comments on the Chemistry of Scotophobin." *Nature* (July 28, 1972).

STOCKBRIDGE, DOROTHY. "Behavior Study Under Way." *Ehrli News* (September, 1973).

STODALSKY, SUSAN S., and GERALD LESSER. "Learning Patterns in the Disadvantaged." *Harvard Educational Review* (1967).

"Student Body Fees for 'Witchcraft.'" San Francisco *Chronicle* (June 27, 1973).

SUGARMAN, DANIEL A. "Face Up to Fear." *Family Health* (September, 1974).

"Suit over Handicapped Children." San Francisco *Chronicle* (April 10, 1973).

SULLIVAN, GAIL BERNICE. "Psychic Research: A New Awareness." San Francisco *Sunday Examiner and Chronicle* (July 1, 1973).

TALLARD, GEORGE A., JACK H. MENDELSON, GABRIEL KOZ, and ROBERT AARON. "Experimental Studies of the Effects of Tricyanoaminopropene on the Memory and Learning Capacities of Geriatric Patients." *Journal of Psychiatric Research,* Vol. 3 (1965).

TARG, RUSSEL, and DAVID B. HURT. "Use of an Automatic Stimulus Generator to Teach Extra Sensory Perception." *International Symposium on Information Theory* (January, 1972).

TAYLOR, ARTHUR M., MARIE JOSBERGER, and SUSAN E. WHITELEY. "Elaboration Instruction and Verbalization as Factors Facilitating Retarded Children's Recall." *Journal of Educational Psychology,* Vol. 64, No. 3 (1973).

————, MARIE JOSBERGER, and JAMES Q. KNOWLTON. "Mental Elaboration and Learning in EMR Children." *American Journal of Mental Deficiency,* Vol. 77, No. 1 (1972).

"Telly War of Films on the Punjab Borders." San Francisco *Sunday Examiner and Chronicle* (May 26, 1974).

TERRACE, H. S. "The By-Products of Discrimination Learning." *Psychology of Learning and Motivation,* Vol. 5 (1972).

TEUBER, H. L., BRENDA MILNER, and H. G. VAUGHN, JR. "Persistant Antegrade Amnesia After Stab Wound of the Basal Brain." *Neuropsychologia,* Vol. 6 (1968).

"Testing Creativity: Suppose Everyone Suddenly Doubled in Height?" *Psychology Today* (December, 1973).

"They Shall Not Pass." *Time* (December 31, 1973).

THOMAS, LEWIS. "Do Nothing 'Til You Hear From Me." *Psychology Today* (July, 1974).

————. "I Am Less Intelligent than My Liver." *New England Journal of Medicine,* Vol. 287 (1972).

THOMAS, LEWIS, "The Lives of a Cell." Review by Dennis Lewis in San Francisco *Sunday Examiner and Chronicle,* August 25, 1974.

TINBERGEN, NIKO. "The Amount of Strain Now Imposed on the Individual May Well Overstretch Man's Capabilities to Adjust." Conversation with the author by Elizabeth Hall in *Psychology Today* (March, 1974).

TOMPKINS, PETER, and CHRISTOPHER BIRD. "Love Among the Cabbages." *Harper's* (November, 1972).

"The Total TV Branch Banks." San Francisco *Chronicle* (February 27, 1973).

TREZISE, ROBERT L. "Are the Gifted Coming Back?" *Phi Delta Kappan* (June, 1973).

TROTTER, ROBERT J. "Can Chimps 'Talk' to Man?" San Francisco *Sunday Examiner and Chronicle* (July 1, 1973).

————. "The Use of Robots—Helping Children to Think." San Francisco *Sunday Examiner and Chronicle* (November 4, 1973).

TROTTER, SAVARETTE R. "Hope for the Autistic Child." San Francisco *Sunday Examiner and Chronicle* (January 21, 1973).

TURNURE, JAMES E., and MARTHA L. THURLOW. "Verbal Elaboration and the Promotion of Transfer of Training in Educable Mentally Retarded Children." *Journal of Experimental Child Psychology,* No. 1 (1973).

488

"TV Doctors for What's Ailing You." San Francisco *Sunday Examiner and Chronicle* (November 24, 1974).

"'TV Eyes' May Help Blind to See." San Francisco *Chronicle* (February 11, 1974).

"Two Girls Sterilized." San Francisco *Chronicle* (June 28, 1973).

"The 'Unfit': Denmark's Solution." *U.S. News & World Report* (March 7, 1966).

UNGAR, G., D. M. DESIDERIO, and W. PARR. "Isolation Identification and Synthesis of a Specific Behavior-Inducing Brain Peptide." *Nature* (July 28, 1972).

UNGAR, GEORGES. "Molecular Approaches to Neural Coding." *International Journal of Neuroscience*, Vol. 3 (1972).

VAN HOFFMAN, NICHOLAS. "Unteachable Kids." San Francisco *Sunday Examiner and Chronicle* (September 23, 1973).

VAN MARTHENS, EDITH, and STEPHEN ZAMENHOF. "Deoxyribonucleic Acid of Neonatal Rat Cerebrum Increased by Operative Restriction of Litter Size." *Experimental Neurology* (February, 1969).

_____, LUDMILLA GRAUEL, and STEPHEN ZAMENHOF. "Enhancement of Prenatal Development of Operative Restriction of Litter Size in the Rabbit." *Life Sciences*, Vol. 11, Part 1 (November 1, 1972).

VAN NUYS, DAVID. "The Consciousness of Edgar Mitchell." *Human Behavior* (January, 1974).

VARGIU, JAMES G. "The Creative Act." *Fields Within Fields*, Vol. 5, No. 1 (1972).

VILS, URSULA. "'Jim and Bob Show'—A Mind Bender." Los Angeles *Times* (February 16, 1973).

"A Visit to the Doctor Machine." San Francisco *Chronicle* (January 22, 1974).

VOGEL, W., KLAIBER BROVERMAN, E. L., G. ABRAHAM, and F. L. CONE. "Effects of Testosterone Infusions Upon EEGs of Normal Male Adults." *Electroencephalography and Clinical Neurophysiology*, No. 31 (1971).

VON HOFFMAN, NICHOLAS. "The New Segregation." San Francisco *Sunday Examiner and Chronicle* (March 26, 1974).

_____. "The View from the Top." San Francisco *Sunday Examiner and Chronicle* (September 23, 1973).

WALCUTT, CHARLES CHILD. "Road to Freedom: Disciplined Reading." *Learning* (November, 1973).

WALKER, P. A., and JOHN MONEY. Review "Prenatal Androgenization of Females" in *Hormones*, No. 3 (1972).

WALLACE, ROBERT. "A Lifetime Thrown Away by a Mistake Fifty-Nine Years Ago." *Life* (March 24, 1958).

BIBLIOGRAPHY

WARRINGTON, ELIZABETH K., and T. SHALLICE. "The Selective Impairment of Auditory Verbal Short-Term Memory. *Brain*, Vol. 92 (1969).

WATSON, PETER. "I.Q.: The Racial Gap." *Psychology Today* (September, 1972).

WEST, LOUIS JOLYON, and JAMES R. ALLEN. "The Green Rebellion." *Sooner Magazine* (November, 1967).

WESTLAKE, PHILIP R. "The Possibilities of Neural Holographic Processes Within the Brain." *Kybernetik*, Vol. 7 (1970).

"What You Experience for Yourself Is the Truth. Something Only Believed Is a Lie." An ad for EST training in the San Francisco *Chronicle*, December 12, 1974.

WHITE, CARROLL T., and LEONARD BONELLI. "Binocular Summation in the Evoked Potential as a Function of Image Quality." *American Journal of Optometry and Archives of American Academy of Optometry* (April, 1970).

———. "Evoked Cortical Responses and Patterned Stimuli." *American Psychologist* (March, 1969).

WHITE, ROBERT J., L. R. WOLIN, L. C. MASSOPUST, JR., N. TASLITZ, and J. VERDURA. "Primate Cephalic Transplantation: Neurogenic Separation, Vascular Association." *Transplantation Proceedings* (March, 1971).

"Who's Retarded?" *Time* (September 4, 1972).

WILLIAMS, ROBERT C. "The Silent Mugging of the Black Community." *Psychology Today* (May, 1974).

WILLIAMS, ROGER J. "You Are Biochemically Unique." *Texas Monthly* (February, 1974).

WILSNACK, SHARON C. "Femininity by the Bottle." *Psychology Today* (April, 1973).

WILSON, PAUL D., and AUSTIN H. RIESEN. "Visual Development in Rhesus Monkey Neonatally Deprived of Patterned Light." *Journal of Comparative and Physiological Psychology*, Vol. 61, No. 1 (1966).

WINOGRAD, TERRY. "When Will Computers Understand People?" *Psychology Today* (May, 1974).

WINTER, RUTH. "Ageless Aging." *Family Health* (November, 1973).

———. "Linking Acting, Acupuncture, and Hyponosis." San Francisco *Sunday Examiner and Chronicle* (June 16, 1974).

WOOD, JIM. "The I.Q. Bias Battle." San Francisco *Sunday Examiner and Chronicle* (September 24, 1972).

WOODWARD, KENNETH L. "When Your Child Can't Read." *McCall's* (February, 1973).

"Women and Doctorates—Men Found Far Ahead." San Francisco *Chronicle* (January 6, 1975).

WRIGHT, GUY. "Retarded Thinking." San Francisco *Examiner* (June 24, 1973).

WURTMAN, RICHARD J. "Biological Considerations in Lighting Environment." *Progressive Architecture* (September, 1973).

YAFA, STEPHEN H. "Zap! You're Normal." *Playboy* (March, 1973).

ZACH, LILLIAN. "The I.Q." *Today's Education* (September, 1972).

ZAMENHOF, STEPHEN, EDITH VAN MARTHENS, and LUDMILLA GRAUEL. "Prenatal Cerebral Development; Effect of Restricted Diet, Reversal by Growth Hormone." *Science* (November 26, 1971).

ZIEGLER, MEL. "The $200 Cure;" "60 Rough Hours in an EST Seminar;" and "The Founder of EST Sells Bliss." A series in the San Francisco *Chronicle*, December 2–4, 1974.

ZIGLER, EDWARD. "On Growing Up, Learning and Loving." *Learning* (March, 1973).

_____. "Project Head Start: Success or Failure?" *Learning* (May, 1973).

ZOBRIST, ALBERT C., and FREDERIC R. CARLSON, JR., "An Advice-Taking Chess Computer." *Scientific American* (June, 1973).

491

PAPERS, SPEECHES AND MISCELLANY

AMERICAN ASSOCIATION ON MENTAL DEFICIENCY. "Number of Professionals in Mental Retardation Work." Personal correspondence from George Soloyanis, executive director. November 20, 1972.

AMERICAN BROADCASTING COMPANY. *Children—A Case of Neglect.* Television documentary produced and directed by Pamela Hill. July 17, 1974.

ARBIB, MICHAEL. "Consciousness: The Secondary Role of Language." Paper presented at the American Psychological Association symposium on Content and Consciousness, December 29, 1972.

ARISTERA PRODUCTS CATALOGUE AND ADDENDA. Left-handed implements and materials. Westport, Connecticut, 1974.

BAGLEY, JOHN D. *A Paradigm for Artificial Intelligence.* IBM Research Report, RC 2345 (#11458), January 20, 1967.

BALL, RACHELL S., and LELAND H. STOTT. "Evaluation on Infant and Preschool Mental Tests." Merrill Palmer Institute, Detroit, 1963.

BERKELEY CENTER FOR DRUG STUDIES. "Impairments of Ego Functions in Psychedelic Drug Users," by Rosbert S. Wallerstein, Stephen M. Pittel, *et al.* Presented at Conference on Drug Use and Drug Subcultures, Asilomar, Pacific Grove, California, February 11–15, 1970.

BOGEN, J. E. "The Right Hemisphere Implications of Athletic Skills." Personal communication, October 13, 1973.

BOND, JULIAN. "Forced Sterilization of Black Welfare Mothers in the South." Poverty Law Center letter, undated.

BONNER, JAMES. "Beyond Man's Genetic Lottery." Speech in the lecture series, "The Next Billion Years." Palace of Fine Arts, San Francisco, August, 1973.

BROCHURE OF THE NEUROPSYCHIATRIC INSTITUTE, UCLA. *The Door to Tomorrow.* For the Mental Retardation Program. Prepared by Sheldon M. Stern, undated.

CALHOUN, JOHN B. *Promotion of Man.* In *Global Systems Dynamics.* Reprinted by the U.S. Department of Health, Education and Welfare, Health Services and Mental Health Administration, National Institute of Mental Health, 1969–70.

CHASE, RICHARD ALLEN. "Human Behavior and Environmental Design; The Design of Learning Environments." Paper presented at the American Association for the Advancement of Science, Washington, D.C., December 29, 1972.

Clarence Darrow. Television drama starring Henry Fonda, written by David W. Rintels from the book *Clarence Darrow for the Defense.* Produced by Mike Merrick and Ann Gregory, directed by John Rich. Dome Productions in association with NBC-TV, September 4, 1974.

COOPER, LYNN A., and R. N. SHEPARD. "Chronometric Studies of the Rotation of Mental Images." Paper presented at the Symposium on Visual Information Processing, Carnegie-Mellon University, May 18–19, 1972.

CROW, JAMES F. "The Measurement and Meaning of Heritability." Unpublished paper, February 6, 1973.

DEUTSCH, MARTIN. "53 Errors or Misinterpretations in Jensen's Article." List submitted to the Committee on Scientific and Professional Ethics and Conduct, American Psychological Association, 1971.

"Education of the Gifted and Talented." Report to the Congress by the U.S. Commissioner of Education, and background papers submitted to the U.S. Office of Education. Government Printing Office, March, 1972.

"Effects of Ribonucleic Acid on Memory Defects in the Aged." Paper by D. Ewen, S. Sued, L. Solyom, B. Wainrib, and H. Bank, presented to the 119th Annual Meeting of the American Psychiatric Association, St. Louis, May 6–10, 1963.

ERNST, H. A. *Computer-Controlled Robots.* IBM Research Report, RC 2781 (#13043), January 30, 1973.

ERTL, JOHN. "Evoked Response with Dyslexic Children." Personal communication, October 3, 1972.

_____. "Neural Efficiency and Human Intelligence." Final Report, Ottawa University (Ontario) Center of Cybernetic Studies, December, 1969.

FULLER, RENÉE. "Intelligence and the Fuller Reading System." Paper presented at the 80th annual meeting of the American Psychological Association, Honolulu, September 6, 1972.

GAZZANIGA, MICHAEL. "The Right Hemisphere Implications of Athletic Skills." Personal communication, November 1, 1973.

HAIGHT-ASHBURY RESEARCH PROJECT. "Ego Functions in Psychedelic

493

Drug Users." Report No. 1 on general impairments, presented at a meeting of the American Psychoanalytic Association by Linda Hilles and Phyllis A. Kempner, 1972.

HANLEY, JOHN, JOHN R. ZWEIZIG, RAYMOND T. KADO, and W. ROSS ADEY. "Some Applications of Biotelemetry." In the *1968 National Telemetric Conference Record* of the Electrical and Electronic Engineers, April, 1968.

HAVENDER, WILLIAM. "A Comment on Arthur Jensen's Critics." Unpublished and undated.

HEBER, RICK. "Rehabilitation of Families at Risk for Mental Retardation." A Progress report on the Milwaukee Project, University of Wisconsin at Madison, December, 1972.

HELSON, RAVENNA. "Comments on the Paper by Nathan Kogan on Sex Differences in Creative and Cognitive Styles." Presented at the Graduate Records Examination (GRE) Conference on Cognitive and Creative Styles in Higher Education. Institute of Personality Assessment and Research, University of California, Berkeley, November, 1972.

HODL, JOHN J., JR. "Computer-Based Intelligence Testing." Report of the Florida State University Computer-Assisted Instruction Center, Tallahassee, February, 1971.

HOLLINGSHEAD, MAYBELLE CLAYTON, and CHARLES CLAYTON. "Comparison of the WISC Patterns of Retarded and Non-Retarded Readers—Indian Youth." July 1, 1971.

HORN, JOHN. "Ethical Issues of Behavioral Science Research: On the Heritability of Intellectual Abilities." A symposium, 51st annual meeting, Western Psychological Association. San Francisco, April 21–24, 1971. As abstracted in *JSAS Catalogue of Selected Documents in Psychology,* Vol. 2, Winter, 1972.

HUNT, J. McVICKER. "Heredity, Environment, and Class or Ethnic Differences." Paper presented at the 1972 Invitational Conference on Testing Problems, sponsored by the Educational Testing Service, Princeton, New Jersey, 1972.

———. "Psychological Assessment in Education and Social Class." Paper given at the Missouri Conference sponsored by the University of Missouri, Columbia, Missouri, April 13–14, 1972.

———. "Sequential Order and Plasticity in Early Psychological Development." Paper presented at the Jean Piaget Society's Second Annual Symposium, Temple University, Philadelphia, May 24, 1972.

JACOBS, ELEANOR A., S. MOUCHLY SMALL, PETER M. WINTERS, and HARRY ALVIS. "Hyperbaric Oxygen Effect on Cognition and Behavior in the Aged." Department of Psychiatry, School of Medicine, State University of New York at Buffalo and the Veterans Administration Hospital, Buffalo, 1971.

JARVIK, LISSY F., "Human Intelligence: Sex Differences." Paper presented at the Symposium on Perspectives on the Nature of Intelligence, Mental Program, Department of Psychiatry, UCLA Medical School, June 5, 1971.

JELINEK, F., L. R. BAHL, and L. MERCER. *Design of a Linguistic Statistical Decoder for the Recognition of Continuous Speech.* IBM Research Report, R C 4815 (21421), April 19, 1974.

JENSEN, ARTHUR R. "A Two-Factor Theory of Familial Mental Retardation." Paper presented at the 4th International Congress of Human Genetics, Paris, September 9, 1971.

———. "Comments on Martin Deutsch's '53 Errors or Misinterpretations in Jensen's Article.'" Rebuttal sent to the Committee on Scientific and Professional Ethics and Conduct, American Psychological Association, 1971.

———. "Ethical Issues of Behavioral Science Research: On the Heritability of Intellectual Abilities." A symposium, 51st annual meeting, Western Psychological Association. San Francisco, April 21–24, 1971. As abstracted in *JSAS Catalogue of Selected Documents in Psychology,* Vol. 2, Winter, 1972.

———. "Improving the Assessment of Intelligence." Paper presented at the Symposium on the Theory of Intelligence at the annual convention of the Western Psychological Association, Portland, Oregon, April 28, 1972.

———. "On 'Jensenism': A Reply to Critics." Address at the American Educational Research Association annual convention, Chicago, April 7, 1972.

———. "Race and Mental Ability." Paper presented at a symposium of the Institute of Biology on Racial Variation in Man, Royal Geographical Society, London, September 19–20, 1974.

KAGAN, JEROME. "Cross-Cultural Perspectives on Early Development." Paper presented at the annual meeting of the American Association for the Advancement of Science, Washington, D.C., December 26, 1972.

———. "Plasticity in Human Cognitive Development." Summary of a paper presented at the American Association for the Advancement of Science, 139th meeting, Washington, D.C., December 26, 1972.

KAMIN, LEON J. "Heredity, Intelligence, Politics and Philosophy." Speech to the Southern Regional Council in Atlanta, March 24, 1973.

KENDRICK, S. A. "An Old Problem Revisited." Speech from the Proceedings of the Western Regional Conference on Testing Problems, San Francisco, May 1, 1970 (Educational Testing Service).

KENISTON, KENNETH. "Drug Use and Student Values." Paper presented at the National Association of Student Personnel Administrators, November 14, 1966.

Leonardo da Vinci. Booklet produced by IBM, text written by Richard McLanathan. Armonk, New York, 1973.

LEVENSKY, KAY. "The Performance of American Indian Children on the Draw-A-Man Test." In the *National Study of American Indian Education,* Series III, No. 2. Final report, March, 1970.

LYON, HAROLD C., JR. *The Other Minority.* A preliminary report on the U.S. Office of Education's effort to help our most promising children. Undated.

Maharaj-Ji: Lord of the Universe. Film by Top Value TV of Los Angeles, aired on KQED-TV, San Francisco, March 8, 1974.

McCARTHY, JOHN. "How Intelligent Can a Computer Be?" In the 1967 Financial Report of Stanford University. Stanford University Press, 1967.

McCONNELL, JAMES V. "A Tape Recorder Theory of Memory." Speech to the Midwestern Psychological Association, Chicago, May 2, 1963.

_____. *The Biochemistry of Memory.* Paper published by *Das Medizinisches Prisma,* No. 3. C. H. Boehringer Sohn, Ingelheim am Rhein, West Germany, 1968.

McGAUGH, JAMES L. *Drug Effects on Learning and Memory.* Paper published by J. R. Geigy, Basle, Switzerland, 1969.

_____. *Drug Facilitation of Memory and Learning.* Paper from *Psychopharmacology: A Review of Progress, 1957–1967.* Public Health Service publication No. 1836, Washington, D.C., 1968.

MONEY, JOHN. "Nativism Versus Culturalism in Gender-Identity Differentiation." Paper written for the American Association for the Advancement of Sciences, Symposium on Sex Role Learning in Childhood and Adolescence, Washington, D.C., December 28–29, 1972.

MOREHEAD, DONALD M. *Early Grammatical and Semantic Relations: Some Implications for a General Representational Deficit in Linguistically Deviant Children.* In *Papers and Reports on Child Language Development,* D. Ingram, ed. Stanford University, 1972.

NATIONAL ACADEMY OF SCIENCES. "Letter to the President," from Bernard Davis. July 7, 1970.

NATIONAL MERIT SCHOLARSHIP CORPORATION. "The National Merit Scholarship Program for Creative Students—Details." Personal communication from its president, Edward C. Smith, July 18, 1973.

———. "The National Merit Scholarship Program for Creative Students—Total Number Given." Personal communication from Virginia O. Chalmers, July 15, 1974.

———. "The Number of Scholarships Given to Academic Students During a 7-Year Period." Personal communication from Edward C. Smith, June 21, 1974.

The New Wechsler Intelligence Scale for Children—Revised, An explanatory brochure. From The Psychological Corporation, New York City, as reprinted from the manual for the Wechsler Intelligence Scale for Children, revised, 1974.

PINES, MAYA. "How the Social Organization of Animal Communities Can Lead to a Population Crisis Which Destroys Them." National Institute of Mental Health, *Mental Health Program Reports—5*. December, 1971.

PITTEL, STEPHEN M. "The Cognitive Capabilities of the Street People."
• Personal communication, October 10, 1973.

THE PRESIDENT'S COMMITTEE ON EMPLOYMENT OF THE HANDICAPPED. *About Jobs and Mentally Retarded People.* Booklet from the committee and the National Association for Retarded Children, Government Printing Office, 1972.

THE PRESIDENT'S COMMITTEE ON MENTAL RETARDATION. *Hello World!* Brochure, Government Printing Office, 1969.

PROCEEDINGS, INTERNATIONAL JOINT CONFERENCE ON ARTIFICIAL INTELLIGENCE. Sponsored by the National Science Foundation and the Institute of Electrical and Electronic Engineers, June, 1973.

"Rental Conditions and Cost of the Ertl Neural Efficiency Analyzer." Form business letter from Bruce G. Oken, president of Associates International, Inc., August 1, 1972.

"Ribonuclease." Section by Robert L. Heinrikson, in *Encyclopedia of Science and Technology*, Volume 11. McGraw-Hill, 1971.

RIEGEL, R. HUNT, FRED W. DANNER, and LINDA J. DONNELLY. "Developmental Trends in the Generation and Utilization of Associative Relations for Recall by EMR and Non-retarded Children: The Sorts Test." August, 1973.

RIESEN, AUSTIN A. "Effects of Visual Deprivation on Perceptual Function and the Neural Substrate." From Symposium Bel-Air II, J. de Ajuriaguerra, ed. Desafferentation Expérimentale et Clinique, Georg & Cie, Geneva, 1965.

RIMLAND, BERNARD. "A Search for Tests of Practical Intelligence." Paper for the Conference on Cultural Factors in Mental Test Development, Application and Interpretation, Istanbul, July 19–25, 1971.

497

_____. "Idiot Savants." Letter to the editor of *Life* magazine, April 8, 1966.

_____. "The Lost Genius Debate." Rebuttal to Ehrlich and Holdern's article in *Saturday Review,* May 1, 1971. Letter undated.

_____. "Nutrition and Related Approaches to Improving Human Potential." Speech at the 51st Annual Meeting of the American Dietetic Association, San Francisco, October 16, 1968.

ROYAL DANISH GOVERNMENT. "Proposal to Law on Sterilization and Castration." Translation by Ingrid Rempel. 1970.

_____. "Sterilization and Castration Act," 1967.

SCRIVEN, MICHAEL. "Ethical Issues of Behavioral Science Research: On the Heritability of Intellectual Abilities." A symposium, 51st annual meeting, Western Psychological Association. San Francisco, April 21–24, 1971. As abstracted in *JSAS Catalogue of Selected Documents in Psychology,* November 2, Winter, 1972.

SPERRY, R. W. "The Right Hemisphere Implications of Athletic Skills." Personal communication, October 2, 1973.

SPRING, CARL. "The MBD Syndrome and Stimulant Medications." Personal communication, January 29, 1973.

Stanford-Binet Intelligence Scale—1972 Restandardization. A brief review by Lynn D. Berntson. Houghton Mifflin Company, 1972.

STUDENTS FOR A DEMOCRATIC SOCIETY. *Jensenism: A Closer Look.* Undated booklet. Berkeley, California.

TAVA, EDWARD G. "The Use of the Wechsler Intelligence Scale for Children in Differentiating Between the Endogenous and Exogenous Mental Defective." Paper presented at the annual meeting of the California Educational Research Association, San Diego, April, 1971.

TUDDENHAM, READ D. "The Intelligent Woman." Personal communication, March 2, 1973.

_____. "A Piagetian Test of Cognitive Development." Paper presented at the Symposium on Intelligence, Ontario Institute for Studies in Education, Toronto, May 8, 1969.

UCLA MENTAL RETARDATION CENTER REPORT ON RESEARCH, 1969–70. Prepared by Stephanie Karsten, 1970.

UNIVERSITY EXPLORER (CHARLES LEVY). "A Lock for Every Key (The Structure of Antibodies)." Radio interview with biochemist Dr. Gerald Edelman of Rockefeller University. University of California at Berkeley series, April 20–26, 1975.

UNIVERSITY OF MICHIGAN. "If the High-IQ Rabbit and the Moderate-Intelligence Tortoise Are Racing to Solve a Problem, Which One Is

Likely to Get the Answer First?" News release by Thomas S. Roberts. March 4, 1969.

Use of Chemically Defined Diet with Non-ambulatory Mentally Retarded Patients. California Mental Health Research Monograph, Phyllis M. Baker, ed. State of California Department of Mental Hygiene. Research Monograph No. 14, 1972.

VIDAL, JACQUES. "Toward Direct Brain-Computer Communication." Paper intended for the *Annual Review of Biophysics and Bioengineering,* October, 1972.

WHITE, ROBERT J. "Preparation and Mechanical Perfusion of the Isolated Monkey Brain." Paper presented to the 4th Symposium, Karolinska (Sweden) Symposium on Research Methods in Reproductive Endocrinology, October 11–13, 1971.

Index

Aaron, Hank, 133, 134
Abstraction, computers and, 397–98
Acting, actors, 139, 140, 143, 146, 151
Action cycle, 371
Action mode of thinking, 119
Acupuncture, 354–55
Adaptive reaction, 415
Adey, Ross, 355
Adrenalin, 340
Adrenochrome, 340
Adrenogential syndrome, 265, 273
Age, and intelligence testing, 207–9
Aging, 336; sexual difference in, 262
Aggression, malignant, 433
Aikido, 37
Alcohol, 336
Alerting system, in social brain, 375
Alexia, 314
Allen, Woody, 413
Allende, Salvador, 388
Alpert, Richard, 345
Alphabet, phonetic, 101–2, 422, 424
American Psychological Association, 16, 232
Amniocentesis, 317, 345
Ampère, André Marie, 305
Amygdala, 27
Analogy, 117
Anderson, Hans Christian, 318
Anti-Semitism, and intelligence testing, 174
Aphasia, 50; and language, 320–21
Appositional thinking, 119
Appreciation system, in social brain, 375
Arbib, Michael, 388–89, 393–94, 398, 400–1, 404
Army Alpha test, 176, 186
Art, artists, 138–56, 224, 343; and creativity, 126, 267; and emotions, 147; evolution of, 82; intelligence and, 131–32

Artificial intelligence, 386, 392, 394–96, 400, 401. *See also* Computers
Artificial perception, 428–29
Artistic language, 141–46
Asimov, Isaac, 46–47
Associative learning ability, 251 *ff.*
Athletics, intelligence and, 133–38; and women, 274
Auden, W. H., 130
Auditory imaging, 79–80
Autism, 308–13
Autonomic nervous system, memory and, 106–7
"Average distribution" concept, 161–62
Axon, 29

Baker, Russell, 365
Balanchine, George, 140
Ball, George, 364
Bane, Mary Jo, 202–3
Barron, Frank, 124, 125, 126, 127, 129–31, 257
Basal ganglia, 133
Bayley, Nancy, 186
Becker, Ernest, 436
Beer, Stafford, 388–89
Beethoven, Ludwig van, 141, 143, 152, 153
Behavior: operant, 223–24; respondent, 223
Behavioralism, 108–9, 110–11
Behavior modification, 348
Belbin, Eunice, 115
Belief system, irrational, 122
Bereiter, Carl, 249
Bergson, Henri, 101
Berkeley Growth Study, 184 *ff.*, 197
Bernstein, Leonard, 140, 151, 152–53
Best and the Brightest, The (Halberstam), 410
Beta waves, 356–57

Bilateralization of brain function, 51, 52–53, 54–74, 103–4, 172–73, 252–53, 318–19; and alexia, 314–16; and duplication of skills, 65–68; and IQ testing, 210, 221–22, 224; and learning, 113–15; and mental retardation, 321–24; and modern evolution, 417–21, 434–37; in normal brain, 69–71; and normative control, 71–74; and psychedelics, 340–41, 342–44; and right-handedness, 50–52; and sexual differentiation, 266–69, 275–76; and sight, 59–64; and thinking, 118–19; and touch, 57–59. *See also* Left hemisphere, Right hemisphere
Binet, Alfred, 160, 168–71, 172, 185
Binet-Simon scales, 170
Biofeedback, 106, 107, 348–51, 355–56, 358, 359–60
Bioplasmic energy, 355
Biotechnology, and future of human intelligence, 345–61
Birth, and intelligence, 333–35
Bisected Brain, The (Gazzaniga), 56
Blake, William, 139
Bland, Alexander, 140
Blau, Abram, 51–52
Boccioni, Umberto, 428
Bodmer, Walter, 228
Bogen, J. E., 56, 58, 68, 71, 118–19, 120, 135, 348, 432
Bonner, James, 302, 345–46, 347
Boolean algebra, 413–14
Boring, E. G., 157, 207, 432
Botticelli, Sandro, 343
Botvinnik, Mikhail, 403
Boulding, Kenneth, 75, 76, 84, 104, 373, 397–98, 415, 418, 423, 430, 437
Boullé, Pierre, 409
Bower, Gordon, 85–86, 87, 91, 93, 94, 96–97, 134, 359
Bower, Roger, 318
Bowers, Faubion, 153, 154
Braginsky, Benjamin, 327
Braginsky, Dorothy, 327
Brahms, Johannes, 144, 149

Brain, Lord, 376–77
Brain, the, 25–48, 331–33, 393–94, 433; bilateralization of function, 54–74, 103–4, 113–15, 118–19, 210, 221–22, 224, 252–53, 266–69, 275–76, 314–16, 318–24, 340–41, 342–44, 417–21, 434–37; components of, 27–28; computerized, 393; emotional, 430–31; evolution of, 76–83; hemispheric dominance, 50–54; localization of function, 69; memory, 31–48; and mental imaging, 75 ff.; neuron, 29–31; normative control of, 71; size and structure, 26, 266–69; social, 370, 374–77, 383, 389; triune nature of, 430–32
Brain stem, 27
Brainstorming, 381
Brain structure, differences in male and female, 266–69
Brain waves, 356–57
Brave New World (Huxley), 342
Break boundary, 418, 423, 437
Brigham, Carl, 177
Broca, Paul, 49–50
Bronfenbrenner, Urie, 337
Brown, Barbara, 119, 349, 350–51, 354, 356, 357
Bruner, Jerome, 94, 337
Buckner, Mayo, 327–28
Buros Mental Measurements Yearbook, 218
Burt, Cyril, 171–73, 179, 182–83
Buxton, Jedediah, 305
Byron, Lord, 27

Calendar savants, 305
Calhoun, John, 367–77, 380, 383, 389
California, University of, at Berkeley, Growth Studies, 184 ff., 197, 212
Camus, Albert, 117
Carlson, Frederic, Jr., 402–4
Carnegie Commission on Higher Education, 257
Carnegie Corporation, 298
Carr, Donald C., 106

501